T0301472

EXITING THE FACTORY

Strikes and Class Formation beyond the Industrial Sector

Volume 2: Non-Industrial Labour
Stoppages around the World

Alexander Gallas

BRISTOL
UNIVERSITY
PRESS

First published in Great Britain in 2024 by

Bristol University Press
University of Bristol
1–9 Old Park Hill
Bristol
BS2 8BB
UK
t: +44 (0)117 374 6645
e: bup-info@bristol.ac.uk

Details of international sales and distribution partners are available at bristoluniversitypress.co.uk

© Bristol University Press 2024

British Library Cataloguing in Publication Data
A catalogue record for this book is available from the British Library

ISBN 978-1-5292-4222-5 hardcover
ISBN 978-1-5292-4223-2 ePub
ISBN 978-1-5292-4224-9 ePdf

Cover design: Andy Ward
Front cover image: iStock/FG Trade
Bristol University Press uses environmentally responsible print partners.
Printed and bound in Great Britain by CPI Group (UK) Ltd, Croydon, CR0 4YY

FSC
www.fsc.org
MIX
Paper | Supporting
responsible forestry
FSC® C013604

Contents

List of Figures and Tables

Figures

Tables

List of Abbreviations

AFL-CIO	American Federation of Labor and Congress of Industrial Organizations
ANC	African National Congress (South Africa)
BDA	Bundesvereinigung der Deutschen Arbeitgeberverbände (Confederation of German Employers' Associations)
BMA	British Medical Association
CC.OO	Comisiones Obreras (Workers' Commissions, Spain)
CDU	Christlich Demokratische Union Deutschlands (Christian Democratic Union of Germany)
CGT	Confederación General del Trabajo (General Confederation of Work, Spain)
CIG	Confederación Intersindical Galega (Galician Unions Confederacy)
CNT	Confederación Nacional del Trabajo (National Confederation of Work, Spain)
COSATU	Congress of South African Trade Unions
CSU	Christlich-Soziale Union in Bayern (Christian Social Union in Bavaria)
DBB	DBB Beamtenbund und Tarifunion (German Civil Service Federation)
DGB	Deutscher Gewerkschaftsbund (German Trade Union Confederation)
ELA	Eusko Langileen Alkartasuna (Solidarity of Basque Workers)
ETUC	European Trade Union Confederation
EVG	Eisenbahn- und Verkehrsgewerkschaft (Railway and Transport Union, Germany)
GDBA	Union of *Beamten* and *Beamten* Candidates at Deutsche Bundesbahn
GdED	Gewerkschaft der Eisenbahner Deutschlands (Union of Railway Workers of Germany)

GDL	Gewerkschaft Deutscher Lokomotivführer (Union of German Train Drivers)
GDP	gross domestic product
GEW	Gewerkschaft Erziehung und Wissenschaft (Education and Science Workers' Union, Germany)
IG BCE	Industriegewerkschaft Bergbau, Chemie, Energie (Industrial Union Mining, Chemicals, Energy, Germany)
ILO	International Labour Organization
IMF	International Monetary Fund
LAB	Langile Abertzaleen Batzordeak (Nationalist Workers' Commissions, Basque Country)
NHS	National Health Service (Britain)
NUM	National Union of Mineworkers (Britain)
NUMSA	National Union of Metalworkers of South Africa
OECD	Organisation for Economic Co-operation and Development
PCS	Public and Commercial Services Union (Britain)
PP	Partido Popular (People's Party, Spain)
PRA	power resources approach
PSOE	Partido Socialista Obrero Español (Spanish Socialist Workers' Party)
RMT	National Union of Rail, Maritime and Transport Workers, Britain
SPD	Sozialdemokratische Partei Deutschlands (Social Democratic Party of Germany)
TUC	Trades Union Congress, Britain
UCU	University and College Union, Britain
UGT	Unión General de Trabajadores y Trabajadoras de España (General Union of Workers of Spain)
USO	Unión Sindical Obrera (Workers' Trade Union, Spain)
VC	Vereinigung Cockpit (Cockpit Association, Germany)
ver.di	Vereinte Dienstleistungsgewerkschaft (United Services Trade Union, Germany)
WTO	World Trade Organization

Preface

From today's vantage point, it is obvious that capitalist development is accompanied by local and macroregional processes of deindustrialization. Smoking chimneys are no longer an everyday sight in the heartland of the industrial revolution, the Northwest of England, and we are used to hearing news about factories being shut or relocated. This raises important theoretical and political questions, which concern both how we understand capitalism, and what we make of the classical socialist idea that organized labour is a force of political progress or even human emancipation. What happens to class relations and working-class solidarity when the factory gates close for good?

In the introduction to this book, contained in Volume 1, I presented two countervailing claims by eminent scholars on this subject matter. The first one came from Manuell Castells, the Spanish sociologist and former minister in the centre-left government of Pedro Sánchez. According to Castells, we find ourselves in a 'post-industrial period' marked by 'informational capitalism' (2010: 225, 18), which fosters individualization and undermines worker solidarity. The late Leo Panitch, a leading Canadian Marxist intellectual and political scientist, took the opposite view. He argued that the decline of manufacturing in the capitalist centres is accompanied by the emergence of new solidarities among workers, which can be found outside of the industrial sector (Panitch, 2001: 367).

Against this backdrop, I wagered that strike research is an ideal area for exploring this issue systematically. After all, labour stoppages are based on the principle of solidarity among workers. If Castells is right, non-industrial labour stoppages should be few and far between, and if they occur, it should be rare for close cross-sectoral links between workers to emerge. The opposite should be the case if Panitch is correct: There should be ample evidence of workers going on strike in non-industrial sectors – and of what I call broad-based, inclusive or expansive solidarity. Accordingly, the research question pursued in my book is this: *What are the class effects of non-industrial strikes – or to what extent do they contribute to working-class formation?*

In Volume 1 of this book, I positioned my project vis-à-vis existing research and laid the theoretical groundwork for addressing my question.

In what follows, I give a brief overview of some of my key points. These will hopefully help my readers orient themselves and make connections once they start engaging with the observations and arguments contained in this volume. And yet, I must utter a warning. There are numerous threads that connect the two volumes, and it is impossible to capture all of them in this short summary. Consequently, I would not recommend reading this or the other volume in isolation. There is a danger of either missing how the non-industrial strikes taking place in the present moment are not just products of circumstance, but linked with structurally inscribed features of the capitalist mode of production – or of grasping just those general features, but not the unique configurations of contradictions that characterize the present conjuncture of crisis.

Notably, my research question refers to a general subject matter. It concerns the nature of contemporary capitalism altogether, not just of specific geographic spaces. Accordingly, I decided to approach it, in Volume 1, from a global labour studies angle. This was to ensure that the global nature of present-day capitalism is taken seriously. After all, global labour studies aspires to studying labour relations and mobilizations of workers across the globe (Brooks and McCallum, 2017; Cook et al, 2020).

Consequently, I started in Volume 1 by reviewing key contributions to the global labour studies literature. I argued that it is clear from this literature that global labour scholars commit to 'being on the side of workers', but that they do not clearly spell out what this means. In other words, their writing contains a normative-critical subtext consisting of side-remarks and scattered ideas highlighting the need to oppose the subjugation of workers and side with labour movements, but little in the way of a systematic line of reasoning explaining why they take this standpoint. With reference to a position in social philosophy called 'qualified ethical naturalism' (Sayer, 2005: 2018), I addressed this shortcoming. I showed that class domination causes workers to suffer, and that being on their side means supporting their practices and strategies of contesting it.

In a second step, I engaged with the power resources approach (PRA) (AKSU, 2013; Schmalz et al, 2018), an oft-used framework in global labour studies. I argued that the PRA-type analyses are compromised in their clarity because of a lack of reflection on their normative foundations. This is visible in the fact that union power is equated with class power, which does not sufficiently pay heed to the fact that union activities can indeed contribute to fortifying capitalist class domination – in particular in cases where workers' organizations become co-opted or their leaders are corrupt. From this, I concluded that global labour scholarship needs a class theoretical foundation.

Accordingly, my third step was to conceptualize class in capitalism. With reference to Karl Marx (1976) and Nicos Poulantzas (1974), I argued that the relations of production characterizing the capitalist mode of production have two poles or class locations, the side of capital and the side of labour. These are constituted by the ownership or non-ownership of means of production – and the fact that the non-owners (or workers) sell their labour power to the owners (or capitalists) for a wage.

Furthermore, the relations of production are antagonistic, meaning that there is an irresolvable clash of interests between the two sides. This concerns how the labour power bought and sold should be expended during the work process, and where limits of its expenditure lie.

And finally, the relations of production are marked by class domination, that is, an unequal access to material and ideational resources: The side of capital is systematically advantaged over the side of labour in terms of owning the product of surplus labour (exploitation); of being able to make binding decisions over what is produced – and how (despotism); and of being seen as possessing the expertise needed to do 'business', which in turn relegates workers to a subordinate position tasked with executing orders from 'above' and separates them from their skills and intellectual capacities (alienation).

Notably, the state is present in the relations of production (Poulantzas, 1978: 17, 27). After all, ownership of the means of production can only exist if there is a legal system safeguarding it – and for this to be there, there also needs to be a state. But this state is not a neutral instance. There is a range of selectivities built into it that tend to unify the side of capital into a power bloc – most importantly, the principle of government. The latter operates under the constraint of having a secure tax base, which is why there is a strong incentive for political leaders to keep capital accumulation going. And likewise, there are selectivities that tend to separate workers from one another. Thanks to the existence of the state, people become citizens endowed with individual rights, which separate them from one another – and members of an imagined community at the national level, which is linked with nationalist interpellations that mobilize them across different class locations.

And yet, the antagonism contained in the relations of production produces conflicts over work, and in these conflicts, workers can strengthen their hand vis-à-vis capital through joining forces. If they do so successfully and across the boundaries of specific groups, single business units or sectors, working-class formation is in evidence. However, capitalist competition, rights-based individualism and nationalism work against class-based solidarity – and labour struggles can have unifying or divisive effects depending on what kind of demands are made, who is addressed, and how things develop. In a nutshell, capitalist development is characterized by a constant 'making', 'unmaking' and 'remaking' of working classes (Silver, 2014: 49).

In the process, trade unions – as organizations facilitating the formation of worker coalitions – play a key role. And thanks to the existence of law and the state, they are faced with a dilemma: They can use their strength for forcing the side of capital to recognize them as legitimate negotiation partners, which means that they can legally contest some of the conditions of how labour power is expended; at the same time, this contributes to fortifying capitalist class domination because union recognition is usually premised on workers accepting the capitalist status quo (see Hyman, 1989: 40). In a nutshell, unions have a 'double character' (Müller-Jentsch, 1981; 2003: 654; see Hürtgen, 2018): They are 'class organizations' (Esser, 1982: 228), but also instances of 'mass integration' (Esser, 1982: 245).

The conceptualization of class briefly sketched here forms the theoretical foundation of this second volume, which is mostly dedicated to empirical research. I use categories informed by it to examine non-industrial strikes around the globe – and to identify patterns that shed light on the research question. And in keeping with my global labour studies angle, I explain in the process how research on strikes and class formation from a global perspective can be carried out.

Part I of this volume is indeed dedicated to capturing the global picture. In Chapter 1, I explain my research design. I do so by drawing upon Philip McMichael's notion of 'incorporated comparison' (1990; 2000), which calls for contextualizing delimited case studies by embedding them in more broad-brush accounts of developments and events at the global level. Accordingly, Chapter 2 is dedicated to capturing neoliberalism with this wider angle. Chapter 3 then specifies the general observations by providing an overview of how the service and public sectors across the world have evolved in this context. Part I concludes with Chapter 4, which complements the contextual information thus produced with a detailed mapping of non-industrial strikes around the world, in the conjuncture of crisis. This is based on newspaper coverage; I examine whether there is evidence for working-class formation.

In line with McMichael's considerations, Part II contains more detailed case studies. I zoom in on Western Europe and compare three strike waves, the railway strikes in Germany (Chapter 6), the junior doctors' strikes in Britain (Chapter 7), and the general and general feminist strikes in Spain (Chapter 8). But before doing so, I provide another contextualization by focusing on how labour relations in the three countries have been developing in the last decades (Chapter 5).

The conclusion contains my final reflections on the book in its entirety. In it, I compare the three cases and link them with the findings from Part I. I then use my findings for a final discussion of Castells' claim and Panitch's counterclaim and end the book by giving an answer to my research question.

PART I

Strike Research from a Global Angle: Collective Action in Response to the Crisis of Neoliberalism

Beyond Methodological Fordism: The Case for Incorporated Comparisons*

The limitations of methodological Fordism

My commitment to taking the global angle seriously is at odds with a lot of research in the fields of political economy and labour studies. Single country case studies and comparative studies of a small number of countries are common currency. Both have contributed significantly to our understanding of different capitalist social formations and the fact that institutions and configurations of actors at the national level matter and differ. Through establishing differences and communalities across national states, they enhance our understanding of what the capitalist mode of production is, and what the specificities of macroregional or national contexts are.

Many of those studies exhibit a research strategy that can be called 'methodological Fordism'.[1] With this term, I refer to a set of methodological choices starting from the implicit assumption that Fordism is the standard mode of capitalist development. This does not mean that all research in this mould studies 'Fordist' or 'post-Fordist' configurations or uses the corresponding terminology. My point is that it has a family resemblance with scholarship that explicitly does so and shares with it a number of guiding assumptions: the primary unit of analysis is the national state; the study of manufacturing and of the labour relations in the sector – frequently referred to as 'industrial relations' (see Nowak, 2021) – are key to understanding national political economies; and contemporary capitalism can be deciphered

---

* This chapter is a revised version of an article contained in *The Handbook on Critical Political Economy and Public Policy*, edited by Christoph Scherrer, Ana Garcia and Joscha Wullweber and published by Edward Elgar in 2023.
[1] See, for example, Esping-Anderson (1990), Hall and Soskice (2001) and Streeck (2009).

by focusing on a relatively small number of highly industrialized core countries.[2] Notably, 'methodological Fordism' entails a specific mode of comparison. It starts from the presumption that capitalism consists of a collection of capitalist national states forming 'discrete bounded units', whose relationship is 'external' (Hart, 2018: 376). In Philip McMichael's words, these units are subjected to an 'analytic comparison' (1990: 389): Clearly delimited cases are compared with the aim of identifying and separating case-specific and common traits. Due to this being research in the field of political economy, these traits are either national or macroregional specificities or transnational invariances. They often refer to *Varieties of Capitalism*, as Peter Hall and David Soskice's influential edited volume on the 'comparison of national economies' is called (2001: v).

Thanks to focusing on institutions and regulation, research of this type tends to exhibit 'a normative orientation to social democracy' (Bruff, 2021: 6). It enhances our understanding about historical or geographical variation within capitalism, but also invites what often prove to be, on closer inspection, inadequate generalizations about its nature from a small number of cases. In particular, analyses that examine 'Fordism' and 'post-Fordism' are indicted for making sweeping statements about the nature of capitalism in the second half of the 20th century. According to critics, they have a tendency for disregarding its instabilities, the specificities of different geographical and historical settings, and the 'path-shaping' role of workers' struggles (Baca, 2004; Gambino, 2007). And conversely, important traits of capitalism become visible only if one takes a longer historical and a broader geographical view – for example, the important fact that work in capitalist social formations often was, and still is, informal, precarious and unfree (van der Linden, 2008; Moody, 2017: 23; Gordon, 2019).

An alternative is offered by the assumption that there is one and the same global and capitalist social order, which exhibits a degree of 'variegation' reflected in specificities located at the macroregional, national, regional or local level (Peck and Theodore, 2007; Jessop, 2014; 2015). In the research process, this translates into a commitment to studying together global political-economic mechanisms and tendencies as well as case-specific configurations – or the global social formation in conjunction with specific national social formations. Against this backdrop, I discuss in this chapter how to conduct empirical research on strikes and class formation from this global vantage point. I approach this challenge by, first, discussing critical problems that occur in the research process (the dangers of subsumptionism, an opportunistic mode of investigation where empirical research is reduced

---

[2] Examples of studies that are explicitly about Fordism are Lipietz (1996), Aglietta (2000), Koch (2006) and Baccaro and Pontusson (2016).

to seeking out evidence in line with one's theoretical assumptions; the limitations of approaching global issues from a quantitative angle; the challenge of reconciling analytical breadth and depth; and the need for selecting suitable cases and data); and, second, drawing upon McMichael's notion of 'incorporated comparison' and outlining my research design based on it.

The trap of subsumptionism

Arguably, empirical research from a global vantage point is only possible if one operates on the grounds of a global conceptualization of capitalism (see Jessop, 2015: 69–72; Bieler and Morton, 2018: 94). If one sees the capitalist mode of production as a global phenomenon from the start – and if one's conceptualization comprises the world market as 'the ultimate horizon of competition' between capitals (Jessop, 2015: 66) – it is unlikely that one mistakes specificities of 21st-century capitalism in North America or Western Europe for general characteristics of capitalism.

And yet, there is the critical problem that by definition, research from a global vantage point is far more removed from macroregional, national, regional or local specificities than research based on theories with a more limited spatial field of validity (see McMichael, 1990: 391). From the perspective of research pragmatics, it is only possible to examine a global research field if one disregards a lot of information and resorts to abstraction and simplification. It is tempting to deal with the wealth of information one is exposed to by equating one's abstract-simple conceptualization of global capitalism with its observable reality, that is, to see observations that conform to one's theoretical assumptions about the nature of capitalism as 'proof' that the latter are full descriptions of social reality. This is often the case with 'encompassing comparisons', which start from global structures and, in a second step, situate cases in them (Tilly, 1984 cited in McMichael, 1990: 386). Using a Jessopian turn of phrase, research designs of this type run the risk of falling into the trap of subsumptionism (Jessop, 1982: 73; 1990: 251). With this concept, I refer to a specific type of methodological opportunism: The function of empirical research is reduced to identifying cases and datasets that are fully in line with the predictions that follow from one's theoretical assumptions; research becomes a tick-box exercise where cases and data are ignored that go against those assumptions. A classic example for subsumptionism provided by Bob Jessop is the 'state monopoly capitalism' (stamocap) literature from the 1970s (1982: 71–2). It presumed, at the level of theory, the existence of a prescribed path of capitalist development culminating in the emergence of state monopoly capitalism and, eventually, socialism (Jessop, 1982: 51).

Due to the multifaceted nature of the social world and the seemingly endless stream of information contained in it, one will usually find it easy to produce some evidence that appears to confirm one's own hunches, preconceptions and predictions (see Sayer, 1992: 60–1). But as any generic detective story tells us, *some* leads are not enough to demonstrate conclusively that a suspect is guilty. In these stories, new information tends to surface all of a sudden that throws into doubt what the protagonists have been assuming up to that point, which forces them to reconsider what they think is the case.

The practical experiences of social scientists resonate with this genre of literary fiction. Research rarely is a linear process in which we first describe our theoretical assumptions and then amass more and more data providing evidence that these assumptions are right. It is quite likely that there will be data directly challenging the latter, and other data that are contradictory and ambiguous and thus difficult to interpret (see Sayer, 1992: 173–4, 222; 2000: 40). The critical problem with subsumptionism is not that researchers make propositions about the social world that are based on theoretical assumptions, but that they select cases and data with a view to preventing such challenges from occurring. In this sense, it is a highly biased practice. Taken to its logical conclusion, subsumptionism renders empirical research superfluous because everything there is to know has already been identified at the level of theory.

This can be illustrated with reference to my research problem. A 'subsumptionist' approach following Castells' observations on the absence of a working class in present-day capitalism would select non-industrial strikes that are occupation-driven and thus can be understood as signalling the absence of solidarity with workers from other sectors. These strikes could be used to show that there is fragmentation among workers and a relative absence of class-based solidarity. A strike that could serve as an example because it has been interpreted in this manner is the labour dispute between Vereinigung Cockpit (VC) [cockpit association], a pilots' union in Germany, and Lufthansa, the national carrier. VC staged 14 strikes at Lufthansa in the years 2014 and 2015, leading to the cancellation of 8,500 flights (Wissenschaftlicher Beirat, 2016: 114; Raehlmann, 2017: 34–6). The reason was that the company was threatening to exit the existing pensions agreement for pilots. Commentators in the media claimed that the pilots were a small band of highly paid employees abusing their capacity to disrupt air traffic to defend their privileges (Sauer, 2014; Obertreis, 2016). If we follow this interpretation – and be it just for the sake of the methodological argument developed here – the strikes had limited expansive effects in sense of creating ties with other groups of workers, in particular outside aviation.[3]

---

[3] For more a detailed account of the strike that comes to more nuanced conclusions, see Chapter 3.

In contrast, the Panitch position is, at the level of theory, that non-industrial labour disputes facilitate class formation. If one acted in a subsumptionist manner, one would select non-industrial strikes appearing to confirm this assumption, that is, strikes led by people with an uncompromising stance towards management and a radical, class-based rhetoric. One could focus, for example, on the frequent stoppages in recent years at London Underground, which are usually led by the National Union of Rail, Maritime and Transport Workers (RMT) (see Connolly and Darlington, 2012; Gordon and Upchurch, 2012; Gallas, 2018: 248). Importantly, the RMT is a union known for its deep hostility to austerity and neoliberal modes of public sector management – plus its commitment to militancy and socialist class politics. At the same time, it is a comparably successful union when it comes to winning concessions for its members. This turns the RMT strikes into a model case for arguing that processes of class formation are taking place in non-industrial labour disputes: its representatives use a language of class and class struggle, and its demands are expandable beyond a narrow constituency of members. Arguably, the RMT is the most clear-cut example of a militant, socialist union in present-day Britain.

Importantly, looking exclusively at the VC or the RMT is not a very good basis for assessing the class effects of non-industrial strikes precisely because of the danger of subsumptionism. Both are specific cases in their national context and in the context of non-industrial trade unionism in deindustrializing countries. Ambiguities and contradictions are not visible to the same degree as in the cases of other unions, which are often less clear about their political agenda or more hesitant when it comes to militancy. The Union of German Train Drivers (GDL), for example, is a militant organization, but it also has an image of a conservative, occupational union when it comes to its politics. In contrast, the Railway and Transport Union (EVG), also from Germany, has been cooperating with management for a long time. But it has become more open-minded about strikes in recent years – and unlike the GDL, it is affiliated with the German Trade Union Confederation (DGB), the main union umbrella in Germany, which, compared to other confederations in the country, has by far the broadest base among workers (Hürtgen, 2016; Birke, 2018; DW, 2018). These examples show that we risk overriding contradictions and ambiguities if we try to settle the debate on the working class with reference to VC or the RMT. Both unions may form part of the picture, but they (or similar cases) should not be the only objects of interest. Consequently, I have decided to examine, in my case studies, strikes that are ambiguous in their class effects: not just the strikes in the German railway sector (Chapter 6), but also the strikes by junior doctors in Britain (Chapter 7) and the general and feminist strikes in Spain (Chapter 8).

My critique of subsumptionism gives rise to the question of what a sound conceptualization of the relationship between theory and empirical research would look like. Scholars operating on the grounds of a critical realist ontology highlight that social systems are open systems (Bhaskar, 1979: 45; Sayer, 2000: 15). This corresponds with my critique of the biased, 'locked' nature of subsumptionist research. As I argued in Volume 1, Chapter 4, critical realism is based on a non-deterministic understanding of social determination: Social systems do not have unavoidable effects that can be determined in advance. They exhibit tendencies with potential effects, but it may be the case that these tendencies remain 'dormant' due to countertendencies, contextual factors, coincidences and countermeasures taken by actors. This suggests that there is a degree of determinacy and contingency to any social setting, which is why theory (usually understood by critical realists as conceptualization) needs to be complemented with empirical research and vice versa (see Collier, 1994: 7–8; Sayer, 2000: 121–4; Blaikie and Priest, 2017: 177).

Correspondingly, it is plausible to assume, at the level of an abstract-simple conceptualization of global capitalism, that strikes facilitate class formation. At the same time, however, this is only a general tendency, which means that the outcomes of any particular strike cannot be predicted firmly on its grounds. It is equally plausible to assume that there are mechanisms, processes and events working against this tendency, which is reflected in the fact that there are strikes deeply dividing workforces and different groups of workers. It follows that if we want to find out about outcomes, we need theory to provide us with guidance on what to look for, and empirical research for finding out about what is happening. This research should reflect, in the way it is designed, the openness of social systems and the difficulty of predicting their effects on actual, concrete social settings (see Sayer, 1992: 138, 142, 190; 2000: 19). Taking the openness of social systems seriously has important implications for case and data selection: One must not look for 'outcomes' that are predicted by one's theoretical assumptions.

In this one respect, critical realist perspectives on empirical research resemble standard 'comparative politics' approaches. While 'comparative politics' usually rest on positivist ontological assumptions that critical realists do not share, it still offers methodological insights from which they can learn. The debate on 'selection bias' is a case in point. Comparatists argue against 'selection on the dependent variable', that is, the identification of suitable cases on the grounds that they fit with the purported explanation (Landman, 2003: 43–7; see Burnham, 2004: 74–8). The critical problem with operating this way is that cases are excluded by default that could falsify the basic assumptions underpinning the research design. If selection takes place on the grounds of identifying the expected outcomes, researchers will only ever find what they know already. In my own terms, they operate in a subsumptionist manner.

The limitations of quantitative research designs

The existence of the subsumptionist trap underscores the need to carefully reflect on how to reconcile the need for a global vantage point of one's research with the need to consider a wealth of data about different strikes that allows us to capture context-related specificities. A standard way to proceed would be to conduct a statistical analysis based on large-n datasets concerning strike incidence that cover a great number of countries. In principle, they leave room for national specificities to deviate from global trends; it is possible for individual items that are compared to diverge significantly from predictions made at the theoretical level. Accordingly, important contributions to strike research operate on the grounds of quantitative research designs (Franzosi, 1995; Silver, 2003).

However, there are practical obstacles to pursuing such endeavours, which result from the specificity of different contexts and the difficulty of making generalizable observations. For many historical periods and geographical spaces, data are not available, and if they are, there are serious doubts over their reliability and comparability (Hopkin, 2010: 297–300; Gall, 2012: 680–2; Dribbusch, 2018). To choose two random examples, there were, in recent years, strikes for higher wages at the main Alaskan public ferry operator as well as political strikes against the authoritarian regime in Belarus. In both cases, people refused to work. But importantly, they engaged in this practice of protest under fundamentally different political, economic and cultural conditions, and had very different goals. In the Alaskan case, it may be easier to discern class effects than in the Belarus case: The dispute concerned the conditions of the extraction of surplus labour. In contrast, the stoppages in Belarus were part of a broad popular protest movement, and the object of the dispute was not labour relations as such but a conflict over the mode of government (DeManuelle-Hall, 2019; DW, 2020). Would it be adequate to see both as instances of strikes that facilitate class formation?

Notably, this is a point not just about strike research. The more global a research project becomes, the more the difficult it is to ensure that data are measured in a similar manner across time and space, and that the categories used are capturing similar events. Large-n quantitative research struggles with temporal and spatial specificities. There is a danger of subsuming diverging events or practices under one and the same category (see Burnham, 2004: 72–3; Hopkin, 2010: 299–300). If one was interested in the degree to which liberalism as a political ideology shapes the policy of governments in different parts of the world, for example, one would quickly find that definitions and interpretations of what liberalism is varies hugely across countries, and that the political demands of self-professed 'liberals' in the US and Germany in the area of economic policy can be construed as opposites – in US politics, liberalism is commonly associated with state interventionism; in Germany, it is usually linked to the idea of a 'free' market. One is then faced with a dilemma: One can either use a neatly defined category, which runs contrary to everyday understandings to such a degree that it becomes incomprehensible for political practitioners and non-experts in at least parts of the world ('liberalism is a political ideology that is advocating state interventions in the economy for the common good'), or one can interpret a category in a broad manner, which may encompass a lot of cases, but may have little meaning and may be hard to distinguish from neighbouring categories ('liberalism is a political ideology that is committed to fostering democracy').

In this context, it is important to highlight that strikes are, to a degree, contradictory events with contradictory effects: While some people are mobilized together in a strike effort and strong bonds between them emerge, others may be frightened by the consequences, unconvinced that it is possible to win or hostile either to individuals involved with the strike or to the idea of using collective force. Sometimes, the motives and strategic calculations of one and the same person can be fairly contradictory; the same goes for groups and organizations (see Herkommer et al, 1979: 57; Fantasia, 1988: 79, 116; Bergmann et al, 2002: 72–7). In a nutshell, strikes tend to polarize social forces along class lines, which contributes to making class relations visible, but they can simultaneously fragment such forces. Examples are the 1984–5 Miners' Strike in Britain (Gallas, 2016: 166–93) and the strike wave at French car maker Talbot from 1982 to 1984 (Piciotto, 1984; Najiels, 2019). It is practically impossible to build a strong base for a strike without excluding, to a degree, individual workers who are against walking out, which means that an expansive mobilization tends to be accompanied by a deepening of some divisions. This explain why militant labour activists are often in favour of both an expansive, class-based strategy and, at the same time, of isolating groups of workers who are not fully behind a strike. It is possible to see this as both an expansive and divisive – and, thus, a contradictory – approach. Such contradictions are hard to capture with quantitative data, which are generated by assigning numeric values to clearly defined variables (Sayer, 1992: 176–8).

This leads on to a more general point. If we follow Althusser (1969), the capitalist mode of production is characterized by contradictions, that is, structurally inscribed mechanisms that work against one another. Most importantly, there is a need for capital to accumulate and for labour power to be reproduced, which creates the antagonism between capital and labour. Consequently, practices and perceptions emerge in capitalist surroundings that lead to conflict and sometimes defy neat categorization.

This line of argument is at odds with the determinism implicit in a great number of contributions to quantitative research. Research designs based on quantitative data usually rest on a deductivist and positivist understanding of causation in the form of 'a relationship between discrete events' (Sayer, 1992: 104). They are based on a clearly defined, causal relationship between an independent and a dependent variable (A causes a, or A → a). The implication is that the social world is constituted by a set of causes that can be isolated from one another through analysis, and that produce clearly defined outcomes (A → a; B → b; C → c; D → d ...). In other words, the causal relation itself is imagined like a natural force that can be identified in isolation through experimental research – for example, the force assumed to be behind the swing of a pendulum or the movement of a billiard ball that is hit by another. It follows that the social world, just like the natural world, is governed by laws that are clearly separable from one another. This also means that it is characterized by atomism and a strong degree of determinacy (Sayer, 1992: 173; Blaikie and Priest, 2017: 67–71; Wullweber, 2019: 290–1).

In contradistinction to positivist positions, critical realists highlight that there is structural causation, and that forces can be present without being actualized or activated. They emphasize the systemic and tendential nature of the social world and the openness of social systems. It follows that research is an open-ended, exploratory process (see Collier, 1994: 7–8; Sayer, 2000: 121–4; Blaikie and Priest, 2017: 177).

Accordingly, critical realists often use qualitative research techniques like interviews, participant observation or textual analysis. These are better suited, all in all, to capture the contradictions of capitalist social formations because they share a 'naturalistic approach' (Yilmaz, 2013: 312; see Blaikie and Priest, 2019: 159–61). Put differently, they allow for detailed, linguistic representations of social reality that are descriptive in nature and limit the need for the abstraction and simplification characterizing the generation of quantitative data. Consequently, they are far more context-sensitive.

But this comes at a price, which is that they only ever present a very limited sample of the different processes, relations and interactions that constitute a case, and that they do not lend themselves to producing broad overviews (see Landman, 2003: 81). As a result, generalization is a serious challenge for qualitative research (see Rapley, 2014: 52–3, Blaikie and Priest, 2019: 211–13). This raises the question of how to reconcile the need to produce general observations with the specificities of the contexts in which social interactions take place.

The method of incorporated comparison

The method of 'incorporated comparison', developed by McMichael (1990; 2000), deals with the need to connect a global perspective with a sensitivity to context-specific divergences – or with the challenge of reconciling analytical breadth and depth. In contrast to the country comparisons common in political science (see Landman, 2003; Burnham, 2004), it sets out to achieve generalizability by examining global settings as well as comparing cases and considering their specificity. The attribute 'incorporated' refers to the fact that the objects of comparison form part of a larger social setting that is being mapped simultaneously and does not exist independently of the former. In this sense, 'incorporated comparison' is a multi-scalar method.

Importantly, McMichael is aware of the dangers of subsumptionism. He stresses that our understanding of global capitalism cannot be fixed at the level of theory to be refuted or confirmed, in a second step, through empirical analysis:

> Rather than using 'encompassing comparison' – a strategy that presumes a 'whole' that governs its 'parts' – it progressively constructs a whole as a methodological procedure by giving context to historical phenomena. In effect, the 'whole' emerges via comparative analysis of 'parts' as moments in a self-forming whole. I call this incorporated comparison. (McMichael, 1990: 386; see also Hart, 2018: 380)

Accordingly, the three main assumptions guiding incorporated comparisons are anti-subsumptionist (McMichael 2000: 671):

> First, comparison is not a formal, 'external' procedure in which cases are juxtaposed as separate vehicles of common or contrasting patterns of variation. Rather comparison is 'internal' to historical inquiry, where process-instances are comparable because they are historically connected and mutually conditioning. Second, incorporated comparison does not proceed with an a priori conception of the composition and context of the units compared, rather they form in relation to one another and in relation to the whole formed through their inter-relationship. In other words, the whole is not a given, it is self-forming. This is what I understand we mean by historical 'specificity.' Third, comparison can be conducted across space and time, separately or together.

In my understanding, this approach resembles archaeological fieldwork. I am not referring here to Michel Foucault's general observation that history is marked by discontinuities and ruptures, and that an 'archaeological' approach to history consists in drawing out the specificities of different 'strata' layered on top of each other (1989: 8). My point refers to the research practices of archaeologists. In Foucault's terms, these consists in excavating 'a mass of elements that have to be grouped, made relevant, placed in relation to one another to form totalities' (1989: 8). Archaeologists chart, compare and systematize traces and remnants of past human settlements and activities – and from doing so, draw broader conclusions about social formations of the past. In other words, they make inferences about wholes by looking at parts – and have to deal with the fact that these parts are, to a large degree, incomplete. This means that they address significant gaps in information by making plausible assumptions about missing parts on the grounds of what has been found.

Correspondingly, social scientists who make incorporated comparisons attempt to produce insights of a global nature on the grounds of incomplete information, that is, through the comparison of a limited number of objects. This can be done by, first, linking empirical research to social theory in the way described earlier, and, second, by zooming in and out, that is, combining fine-grained case studies with broad-brush descriptions providing overviews. With reference to my object, I propose developing categories for assessing class formation on the grounds of materialist class theory, putting them to use by mapping non-industrial strikes around the world, and supplementing this mapping with detailed case studies of large-scale strikes or strike waves.

Importantly, this mode of comparison is anti-subsumptionist because it does not start from presuming the existence of a functionally integrated whole, whose workings are illustrated by the cases. McMichael says that an incorporated comparison serves to reconstruct an 'emergent totality' (1990: 391), which implies that a full picture is not the precondition, but the outcome of a detailed research process. The role of theory in the research process is not to give full explanations of what is going on, but to guide researchers in the search for such explanations.

The reference to 'emergence' demonstrates McMichael's implicit affinity with critical realism. It implies that we are dealing with a whole at the level of the actual, which is constituted by the activation (or lack thereof) of deep structures through concrete practices in settings conditioned by institutions. This corresponds with McMichael's critique of the positivist assumption that cases used in a comparison can be seen as discrete, separate entities (1990: 389; 2000: 672). Following him, they are always conditioned by a whole that connects them and has effects on how they evolve. At the same time, the workings of this whole are not presupposed in a strong sense. This means that there is space for an open-ended research process.

Large-scale strikes and multiple data types: reflections on case and data selection

My general observations on incorporated comparison as a method bring me to the question of what criteria should be used for case and data selection. Concerning cases, one could focus on Western Europe. This is not an arbitrary choice, or a choice reflecting research pragmatics, namely that fact that I am based in Germany. It is an ideal research setting for my question because, globally speaking, it was the first macroregion around the world to become industrialized and, likewise, the first to witness sustained processes of deindustrialization. Accordingly, the country at the forefront of both processes is located in the region: Britain spearheaded the industrial revolution, but in technologically advanced areas, it fell behind Germany and US as early as the second wave of industrialization starting in the late 19th century – and went through a sustained decline in manufacturing output and employment relative to other sectors from the 1960s onwards (Hobsbawm, 1968: 172–94; Kitson and Michie, 2014: 10).

Since my aim is to identify developments concerning class relations, the most important criterion is generalizability, that is, a choice of cases where it is reasonable to assume that they are somewhat typical and contribute to larger tendencies. In light of this, it makes sense to go for a 'most different' comparison examining country cases varying greatly in terms of strike incidence, namely a country with low (Germany), medium (Britain) and high strike incidence (Spain) (see Figure 5.3 and Table 5.3). Furthermore, these countries are also useful choices because each of them is described, in the literature, as standing for one the three varieties of capitalism dominating in the macroregion[4]: Germany is a coordinated market economy; Britain a liberal market economy; and Spain a Mediterranean mixed type.

The resulting case studies need to offer thick descriptions of strikes in the three countries (see Vromen, 2010), but these have to be complemented with a less detailed mapping of strike activities not just in other Western European countries, but around the globe. This is necessary to ensure that it is possible to differentiate potential macroregional from truly global developments, and to check whether observations made with reference to the cases can also be made elsewhere. Through such a broad contextualization, one avoids the trappings of methodological Fordism and refrains from treating country cases as discrete, unconnected units. The aim is to produce a comprehensive picture of dominant patterns concerning the links between workers that emerge in strike efforts across the globe.

Importantly, comprehensive does not mean complete. What emerges is a transnational account of strikes with a focus on Western Europe, that is a broad-brush, rough description of strikes around the world substantiated with reference to the Western European cases. Put differently, the mode of incorporated comparison proposed here has global ambitions, but modest ones. It allows one to lend credence to tentative observations on worldwide developments with the help of more detailed and saturated analyses of specific cases in a macroregion.

---

[4] See, for example, Hall (2018) or Frege and Kelly (2004).

In terms of the actual strikes chosen, one could opt for selecting strikes and strike waves with pertinent effects. This is the case, in the area of strike research, if stoppages involve a lot of people – and if they are discussed in the political scene and the news media (see Gallas, 2018: 239). It is plausible to assume that strikes have a significant social impact if they become politicized and an object of public debate. This is because, first, such strikes are visible to workers outside the sector where they originate, which is important for arguing that they have the potential to expand beyond a narrow constituency of workers, and, second, because they affect society as a whole. In my view, these represent two necessary but not sufficient conditions for strikes to contribute to class formation. Conversely, it is hard to argue that stoppages have a significant impact on class relations if do not reach other workers and do not have effects beyond local settings.

It can be gauged whether the first criterion is met by assessing how striking workers reach out to other groups of workers, how these other groups react, and how all of this affects organized labour. For example, it can be argued that a strike is visible to other workers if union leaders from other sectors comment on it. The same can be said if there is evidence of conversations on picket lines with other workers or among colleagues who belong to other unions or occupational categories. And of course, a stoppage is also visible if there are collective responses to it like demonstrations. Importantly, it does not matter whether these reactions are supportive, dismissive or indifferent.

The purpose of the second point is to ensure that the significance of strikes goes beyond local effects. This criterion is met if there is extensive coverage in the national news media of the strike, and if its effects reach the political scene. For this purpose, it is useful to check whether a dispute has been covered at least three times in three different national newspapers with a conservative, liberal and socialist orientation, respectively, and if leading politicians representing conservative, liberal and socialist worldviews have commented on it. Admittedly, it may very well be the case that strikes taking place 'under the radar' and not meeting these criteria have a profound impact on class relations at the national level, but this is very hard to gauge.

In keeping with the general theme of deindustrialization, it makes sense to examine stoppages that diverge from the image of the 'classical' industrial strike in at least one crucial respect. Concerning the *model of trade unionism*, the strikes in the German railway sector are a suitable case. They were driven by an occupational and not an industrial union, the GDL. As regards the *social base*, the 2015 to 2019 junior doctors' dispute in England springs to mind. It was carried out by professionals, not by blue-collar workers. When it comes to *demands*, the general strikes in Spain in the 2010s, including the feminist general strikes, are highly relevant because their goals were not primarily economic in the sense of concerning wages and working conditions, but political in nature. The aim is to identify, through a systematic comparison of disputes in these countries, general trends concerning strike activities in the research space.

Furthermore, the identification of suitable data should not follow the subsumptionist template. In qualitative research based on case studies, this means that in principle, any kind of available information relevant to the research topic needs to be considered (see Blaikie and Priest, 2017: 192) – and that sources of information, for example interview partners, descriptive statistics or observations, should not be selected on the grounds of fitting particularly well with one's theoretical assumptions. Accordingly, I used wide range of sources of information for this book:

- statistics on strike incidence, public attitudes towards specific stoppages (opinion polls) and key socioeconomic markers (wage levels, inequality, unemployment, and so on) that help elucidating the context in which strikes take place;
- online accounts of strike action, for example, social media postings, newsletters or blogs;
- coverage of strikes in the news media;
- press releases from political parties, employers' associations and trade unions;
- public statements from people involved with strikes; and
- background interviews with workers actively involved in organizing strikes.[5]

To avoid subsumptionism it is also important to terminate data collection only once a degree of saturation of one's analysis is reached, that is, if there is a repetition of patterns across different materials and the gains in knowledge made through adding material are limited (see Kvale, 1996: 101– 3; Rapley, 2014: 60). This is the point when we can say that evidence has been produced. Importantly, however, this does not mean that the resulting analysis is set in stone once and for all, as Norman Blaikie and Jan Priest point out: 'The argument for affirming evidence rests on the preponderance of confirming data and the absence of contradictory data, notwithstanding the possibility of as yet undefined alternative explanations' (Blaikie and Priest, 2017: 192).

Through examining these cases and data, it becomes possible to give a meaningful response to the research question. A good indicator for the existence or absence of processes of class formation in the context of strikes are the forms of solidarity prevalent in them. For this purpose, it is necessary to look at *demands*, *constituencies* and *mobilizing dynamics* that are visible when workers go on strike. If the demands made by them are,

---

[5] For a list of the interviewed, see Appendix B.

in principle, transferable to other branches or sectors or concern workers in general, if there are ties to workers that are outside of the original constituency addressed, and if there is a mobilizing dynamic characterized by broad popular support, expansive solidarity – or 'class feeling', to use Luxemburg's term – is in evidence. This can in turn be taken as an indicator for the existence of processes of working-class formation. The opposite scenario emerges if workers engaged in a strike effort focus their demands on highly specific issues to do with their workplace, branch of the economy or sector, which means that they are hard to transfer elsewhere, if there are no signs of connections to other groups of workers, and if popular support is limited. Consequently, it is necessary to centre the comparison of the three cases and the mapping of strikes around the world on the forms of solidarity visible in them and establish what kind of pattern dominates across cases and countries. In the light of the contradictions surrounding strikes, it is necessary to carefully weigh up whether expansive or exclusive forms of solidarity predominate and leave room for ambivalences by allowing oneself, in principle, to give a qualified response.

The case for a multi-scalar analysis

The research design and the criteria developed here for case and data selection – based on an 'incorporated comparison' and in line with critical realist assumptions – ensure that the research process remains open. It is possible, on their grounds, to circumnavigate the trap of subsumptionism and address the challenge of reconciling generality and specificity. With the help of McMichael's approach, one can move beyond methodological Fordism with its focus on the national state, a small number of core countries and on manufacturing. As I demonstrated with reference to my research design concerning non-industrial strikes and class formation, it is possible to capture, in one's research, the global yet variegated nature of contemporary capitalism.

Unsurprisingly, this creates new challenges. For one – and in contrast to positivist comparative politics approaches – incorporated comparisons are not based on easily transferable frameworks such as the 'most similar' and 'most different' research designs often used in political science. This is not an argument against using their underlying logic in processes of case selection, which I employed when I chose the cases presented in this chapter. But to overcome the limitations of analytic comparisons, this logic has to be embedded in a multi-scalar approach to analysis: each project requires a unique approach to 'zooming in and out' and working across scales; detailed case studies have to be combined with less detailed descriptions of key institutions, events and developments from a global vantage point. Second, the aspiration to conduct global research is also a burden for researchers. They need to acquaint themselves both with highly abstract-simple theories with a global field of validity and a wealth of empirical material, which is difficult to handle from a pragmatic point of view, and there are bound to be large gaps in their projects. A mapping of non-industrial strikes around the world plus a comparison based on detailed cases in Western Europe produces a comprehensive account of what is going on, but comprehensive does not mean without gaps. Nevertheless, this chapter is also a plea for scholarship that is trying to shoulder this burden.

2

A Catastrophic Disequilibrium: Neoliberal Capitalism in Crisis

A conjunctural approach to the current crisis

Observers discussing the present-day, multifaceted crisis of global capitalism are sometimes invoking the gory imagery of horror films. After the global banking crisis had struck in 2007 and 2008, Chris Harman (2009) and Jamie Peck (2010) spoke of 'zombie capitalism' and 'zombie neoliberalism', respectively. Around a decade later, Raul Zelik reclaimed this trope (2020a). Witnessing the acceleration of climate change and the lack of decisive interventions to slow it down as well as the COVID-19 pandemic, he referred to the people suffering under the yoke of global social order the 'undead of capital'. This is reminiscent of some of the metaphors employed by Marx in the first volume of *Capital* (1976), who stated that '[c]apital is dead labour which, vampire-like, lives only by sucking living labour, and lives the more, the more labour it sucks' (Marx, 1976: 342; see Carver, 1998: 14–20).

The purpose of using these metaphors is obvious. They highlight the fact that we are in a nightmarish situation. Global capitalism lives off the toil of workers around the world, depriving them of their vitality and their ability to actively take control of their lives. But despite the fact that more people than ever are sucked into the system of wage labour and have to submit to the imperatives of capital, it is still teetering on the brink of collapse. Turning people into zombies, it keeps on surviving – but is becoming weaker and weaker in the process. Zelik puts it this way:

> The zombie is about a loss of control and absolute heteronomy: One lives and is still dead. The fear of this is even greater because identity in bourgeois society is based on autonomy and self-control. However, our experience of being-in-the-world hardly conforms to this despite

all the rhetoric of freedom. We are fascinated by the undead, because we are so used to the feeling of being externally controlled. (Zelik, 2020a: 23)

Implicit in this imagery is a specific claim concerning crisis containment: The power blocs around the world are unwilling to, or incapable of, shaking off the neoliberal orthodoxies of crisis management – bailouts for corporations, austerity for the broader populations and market-based attempts to address climate change, for example, emissions trading. This is reinforcing the crisis and is possibly damaging global capitalism and the natural environment beyond repair.

I do not object to the point that the prevailing modes of crisis management are deepening the crisis, and I agree that climate change poses an existential threat to humankind as it has been existing since the onset of industrialization. Nevertheless, I am not convinced by the zombie imagery. It suggests that we are locked into the existing political-economic regime, and that there is little likelihood of change – only a permanent process of weakening – until we reach the stage of final collapse. It is based on a strong sense of continuity and on a teleological assumption: The notion that neoliberalism will persist, and that capitalist development will result in the eventual collapse of the capitalist mode of production. With reference to the COVID-19 pandemic, Zelik contends that '[i]t is part of the truth that this crisis represents a moment of openness, in which almost everything is opened up to question' (2020a: 10). If that this is indeed the case, using zombie metaphors creates the danger of covering up ruptures and openings in the current conjuncture, and of underestimating the agency and creativity of both pro- and anti-capitalist social forces. Consequently, it would be a mistake to assume that we are witnessing more of the same, only worse. Importantly, it would be just as problematic to suppose that the current shifts and changes are automatically strengthening the hand of labour. It is worth emphasizing that novel economic and political arrangements can be more oppressive than existing ones.

Highlighting the possibility of ruptures, I propose looking at the present crisis from a conjunctural perspective. This stresses a degree of openness of the historical situation, and the absence of a detailed script describing how things will evolve from where we are. Importantly, I agree with Zelik and others that the globally dominant, neoliberal political-economic regime is fragile – and that its collapse is indeed a genuine possibility.

This assessment comes with a practical challenge. It is difficult to provide a definitive account of an object that is global and has been existing for several decades. Any attempt to provide a full picture would overburden this monograph. Consequently, I limit myself in this chapter to making some rather impressionistic remarks concerning key developments in global capitalism since the Second World War. I will neither include a broad range of data nor aim to create a complete picture.

In line with my interest in strikes and class formation, I focus on aspects that are of high relevance for workers, and that are informed by my class theoretical perspective. For example, I am more interested in the development of global employment and the rate of global economic growth than in the latest 'innovations' in the field of securitization or the significance of cryptocurrencies for global financial markets. In line with my method of 'zooming' in and out, I neither claim that my detailed case studies in the next part prove, in a deductive manner, the veracity of my more general pronouncements in this and the succeeding chapter, which provide contextualization. Nor do I argue that these pronouncements can be derived, in an inductive fashion, from the case studies. What I show is that there is a fit between my theoretical arguments, which are based on my conceptualization of class; my general observations, which are based on a review of global political economy literature plus some existing statistical data; and my detailed case studies, which result, to a stronger degree, from first-hand empirical research. Operating this way, I argue that it is plausible to assume that there are general trends.

Neoliberalism against organized labour

Before I start discussing how neoliberalism evolved and entered its present crisis, it is necessary to reflect on some of the concepts used in my analyses. What does the term 'neoliberalism' mean, what is a crisis, and what kind of crisis are we faced with in the present moment?

In my view, neoliberalism is a global political-economic regime, that is, an ensemble of institutionalized strategies existing in all parts of the world that bear a family resemblance and thus reinforce one another. It is based on the assumption that the market is the most efficient mode of allocating resources across society, and that a market-based society is also desirable because it preserves individual freedom. From this, neoliberals infer that markets should be 'free', that is, that it is necessary to shield their outcomes from economic and political interference – for example, from monopolistic corporations, trade unions or state apparatuses. Conversely, they advocate protecting the interests of property owners, reducing taxes and redistributive measures, relaxing regulations and expanding markets. Accordingly, a key strategy of neoliberals is to naturalize competition and market outcomes – for example, with the help of bilateral or multilateral free trade agreements, which usually cannot be abandoned by a single contracting party and thus create binding rules and regulations that are very difficult to alter. If subsidies or the nationalization of firms are banned under free trade agreements, a government altering market outcomes is in breach of its legal obligations.

Through enshrining rules that protect market outcomes, neoliberal political projects protect capital and work against democracy (see Scherrer, 2014: 348; Šumonja, 2021: 220).

The economist Friedrich August Hayek, one of the main advocates of neoliberalism, describes the market mechanism thus:

> The fact is simply that we consent to retain and agree to enforce uniform rules for a procedure which has greatly improved the chances of all to have their wants satisfied, but at the price of all individuals and groups incurring the risk of unmerited failure. ... It is the only procedure yet discovered in which information widely dispersed among millions of men can be effectively utilized for the benefit of all – and used by assuming to all an individual liberty desirable for itself on ethical grounds. It is a procedure which of course has never been 'designed' but which we have learnt gradually to improve after we had discussed how it increased the efficiency of men in the groups who had evolved it.[1] (Hayek, 1973–7: 71)

The assumption that the free reign of the market is likely to lead to beneficial outcomes for all is diametrically opposed to the primary principle behind working-class formation, the principle of solidarity, which aims at cutting out competition between workers and thus obstructs the market mechanism. In this sense, neoliberal political projects work against working-class interests. In a nutshell, neoliberalism is directed against organized labour (Candeias, 2004: 78). Accordingly, Hayek paints unions in a very negative light, that is, as privileged organizations exempt from the rule of law (1960: 267). His close colleague Milton Friedman flips the capitalist relations of production when he ascribes 'monopoly power' to unions – with the obvious implication that monopolies need to be broken up (1962: 116).

If I speak of neoliberalism as a political-economic regime, I refer to an object located at the level of the social formation with a global extension. It consists in a network of mutually reinforcing, institutionalized strategies that have been created, promoted and consolidated by power blocs and representatives of capital from all over the world from the 1970s onwards. The network emerged in a handful of countries that were at the forefront of political-economic change, most importantly Britain, Chile and the US, and then spread all over the world. Neoliberalism reached global dominance in 1990s – after the Soviet bloc had collapsed, and when centre-left governments started to embrace the idea of the 'free' market.

---

[1]   For a detailed critique of Hayek, see Gallas (2015).

This raises the question of how political forces promoting neoliberalism were able to secure broad popular support and, more specifically, support from people located on the side of labour. It is worth clarifying in this context that the incompatibility of neoliberalism with working-class interests does not mean that it is impossible for individual workers to benefit from processes of neoliberalization. Quite the contrary – it is part and parcel of such processes that workers become divided, with some 'winning' and others 'losing'. The Thatcher government, for example, sold off council houses on a grand scale to tenants at subsidised prices (see Gallas, 2016: 145–6), which drove a wedge between workers who could afford to buy their houses and those who could not, and between the generation that was able to purchase their homes and later generations who were not afforded this opportunity and found themselves in a rental market with limited options and little legal protection.

An organic crisis

Commentators quite frequently invoke a 'crisis of neoliberalism' with reference to the current conjuncture of global capitalism and explain in great detail what is happening to the existing political and economic institutions and key social forces in the process (Brie, 2009; Aalbers, 2013; Jaffee, 2020). But they rarely explain what the ubiquitous term 'crisis' means. From my vantage point, it refers to situations where the strategies of dominant forces inside the power bloc cause frictions to such a degree that comprehensive additional interventions are required to reproduce the capitalist mode of production, the institutions underpinning the existing social formations as well as the existing relations of social domination. In other words, it becomes necessary to mobilize additional material and ideational resources to ensure that day-to-day routines in the affected areas can somehow continue, and often, this is still not possible to the full extent. Depending on the extension and magnitude of the crisis, the interventions required can differ – from attempts to stimulate the economy to measures strengthening the repressive state apparatus that are aimed at quelling protests.

This raises the question of what kind of crisis neoliberalism is faced with. Using a Gramscian term, I argue that there is an 'organic crisis' of global neoliberal capitalism (Hall, 1979: 15–16; see also Gramsci, 1971: 318). The attribute 'organic' highlights the fact that economic, political and cultural crisis dynamics align with, and reinforce, one another. In other words, an organic crisis is a comprehensive crisis that requires drastic, atypical measures and changes to ensure the continued existence and dominance of the capitalist mode of production and the relationships of domination linked with it, including class relations. Importantly, the atypical nature of the crisis management needed creates ruptures in the dominant political-economic regime. An organic crisis is not merely a cyclical crisis, which is followed by a number of adjustments and a return to the status quo ante, but a situation in which a wholesale 'regime shift' occurs (Jessop, 2002: 169). In this sense, I contend that capitalism in the West, which was characterized by settlements between capital and labour at the national level and varying degrees of state interventionism to protect them, was facing an organic crisis in the 1970s that led to the emergence of neoliberalism (see Harvey, 2005: 12; Bieling, 2011: 95–7).[2] Likewise, I argue that present-day, neoliberal capitalism also finds itself in an organic crisis.

An important qualification is that it is too early to say what the outcomes of this crisis will be. It is by no means clear that a new, coherent regime will replace neoliberalism; my claim is that some of the pillars on which it rests are crumbling in the situation of crisis. Arguably, a chaotic, incoherent conjuncture of permanent crisis has emerged where some aspects of the neoliberal regime are still more or less intact, and others have ceased to exist. This has important implications for the reproduction of class domination and, as a consequence, for labour.

The collapse of settled capitalism

To make sense of the current conjuncture, it is necessary to look at longer-term developments that produced the conditions of the present day. From a Marxian vantage point, historical developments inside capitalist social formations reflect, to a significant degree, attempts of power blocs to address the inherent instability of capitalist relations of production, and the contestations to capitalist class domination that they give rise to. In light of this, it is worth tracing how the rise and decline of neoliberalism reflects class conflict and shifting class political strategies.

A useful starting point is the work of the US engineer Frederick Taylor, who had argued, at the beginning of the 20th century, that the efficient

---

[2] The temporality of reactions to the crisis, that is, of the processes of neoliberalization occurring in response to it, played out differently across countries. It can be described with the help of a typology developed by Jessop (2002: 169). Vanguard countries such as Britain, Chile and the US experienced neoliberalization first as a 'regime shift', that is a series of sharp shocks in the second half of the 1970s and the 1980s, and then a long phase of consolidation from the 1990s onwards. In countries with more consensus-based political systems, this order was reversed. A good example is Germany: In the 1980s and 1990s, a long string of 'neoliberal policy adjustments' were implemented. This was followed by the sharp shock of the Agenda 2010 policies, which the 'red-and-green' governments under Schröder pursued in the early 2000s. For the transition countries formerly belonging to the Soviet bloc, neoliberalization amounted to a 'radical system transformation', which occurred straight after the collapse of Soviet-style socialism in Eastern Europe in the late 1980s.

organization of production required a degree of simplification of each task so that a trained, 'intelligent gorilla' could carry it out (1919: 40). Reflected in the emergence of the assembly line in the US car industry, 'Taylorism', with the strict discipline it imposed on workers, soon became a dominant strategy of organizing manufacturing. However, it reached a limit from the mid-1960s onwards when workers in in countries such as Britain, France, Italy and West Germany increasingly resisted the Taylorist discipline imposed on them, and labour unrest intensified (Nowak and Gallas, 2013). This amounted to a rupture with the settlements between capital and labour instituted after the Second World War in the Global North, which had traded union acquiescence to the (often Taylorist) discipline characterizing the industrial work process for full employment as well as increasing wages and improving living standards. Settled capitalism had been sustained through manufacturing and productivist cycles based on the production of relative surplus value. Increases in productivity, achieved through imposition of Taylorist discipline on the shop floor, translated both into extra profits and wage increases, and a significant share of the profits was reinvested into the industrial sector.[3] In the Global South, various governments attempted to pursue developmentalist agendas that resembled the Northern strategies. They promoted strategies of import-substitution industrialization that were also aimed at establishing productivist cycles (see Wallerstein, 2005).

In the 1970s, global capitalism entered a conjuncture of crisis, which mirrored the labour unrest on the shop floors and the fact that the productivist cycles had broken. At the economic level, this conjuncture was characterized by 'stagflation', that is, economic stagnation combined with high inflation. In 1973, the first oil crisis hit oil-importing countries, and global economic growth collapsed in the subsequent two years. Around the same time, there were warnings of a 'global unemployment crisis' (Grant, 1971). In West Germany, for example, unemployment shot up from 0.7 per cent in 1970 to 4.7 per cent in 1975 (Sell et al, 2020); and in the US, it rose from 4.9 to 8.5 per cent over the same period.[4] At the global level, adequate data are hard come by, but the collapse of growth plus processes of mechanization

---

[3] In this usage, the attribute 'settled' has a double meaning: It highlights how capitalism was based on settlements between capital and labour, and how these settlements emerged at the national level and were sustained through interventions at the level of the national state. I prefer 'settled capitalism' to more well-known characterizations such as 'embedded liberalism' and 'Fordism' because neither liberalism nor Fordism were regimes dominant in all of the Western world during the postwar era, and because settled capitalism highlights the specific configuration of class relations at that time.

[4] https://data.bls.gov/timeseries/LNU04023554&series_id=LNU04000000&series_id= LNU03023554&series_id=LNU03000000&years_option=all_years&periods_option= specific_periods&periods=Annual+Data [Accessed 14 October 2022].

and automatization in manufacturing indicate that there was a jobs problem far beyond West Germany and the US.

For labour, the era of stagflation was a crisis of employment and income plus a crisis of work organization. Workers articulated their frustration with having to bear the brunt of downturn and having to submit to the discipline of Taylorist production through going on strike. Many of their actions were militant, wildcat strikes that occurred outside of the existing legal frameworks for labour disputes. A case in point is the string of stoppages that shook West Germany in September 1969, which mainly affected the steel industry. It initiated a broader wave of disputes involving more than 1.2 million workers and culminated in the 1973 migrant worker strike at Ford (Schumann et al, 1971; Birke, 2007: 219, 274–304). These stoppages are significant because they occurred in a country that had cultivated a reputation for industrial 'peace', that is, a corporatist, legalistic, negotiation-based approach to labour relations supported by capital, labour and the state. Importantly, the preparedness to take militant action was not specific to Western Europe. In the 1970s, there were instances of labour unrest around the world. For example, there was a wave of strikes of Black and Indian workers in Durban, South Africa, in 1973 that involved almost 100,000 workers and hit major industrial compounds in the city, reflecting frustration with low wages and poor working conditions and expressing open opposition to the Apartheid regime. This constituted an important step in the labour-based resistance to Apartheid that contributed significantly to the regime's eventual downfall (Horn, 2003; Lichtenstein, 2015: 114–20). In India, there was a wave of railway strikes, culminating in a large-scale stoppage in May 1974, which lasted for 20 days, and in which a number of workers in the low seven figures participated (Samaddar, 2015; Choudhury, 2017).

For capital, there was a crisis of profitability – a situation characterized by capitalists searching for opportunities for investment where they were able to obtain a high profit margin. There were not just issues with the labour process and people's refusal to submit to the discipline of Taylorism; the pressure on jobs and, as a result, on wages meant that demand was weak. All in all, we can speak of an emerging overaccumulation crisis, that is, a situation where the profitable reinvestment of capital became a problem.

The economic tensions were compounded by an impasse at the political level: Right-wing authoritarian, anti-labour forces and socialist, pro-labour forces both made advances and were defeated in the era of stagflation, and how events evolved depended on time and place. In Chile, the *coup d'état* in 1973 under the leadership of Augusto Pinochet ended the left-socialist government of Salvador Allende; in Argentina, the right-wing General Jorge Rafael Videla installed a military dictatorship in 1976. In 1977, the right-wing Likud, for the first time in history, won an Israeli election and its leader, Menachem Begin, became prime minister. Roughly around the same time, the military dictatorships in Greece, Portugal and Spain were disintegrating; in particular, the Carnation Revolution in Portugal amounted to a successful popular mobilization against the ruling far-right clique. In Britain, the Labour Party won two elections in 1974 with a left-socialist manifesto and against the backdrop of a militant and successful miners' strike, and the Soweto Uprising in 1976 demonstrated that the hold of the Apartheid regime over the Black population in South Africa was weakening.

At the level of culture, the existence of tensions and contradictory developments was also visible. Mass migration into Western Europe and the emergence of new immigrant communities resulted in a re-composition of the labour force and started to challenge traditional notions of belonging and national identity. In the US, the civil rights movement had successfully challenged segregation, which also created opportunities for new solidarities, new demands and worker organization across racial lines (Roediger, 2017: 10). This triggered a racist backlash, which was reflected in the rise to prominence of far-right politicians such as Enoch Powell in Britain or George Wallace in the US (Carter, 1996; Hall et al, 2013: 244–6; Gallas, 2016: 81–3).

The radical movements of workers, students, people of colour, anti-militarists, women, gay people, people concerned about the natural environment and others that had emerged from the 1960s onwards in places as diverse as Mexico City, Paris and Prague facilitated the rise of anti-authoritarian attitudes. On the one hand, these attitudes worked against acquiescence and conformist behaviour and promoted rebellion; on the other hand, they fostered individualistic and anti-state orientations and lifestyles that were hard to reconcile with strong notions of class-based solidarity and the importance of acting together in mass movements (see Boltanski and Chiapello, 2005: 167–216; Guldi, 2019). Around the same time, second-wave feminism began to challenge the dominant understandings of gender relations, marriage and sexuality – and with it, the ignorance of organized labour towards reproductive labour (Arruzza, 2013: 49–55, 69–78).

The rise of the 'New Left' led to fierce backlashes from social conservatives, who created a discursive link between the economic and political crisis tendencies and lifestyle changes and created imaginaries of social decline. Obviously, these developments played out in different ways in different countries and different parts of the Western bloc. For example, figures like Mary Whitehouse in Britain and Jerry Falwell Sr. in the US, who promoted a restoration of 'family values', were linked to evangelical Christianity. In other countries, this role fell to representatives of the Catholic Church, for example to Patricia Bartlett in New Zealand, a former nun, or to far-right activists like the Nouvelle Droite in France, a circle of intellectuals around Alain de Benoist that was deeply opposed to both Western liberalism and the advance of the left. But what can be said was that there was a general push towards cultural liberalization as well as fierce opposition to it from the right – which roughly mirrored the contradictory developments at the political level (see Bar-On, 2008; Banwart, 2013; Hall et al, 2013: 247–53, 286–7, 314; Brookes, 2018).

In a nutshell, this was a conjuncture where neither left-socialist nor right-authoritarian forces were capable of consolidating advances; in fact, it was a chaotic situation where either side was managing to damage the other without making decisive gains, paving the way for a fundamental political realignment. In the Gramscian tradition we can speak not just of an organic crisis, but also of 'an equilibrium of forces heading towards catastrophe' (Gramsci, 1971: 219).

The emergence of neoliberalism

In a conjuncture marked by intensifying class struggles and stagnant productivity, governments – led by the US – initially reacted with expansionary strategies in the fields of monetary and fiscal policy. This created inflationary pressures and pushed up public debt. Under conditions of the Bretton Woods system, fiscal expansion in the US – fuelled by the Vietnam War and Lyndon B. Johnson's 'Great Society' agenda – led to a significant increase in the amount of dollars circulating outside the US (Helleiner, 1994: 86–7; Cleaver, 1995: 155).[5]

The Bretton Woods system collapsed in the early 1970s. In 1971, gold convertibility of the US dollar was suspended, and in 1973, a system of freely fluctuating exchange rates emerged. This development paved the way for the liberalization and globalization of financial markets. The collapse of Bretton Woods meant that there was no longer an obligation, on the side of central banks, to keep their currencies within a band to the dollar and impede capital flows across borders (see Eichengreen, 1996: 93–135; Bieling, 2011: 84–7). This was in keeping with what economist Milton Friedman had been advocating since 1950 (Friedman, 1962: 67). In contradistinction to Keynesians, he argued that the primary task for governments in the broader area of economic policy was to fight inflation (Friedman, 1962: 38), and

---

[5] After the Second World War, the monetary order of the West had emerged out of the 1944 Bretton Woods agreement between 44 countries that represented the Allies. It led to the creation of the International Monetary Fund (IMF) and the World Bank. Under it, currencies were pegged to the US dollar, which was convertible into gold. A system of capital controls protected governments from balance-of-payments pressures and enabled them to adjust their pegs to the dollar in a controlled manner if that was necessary. It enabled central banks and governments to achieve a degree of independence in the field of monetary policy (Eichengreen, 1996: 136; Scherrer and Kunze, 2011: 64).

that capital controls, trade barriers and fixed exchange rates hampered the capacity of markets to correct themselves (Friedman, 1962: 67–9).

The Bretton Woods episode shows that in an unstable situation, space for a fundamental political realignment emerged. Intellectuals like Friedman and Hayek and think tanks like the Mont Pelerin Society and the London-based Institute of Economic Affairs had been promoting economic liberalism-cum-authoritarianism as a path to the eradication of economic crisis tendencies for decades, but their agenda gained traction in the 1970s (Harvey, 2005: 19–22). Neoliberalism combined traditional themes of the right like toughness on crime, nationalism and the need to work hard with economic liberalism and some of the individualist themes that had become more pertinent in the context of revolt of 1968; its proponents presented themselves as offering an alternative to both the socialist left and 'settled' Conservatism.

In a move that can be seen as a form of 'authoritarian populism' (Hall, 1979: 15), neoliberal politicians claimed to be champions of the people, promoters of 'law and order' and enemies of 'shirkers' and vested interests – and did so from positions of power inside the state. They claimed to be untainted by the collapse of the postwar arrangements, which had been supported, in many countries, by both the centre-left and the centre-right; as supporters of everyone aspiring to 'get ahead' in life through 'hard work'; as 'anti-collectivists' and 'anti-statists' standing up for 'freedom'; and – ignoring the fundamental difference between subaltern, popular positions and those inside the power bloc – as antagonists of those from the left and right who were allegedly benefiting from the status quo, be they industrialists in receipt of subsidies, trade union leaders presiding over closed shops or welfare recipients refusing to work (Hall, 1979; Gallas, 2016: 146–7). The neoliberal interpretation of the crisis was perfectly captured in a campaign poster used by the British Conservative Party in 1978 – by which time Margaret Thatcher had assumed its leadership – which showed a stylized dole queue and simply said 'Labour isn't working'.

Important political staging posts on the path of neoliberalism to becoming the globally dominant political-economic regime were the anti-socialist coup in Chile, which turned the country into a laboratory of neoliberalism under the guidance of economists trained at the University of Chicago; the decision of the leadership of the Chinese Communist Party in 1978 to start liberalizing the Chinese economy; the election victories of Margaret Thatcher in Britain and Ronald Reagan in the US in 1979 and 1980, respectively, who soon became figureheads of the 'new right'; the *coup d'état* in Turkey in 1980, which led to a ban on parties and unions, fierce repression against left-wing and labour activists and a liberalization of the Turkish economy under the guidance of the IMF; the fact that in 1983, the Mitterrand government in France – at the time, a coalition of socialists and communists – caved in to the pressures of financial capital, which had started to move against the franc, and prioritized the fight against inflation over an agenda of social democratic transformation; the collapse of Soviet-style socialism around 1989 in Eastern Europe, which meant that the hand of organized labour in capitalist countries was no longer strengthened by the need to hold back the 'Red Scare'; and the fact that a string of social democratic and left-liberal presidents and prime ministers of countries that were hubs of the global economy accepted, in the wake of this collapse, key tenets of economic liberalism, among them P.V. Narasimha Rao in India, Bill Clinton in the US, Thabo Mbeki in South Africa, Tony Blair in Britain and Gerhard Schröder in Germany (see Harvey, 2005; Dogan, 2010; Karadag, 2010; Gallas, 2016; Zelik, 2020a: 96–102).

At the cultural level, the changes were felt in the promotion of individualism and consumerism – attitudes that were not just fully consistent with economic liberalism, but that reflected, to a degree, the anti-authoritarianism and anti-traditionalism of the period around 1968. They became articulated with at least three more traditionalist themes that the 'new right' had inherited from the 'old right', which had existed before the postwar settlements between capital and labour: nationalism and patriotism; an emphasis on 'self-improvement' through hard work; and a call for 'law and order', which facilitated the expansion of repressive state apparatuses in many countries. Governments tended to justify this process with reference to the need to crack down on crime as well as on left-wing 'extremism' and militant segments of organized labour; the latter pattern, however, receded into background once the Soviet bloc had collapsed and the left and the unions had been forced onto the retreat (see Hall, 1979; Hall et al, 2013; Gallas, 2016: 280–1).

The emerging neoliberal regime was institutionalized by what was soon to be known as the 'Washington consensus' – a number of political-economic commitments made by governments around the world and by international institutions, most importantly the IMF, the World Bank and the World Trade Organization (WTO). Among these commitments were the creation of global financial markets and production networks – a move that can be seen as fostering economic globalization; a general emphasis in economic policy on individual advancement and 'free' markets, including the privatization of publicly owned corporations and public services; the promotion of free trade and multilateralism at the level of international politics; the adoption of a restrictive approach to public spending; the endorsement of approaches in monetary policy aimed at keeping inflation low; and the rejection of state interventionism in economic matters and collectivism in labour issues (Harvey, 2005: 93; Gamble, 2009: 84–7; Bieling, 2011: 100).

Following Peter Gowan, the social shifts facilitated the emergence of the 'new Wall St system' (Gowan, 2009), that is, a self-reinforcing transnational financial system that operated at a distance from the real economy. The 1970s crisis had ushered in two changes that contributed to this emergence: the suspension of gold convertibility meant that there were no formal limits to the expansion of the money supply; and the emergence of floating exchange rates amounted to private investors now carrying currency risks connected to international trade (Gowan, 2009: 7). In the centres of capitalism, governments decided step-by-step to remove capital controls, which operated as an obstacle to ensuring such risks (Candeias, 2004: 112). Subsequently, a transnational, open financial system emerged that facilitated the creation of speculative bubbles.

Part of the process were shifts of power relations inside power blocs around the world. Once financial markets had been liberalized and central banks had decided to increase interest rates, enormous profits could be made through financial investments. This contributed to the adoption of finance-led accumulation strategies and the rise of financial capital, which became the dominant fraction of capital in most countries.

Industrial corporations were not just hit by privatization and the abolition of subsidies, but also by the growing competition of finance. This created significant additional pressure to push up profitability – investors increasingly had the option of divesting their capital and moving it into the financial sector. In principle, there were four main routes for capitalists to increase profits – or four 'fixes', to use Silver's terminology: First, the 'technological fix' (Silver, 2014: 51), that is, the use of automation and computer technology to alter the labour process and push up productivity; second, the 'spatial fix' (Silver, 2014: 49), that is, the shifting of production to countries with lower wage levels and, as a result, production costs; third, the 'product fix' (Silver, 2014: 62), that is, the shifting of production into new areas; and, fourth, the 'financial fix' (Silver, 2014: 64), that is, the decision to move investments from production to financial assets. One may want to add that once organized labour became weaker both thanks to strengthening financial capital and governments openly attacking unions as well as the institutions of the welfare state, there was also a 'political fix', that is, corporations pushing for, and making use of, shifts in the regulation of labour relations as well the tax regime to restore profitability. This was done by employing union busting techniques and obstructing the organization and collective action of workers; by cutting social wages and thus creating precarity on the side of workers; and by evading taxation and paying less tax overall (see McNally, 2009: 60). Finally, there was also a 'proletarianisation fix', that is, the dispossession of agricultural workers, mostly in India and China, that significantly increased the global reserve army of labour (McNally, 2009: 52, 60). This added significantly to the pressure on workers who had jobs.

The result was that economic inequality increased significantly in many of the countries experiencing neoliberalization and the insertion into a global political economy dominated by finance, for example in Britain, China, India and the US.[6] Furthermore, the international division of labour changed significantly (Candeias, 2004: 168–77; McNally, 2009: 51–2). In various countries of the Global North, areas of production began to predominate that were based on the use of high tech and skilled or even highly qualified workers; less technologically advanced forms of manufacturing were often relocated to countries in the Global South, the classical example being, as Silver argues in *Forces of Labor*, the car and garment industries.

These processes of deindustrialization and industrialization, which were part and parcel of the overall neoliberalization of the global political economy, were accompanied by the restructuring of labour relations. In other words, neoliberal governments attacked militant trade unions. In Britain, the Thatcher government chose to restrict trade union rights and go after organized labour. The key confrontation was the 1984–5 Miners' Strike, which was the response of the National Union of Mineworkers (NUM) to the decision of the Thatcher government to run down this state-owned industry. It ended with the defeat of the union. In the US, the Reagan administration also sought open confrontations with organized labour. Notably, it fired 12,000 air traffic controllers and banned them from public service for life after they had walked out in 1981, and subsequently legally restricted the room for manoeuvre of unions. In Chile, one of the first countries to adopt neoliberalism after the *coup d'état* in 1973, the Pinochet dictatorship suppressed the socialist labour movement, but was not successful in co-opting anti-communist unions. Nevertheless, the 1979 Labour Plan significantly restricted the ability of unions to legally go on strike. In South Korea, an important hub of global industry, the transition to democracy in the 1980s was accompanied by the institution of a draconian regime of labour repression. In Nigeria, the 2005 Trade Union Amendment Act was inspired by the Thatcherite anti-union legislation and also created significant obstacles for workers who wanted to go on strike legally (Cohen, 2006: 65; Álvarez Vallejos, 2010; Gallas, 2016; Aborisade and Povey, 2018; Avarena Carasco and Muñoz, 2018: 134; Ji, 2020). The terrain on which class formation took place shifted drastically over the course of the 1980s and 1990s, both in the North and South.

The increasing economic inequality and the restructuring of labour relations show clearly that capital was the beneficiary of neoliberalization, and that labour lost ground. Against this backdrop, I agree with Harvey's assessment that neoliberalism amounts to 'a successful project for the restoration of ruling-class power' (Harvey, 2005: 203). Nevertheless, it is

---

[6]   https://data.worldbank.org/indicator/SI.POV.GINI?locations=1W-CN-IN-US-GB&name_desc=true [Accessed 9 October 2022].

worth stressing that this process of restoration was met with fierce resistance. At the forefront were public sector unions active in areas and industries controlled by the state that came under direct attacks thanks to neoliberal restructuring. Prime examples are the 1984–5 Miners' Strike in Britain, in which the NUM battled against the plan of the Thatcher government to phase out coalmining, a nationalized industry; and the successful public sector strike wave in France against the Juppé plan in 1995, which aimed to cut pensions for people employed by the state. As neoliberalization deepened and spread out, the mobilization against it became less specific. With the 1999 'Battle of Seattle', the alter-globalization movement moved to the forefront, which was a very broad coalition against the restructuring of the global political economy on the grounds of free-market ideas (Zinn, 2003: 672–4; Scherrer and Kunze, 2011: 105–6, Gallas and Nowak, 2012: 47–8; Gallas, 2016: 166–93). Importantly, struggles of industrial workers did not vanish in this process. Viewed from a global vantage point, they moved with capital, which was relocated to newly industrializing countries (Silver, 2003; 2014; see Chapter 3).

The neoliberal turn of social democracy

The contestations to neoliberalism reflect the antagonistic nature of class relations in capitalism, and the fact that there were limits to popular consent in the first phase of neoliberalization. In the 1990s and early 2000s, an important political shift occurred. After Conservatives had won a string of elections and the resistance to neoliberalism visible in the first phase started to wane somewhat, social democratic and centrist forces started to embrace free market ideas. What emerged was a 'progressive neoliberalism' (Fraser, 2017), which connected the notion of a 'free economy' and the preservation of existing power blocs with a commitment to fostering 'equality of opportunities' through measures aimed at protecting individuals from discrimination in market settings, strengthening 'employability' through education and training and alleviating some of the market outcomes that badly affected disadvantaged groups. According to Nancy Fraser (2017), '[t]he progressive-neoliberal bloc combined an expropriative, plutocratic economic program with a liberal-meritocratic politics of recognition'.

Its emergence was a direct reaction of centrist and centre-left forces to the pressure enacted on politicians through the growing economic significance and political influence of financial capital. Initially, centre-left politicians embraced ideas of the 'new right' out of opportunism and for strategic reasons. They believed that they would be able to buy time and expand their room for manoeuvre if they displayed faith in free market doctrines and met the expectations of financial investors. Dennis Healey, Chancellor in a Labour government under James Callaghan in mid-1970s Britain, is a prime example. He was an ' "unbelieving" monetarist' (Stephens, 1996: 11), accepting an IMF loan in 1976 that was offered on the condition of taking a deflationary approach to monetary and fiscal policy. Upon leaving office, he confessed that his commitment to fiscal restraint and his preparedness to allow unemployment to increase was entirely tactical, that is, an attempt of managing the expectations of financial investors in order to protect the pound, and not something done out conviction (Gallas, 2016: 123). Likewise, the right turn of the Mitterrand presidency appears to have been an attempt to address the fact that there was massive pressure from financial capitalists, who had begun to sell francs and move capital out of the country. In the end, the French government abandoned its reform agenda, which was based on nationalizations, infrastructural investment and the introduction of the 35-hour working week (Zelik, 2020a: 99–101).

Once neoliberalism and the 'new right' became more normalized, centrists and moderates reconsidered their options and started to fully embrace 'new right' ideas, just like the many important forces on the right had accepted Keynesian in the immediate postwar decades. Part of the process was a series of election victories for right-wing forces, namely, the British Conservative Party and the Republican Party in the US. Thatcher was in office from 1979 to 1990, winning three general elections in a row, and Reagan from 1981 to 1989, serving a full two terms. And their successors also stood for free market beliefs – George H.W. Bush, elected in 1988, had been vice-president under Reagan, and John Major, who took over from Thatcher in 1990 and was re-elected in 1992, had served in Thatcher's cabinet as Chancellor of the Exchequer. The fact that Soviet-style socialism collapsed in the late 1980s and early 1990s was interpreted, by many commentators, as a final victory for capitalism and Western-style 'liberal democracy'.[7] In light of this, it is not surprising that leading centrist and centre-left forces called for 'new realism' – a term used by the right-wing of the Labour Party and the trade

---

[7] Francis Fukuyama's *The End of History and the Last Man* (1992) is probably the most fervent scholarly statement declaring that the socialist challenge to capitalism and liberal democracy had ceased to exist after the fall of the Berlin Wall. Fukuyama echoed a famous dictum by Thatcher when he stated that according to Hegel, 'there were no alternative principles or forms of social and political organization that were superior to liberalism' (Fukuyama, 1992: 64; see also Gallas, 2016: 120). Indeed, he suggested that human history may have reached an endpoint with the collapse of Soviet-style socialism (Fukuyama, 1992: 293–4). Given his alignment with the Rand Corporation, a 'new right' think tank, his belief in the superiority and supremacy of 'the market' and representative democracy is not surprising. But at the time, similar claims could be heard from intellectuals less clearly placed on the right. Hans-Magnus Enzensberger (1991), for example, a leading West German intellectual supporting the 1968 student movement, called for an ultra-pragmatic approach to politics and an end to utopian thinking once the authoritarian regime in East Germany had collapsed.

unions in Britain from the 1980s onwards to refer to the decision to seek accommodation with neoliberal forces (Gallas, 2016: 233).

India was a pioneering country when it came to establishing a social democratic variant of neoliberalism. From 1991, Rao headed a Congress-led government that embarked on eradicating the socialist elements in the Indian mixed economy. Similarly, the 'New Democrats' in the US, which came into office after Bill Clinton's election victory in 1992, married a commitment to 'diversity' and 'meritocracy' with a staunch belief in free markets and financial liberalization (Fraser, 2017). Britain, Germany and South Africa followed a few years later, with governments led by the Labour Party, the Social Democratic Party (SPD) and the African National Congress (ANC), respectively, embracing free-market ideas. Indeed, Thatcher was quoted in 2008 as having stated that Tony Blair – prime minister of Britain from 1997 to 2007 – and 'New Labour' – the remodelled Labour Party under his leadership – had been her greatest achievements (Gallas, 2016: 280). The electoral victories of centrist and centre-left parties in the 1990s reflected the fact that neoliberalism had become dominant, but that neoliberalization had caused deep grievances.

The worldview of progressive neoliberalism is captured in a paper published in June 1998 by the new British prime minister Tony Blair and the soon-to-be chancellor of Germany, Gerhard Schröder. Similar to the 'New Democrats', they claimed to pursue a 'Third Way' between the doctrines of the 'new right' and the 'old' social democracy. In other words, they claimed to occupy a 'New Centre', which was also based on a commitment to free markets, anti-discrimination and meritocracy:

> [W]e need to apply our politics within a new economic framework, modernised for today, where government does all it can to support enterprise but never believes it is a substitute for enterprise. ... The promotion of social justice was sometimes confused with the imposition of equality of outcome. The result was ... the association of social democracy with conformity and mediocrity rather than the celebration of creativity, diversity and excellence. (Blair and Schröder, 1998: 2–3)

In principle, progressive neoliberals recognized the fact that capitalism had some unjust outcomes (see Blair and Schröder, 1998: 4). But they decided to abandon attempts to address imbalances through steering the economy, to reduce inequality through redistribution or to shift class relations in favour of labour. Put differently, they accepted the premise that high growth rates required 'free' markets, and – in line with what Friedman and Hayek had been saying all along – that prosperity could only be achieved through a 'trickle down' of wealth from the top, heavily constraining the room for state interventions. Peter Mandelson, one of the architects of 'New Labour' in Britain, famously quipped that he was 'intensely relaxed about people getting filthy rich as long as they pay their taxes' (cited in Joyce and Sibieta, 2013: 179), and Gerhard Schröder was called 'der Genosse der Bosse' (the comrade of the bosses) because his policies – among them corporate tax cuts, labour market liberalization and the reduction of unemployment benefits – were so obviously in favour of capital and to the detriment of labour.

As the Blair–Schröder paper clearly stated, the aim of political interventions was to ensure fair competition and equality of access, but not equality of outcomes. Accordingly, social policy in the progressive neoliberal mould was about ameliorating the worst effects of the market economy and ensuring that people were well-educated, employable and prepared to enter the labour market. This meant that people out of work should receive training and advice, but what was also needed were measures that forced them to keep on actively looking for work, no matter what the wages and working conditions of the jobs on offer were (the principle of 'welfare-to-work') (see Blair and Schröder, 1998: 10).

At the same time, social democratic and moderate governments continued to draw from the class political repertoire of the 'new right', which had already been emerging in the 1980s, and which reflected the growth of global financial markets. They facilitated the access of middle- and low-income groups to mortgages and consumer credit, which were available thanks to financial liberalization. The political scientist Colin Crouch has called this approach to producing consent, particularly visible in Britain and the US, 'privatised Keynesianism' (Crouch, 2009). The notion that people should be turned into asset-owners had, for a long time, been part and parcel of neoliberal projects. Thatcher's inner circle, for example, promoted 'popular capitalism' and actively worked to turn workers into house- and stockowners, which had the effect of sowing division on the side of labour and obstructing class formation (Gallas, 2016: 145–7; see also Scherrer, 2014: 349). In the US, the expansion of the mortgage market to poor people, who often had ethnic minority backgrounds, was fully compatible with the decision of the Clinton administration to limit benefits and expand the market mechanism, and the conviction of the administration of George W. Bush that home ownership should be the standard mechanism providing access to housing (Dymski, 2009: 166; Panitch and Konings, 2009: 74).

Importantly, the proliferation of narratives and financial practices that addressed workers as asset owners and consumers, combined with the shifting rhetoric of centre-left political forces, contributed to challenging the popular narratives that people had used to make sense of their position in the social fabric. The Blair–Schröder paper neither referred to 'class' nor 'inequality'. Instead, there was talk of 'marginalisation and social exclusion' (Blair and Schröder, 1998: 4), invoking the image of a more or less equal society where some people unfortunately had been pushed to the side-lines.

What was ignored completely in the imaginary of society thus created was the significant degree to which processes of neoliberalization contributed to increasing economic inequality (see Piketty, 2014: 294–6; Gallas, 2016: 278).

The political relevance of this shift in terminology cannot be overstated. As the sociologist Didier Eribon observes with reference to the case of France:

> The parties of the left, along with party intellectuals and state intellectuals, began from this moment forward to think and speak the language of those who govern, no longer the language of those who are governed. ... All this was nothing other than a hypocritical and underhanded strategy meant to invalidate any approach to these problems that used terms such as oppression and struggle, or reproduction or transformation of social structures, or inertia and dynamism within class antagonisms. (Eribon, 2009: 129–30)

In a nutshell, people had been stripped of a language of class and a political option to understand their situation and create collective political agency. The rhetoric of progressive neoliberalism contributed to making invisible working-class forces. But this did not mean that people no longer suffered from the effects of the organization of work across society – and from capitalist class domination. In this situation, Eribon argues, some people experienced a warped sense of agency by doing something that the promoters of progressive neoliberalism declared – for understandable reasons – unacceptable, that is, voting for the far right (2009: 131–2; see Dörre, 2018).

This had serious implications for organized labour. The neoliberal turn of the centre-left also meant that it became increasingly difficult for organized labour to work through official political channels with the aim of effecting change. The link between social democracy and organized labour became weaker, with some trade unions openly advocating anti-neoliberal political platforms and positioning themselves clearly to the left of the social democratic party leaderships. In some cases, unions – particularly those with a more militant bend – openly protested against governments led by social democratic parties. This led to splits and realignments. In Britain, branches of the RMT decided to support the Scottish Socialist Party financially. This resulted in the Labour Party expelling the RMT from the alliance of unions directly linked with it. Similar tensions led the Fire Brigades Union to cut its official ties with the party. In Germany, an emerging split between left-wing circles linked to organized labour and the SPD became institutionalized when disaffected social democrats and trade unionists teamed up with the mostly East German, post-Communist Party of Democratic Socialism to found the Left Party in 2007. And in South Africa, the main union federation, Congress of South African Trade Unions (COSATU), expelled its largest affiliate, the metalworkers' union, National Union of Metalworkers of South

Africa (NUMSA), in 2014. This was a consequence of the latter calling for COSATU to cut its ties with the ANC and the South African Communist Party and withdrawing its support for the latter two parties. The 'tripartite alliance' between COSATU, the ANC and the Communist Party had emerged in the fight against Apartheid and has been the coalition behind all South African governments since Mandela became president in 1994.

The global financial crisis

The dominance of neoliberalism – including its 'progressive' form – was ruptured at the global level when the global economic crisis hit. It first arrived in 2007 in the form of what was called a 'subprime mortgage crisis' in the US. 'Subprime' mortgages were high-risk loans offered to people on low incomes. The crisis hit when the latter defaulted on their loans due to increasing interest rates, which was a historical first: it was a finance-induced slump that impacted on the poorest segments of the population straight away; it did not have to be translated into a broader economic crisis for them to be affected (Lapavitsas, 2009: 114). In this sense, there was a direct connection between the way the crisis played out and the prevalent class politics of the neoliberal power blocs in the US and beyond. It reflected the proliferation of privatized Keynesianism.

The expansion of private debt through subprime mortgages had catastrophic consequences and quickly affected the financial system in its entirety because the 'subprime' loans had been 'securitized', that is, repackaged with other loans and sold to third parties. Risks had spread across the globe and had been rendered invisible. Consequently, defaulting 'subprime' mortgages created 'contagion' in other parts of the financial sector (see Gamble, 2009: 21–6; Harvey, 2010: 1–2). In the US, the 'subprime' mortgage crisis led to loans of all types drying up, including those considered low risk, within the space of six months. Peter Gowan infers that there was a bubble in the entire financial sector, not just in the area of mortgages (2009: 5, 18). In other words, the mortgage crisis was only a symptom of a crisis of the credit mechanism. Securitization had not just contributed to the massive expansion of credit, but had also covered up liability.

Accordingly, the rate at which banks extended loans to other banks was suddenly out of sync with the rates central banks charged for loans to retail banks, indicating a general loss of trust inside the banking sector. Banks struggled to get credit from other banks, which posed a threat to their day-to-day operations because this deprived them of liquidity. The most visible instance of this first stage of the crisis was the run on the British mortgage bank Northern Rock in September 2007, which had found it increasingly difficult to secure loans for the mortgages it offered through borrowing money from other banks (see Gamble, 2009: 21–6; Harvey, 2010: 1–2).

In a second step, governments and central banks decided to bail out those banks to the tune of billions and prop them up through making available money for free or at very low interest rates (Gamble, 2009: 13–35; Harvey, 2010: 1–6). In September 2008, the US-based financial services firm Lehman Brothers went bankrupt, which created fears that the global economy would collapse. This led to state interventions on an even grander scale, including measures to stabilize demand and combat the recession that the global economy had entered. In the Global North, governments nationalized several large retail banks and mortgage lenders to prevent the financial system from collapsing.

As a result, public debt shot up – in 2019, public debt in the Global North was higher than in 2008 in 90 per cent of countries, and the increase amounted to more than 30 percentage points in a third of them (Moreno Badia and Dudine, 2019). The use of public coffers to contain the crisis transferred it onto the level of the state. This was in line with Harvey's claim that 'capital never solves its crisis tendencies; it merely moves them around' (2011: 11). In his view, crises occur when capital accumulation hits barriers – and barriers are never fully removed, they are shifted.

Inside the Eurozone, the crisis became a sovereign debt crisis. Doubts had emerged whether some of the Eurozone countries, in particular Greece, Ireland, Portugal and Spain, would be able to continue to service public debt, which obstructed these countries from borrowing money. This threatened the existence of the European monetary union because member states were struggling to finance their day-to-day activities through loans (Lapavitsas et al, 2010; Lucarelli, 2012). The Troika of the IMF, the European Central Bank and the European Commission negotiated loans with the crisis countries but coupled those loans with the obligation on national governments to impose swingeing public expenditure cuts. This had a pro-cyclical effect and deepened the economic downturn in those countries. After the όχι referendum in July 2015, the Tsipras government in Greece – led by the SYRIZA party, the 'coalition of the radical left' – had a mandate to end austerity, which would have required leaving the Eurozone. But it decided against this risky path, which would have required not just re-establishing a national currency and coping with a likely hike in prices for imported goods, but also the nationalization of key firms in danger of collapsing, a systematic industrial policy to enhance productivity and boost exports and the imposition of capital controls (see Lapavitsas et al, 2010: 8; Boukalas and Müller, 2015).

The magnitude of the global financial crisis is visible in the fact that unlike the 1980s Latin American debt crisis or the 1997 Asian financial crisis, it emerged in the 'heartlands' of neoliberal, financial capitalism – Britain and the US – and did not spare any of the larger macroregions of the globe (see Gowan, 2009). The globalized nature of the banking system and of financial markets meant that it quickly spread all over the world, which points to the fragility of global neoliberal capitalism.

Collapsing neoliberalism?

Looking at the conjuncture of crisis from today's vantage point, the institutions underpinning the global financial system have not been restructured much since 2007. The bailouts and a flood of cheap money may have prevented the financial system from collapsing; indeed, they created a boom in the stock market. But critical observers point out that attempts to re-regulate the financial sector have been limited (Rixen, 2013; Christophers, 2016); that the 'too big to fail' problem – the existence of financial corporations whose collapse can threaten the continued existence of the entire financial system – has not been addressed properly; that profitability in the banking sector remains weak (Bell and Hindmoor, 2018); and that attempts to act against financial crime have been lacklustre (Ryder, 2016). This suggests that we are dealing with an ongoing global financial crisis, which has been tackled with means that fortify the status quo and contain the crisis tendencies temporarily but fail to tackle its institutional underpinnings.

The strong institutional continuity in the area of finance is also visible in the fact that the dominant responses of governments in the Global North to the economic fallout from the COVID-19 pandemic resemble the earlier strategies of crisis management. They opted for another round of large-scale bailouts for corporations as well as limited aid for people on low and middle incomes – and central banks continued to make available free or cheap money. As a result, asset prices and financial markets stabilized. Attempts to rein in the financial sector and curb its political influence are still nowhere to be seen. This suggests that finance-oriented accumulation strategies continue to dominate at the level of economic, fiscal and monetary policy, and that financial capitalists have so far been able to defend the deep integration of finance across national boundaries and their leading position in the global political-economic regime. This is visible in the fact that they have managed to offload the costs of the crisis onto the shoulders of subaltern people (see Scherrer, 2011; Palley, 2016: 124–7).

Again, crisis management is centred on mobilizing public money on a grand scale and, in some cases, using the subsequent hikes in public debt as a justification for the politics of austerity. This raises the question of how long governments can continue with modes of crisis management that benefit capital but lead to severe cuts to state expenditure on social infrastructures. What is at stake here is the functioning of 'free' markets and the dominant discursive patterns used to justify neoliberal economic policy, according to which state apparatuses have to restrain public spending and refrain from intervening in economic processes to correct market outcomes. Policies geared towards protecting asset prices and exposing public coffers to round after round of cuts not only consolidate the existing high levels of economic inequality, but also demolish the existing social infrastructures, neither of which is a good foundation for generating consent from subaltern forces. So are there signs that neoliberalism could collapse under the weight of the economic inequality it has created?

From 2007 onwards, several long-standing economic, political and cultural institutions and arrangements characterizing social formations across the globe have been eroding, and some are even on the brink of breaking down. There is no openly announced retreat from neoliberalism, and political interventions are still, to a strong degree, based on the notion that free markets produce prosperity. Nevertheless, there are signs that institutions and arrangements underpinning the Washington consensus are under attack. This is visible in the political scene, where Britain has departed from the EU, and where authoritarian populist leaders such as Jair Bolsonaro, Rodrigo Duterte, Boris Johnson, Sebastian Kurz, Viktor Orbán, Narendra Modi and Donald Trump have persistently been attacking the rule of law and representative democracy (see Book et al, 2020). But my observation also applies to economic policy, where the dominant strategies of crisis management – most importantly stimulus programmes, bailouts and nationalizations – go against the neoliberal rhetoric of the 'free market'; to trade policy, where the Trump administration in particular has been fiercely critical of the institution facilitating free trade at the global level, the WTO; and to central banking, which is characterized by interest rates that have been close to zero or even negative for a long time and by the creation of purchase schemes that allow investors to sell junk bonds. Next to these political-economic crisis tendencies, there are sizeable dislocations in the realm of culture, namely, the 'culture wars' over values, identity and belonging stoked, first and foremost, by the far right and played out in the press and on social media. They point to processes of cultural-political fragmentation and polarization that affect both the political scenes and the legal systems across the globe, for example in the areas of reproductive rights or migration policy. Many of the economic, political and cultural institutions underpinning neoliberalism are under attack.

Taken together, these processes bear the hallmarks of an organic crisis (see Fraser, 2017). What sets the current conjuncture apart from the 1970s crisis and magnifies the challenge of returning to the status quo ante is that the economic, political and cultural crisis tendencies are accelerated and inflated by climate change and the COVID-19 pandemic. The current crisis is not just a social crisis, but a crisis of 'society-nature relations' (Brand and Wissen, 2013). There is an alignment and reinforcement of crisis tendencies that are, at the same time, intrinsic to social systems and a product of the interactions between natural and social systems. This gives the present crisis a distinct material force (Cook et al, 2020: 75, 81), which is reflected in the emergence of highly specific and unnegotiable containment conditions – the need to drastically cut carbon emissions to slow the heating of the planet and the need to drastically interrupt social interactions if one wants to prevent the virus from spreading.

The effects of climate change and the COVID-19 pandemic can be captured with reference to scale and speed. Climate change is upscaling the existing crisis tendencies. The climate crisis is a truly global and universal crisis – or a crisis without any national boundaries. It is putting the survival of humankind as it has been existing since the industrial revolution under threat, and it requires fast, comprehensive interventions at a global scale. In other words, national or macroregional solutions will not work. The COVID-19 pandemic has also accelerated and magnified the already existing crisis tendencies significantly and has not been used for curbing carbon emissions for good (see Satgar, 2018; Harvey, 2020; Zelik, 2020b: 349).

The growth imperative of capitalist mode of production and the absence of a world state, that is, a political body with global reach capable of making binding decisions, turn managing the climate crisis into a daunting task. As a result, I contend that we are in the midst of a global, organic crisis of neoliberal capitalism. There appear to be 'incurable contradictions' that make it hard to envisage the return to the status quo ante (Bieling, 2018: 167).[8] Due its all-encompassing nature, this organic crisis amounts to a rupture with the neoliberal political-economic regime, that is, the dominant ensemble of strategies protecting the capitalist mode of production and the relations of social domination inherent in it, among them class relations. In other words, the existing arrangement of class relations is at stake, and there are bound to be ruptures in this arrangement.

Importantly, organic crises can still be crises within, rather than crises of, capitalism. The demise of neoliberalism is not an even, linear process affecting every aspect of the global political-economic regime to the same degree. It remains an open question to be decided in the coming years whether the already visible changes will soon coalesce into a wholesale regime shift and the advent of a new regime, or whether we are faced with a protracted,

---

[8] While I agree with Bieling that we are dealing with an organic crisis, I depart from his analysis in one respect: He argues that an organic crisis is characterized by the absence of a consensus to social domination by subaltern forces (Bieling, 2018: 167); I contend that there is a range of political arrangements that are not based on a full consensus – and that the existence of such an arrangement does not indicate, by default, that there is crisis. Consensus may have existed in the era of 'settled capitalism' in a number of Western European countries. But if we take a global, long-term perspective on the history of capitalism, these cases are the exception, not the rule.

permanent crisis and a slow-motion demise of the existing regime, as the 'zombie' metaphor suggests.

Polarization and fragmentation

If my observation is right that the existing economic, political and cultural institutions are, to varying degrees, under attack, it follows that the present configurations of class relations, which are made durable through those institutions, are fragile. In this sense, the current conjuncture is fundamentally different from the hey-day of neoliberalism in the early 2000s. There are very serious dangers, but also certain opportunities for labour.

The dangers do not just simply consist in the income and job losses induced by a deep economic crisis and their debilitating effect on labour. For the past 15 years, governments across the globe have continued to pursue neoliberal agendas insofar as they have tended to opt, in their crisis management, for restoring the profitability of investments for capital. In many countries, they have attacked – through cuts to state expenditure – public infrastructures that benefit workers, for example, educational facilities, legal aid, libraries and public healthcare provision.

In addition to these pressures, the pandemic hit workers badly. Class divisions resulted in a highly uneven exposure to health risks. Whereas people with high formal qualifications often had the privilege of retreating into the safety of their homes and working from there, many of those who did not fall under this category were less fortunate: they continued to operate in cramped workplaces and had to use public transport to get there. The economic downturn caused by the pandemic had drastic repercussions in particular on precarious workers. During the beginning stages of the health crisis, the International Labour Organization (ILO) announced that '1.6 billion workers in the informal economy – that is nearly half of the global workforce – stand in immediate danger of having their livelihoods destroyed' (ILO, 2020).

The sustained increase in unemployment was also a critical problem for organized labour. Unions were weakened through members losing jobs, and workers were often less willing to take risks and get involved in collective action because the labour market was challenging. In addition, restrictions on people's movements and right to assembly, understandable as they were from an epidemiological point of view, prevented the organization and mobilization of workers.

Against this backdrop, there are signs of a rightward shift at the level of politics in recent years – again a development that was accelerated by the COVID-19 pandemic, whose handling by centrist governments was portrayed by the far right as an encroachment on freedom. At the moment, authoritarian populists can build on broad popular support in a range of different countries, and they are backed by a significant number of workers. As I have already argued, there has been an authoritarian streak in neoliberal projects from their inception, which curbed workers' agency through imposing restrictions on their modes of collective organization and mobilization. But right-wing political leaders are currently taking authoritarianism to a new level through open disdain for the mechanisms of representative democracy and attacks on the rule of law. Infamous instances are Johnson's prorogation of parliament in 2019 and Trump's botched *coup d'état* on 6 January 2021. Despite often resorting to a top-down mode of decision-making, neither Reagan nor Thatcher can be said to have used similar measures.[9]

Importantly, the rise of authoritarianism also points to limitations of producing consent with the help of the dominant strategies of crisis management. Lately, there have been consistent attacks on the right to strike both by national governments and at the level of the ILO (Tzouvala, 2016; Xhafa, 2016; Frey, 2017; Runciman, 2019). This would not be a strategy worth pursuing if there was no potential of strikes to disrupt the accumulation of capital and social life in general. To reiterate a point made by the proponents of the PRA: through being located where they are in the labour process, workers can exercise class power, and this is true even in a conjuncture of crisis, which is why labour is considered a potential threat to capital even then.

Next to this principled point about worker agency in capitalism, one may want to add that there are developments that could benefit organized labour. For example, the neoliberal narratives of general prosperity through a 'trickle down' of wealth and of opportunities for all have lost traction in a situation marked by a sustained increase in economic inequality – and by workers, not capitalists, bearing the brunt of the recurring crises. The British non-governmental organization Oxfam estimates that while 99 per cent of people around the globe experienced income losses during the COVID-19 pandemic, the ten richest men in the world doubled their wealth; and that large supermarket chains also benefited considerably (Oxfam, 2021; 2022: 16). Likewise, big pharmaceutical corporations enjoyed massive windfall profits through the worldwide vaccination drives (Nichols, 2022). Once again, the losses of capital were socialized and the losses for labour were privatized under conditions of a deep crisis. Such circumstances make it difficult to keep alive the mantra of meritocracy that has been underpinning neoliberalism since its earliest stages.

---

[9] It is worth mentioning in this context that the Thatcher government dissolved six metropolitan councils plus the Greater London Council in 1986 (Gallas, 2016: 195). But importantly, there were no comparable efforts at the national level.

Against this backdrop, it not surprising that neoliberalism has been hitting political limits in recent years. This becomes visible if one considers that novel socialist projects have emerged in the heartlands of neoliberalism, namely Britain, Chile and the US. These projects are associated with the names of Jeremy Corbyn, Gabriel Boric and Bernie Sanders. In addition, it is noteworthy that there was a close link, in the COVID-19 pandemic, between the proliferation of casual work and the patterns in which infections were spreading. This was the starting point of public debates on the need to recognize the importance of, and remunerate better, badly paid jobs that suddenly were seen as being 'essential' (Cook et al, 2020).

The limitations of neoliberal politics point to a certain weakness of capital in the present moment – not in terms of exercising control over the labour process or economic processes more generally, but in terms of facilitating the production of consent at the political level. During the hey-day of neoliberalism, there was a broad party-political support for it, which was reflected in moderate and centre-left parties like the ANC, Congress, the Democratic Party, the Labour Party, the SPD, the French Socialist Party and, to a degree, the Brazilian Workers' Party embracing free-market ideas. In the current crisis, there is polarization: the broad alliances sustaining both centre-left and centre-right parties have come apart, which is visible in the formation of breakaway groups or the emergence of forceful political competitors, but also in infighting and drastic agenda shifts. The emergence of the German Left Party, Podemos and SYRIZA, the rise of the German and the French Green Parties as well as the rise of a popular, anti-neoliberal bloc in Chile have weakened the prospects of the traditional social democratic outfits in those countries, and the same can be said of far-right forces and their conservative counterparts like Vox and the People's Party in Spain and National Rally and the Republicans in France. Whereas the Tories, the US Republican Party and the Austrian People's Party have embraced anti-democratic, far-right agendas, the Labour Party under Corbyn and the left-wing of the Democratic Party under Sanders have attempted to revitalize democratic socialism and continue to influence – despite recent setbacks – the debates over the course of their respective parties.

To further complicate things, polarization should not be taken to suggest that centrist, neoliberal political platforms are eroding or that the right or left is consolidating their control of the political scene. It is more the case that political fortunes have been shifting rapidly in recent years. Joe Biden was able to successfully rebuild a moderate alliance after Hillary Clinton lost the presidential election in 2016; and conversely, Trump went from a surprise victory to a trouncing defeat within the space of four years. Likewise, Olaf Scholz became chancellor of Germany in 2021 with the help of a centrist coalition. The example of Jeremy Corbyn is dramatic because it shows how quickly support for a political platform can evaporate in the current conjuncture. Within the space of two years, he went from forcing Theresa May into a minority government thanks to a strong election result to being routed at the next election. This shows that polarization is accompanied by fragmentation, that is, the rapid disintegration and re-emergence of political forces dominating the political scene.

Gramsci had talked of an 'equilibrium with catastrophic prospects' (1971: 222) with reference to a situation where the traditional political forces of capital could no longer impose their rule and the forces of the working class could not yet take over because both sides were equal in strength. This shows that class relations of forces do not develop like a zero-sum game where the strength of capital automatically translates into the weakness of labour and vice versa. Following Gramsci, there can be an equality in strength. He argued that this had distinctive political consequences because it paved the way for 'Caesarism' – a form of political rule where 'a great personality is entrusted with the task of "arbitration" over a historico-political situation characterised by an equilibrium of forces heading towards catastrophe' (1971: 219). Put differently, a catastrophic equilibrium invites forms of dictatorship that are based on charismatic leadership.

In the Great Crisis, we seem to be dealing with a reversal of Gramsci's 'catastrophic equilibrium' – an equality in weakness. For the side of labour, this is visible in the decline of trade unionism and labour parties. But possibly, capital also finds itself in a position of weakness. As I have argued in Volume 1, Chapter 5, concessions won by labour have not just strengthened the hands of workers and have improved their working and living conditions, but have also rendered the capitalist mode of production durable. If capital 'overpowers' labour to a degree that such concessions are stripped away on a grand scale, this durability is undermined – and the dynamic of capital accumulation starts to endanger the mode of production. Put more simply, capital is beginning to eat into itself. Miloš Šumonja, a Serbian scholar, speaks of the 'suicidal tendencies of untamed capitalism' in this context (2021: 216).

There is a range of symptoms in the present conjuncture that could be read as reflections of these crisis tendencies, which encompass the global social formation: first and foremost, the climate catastrophe; the COVID-19 pandemic, which possibly has been caused by the encroachment on wild nature caused by the expansion of capitalism and the resulting zoonoses (Malm, 2020: 31–50; Peet and Peet, 2020); shortages in labour power and raw materials; the continued inflation of the financial sector, the price shocks experienced by consumers and the inability of central banks to step in through tightening their monetary policy; the attacks on liberal democracy in its heartlands, namely Britain and the US; and the campaigns of the far right to reject 'globalism' and declare 'culture wars' on liberalism and the broad left, which have been garnering mass support in some countries and contexts. Arguably, power blocs across the globe have been struggling to develop and pursue coherent strategies that are based on stable and broad popular support, which leads to constantly changing political configurations.

Under these conditions, many of governments resort to authoritarian, top-down forms of decision-making and repression against forces of dissent, no matter whether they are led by moderate or far-right forces. And there are significant advances of the right and right-wing leaders who resort to 'Caesarist', personality-based modes of leadership. But importantly, their projects often do not reach a consolidation stage. Trump lost the presidential election in 2020, and Johnson and Kurz were forced to resign while I was writing this book. Part of the picture is also the temporary rise of Corbyn and Sanders, tied to the emergence of closely knit, grassroots movements – and how they managed to influence, to a degree, political debates in the centre and on the right. Last but not least, centrists like Biden and Scholz have been winning elections and have managed to build broad coalitions around their government projects. At the same time, Biden quickly lost popularity after his inauguration, and tensions were apparent in Scholz's coalition right from the start.

In light of this, I propose talking of a 'catastrophic disequilibrium', that is, a chaotic situation in which class relations are unstable – and both capital and labour act on the grounds of a position of weakness: Capital because there is no new project in sight capable of addressing the multifaceted crisis and of producing consent on a scale that goes beyond a small constituency of die-hards. And labour because the devastation caused by neoliberalism and the Great Crisis mean that workers' organizations have been weakened considerably thanks to fierce repression and drastic socioeconomic change, most importantly, processes of deindustrialization and precarization.

In line with my conjunctural, anti-deterministic thinking, a disequilibrium can turn into a terminal crisis, but there is no necessity for this to happen. This is what is setting apart my terminology from the 'zombie' metaphors that I criticized at the start of the chapter. Importantly, the historical openness of the conjuncture means that there are avenues for advances of labour. But again, it would be wrong to assume that they will be taken no matter what happens next. What can be said, in any case, is that workers around the globe are developing collective agency in the conjuncture of crisis. This is the topic of Chapters 5 to 8.

3

Shifting Conditions of Struggle: The Service and Public Sectors in the Age of Neoliberalism

Spatial fixes and the rise of the service sector: changes in the global division of labour

As I focus on processes of class formation outside manufacturing, it makes sense to examine how the division of labour across sectors has been developing around the globe. I want to assess whether my focus on service and public sector work is justified – and whether my research heuristic captures relevant developments. The ILO is collecting and aggregating data on the size of three sectors of the global economy – agriculture, industry and services – which can be used for this purpose. The figures refer to the number of people employed or self-employed in each sector.

Undoubtedly, there are questions worth asking about the validity of the ILO data. The categories used are based on the empiricist assumption that the sectoral location of any worker can be read off from the 'main activity' of the business unit where they work. Following the logic of the ILO, the high-level asset manager working for a hedge fund, the independent business lawyer advising her for hefty fees and the janitor cleaning both of their offices and earning the minimum wage are all working in the service sector. And a similar point can be made about reliability. Data are gathered from all corners of the world and from a great number of sources. Nevertheless, I contend that the ILO figures still have a use value if one is clear about the fact that they provide a very rough sketch and not a fine-grained picture.[1]

---

[1]   The charge of empiricism refers to the fact that the ILO assumes the sectoral location of workers to be transparent, and that all workers in one business unit to belong to the same sector: 'Data are disaggregated by sector economic activity, which refers to the main activity of the establishment in which a person worked during the reference period and does not depend on the specific duties or functions of the person's job, but on the characteristics of

The data are available in the form of absolute and relative numbers. Since it is likely that the global workforce develops in tandem with the global population, the absolute figures say little if they are not related to population growth. According to UN estimates, there were 5.49 billion people on the planet in 1992, and this number has increased to 7.84 billion in 2020.[2] This amounts to an increase of 42.8 per cent.

It can be gleaned, first, from the numbers that there is a strong increase in services. In absolute terms, they have increased from 803 million people in 1992 to 1.622 billion in 2019. This is a rise of 102 per cent, which is exceeding the global population increase by far. The increase translates into the share of the sector in the global workforce going up from 34.7 to 50.9 per cent over the same period (see Figure 3.1). One factor behind this development is the fact that the dominant accumulation strategy in the neoliberal era is finance-driven accumulation, and that the urban infrastructure of finance extends far beyond banks. It relies on IT specialists and lawyers – and also on a range of other services, often performed by migrants and women, that can safely be located on the side of labour. Typical sectors are catering, childcare, cleaning, entertainment, retail and transport (see May et al, 2007; Wills et al, 2009). Another factor, mentioned by Kim Moody with reference to the US, is that maintenance work has often been outsourced in recent years, which means that it is counted in the statistics as service sector work (2017: 20–1).

Second, the numbers for industry are 503 million in 1992 and 693 million in 2020, an increase of 37.7 per cent. If we factor in population growth, this means that industry has remained static – at least at the global level. Accordingly, the share of people working in the industrial sector is the same in 1992 and 2020 – 21.7 per cent (see Figure 3.1). Of course, this does not rule out the

---

the economic unit in which this person works' (ILO, see data source for Figure 3.1). This may be a simplification needed to keep data collection manageable, but it can obviously lead to distortions, as I have argued with reference to the variety of jobs and positions in workplace hierarchies that can be found in one and the same sector. Besides, there is no attempt, in the ILO data, to account for the facts that a lot of people are involved in different activities in one and the same workplace; that the boundaries between sectors are often opaque (for example, labour processes in agricultural factories resembles those in manufacturing); and that certain activities are necessary for the production of goods but do not alter the latter's physical constitution (for instance, transport). Besides, there is no distinction in the ILO framework between self-employment and employment, and no breakdown of jobs according to whether workers have decision-making capacities and expertise or not. All of this suggest that the ILO data do not directly capture a global workforce in the sense of labour as a class grouping. But this does not mean that they are useless. Even if they do not capture class relations, they show roughly how work is evolving across the globe, and what kind of work processes people are involved in.

[2] https://tinyurl.com/4n5wcs2r [Accessed 9 October 2022].

Figure 3.1: The global sectoral division of labour (in per cent)

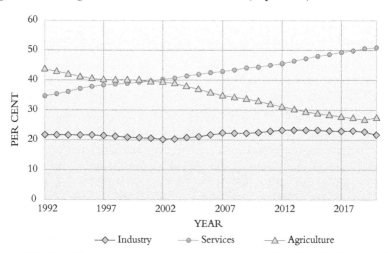

Source: ILO, Trends Economic Models, Employment by Sector (Weso Data Finder), https://
www.ilo.org/wesodata/chart/94z-RahAi [Accessed 14 October 2022]

Silverian scenario of certain zones of the global economy experiencing
sustained processes of the deindustrialization, which have been compensated
for by the industrialization elsewhere. It is possible to break up the figures
with the help of the income country groups as defined by the World Bank,
which are based on gross national income. The resulting numbers back up
Silver's observations on companies in manufacturing seeking 'spatial fixes' by
relocating abroad (2003: 46; 2014: 49–50). The share of industrial work has
not changed much in low-income and upper-middle income countries if we
compare numbers for 1992 and 2020 (from 10.1 to 10 and from 23 to 24.5
per cent, respectively). But it has increased significantly in the upper-middle
category from the turn of the century until the Great Crisis hit (from 22 to
27.2 per cent between 2002 to 2012) and has also been growing sizeably from
this point until the COVID-19 pandemic started in lower-middle income
category (from 15.3 per cent in 1998 to 22 per cent in 2019). At the same
time, there has been a sustained industrial decline in the high-income group
since 1992 (from 30.7 to 22.7 per cent in 2002) (see Figure 3.2).

Next to referring to the effects of spatial fixes based on outsourcing, the
relatively steep fall of employment in manufacturing in the centres of capitalism
can be explained with the help of productivity increases. As Kim Moody
observes with regard to the US, productivity increases in manufacturing have
been outstripping by far those in the service sector in recent decades, and this
has resulted in de-manning in the sector (2017: 18–19). Importantly, however,
the availability of new technology does not explain fully why workers are laid
off. It is necessary for relations of forces to exist between capital and labour that

Figure 3.2: Share of industry in the global workforce according to income country groups (in per cent)

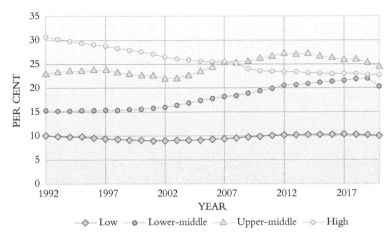

Source: ILO, Trends Econometric Models (Employment by Sector), https://www.ilo.org/wesodata/chart/94z-RahAi [Accessed 14 October 2022]

allow management to do so on a grand scale. Consequently, what also needs to be considered are the attacks on organized labour orchestrated by governments and capital in the neoliberal era. These often affected the strongholds of union movements in the industrial sector. Britain is the textbook case for how union busting via deindustrialization works. The Thatcher government invoked the 'union problem' in this context, that is, the existence of militant and well-organized unions in the industrial sector. It also made the conscious decision to accelerate industrial decline through removing capital controls and thus exposing firms to international competition as well as downsizing and privatizing state-owned corporations (Gallas, 2016: 4). In so doing, it forced organized labour in its industrial strongholds to launch defensive strikes, which in turn created a justification for attacking militant trade unionism. This applied, in particular, to sectors such as coalmining and steel, culminating in the 1984–5 Miners' Strike (Gallas, 2016: 132, 151–2; 166–99; see also Cohen, 2006: 55–6). In Britain, jobs in manufacturing plummeted from 7.9 million in 1971 to 2.9 million in 2016 (Berry, 2016: 6).

All in all, there is evidence for industrial decline in high-income countries, and for industrial production shifting away from there. But there are no signs that industrial production is about to vanish. In absolute numbers, the size of the global industrial workforce is greater than ever. Against this backdrop, it is important to bear in mind that I operate with a research heuristic because I discuss the Castellsian claim that class formation is absent outside the industrial sector – and not because I subscribe to the more far-reaching claim that we have entered a post-industrial age, and that industrial work is about to become obsolete.

Third, there is a clear trend concerning agricultural employment. It dropped from 1.009 billion people in 1992 to 874 million in 2020, which is a decrease of 15.4 per cent. Considering population growth, this is a significant decline. Expressed in relative numbers, this amounts to a drop from 43.6 to 24.7 per cent (see Figure 3.1). What comes into view is a sustained, albeit geographically uneven, trend: The output per worker in agriculture has been increasing significantly since the 1960s (see Scherrer, 2018: 219), which explains why fewer agricultural workers are needed despite global population growth. Considering the stagnation in industrial employment, it is not surprising that in the Global South, many of the workers leaving agriculture behind ended up in the service sector – and in informal jobs (Scherrer, 2018: 210). Importantly, agricultural work reflects, in pockets of the global capitalist economy, the existence of contradictory class locations. A vast number of smallholder farmers are not waged workers (see Scherrer and Verna, 2018: 1) – and they may or may not own the land they work on as well as relying on the work of unpaid relatives or hired helpers. For reasons of reducing complexity and in line with the developmental trend described, I have chosen to disregard agricultural work when I address the question of class formation.

In a nutshell, what has been happening in the last three decades has been a 'tertiarization' and de-agriculturalization, but not a deindustrialization of the global workforce. Non-industrial and non-agricultural employment is a lived reality for a very large group of people who are located on the side of labour. Furthermore, the numbers underscore that all three sectors continue to be crucial for the reproduction of global capitalism; that services have grown considerably in importance; and that agriculture still matters for employment but is less significant than it used to be.

In this context, it is worth mentioning that numerous scholars also refer to a 'tertiarization' of strikes (Bordogna and Cella, 2002: 599–602; Vandaele, 2011: 31–2; Gall, 2012: 18; Bewernitz and Dribbusch, 2014; Köhler and Calleja Jiménez, 2014: 753; Lacalle, 2015: 102; Lesch, 2015: 3; Luque Balbona and González Begega, 2017: 101–2). Global numbers on strike incidence are hard to come by, but there is scattered evidence from Western Europe that lends credibility to this claim: a long-term comparison of strike incidence in the Italian metal industry as compared to the transport sector (Bordogna and Cella, 2002: 602); the fact that service sector workers were responsible for 82 per cent of strike days in Germany between 2004 and 2013 (Bewernitz and Dribbusch, 2014: 396); and the sustained increase of the relative share of service and public sector strikes in overall strikes in Spain in recent years (Lacalle, 2015: 107; Luque Balbona and González Begega, 2017: 102). Taken together, the numbers and observations discussed demonstrate that it is impossible to examine class formation in present-day capitalism without considering the service sector.

State service and neoliberalism: the continued importance of the public sector in contemporary capitalism

In Volume 1, Chapter 6, I emphasized how the capitalist relations of production cannot exist unless there is a capitalist state. I added that for the former to exist as a reproducible ensemble of relations at the heart of the mode of production, various state apparatuses have to be in place (see Volume 1, Table 5.4). For these apparatuses to be operational, a great number of people need to work. Consequently, waged work in capitalist social formations is not just work for capitalists. A sizeable part of the workforce operates on behalf of those state apparatuses and is paid out of tax income or other state revenues. Workers who are publicly employed play an important role in any capitalist social formation. If one wants to understand class relations in contemporary capitalism, they need to be considered.

This raises the question of where the sectoral location of the public employees is. The ILO framework is based on a categorization *ex negativo* – the presence or absence of a tangible labour product is what divides industry from services. From the point of view of the ILO, the answer is simple: publicly employed workers belong to the service sector.

If we follow Marx in *Capital* volume 2, things are more complicated. According to him, goods production takes place if a labour product is made that is consumed after production is finished; the delivery of a service occurs when production and consumption take place at the same time (Marx, 1978: 135). It follows that the tangibility or intangibility of goods is of secondary importance for defining sectors, what is important is the relationship between production and consumption. Indeed, the production of goods, no matter of what form, can be grouped together and set apart from service delivery. It follows that the dividing lines between goods production and services differs from those that are implied by the ILO definition. In the latter, a coder earning his keep by developing software or a guitarist doing so through recording music deliver services; in the Marxian understanding, they produce goods. With his definition, Marx highlights how relations between producers and consumers diverge when different types of work are carried out. When goods production occurs, consumers and producer tend not to interact directly; in the case of service delivery, encounters are often unavoidable.

At first, it may appear that adopting one definition or the other is merely a matter of taste or an academic finger exercise. However, the Marxian definition matters greatly for my purposes because it captures different conditions for collective action. Where workers encounter consumers directly, there is often a degree of dependency of the latter on the former. This is particularly pronounced in, but not exclusive to, the field of remunerated care work. When care workers go on strike, this raises the question of who looks after their clients. When auto workers go on strike, the worst that usually happens for car buyers is that they have to wait a little until they can purchase the model of their choice. If we follow Marx, service sector strikes tend to affect customers and clients directly – and as such, they can be highly disruptive (see Luque Balbona and González Begega, 2017: 102). This can strengthen the hand of the workers because it may force employers to the negotiation table and to settle, but it can also be used to turn people against striking workers. Consequently, there is a lot of potential for broader social conflicts – and, consequently, for the politicization of strikes – and also for new alliances between the providers and users of services. In a nutshell, relations between producers and consumers matter for the dynamics of struggle, and this can be captured with the help of the Marxian definition.

But to return to the initial question – what does following the Marxian path imply for the sectoral location of publicly employed workers? In my view, there are two takeaway points. First, many activities carried out by publicly employed workers neither produce a good to be consumed after production, nor a service consumed while it is produced. Traffic wardens, soldiers, gardeners looking after public parks or civil servants working for a ministry neither belong to the first nor to the second category. Many may see themselves as serving 'the community', 'the public' or 'the nation', but these are imaginary collectives with fuzzy boundaries that are hard to construe as customers. And if we follow Poulantzas' understanding of the capitalist state, notions that state bodies are safeguarding the common good should be rejected anyway (which is not to say that subaltern people may benefit from activities carried out on behalf of state bodies). Consequently, I propose adding to goods production and services a third category of work – *Staatsdienst*, to use a term commonly used in German, or 'state service', that is, activities that facilitate the reproduction of the existing social order. As a consequence, I speak of the 'service and public sectors' when I refer to non-industrial work.[3]

Second, there are also various activities of publicly employed workers that can be seen as services: education, care in its multiple forms, citizens' advice, public transport, mail and communication, maintaining the water and energy supply, and so on. The status of these activities as services is also confirmed by the fact that in all these cases, there are private-sector equivalents. And there are even some activities that amount to goods production. This does not just apply to workers in state-owned factories and mines, but also to

---

[3] Obviously, this omits the agricultural sector, but I contend that this is justified for reasons of complexity reduction (see the preceding section).

state-employed IT specialists writing code that is used by public bodies, state-employed orchestras that record music and scholars working for public universities who write books on class formation. It follows that sectors cannot be distinguished neatly because, in many cases, people mix different types of work in their activities. Scholars, for example, produce goods, provide services, in particular teaching and student advice, and also deliver state services in the form of committee work. Nevertheless, what can be said is that in certain branches of the economy, certain types of work predominate, which is why it makes sense to speak of an industrial sector, a service sector and a state or public sector.

In this context, it is worth emphasizing, against popular misconceptions, that neoliberalization is not about forcing the state onto the retreat. Undoubtedly, networks of governments, politicians, bureaucrats and intellectuals of the power blocs (who are often 'advisers' from think thanks and consultancies) have been working in the last five decades to restructure state apparatuses profoundly, for example, by cutting the social wage, privatizing public enterprises, liberalizing financial and labour markets and imposing on them private sector management techniques and internal markets. Furthermore, governments have adopted authoritarian modes of decision-making, have undermined some of the procedures of representative democracy and have fortified repressive state apparatuses (Gamble, 1994; Peck, 2003; Kannankulam, 2008). But this does not mean that the public sector has lost its importance. In different countries across the globe, the share of the gross domestic product (GDP) representing the wage bill of public sector workers has been more or less stagnant since the turn of the millennium (see Figure 3.3). And likewise, the share of public sector workers in the overall workforce has not changed much since the crisis hit the Global North. In 2007, this number was 18.2 per cent in Organisation for Economic Co-operation and Development (OECD) countries on average; in 2019, it was 17.9. In a nutshell, the public sector continues to play an important role for employment (see Figure 3.4).

Against presumptions that industrial workforces are at the heart of organized labour, it needs to be added that in present-day capitalism, public sector workers are far more inclined to join trade unions than private sector workers. The database on Institutional Characteristics of Trade Unions, Wage Setting, State Intervention and Social Pacts (ICTWSS) contains information on labour relations across the globe for a number of variables, among them trade union density among privately and publicly employed workers. Table 3.1 contains the newest figures, at the time of writing, for all the countries for which both variables are contained in the database. They show a very clear trend: It is visible that in every single country listed, trade union density among public sector workers is far higher than for people employed in the private sector – between

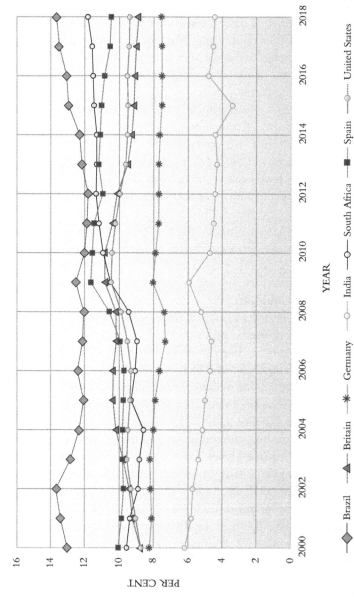

Figure 3.3: Public sector wage bill as a share of gross domestic product (in per cent)

Source: World Bank, WWBI, Wage Bill as a Share of GDP, https://tinyurl.com/yhrs375s [Accessed 9 October 2022]

Figure 3.4: Public sector employment as a share of total employment (in per cent)

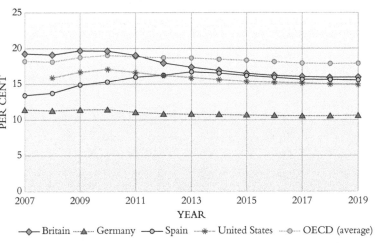

Source: OECD, Government at a Glance, 2021 Edition, https://stats.oecd.org/Index. aspx?QueryId=107595 [Accessed 9 October 2022]

1.6 percentage points in the case of Belgium and 82.3 percentage points in the case of Costa Rica.[4]

How can the greater propensity of publicly employed workers to unionize be explained? If we follow Poulantzas' understanding of the capitalist state, working-class forces are present in it, albeit in a subaltern position (1978: 141–3). This means that the side of the employer cannot simply be equated with capital. The state tends to be under stronger public scrutiny than private sector firms because it is funded, to a good part, out of tax revenue, and notions of the 'common good' and the 'rule of law' often play a more important role when the activities inside its apparatuses are assessed. At the same time, the tax revenue of the state tends to be a steadier source of income than the revenue generated by private sector firms, which usually translates into greater job security than in the latter, where precarious work tends to be more widespread. Both factors explain why joining a trade union is usually less risky than in the private sector, and why workers perceive unions as organizations that support them.

---

[4]   Of course, there are limitations to this sample. It only contains 15 countries, and out of those, 12 are high- and three are upper-middle-income countries, which means there is a strong northern bias; it aggregates numbers from different sources, which may vary in terms of their reliability and validity; and the numbers for Finland, Norway, Sweden and the US are at least two decades old. Thanks to the very clear trend contained in the data, I contend that they still provide evidence for the strength of public sector trade unionism.

Table 3.1: Union density (in per cent)

Country	Year	Privately employed workers	Publicly employed workers
Austria	2017	21.2	42
Belgium	2016	51	52.6
Costa Rica	2019	4.4	86.7
Denmark	2016	59.9	81.5
Finland	2000	64.5	98.4
Germany	2015	15.4	23.3
Japan	2019	15.8	25.7
Latvia	2016	6.2	31.5
Netherlands	2016	15.5	21.5
New Zealand	2018	10	62
Norway	1985	42.5	92.6
Russia	2016	15	80
South Africa	2005	32.2	67.2
Sweden	1985	75.4	92.6
USA	1981	18.5	32.2

Source: https://www.oecd.org/employment/ictwss-database.htm [Accessed 9 October 2022]

Importantly, it needs to be added that public sector workers in many cases inhabit contradictory class locations, which is reflected in the fact that public sector unions are often occupational unions or professional associations. Furthermore, there are, in many countries, strike bans on certain groups of publicly employed workers. Consequently, it should not be inferred that the high union density among publicly employed workers necessarily translates into militancy.

Nevertheless, many of the large-scale strikes and strike waves in the conjuncture of crisis that caused significant public debates were carried out by people in public employment. Among them are the 2010 public sector strike in South Africa; the large, cross-sectoral strikes against austerity that occurred in the wake of the Great Crisis in many Western European countries; the frequent teachers' strikes in the US in recent years; the general strikes against inequality and neoliberalization in Argentina and Chile; and the large-scale one-day general strikes in India, which involved publicly employed workers in great numbers (see Chapter 4 and Gallas and Nowak, 2012; Nowak and Gallas, 2014). Arguably, the politics of austerity as a dominant mode of crisis management turned state apparatuses into key sites of class struggle, with publicly employed workers on the frontline of struggles against jobs cuts, deteriorating working conditions and cuts to the social wage.

And if we zoom in on Western Europe, this picture is confirmed. Reflecting the numbers cited, much of the labour militancy visible in Britain in recent years came from state-employed workers. This does not just concern the strikes against pension cuts in the early 2010s, but also the Royal Mail strike in 2009, the frequent strikes at the London Underground and the strikes in higher education in 2013 and from 2018 onwards (Gallas, 2018: 245–9). Obviously, the junior doctors' dispute, which lasted from 2015 to 2019 and brought strikes in its first two years, also falls under this category (see Chapter 7). In Germany, there was a large strike wave in the public and service sector in the year of 2015 (Birke, 2018), which affected the railway and postal services as well as social workers and childcare workers (see Chapter 6). And in Spain, the general strikes against austerity, again in the early 2010s, involved both privately and publicly employed workers. Furthermore, there were also two waves of protests and strikes on the terrain of the state – the *marea verde* [green wave] in the area of education and the *marea blanca* [white wave] in the area of healthcare (Huke and Tietje, 2018) (see Chapter 8).

Ecological dominance: working–class formation in the public sector

In the light of the strength of organized labour in the public sector, it could be argued that it is a key site of working-class formation. But viewed from a class theoretical angle, labour relations in the public sector do not map neatly onto the capitalist relations productions as described in Volume 1, Chapter 6. Do state bodies and state officials represent the side of capital and the people employed by them the side of labour? There are three conceptual issues that complicate an affirmative answer to this question.

First, a significant number of public sector workers are professionals who have decision-making capacities concerning their work such that their activities do not easily fit with the despotism claim, for example, medical doctors working for public health services, teachers working for state schools or academics working for public universities. And likewise, professionals of this type possess ample opportunities for developing their practical and intellectual faculties and presenting themselves as state-approved experts, which does not sit easily with the alienation claim (see Hoff, 1985: 218). It follows that many publicly employed workers inhabit contradictory class locations. Their strike activities can contribute to working-class formation – but this is only possible if there is evidence of processes of adsorption dragging their activities towards the side of labour, as I have argued in Volume 1, Chapter 6. This conceptual complication translates into a challenge for research practice: Investigating public sector strikes requires one to first carefully assess the class locations of the workers involved – and if those locations are contradictory, to examine whether there are indeed indications of adsorption. Only then, it is possible to say what the class effects of the strike activities in focus are.

Second, as I argued in the preceding section, state bodies and state officials acting as employers cannot be safely placed on the side of capital. If we follow Poulantzas and see the capitalist state as the material condensation of class relations of forces between capital and labour, working-class forces are also present inside the state, albeit in subordinate positions. Accordingly, the decisions taken by state officials are not simply reflections of the interests of capital, even if the selectivities of the capitalist state favour strategies that are conducive to the reproduction of capitalist class domination. In other words, there are incentives for state officials to act in a pro-capitalist manner, most importantly the fact that the tax base usually funding the state requires capital accumulation. But it cannot be taken as a given that they follow these incentives – all the more if they have strong links with working-class forces.

Third, publicly employed workers, in many cases, do not produce commodities that are sold in a market. They either perform state-services or services – and the latter are usually available for free or for a stipulated fee that does not represent a market price because private sector competition is very limited or fully absent. This is possible because publicly employed workers are paid out of government receipts, a large share of which usually come out of taxes, and do not have to generate their main income with the help of revenue created in markets in goods and services. Accordingly, state bodies are usually not driven by the profit motive, which means that competitive pressures tend not be felt by people working for them to the same degree as by people working for for-profit, private sector firms (Projekt Klassenanalyse, 1973: 294; Armanski, 1974: 14; Gough, 1979: 104). Importantly, it can be inferred from the fact that most publicly employed workers do not produce commodities that they do not produce surplus value. After all, for the latter to be realized, a commodity has to be bought and sold (Marx, 1976: 437). The absence of surplus value production raises the question whether publicly employed workers are subject to exploitation at all.

Despite these conceptual complications, there are good reasons to see labour relations in the public sector as capitalist relations of production. Using a Jessopian term (Jessop, 2000), I contend that capitalist social formations are characterized by the 'ecological dominance' of the capitalist mode of production over the overall social division of labour. Following Marx, the organization of work in a social order provides a clue as to how the latter is shaped in its entirety. It only makes sense to call social formations 'capitalist' if the organization of work in them is dominantly capitalist. This is the determination in the first instance discussed in Volume 1, Chapter 5.

But what does 'ecological dominance' mean in this context? With this term inherited from biology, Bob Jessop refers to 'the capacity of a given system in a self-organizing ecology of self-organizing systems to imprint its developmental logic on other systems' operations ... to a greater degree than the latter can impose their respective logics on that system' (Jessop, 2000: 329). When we talk about class, we start from relations, not a system. The latter term suggests a degree of durability that the capitalist relations of production, if taken in isolation, do not possess. Nevertheless, what we can glean from Jessop is that in the capitalist mode of production, the capitalist relations of production are dominant in the sense that they serve as a norm for the organization of work across society.

Labour market statistics are a simple indicator of this dominance. They illustrate the degree to which private sector employment is the prevalent form of work. If we go by the numbers on the OECD, Britain, Germany, Spain and the US contained in Figure 3.4, the share of privately employed workers in the overall workforce by far outweighs that of publicly employed workers. Of course, numerical strength does not automatically translate into societal dominance. But there is also a qualitative argument for why such quantitative reasoning applies in this case. In capitalist social formations, labour markets tend to be integrated. This means that workers, if they seek employment, are free to try entering whichever sector they see fit. They can either work for private corporations or for public entities. If the state service sector is small compared to the goods production and service sectors, there is a strong incentive for state bodies not to 'overpay' its employees in comparison to privately employed workers because they would potentially have to face accusations of favouritism and 'wasting' taxpayers' money, which are particularly forceful if there are mechanisms of representative democracy. And as I have discussed, there is also a strong incentive – due to the dependence of the state on tax revenue generated in the private sector – to create stable conditions of accumulation for capital. One important factor is a permanent supply of labour power for private sector companies, which would be threatened if people generally sought employment with state bodies. A similar point can be made with reference to planning and dividing up work-related tasks. It is easier to bring the outcomes of public service provision in line with government plans and strategies if decisions are imposed in a despotic, top-down manner. And finally, the order of knowledge is guaranteed by the state anyway, which means that the division between state-approved experts and laypeople applies inside and outside state apparatuses. It follows that there are strong incentives for governments and state officials to create labour relations in the public sector that resemble those in the private sector, which also means that the conditions of work are comparable. It can be argued that ecological dominance means that the capitalist relations of production also extend to the public sector – despite the fact that it is harder to identify the side of capital in this configuration. Ian Gough, in his classic study of *The Political Economy of the Welfare State* (1979; see Armanski, 1974: 14; Poulantzas, 1974: 212), makes this exact point:

> The hours, pace and intensity of labour within state services are likely to approximate those in the private sector through the mobility of labour between the two sectors, aided by the adoption of private-sector managerial techniques within the state. And rates of pay have also tended to converge. ... Consequently, it is likely that the ration of surplus labour, or the rate of exploitation, is converging over time between the two sectors. One can express this more abstractly by observing that the capitalist mode of production is dominant within all capitalist societies, hence it will increasingly determine the labour process and relations of production within other sectors ... in such societies, including the state sector. (Gough, 1979: 166)

The implication of Gough's considerations is that surplus labour is extracted from public sector workers just like private sector workers (Carchedi, 1977: 132; Gough, 1979: 119). Accordingly, publicly employed workers experience the antagonism to capital, but do so in an indirect manner, that is, in the form of pressures imposed on them by their managers with the help of budget restrictions or efficiency drives. Even if there is no surplus value to be realized through the sale of a commodity or service, the working conditions are similar, which is why it is justified that he speaks of exploitation. In a nutshell, exploitation takes place when surplus labour extraction takes place, and for this to happen it is not necessary that surplus value is produced (see Poulantzas, 1974: 212). Consequently, the relations of production, in terms of the regime of ownership, the division of tasks and the order of knowledge, are the same for many privately and publicly employed workers – and if the latter are faced with exploitation, despotism and alienation, they can be safely placed on the side of labour.[5]

---

[5]   As I have argued, it may be the case that state bodies trade higher job security and more secure pensions for lower pay compared to private corporations, which explains higher union density and reflects the fact that labour is present inside the state. But these nuances, which balance one another out, do not change the fundamental fact that exploitation, despotism and alienation can be found inside state bodies. Consequently, I argue that a significant number of publicly employed workers are clearly located on the side of labour.

In sum, there is a workforce in the public sector that is partly located on the side of labour, and partly in contradictory class relations. If there is labour unrest inside the state, working-class formation is possible and likely – with the qualification that there have to be configurations, for the latter groups, that result in adsorption. But there is no principled reason to exclude publicly employed workers from my discussion of class formation in non-industrial sectors, quite the contrary.

The extension of labour as a class grouping

In my class analysis of service and public sector employment, I depart from Poulantzas. He presumes that for people to belong to the side of labour in terms of their class location, they do not just have to be faced with exploitation, despotism and alienation, but also have to be productive workers, that is, producers of surplus value (1974: 204). In other words, Poulantzas distinguishes, in the area of structural class determination, between 'wage earners' who are 'directly exploited' because they produce surplus value, and those who are only 'exploited' indirectly because they carry out surplus labour, but do not produce surplus value (1974: 212). According to Poulantzas, the latter grouping includes most people employed in what I call services and state services (1974: 193, 212–14) – and their class grouping is not labour, but the 'petty bourgeoisie' (1974: 191–336). If I was following Poulantzas in this respect, it would signify that Castells is right, and that there is no reason to presume that there are significant processes of working-class formation in the service and state-service sectors.

But there are critical questions to be asked. Poulantzas agrees that in both cases people's remuneration is limited to what they need to reproduce their labour power (1974: 212). So why make a difference between the two groups? Poulantzas' answer is that only productive workers experience the distinct competitive pressures and the resulting 'constant "revolutionization"' of the means of production' that characterize labour processes exposed to relative surplus labour production (1974: 310).

There appear to be two reasons why Poulantzas believes that this makes a fundamental difference. First, he says that only productive workers have 'long-term interests' that are 'revolutionary' (1974: 204). He does not explain why this should be the case – and the answer is not obvious if we consider that he speaks of 'exploitation' with reference to people working in services and state services. Thomas Goes, in his reconstruction of Poulantzas' class theory (2019), comes to Poulantzas' support and makes what can be termed a 'don't bite the hand that feeds you' argument. Following Goes, publicly employed workers have an interest in the continued existence of the capitalist state because their livelihoods depend on it (2019: 82). In other words, it is not in their interest to adopt revolutionary politics because if they did, they would put their own reproduction at risk. In my view, this is not a particularly convincing point. It does not explain why wage earners in industry are fundamentally different from those in services – and Goes, indeed, appears to see this issue and moves beyond Poulantzas by arguing that the workers in services, but not publicly employed workers, are productive workers (Goes, 2019: 64). Even more importantly, Goes' point could be taken up to deny productive workers in Poulantzas' understanding any revolutionary credentials. After all, their livelihood depends on the continued existence of the firms they are employed by. In line with their immediate interest in reproduction, trade unions have, throughout the history of capitalism, entered concession bargaining in situations where firms have been struggling financially, which means that they have placed the continued economic existence of the latter over wages and working conditions. We may say that they do not act in line with workers' fundamental interests when they do so, but the exact same argument could be made to defend publicly employed workers who are in favour of the state because they rely on it for their incomes for the time being. It follows that there is no fundamental difference between privately and publicly employed workers when it comes to divergences, at the conjunctural level, between immediate and fundamental interests. Consequently, Poulantzas' move to exclusively pin an interest in revolution on productive workers is unjustified.

Second, Poulantzas does more than just making principled points about interests. He also suggests that the experience of surplus value production creates a proclivity, on the side of workers engaged in material production, to subscribe to revolutionary politics, which sets them apart from other wage earners. In his view, the specific pressures imposed on those workers in the labour process – he invokes the Marxian expression 'bodily appendage of the machine' – explains why they are different (1974: 310). This argument, however, ignores the degree to which competitive pressures also exist in the service sector – one only needs to think of the highly mechanized labour processes of call centre workers or checkout operators in supermarkets. In line with Goes, I would indeed emphasize that services are usually commodified, and that many people working in services are wage earners. I do not see reasons for assuming that a service offered for a price in the market and delivered by someone employed by a capitalist should not count as an act of surplus value production. It follows that productive work is not exclusive to the production of tangible goods and, by implication, the same can be said about the production of relative surplus value. This goes against Poulantzas' narrow understanding of productive work and his presumptions concerning the purportedly exclusive experiences of producers of tangible goods. Why should workers in call centres or supermarkets, who operate on the grounds of rhythms set by computers, not be seen as appendages of machines?

And thanks to the ecological dominance of the capitalist relations of production, similar pressures also exist in state services – even where the production of relative surplus value is absent because there is no commodity to be produced. Indeed, governments have been introducing, for a long time, entrepreneurial management techniques, spending limits and internal markets (see Harvey, 2005: 47, 61; Gallas, 2016: 138, 240; Knafo, 2020). Finally, the argument concerning the revolutionary proclivities of productive workers neglects the fact that relative surplus production forms the economic basis for class compromises in the form of productivist pacts and political reformism (see Volume 1, Chapter 5).

In sum, I question the presumption that workers in services are unproductive. Furthermore, I contend that even if we accept that workers in state services are unproductive, there is no valid reason to assume that they are fundamentally different in terms of their interests or political attitudes from productive workers. As Poulantzas points out, there is a range of ideological patterns working in favour of the capitalist status quo that are being adopted by publicly employed workers, for example, bureaucratism (1974: 274), reformism (1974: 290), technocracy (1974: 292), meritocracy (1974: 293) and statism (1974: 310). But one can argue, with reference to the potential compromises that become possible on the grounds of the production of relative surplus value, that privately employed workers are also inclined to adopt these patterns, maybe with exception of the first. Consequently, I contend that all workers experiencing exploitation (defined as the extraction of surplus labour), despotism and alienation find themselves in the same class location and belong to labour as a class grouping. And even if there is a range of mechanisms working in favour of the status quo, they experience the antagonism to capital either directly or indirectly, which represents a potential for revolutionary politics. If we follow Luxemburg and Althusser, revolutions take place when contradictions fuse at the level of the conjuncture (see Volume 1, Chapter 7). This is why the mere existence of mechanisms rendering the mode of production durable is not an argument against the possibility of a rupture with it.

4

Outside the Factory Gates: Strikes in Non-Industrial Workplaces around the World

Mapping: a qualitative research technique for global labour studies

Governments around the world have been managing the Great Crisis by adopting the politics of austerity. Public spending cuts tend to have drastic effects on workers because they usually translate into social wages being slashed. They are often particularly harmful to people employed in the public sector who may be faced with redundancies, worsening working conditions and direct wage cuts. Against this backdrop, it is unsurprising that large, disruptive strikes have been occurring frequently in non-industrial settings in recent years. Complementing Silver's point that labour unrest travels when industries relocate, it can be observed that in many countries, militancy in the public and service sectors has been pronounced, sometimes more pronounced than in manufacturing. In various contexts, public and service sector unions take a leading role in their respective labour movements – and the workers involved do not conform with the image of the striker created by Hyman's book cover from the 1970s, which shows a White, middle-aged male miner (see Volume 1, Introduction).

In this chapter, I map labour disputes from around the world that have been taking place in the public and service sectors during the conjuncture of crisis. I take inspiration from my colleagues Franziska Müller, Simone Claar, Manuel Neumann and Carsten Elsner, who have mapped African renewable energy policies (Müller et al, 2020) – and from Silver's approach in *Forces of Labor* (2003), where she uses a dataset based on newspaper coverage of strikes to identify patterns of labour unrest. I understand mapping in a metaphorical sense, that is, as a qualitative research technique that creates systematic but heavily simplified and 'flat' representations of multi-dimensional objects, which are mostly linguistic. For example, mapping can take the form of a table where large numbers of cases are grouped according to patterns. Due to the simplicity of these representations, mapping is well-suited for producing the contextualizations that incorporated comparisons require. It allows one to cover geographical areas with large extensions.

In my understanding, mapping is a three-stage process. One starts by collecting data and creates a dataset that includes information on some key traits of one's object. After that, one classifies the data through a coding exercise. The codes can be generated in an inductive manner by identifying prevalent patterns in the data, or in a deductive manner by deriving them from a theoretical framework. The last step is interpreting the codes by relating them to the research question.

Accordingly, my research presented in this chapter is based on a dataset, which I have created through the 'strategic' sampling of news media coverage of strikes in services and the public sector. It represents a collection of 'extremely varied' cases around the globe in the conjuncture of crisis (Danermark et al, 2002: 170). The investigation period is January 2007 to October 2020. Variation here refers to the geographical locations, sectors and constituencies of strikes. My goal has been to include stoppages from all over the world, from a large variety of sub-sectors of the public and service sectors and with a range of aims and demands. I have included general strikes in the sample because they have been an important mode of resisting the politics of austerity provided there was evidence of a widespread involvement of service and public sector workers (see Gallas et al, 2012; Nowak and Gallas, 2014).

I created my database by searching the online archives of widely read quality papers from across the globe for coverage of non-industrial strikes and entered key information on them in a spreadsheet.[1] I chose a paper each from Africa, Asia, North America and South America plus the three Western European countries covered in my more detailed case studies in Part II, namely, *The Mail & Guardian* (Johannesburg), *The Times of India* (Mumbai), *The New York Times*, *Página12* (Buenos Aires), *The Guardian* (London), *Die Tageszeitung* (*taz*, Berlin) and *Público* (Madrid). My choice of papers reflects the need for geographical balance, my knowledge of languages, questions of online accessibility and the need to work with papers that are known for operating on the grounds of a sound factual basis and for being interested in labour disputes. The latter point explains why the selection of

---

[1]   The types of information entered were country; region; branch of the economy; duration; date; number of participants; unions involved; reasons, demands and outcomes. Furthermore, I added links to the source(s) and information on whether one of the newspapers examined systematically was located in the country where the strike took place plus an overall count and a count per country. For further information on my online search and the creation of the database, see Appendix A.

papers shows a certain political bias – they all have a reputation for leaning either toward centrist or left-of-centre politics.

Once I had completed searches of newspapers and produced a sample, I compared the countries contained in it with a list of the G20 countries. This demonstrated that there were still uncharted territories of high significance for the global political economy. My sample did not contain information on strikes in six G20 countries, namely, Canada, Indonesia, Mexico, Japan, Saudi Arabia and South Korea. I decided to conduct additional online searches of two websites dedicated to collecting media coverage and press releases on labour struggles and the activities of unions from across the world, namely, labourstart.org and labournet.de. To reduce bias, I stuck to media coverage and chose not to include in the sample press releases and statements from labour organizations documented on the two sites. Whenever I found information on stoppages that were not the main topic of the article in question, I conducted an online search for additional information on those particular actions. I complemented this with information on strikes covered in the news media that I found when I researched my three cases.

In the end, I had a sample consisting of 387 strikes, which were located in 56 countries and autonomous territories (see Figure 4.1).[2] Obviously, the size of the sample meant that it was not representative, and three G20 countries were still missing. But I decided that the geographical breadth of the coverage was enough for creating a comprehensive, if incomplete, picture. After all, it contained information from all six continents and 17 of the major political economies around the world. Unavoidably, the two online platforms used in the second search referred to articles in other newspapers than the seven initially selected, which means that the number of new outlets included in the dataset increased and became more arbitrary. Despite its limitations, my sample provides a useful overview of non-industrial strikes around the world. It may not be possible to infer much from creating global aggregate numbers concerning strike incidence on its basis, that is, from declaring, in a simplistic quantitative fashion, that (x) of

---

[2] By 'autonomous territories', I refer to territories not fully integrated into national states due to their geographical location outside the mainland, their specific economic conditions and their autonomous forms of government. Due to this distinctiveness, they form separate items in the sample. In it, there are four such domains – French Polynesia, New Caledonia, Wallis and Futuna, as well as Puerto Rico. The former three are Pacific territories belonging to France that span several archipelagos, enjoy political autonomy and have their own currency – and whose GDP per capita is considerably lower than that of the French mainland. Puerto Rico is an archipelago in the Caribbean that belongs to the United States, but that remains 'unincorporated' and is subject to 'local self-government'. Its citizens are not allowed to vote in US presidential elections, and its GDP per capita is also significantly lower than that of the US mainland (CIA, 2022).

Figure 4.1: Geographical coverage of sample

Source: Own illustration

the items in the sample exhibit characteristic (y). After all, the sample varies significantly in its coverage of different countries and parts of the world, and it does not contain strikes that occur under the radar of media coverage. But it is feasible, especially if there is a larger number of items for a single country, to identify patterns at the national level. And it is also possible to say that a certain pattern can be found in (x) out of (y) countries. I contend that it is plausible to assume that the patterns identified this way refer to general trends if observations at the national level overlap between countries, can be verified with reference to the more detailed case studies, which can be found in Part II, and are compatible with my theoretical considerations.

To determine patterns in my sample, I embarked on a coding exercise. In this effort, I followed Victoria Elliott's understanding of coding, who argues that it is a way of 'indexing or mapping data, to provide an overview of disparate data that allows the researcher to make sense of them in relation to their research question' (Elliott, 2018: 2851). I started with a deductive move and derived a number of categories from earlier research that I had undertaken, partly with my colleague Jörg Nowak, with the aim of identifying key characteristics of mass strikes (Nowak and Gallas, 2014: 311–12; Gallas, 2018: 239–40; 2020: 184; Nowak, 2019: 49–50). In line with my research question, I focused particularly on a category called 'class effects', which was supposed to gauge whether strikes have class relevance. My aim was to assess whether inclusive solidarity was in evidence, which could have been taken to point to the existence of processes of class formation.

During the coding process, it became clear to me that it was impossible to directly gauge 'class effects', at least for the majority of strikes.[3] This could be taken to indicate that there was simply no evidence that these effects existed. But there was also the possibility that the category was too abstract to be applied to the concrete but limited information contained in the sample. Accordingly, I decided to drop the category from my considerations without seeing it as a foregone conclusion that there was no evidence of class formation.

Instead, I decided to focus on another category, namely 'character of aims'. In line with my focus on the different dimensions of the class struggle in Volume 1, Chapter 5, it referred to how different dimensions of the social world were addressed through aims formulated before and during stoppages. Accordingly, the codes were 'mostly economic', 'economic and politicized', 'organic' and 'political in a narrow sense'. Importantly, they referred to aims, not effects, which often cannot be neatly classed as being either 'economic' or 'political'.

---

[3] For more detailed information on the coding process and my codes and categories, see Appendix A.

The first code, 'dominantly economic', referred to strikes that occurred in a clearly defined workplace, business or sector or were targeting a clearly defined group of workers making demands vis-à-vis their employer that concerned their conditions of work or employment. The classic case of the collective bargaining strike over wages and conditions falls under this category, but also strikes for union recognition, a collective bargaining agreement or against job cuts (provided they remain outside the realm of political debate altogether or political debate remains limited to 'insiders'). The second code applied to strikes based on economic demands that became heavily politicized and led to debates about work in the respective sector and beyond – either because the employer was the state, or because they were particularly disruptive. The third code, 'organic', refers to strikes with a large extension along class lines, an articulation of economic and political demands and a mobilization along class lines. They differ from 'economic and politicized' strikes insofar as they are broad, and their leaders attempt to speak for workers as a class. Last but not least, there was also a fourth code, 'mostly political', which refers to strikes for political aims that are not directly related to economic issues or issues of work, for example, strikes against *coups d'état*. All in all, the distinction between the different codes was fuzzy sometimes, in particular when it came to differentiating between 'mostly economic' and 'economic and politicized' strikes. However, there were no cases where it was impossible to decide which category a certain strike belonged to.

The codes in themselves did not reveal a class dimension of the strikes, but I decided to investigate whether it was possible to approach it in an indirect fashion. My hunch was that looking at the 'character of aims' category could potentially reveal, in conjunction with the additional information captured by the other categories, connections of striking workers with other workers and demonstrate that there were attempts to mobilize workers as a class. I assumed that if strikes had a political dimension and thus, by definition, addressed the organization of society as a whole, it was possible that they were broad enough in their demands to be seen as having expansive class effects. To examine this assumption, I checked whether the codes contained in the 'character of aims' category could be connected with a set of codes that I established through an inductive move, that is, by identifying strike patterns based on their aims and constituencies. My hope was that this would provide me with more fine-grained depictions of different strike patterns and would enable me to make meaningful observations about class effects.

I was able to link the four codes contained in the 'character of aims' category with five strike patterns:

(1) The 'mostly economic' code refers to two different patterns – first, the standard collective bargaining strike, which concerns wages or working

conditions in a business unit or branch of the economy, and, second, the extension strike, which is about trade union recognition and has similar constituencies;

(2) the 'economic and politicized' code is connected with the expansive-politicized strike, which is about economic aims but evolves into a political conflict over social and economic policy or the role of organized labour in society;

(3) the 'organic' code links with the class-based strike, in which workers are not mobilized just as a workforce or a class fraction, but as an imagined working class as a whole, for example, in general strikes; and

(4) the 'mostly political' code is associated with the exclusively political strike, where the mobilization of workers' power is a vehicle for advancing political causes that are only indirectly connected with work (see Figure 4.2).

Establishing these links enabled me to discuss the class question with reference to patterns that were more fine-grained than the codes produced through the 'character of aims' category. Furthermore, this approach had the advantage of introducing an inductive element into my framework, which created an openness to the research process in line with my critique of subsumptionism (see Chapter 1; Belfrage and Hauf, 2015: 335). In what follows, I discuss the five strike patterns in conjunction with the question of which dimension of

Figure 4.2: The 'character of aims' category

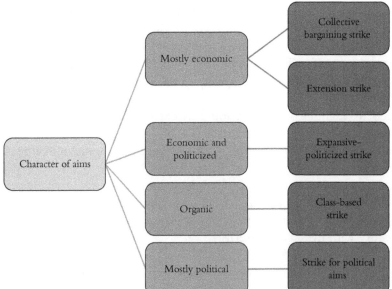

the social world is addressed, and make general observations, to the degree to which they are possible, about class effects.

'Bread and butter' strikes: collective bargaining and the resort to militancy

Collective bargaining strikes are 'mostly economic' strikes over 'bread and butter' issues such as pay and working conditions and have clearly defined constituencies, namely workforces in a business unit or a branch of the economy. If they occur in the public sector, they can also be sectoral. They start with the intention of strengthening one's negotiation position vis-à-vis employers. By definition, they do not directly touch upon broader political questions like regulation, redistribution or economic and fiscal policy; strikes that do are captured by the other three codes.

There are plenty of collective bargaining strikes in the sample – from workers employed by the state media in Antigua walking out who were demanding the payment of outstanding overtime pay, improvements to working conditions and the firing of the general manager to a strike of Zimbabwean cricketers over pay arrears (Ap, 2014; *Daily Observer*, 2018a; 2018b). If we look at the seven core countries in the sample, collective bargaining strikes constituted the most prevalent type of stoppage in Germany, India and South Africa. This suggests that they constitute a standard strike pattern in capitalist social formations.

By definition, class agency remains, in collective efforts of this type, somewhat limited. Strikes attracting a lot of support from other groups of workers tend to become the object of broad political debate, to which 'the mostly economic' code does not apply. Furthermore, the separation between the economic, the political and the cultural dimension characteristic of capitalist social formations in times of stability remains intact. It is functional for the reproduction of class domination because it amounts to labour accepting the control of capital over the labour process, and the specific 'expertise' assigned to the side of capital through the division between mental and manual labour. If strikes of this type remain isolated, they tend not to shift the relations of forces between labour and capital and not to pose a threat to the continued existence of capitalist class domination. But they may change in terms of their aims over time or inspire other strikes – and shift the attitudes of workers as well as creating cross-sectoral bonds between them. As such, their existence cannot be taken as evidence of processes of class formation, but they still matter because they can create favourable conditions for the latter to emerge.

But what does this imply for Castells' claim and Panitch's counterclaim? Two observations are noteworthy: For one, collective bargaining strikes happen all the time and across the globe in the service and public sectors, which also means that they are by no means exclusive to the industrial sector. The sample contained strikes of this type in 32 out of 56 countries covered by it. And notably, all the remaining countries were countries with five or fewer items in the sample. It follows that the number of items for those countries is far too small to infer that 'mostly economic' strikes are rare.

This observation goes against Castells' suggestion that the side of labour in the post-industrial age is characterized by the isolation of workers. In other words, unions are active in non-industrial sectors, and they go on strike. It may be the case that they face specific obstacles, and that strike incidence in deindustrialized settings has not made up so far for the decline in strike incidence in manufacturing. But this does not mean that struggles around work do not exist. Admittedly, this is not a proof for Panitch's counterclaim because it could still be the case that the emergent forms of collective action remain fragmented along branch or sectoral lines and thus do not exhibit expansive solidarity.

A second significant observation is that while it was usually not possible to read off an expansive dimension from these strikes, that is, a 'class feeling' that creates links to other groups of workers and broader struggles, the opposite also held. There were few signs of strikes in this category being divisive. Examples of divisive strikes are highly disruptive stoppages carried out by workers in highly privileged positions or stoppages driven by inter-union competition. But these were few and far between. The only examples in the sample that could be understood in this manner are the frequent strikes of pilots in Europe, which have been construed in the media as strikes by privileged workers (see Chapter 2), and the strikes by train drivers in Germany, which were presented as instances of inter-union competition. But in neither case is this the whole story: the transnational pilots' strikes at Irish budget carrier Ryanair were followed by transnational strikes of flight attendants at the same company, which suggests an expansive pattern, and the train drivers' strike forced the non-striking union, which had closely cooperated with management, to embrace militancy again, which arguably strengthened railway workers in Germany (see Chapter 6). It follows that there were signs of emergent collective agency along class lines even in cases that should be typical instances of strikes with divisive effects.

Extension strikes: collective action in novel branches of the economy

It follows from Castells' claim that organized labour should be particularly weak in those parts of the post-industrial economy that exemplify the alleged shift to 'informational capitalism', that is, those that heavily rely on digital infrastructures. To test this claim, I examined the pattern of the extension strike, which can be connected with the 'mostly economic' code. Extension strikes, which tend to take place at the level of a business unit, demand that usually individualized labour relations become subject to regulation, reorganization or collective negotiation, for example, through the recognition of formally self-employed workers as employees, insourcing or union recognition. Notably, many of the strikes in the sample exhibiting this pattern were located in novel, heavily digitalized branches of the economy.

Examples were a strike over several weeks by call centre workers in Hanover, Germany, demanding higher wages and a collective bargaining agreement in 2013 (Schwarz, 2013); a successful six-week strike in Norway of delivery riders working for Foodora who won a collective bargaining agreement (NIE, 2019); a stoppage of formally self-employed riders working for Deliveroo in London, which lasted for several days and was about the company's pay system in 2016 (Osborne and Farell, 2016); and the case of Uber drivers in Geneva in Switzerland, who went on strike in November 2017 with aim of being recognized as employees (Bardertscher and Kurz, 2017). These strikes underscore that a key point of contention in this field is the difference between people seeing themselves as wage earners and their legal status as self-employed workers.

An important site of collective action in this context is also the online retailer Amazon – both because it is a multinational corporation whose business model is based on heavily digitalized labour processes and interactions with customers, and because it has a long history of refusing to recognize unions and negotiate with them (Apicella and Hildebrandt, 2019: 173–5; Boewe and Schulten, 2019: 15–22). Importantly, the labour process at Amazon has been described thus: 'Labour in Amazon's distribution centres exhibits certain characteristics of digital Taylorism, converting elements of sales work into factory-like labour' (Apicella and Hildebrandt, 2019: 174). As such, Amazon is an excellent test case for Castells' claim that informalization undermines the collective agency of workers.

Indeed, the sample captures a transnational wave of extension strikes for union recognition and collective negotiations at Amazon distribution centres in recent years. It contains more than a dozen stoppages, which took place in Britain, France, Germany, Italy, Poland and Spain. In some cases, the strikes were transnational. The first stoppage at Amazon took place in April 2013 in the small German town of Bad Hersfeld. Hundreds of workers, mobilized by the public and service sector union Vereinte Dienstleistungsgewerkschaft (ver. di), walked out for a one-hour workers' assembly in front of the local Amazon distribution centre to demand negotiations over a collective bargaining agreement (Verkehrsrundschau, 2013; Boewe and Schulten, 2019: 5). This was followed by a one-day strike a month later in Bad Hersfeld and Leipzig, in which 1,700 people participated (DW, 2013). In June 2015, another warning strike in Bad Hersfeld was supported by a go-slow in Poznán, a Polish city, which was of high strategic relevance because the company had been relaying the distribution of ordered goods from Germany to Poland when strikes had been occurring (*Die Zeit*, 2015a; Boewe and Schulten, 2019: 31–2). Another noteworthy strike took place in Castel San Giovanni in Italy, where Amazon's main Italian distribution centre is located. It happened on 24 November 2017 – on 'Black Friday', a so-called 'shopping holiday' where retailers across the globe offer sizeable sales and discounts. In May 2018, the company struck its first agreement with unions, which covered work hours and night shifts in this centre (Bock, 2018; Labournet, 2018). Amazon and the other examples suggest that non-industrial workers – even in heavily digitalized areas – organize and go on strikes.

In existing, non-industrial branches of the economy, privatization, market liberalization and foreign direct investment have tended to intensify competition, to which corporations have reacted with creating subsidiaries and outsourcing specific tasks. These operations allow them to circumnavigate existing networks of solidarity among workers, reduce labour costs at the latter's expense and reinforce workplace control. Where such networks do not exist, outsourcing makes it harder for workers to act collectively and engage in acts of solidarity (see Harvey, 2005: 59, 65–6; Luckett and Pontarelli, 2016; Dor and Runciman, 2022). Nevertheless, the sample shows that some workers in outsourced units respond by taking collective action.[4] The successful #outsourcingmustfall movement in 2015 and 2016 at universities across South Africa is emblematic of such a reaction. A wave of student protests against tuition fees with the slogan #feesmustfall was accompanied by workers protesting and going on strikes against university managements that had chosen to outsource tasks such as cleaning, catering and gardening to cut labour costs (Nkosi, 2015; Luckett and Mzobe, 2016; Luckett and Pontarelli, 2016). And there are more examples from South Africa. In 2014, postal workers, through a

---

[4]   There are several other items in the sample that refer to strikes against outsourcing, which, however, do not fall under the pattern discussed here because they are not about extending the reach of organized labour but defending positions that have been conquered through earlier struggles. There were 14 short strikes by pilots at German national carrier Lufthansa in 2014–15, which were, among other things, about thwarting plans of the company to outsource some of their work to a subsidiary of the company, the budget airline Eurowings (*taz*, 2015). Workers in the Indian banking sectors went on short, symbolic strikes against privatization and outsourcing at Indian public banks in December 2014, September 2015 and February 2017 (TOI, 2014; 2015; 2017; Salomi, 2015). Furthermore, there was a large-scale, two-day general strike in India in 2019. It was directed against the restructuring of labour law under the Modi government involving 10 union umbrellas and up to 200 million people – although this number is disputed and might be too high (Shyam Sundar, 2019; Woodcock, 2019). In this context, an article in the *Times of India* (*TOI*) (2019) reports on how postal workers in particular were dismayed at the prospects of outsourcing in the sector.

four-month strike, forced the government to offer full-time, permanent contracts to part-time and casual workers (*SA News*, 2014). In early 2018, workers at the central medicine depot for public hospitals in the Northwest of the country went on a drawn-out strike, demanding, among other things, higher wages and the dismissal of the head of the public health service in the area, but also the insourcing of casualized workers (Msomi and Team, 2018).

Importantly, there were similar strikes in Europe. Several stoppages took place in London where cleaners and security guards working at universities demanded equal pay and conditions and insourcing. At University College London, this campaign was successful (Farrow, 2017; Hayns, 2017a; 2017b; Chapman, 2019; Booth, 2020). Furthermore, struggles for insourcing also occurred in Germany. There was a dispute running over several months in late 2018 and early 2019 and an eight-day strike of physiotherapists and occupational therapists at hospitals in Berlin. They were employed by subsidiaries of healthcare companies running the hospitals and demanded an end to unequal pay and conditions, which led to their insourcing (Teweleit, 2018; Heine, 2019a, 2019b). Similarly, a short warning strike took place in Berlin of healthcare workers employed with hospitals demanding a wage increase, a limitation of work hours for paramedics and the equalization of pay and conditions for workers at subsidiaries and parent companies (Rothenpieler, 2020).

The examples show two things: First, changes to corporate arrangements that occur in the context of neoliberalization may have drastic effects on labour relations. They produce conflicts and, in a number of cases, lead to collective action by workers, no matter whether these are employed in manufacturing or elsewhere. We can identify indications of working-class formation in the British, German and South African cases because workers act against the individualization and fragmentation of labour relations, create bonds across business units, that is, between 'regular' and outsourced workers, and forge broader alliances: in the case of #outsourcingmustfall the alliance between students and outsourced workers, in the case of the London strikes, the cooperation between the security officers and the cleaners, and in the case of Berlin, the links between workers inside the healthcare sector and across different groups and employment statuses.

Second, it is noteworthy that some of the workers involved are people located in contradictory class locations, for example pilots, therapists and bank workers. The fact that these groups protest outsourcing and corporate strategies that result in the flexibilization and precarization of work can be seen as creating the ground for their adsorption to broader working-class networks, even if it is necessary to check in each individual case how strong the ties between them and people located in working-class locations are. In the case of the Berlin healthcare workers, the coverage indicates a fairly strong degree of adsorption because the more specific issues of therapists were integrated into broader struggles of healthcare workers across the sector.

Expansive-politicized strikes: economic demands and class politics

It is characteristic of the first two strike patterns discussed that their aims rest on a clear-cut distinction between the economic and the political dimension of capitalist social formations, and that they are located on the economic side. As has been discussed, the separation of economic from political and cultural class struggle is functional for the reproduction of capitalist class domination. It limits the scope of collective action by workers and prevents them from addressing the hierarchies of decision-making and knowledge characteristic of class domination. In other words, the power workers exercise when they act together is confined to the economy and affects other areas of the social formation only indirectly (see Volume 1, Chapter 5).

Notably, this is different in the case of the third strike pattern, which is linked with the 'economic and politicized' code. The expansive-politicized strike starts from economic demands, but these also take on a political dimension thanks to the context in which they are voiced. Either the demands are economic and politically charged from the beginning, or workers start to politicize their demands while the stoppages take place.

The public sector is particularly relevant for the first scenario. After all, workers are employed by state bodies. As a result, their pay and conditions are directly linked to political decisions over what kind of public services should be offered, how the public sector should be funded, and what rights and obligations publicly employed workers have. This means that collective negotiations are prone to politicization by default.

This general tendency becomes even more pronounced in the age of neoliberalism. Wage levels and working conditions in the public sector, as well as the pressures faced by public sector workers, are in many cases outcomes of processes of neoliberalization. From the 1970s onwards, neoliberal governments have attacked public sector unions and have restrained their ability to act. They have privatized public companies and services – and this has often resulted in job cuts, wage depression, the worsening of working condition and the erosion of mass bases of unions. Furthermore, they have imposed 'new public management' techniques on state bodies, which are based on the assumption that work processes and service provision in the public sector should be modelled on private sector, for-profit firms. Finally, they have embraced the politics of austerity, which came in waves of cuts to state expenditure (Peters, 2012; see also Gallas, 2016: *passim*). As a result, public sector workers often invoke broader political issues around the nature and purpose of public expenditure, public services and public goods when they legitimize their claims.

A notable, long-running dispute in this context has been taking place at Charité, the university hospital system owned by the German federal state of Berlin, from 2011 onwards. It is 'the first [labour] struggle at a German hospital ... that was carried out not for more money, but for more staff' (Tügel, 2017: 37). The prelude was an enforcement strike over pay involving nurses and healthcare workers (Heine, 2011; Gester, 2012), which was not politicized in a strong sense. A few years later, several rounds of strikes ensued, which focused on understaffing and were politicized: a two-day warning strike in April 2015 (*Ärzteblatt*, 2015; Heine, 2015); an enforcement strike that in the end lasted for ten days in June 2015 (Mernania, 2015; *SZ*, 2015); a one-day warning strike in August 2017 (*Ärzteblatt*, 2017a; *Ärztezeitung*, 2017a; DLF, 2017); and a one-week, symbolic strike in September 2017 (*Ärzteblatt*, 2017b; 2017c; *Ärztezeitung*, 2017b). The workers frequently used the slogan 'more of us is better for everyone' to describe their cause and protest the understaffing at Charité hospitals and its effect both on their working conditions and on patient care. They used to their advantage the fact that hospital managements are forced to refrain from allocating beds to patients if not enough staff is present to care for them. In 2016, the striking workers won an agreement that secured better patient–staff ratios. But at the time of writing, workers were still demanding change because they argued it had not been implemented properly, which is why there were new rounds of strikes (ver.di, nd; Heine, 2021).

Another example is a one-day general strike involving a significant number of public sector workers in South Africa in February 2019. The strike was organized by South Africa's main union federation, COSATU, and it was legal because it was deemed a stoppage over 'socioeconomic' issues. Despite this official label, it can be said to have been political because its two main demands were addressed at the government: to ensure that there are no job cuts and a further deterioration of the unemployment rate, and to refrain from privatizing Eskom, the national energy public utility (EFE, 2019; Nieselow, 2019).

The second scenario of a politicization *ex-post* is often visible if strikes trigger a hostile counterreaction from the repressive state apparatus or become the object of debate between pro- and anti-labour forces in the political scene. This happens in particular if they significantly disrupt routines in the economy or everyday life. In this context, the political-legal environment matters in which the strikes take place.[5]

---

[5]   This echoes Luxemburg once more. In her tract on 'The mass strike', she describes a stoppage of workers in St Petersburg that occurred in 1896. They protested against a compulsory and unpaid three-day holiday on the occasion of the coronation of Czar

If this environment is very repressive, strikes become politicized by default because workers know that they are defying the repressive state apparatus when they walk out. The sample contains, for example, a wave of strikes at US supermarket chain Walmart in China against a new scheduling system (Hernandez, 2016). As such, this protest was about a specific, work-related grievance. But it had a wider, political meaning because it was based on a bottom-up, grassroots form of organizing – and because this goes against the repressive regime of labour relations in China. In the country, the authorities suppress independent forms of labour organization taking place outside the business-friendly All-China Federation of Trade Unions (Pringle, 2016: 126). Consequently, the wave of action at Walmart in China can be said to have been a political statement by default. If strikes are banned, workers staging one declare that they defy the repressive state apparatus. They demonstrate that going on strike is a practice that cannot and should not be outlawed. In this scenario, economic aims become politically charged.

A second example of this pattern from the sample is a three-day strike of metro drivers in Tbilisi, Georgia, in June 2018. After workers had demanded higher wages from the city council and had connected this with a strike threat, a court barred them from stopping work. They responded with a hunger strike, which made them unfit to work and resulted in the metro network being shut down. In this case, an attempt by the authorities to impose a strike ban and the decision of workers to act in defiance and continue with their action turned into a confrontation between workers and the state over the right to strike. In other words, the workers politicized their strike aims when they decided not to yield. The stoppage was framed, after both sides had come to a settlement, by labour activists as setting an example for future action by public sector workers in Georgia (Labournet, 2018; OC Media, 2018).

And third, there was also a wave of strikes by US teachers and education workers in 2018–19 (Blanc, 2019; 2020). It started in West Virginia, where teachers did not have, under the dominant interpretation of the law, a right to strike and enter collective bargaining. Twenty thousand teachers went on a nine-day wildcat strike for higher wages, which led to threats from the state's General Attorney to take legal action against them. The fact that workers did not call it off in reaction to those threats means that it became not just a strike over wages, but over the political question whether they have the right to unionize and negotiate their wages and working conditions collectively. It was successful insofar as the striking teachers enjoyed significant public

---

Nicholas II, which led to fierce state repression. Luxemburg describes the resulting process of politicization thus: 'the strike was outwardly a mere economic struggle for wages, but the attitude of the government and the agitation of the social democracy made it a political phenomenon of the first rank' (Luxemburg, 2008: 122). Following Luxemburg, the interventions of state bodies and political actors are important drivers of politicization.

support and secured a 5 per cent raise although some of them did not see this as sufficient (Bidgood, 2018; Bidgood and Robertson, 2018; Rhodan, 2018).

Importantly, the strikes are also evidence of a process of adsorption of workers in a contradictory class location. They were construed as showing a way forward for US workers in hostile environments across branches and sectors, and not as an action by a special interest group. There was community support, but also solidarity notes from other unions, and unionists from other sectors turning up at rallies (Blanc, 2019: 84–5). MaryBe McMillan, the president of the main US union federation American Federation of Labor and Congress of Industrial Organizations (AFL-CIO) in North Carolina, described the character of the strikes thus:

> I think the more the media covers uprisings in red states like West Virginia, Oklahoma, and Kentucky, the more people see that despite the legal obstacles and challenges that workers face in these states, there is a real interest in rising up against the horrible repressive laws that are in those states. (cited in Elk, 2018)

This demonstrates that the action resonated with other sections of organized labour. It created 'class feeling', to use Luxemburg's term.

All three strikes have a class political dimension because in embracing militant action and defying existing laws, the workers were also taking a stand for the right to organize and strike. In other words – and as was expressed by the labour activists in the Georgian case – they were setting an example insofar as they showed that it is possible for workers to act collectively, and that it is justified to do so. The strikes in question are expansive because they concerned class relations in their entirety.

In political contexts that are less repressive against organized labour, politicization can also happen through the intervention of political decision-makers in strikes, sometimes with the aim of questioning their legitimacy, and workers carrying on nonetheless. A standard example are the strikes in the German railway sector, which are discussed in the next chapter, and which led some leading politicians to first denounce them and then to push for passing a bill in the Federal Parliament that aimed at banning strikes of what were deemed minority unions in a business unit.

A less hostile reaction, but a political reaction nonetheless, occurred in September and October 2009 when sanitation workers in Leeds in the North of England stopped work over pay cuts and productivity increases, accompanied by firefighters and bus drivers in neighbouring cities. The then Prime Minister Gordon Brown intervened, telling workers and employers to restart negotiations (Wainwright, 2009). With his intervention, Brown did not suggest that the activities of the strikers were illegitimate or illegal. He called for restraint and for sacrificing militancy for what he implicitly assumed to be the 'greater good', that is, an end of disruptions to public services. Nevertheless, his intervention can be seen as a reaction that displayed hostility towards labour. Brown questioned the tactics of the striking workers, and he felt the need to get involved. The fact that workers carried on anyway demonstrates how the strike became politicized.

An example of a process of politicization through political intervention that turns the logic of delegitimization on its head can be found in Antigua and Barbuda, an island country in the Caribbean with roughly 100,000 inhabitants, where a short strike in 2018 by workers at a psychiatric hospital over conditions and outstanding overtime pay also resulted in the intervention of the prime minister. In contrast to his namesake from Britain, Gaston Browne decided to get involved personally and to lead negotiations with union representatives. Here, the forcefulness of workers politicized their action. This happened in the form of an intervention from above that attempted to defuse the situation by giving the workers assurances that their grievances would be addressed (*Daily Observer*, 2018c).

There was also a class political dimension to each of these three disputes despite their initially economic motivation. This was because they occurred under specific political circumstances. Despite being couched in economic terms, the workers' demands, through their context, concerned labour relations in society as a whole and the role of workers in them. In this sense, the significance of the strikes extended beyond the workplaces where they took place, which is why it is justified to speak of expansive strikes.

In sum, the different instances of the economic and politicized strike can be seen as indicators of processes of class formation. The key point here is that struggles over specific grievances become linked with wider issues over how work in society should be organized, and who should benefit from the fruits of that work. In this sense, they can also be seen as reflections of 'class feeling'.

Class-based strikes: mobilizing workers across society for economic and political aims

There is a fourth strike pattern, which is also economic and political. Concerning its character of aims, it is connected with the 'organic' code, and in contrast to the expansive-politicized strike, 'class feeling' is easily discernible. It is based on broad, cross-sectoral mobilizations of workers – often in the mode of a general strike – and combines economic with political demands that are couched in class terms. Accordingly, it often involves both private and public sector workers, and it is also not restricted to non-industrial workers. But since the latter tend to play an important role, the class-based strike is still highly relevant for the question of class formation beyond industry.

Due to its encompassing and economic-political character, the class-based strike by default involves a confrontation between organized labour and not just capital but also the government, which is usually seen as prioritizing the interests of capital over the interests of workers and subaltern people in general. It often addresses the existing accumulation strategies by targeting areas such as social, economic, fiscal and monetary policy.

The 'class-based strike' in my understanding resembles Luxemburg's 'mass strike' in that it is a class-based form of mobilization. But there is one crucial difference: For Luxemburg (2008: 147), the mass strike is a form of struggle that emerges in revolutionary conjunctures; in contrast, the strikes I refer to here are not limited to a specific conjuncture and can be both offensive and defensive, and both aimed at protesting specific political decisions or agendas and at toppling a government.

The sample contains class-based and organic strikes in Argentina, Belgium, Brazil, Botswana, Chad, Chile, Costa Rica, Finland, France, French Polynesia, Greece, India, Italy, Morocco, Portugal, Puerto Rico, Spain, Switzerland, Tunisia and Turkey – all in all 20 out of the 56 countries covered. The geographical spread – countries or autonomous territories in all six continents are listed – shows that organic strikes are by no means exceptional but normal events in the current conjuncture.

Notably, most of the class-based strikes in the sample are defensive and symbolic. They represent a hostile counterreaction to government plans that are seen as being detrimental to workers. The sample may comprise 20 country cases where class-based strikes have been taking place, but only in five cases, these were offensive strikes, and only in six, enforcement strikes. This calls for more detailed reflection.

As a direct, broad exercise of workers' power used to advance economic and political aims, class-based strikes can potentially disrupt the economy to such a degree that they inflict significant damage on capital and question the existing mechanisms of political decision-making. In so doing, they raise the question of democracy. Political strikes have long been criticized for being anti-democratic. They are alleged to represent a mode of using force that has not been legitimized through the standard institutions of representative democracy (see Hain, 1986: 12; Gallas and Nowak, 2012: 25). A term existing in German legalese is 'Parlamentsnötigung', that is, coercion imposed on the parliament, which is usually exercised through a general or a political strike (Hensche, 2012: 221). Legal scholars close to labour have responded to these claims by stressing that political strikes are a necessary corrective to capitalist class domination (Abendroth, 1954: 54; Hensche, 2012: 221–2). After all, the latter is based, at the level of the labour process, on despotism and thus is highly anti-democratic. In this sense, class-based strikes are a 'weapon in the fight for democracy' allowing workers to redress

83

somewhat the systemic imbalance between capital and labour (Gallas and Nowak, 2012: 32).

In a nutshell, class-based strikes move beyond the separation of economic and political class struggles, which makes a genuine rupture with the status quo more realistic. Implicitly, they pose the famous question that the British Prime Minister Ted Heath, a Conservative, asked in 1974. Faced with the second miners' strike within the space of just two years, he called a general election under the slogan 'Who governs Britain?' – and lost (Cohen, 2006: 29; Gallas, 2016: 77).

Nevertheless, class-based strikes run a risk: Unless they are short and symbolic (and in certain legal environments even if they are), they can trigger draconian responses from the repressive state apparatus. The high economic, political and legal stakes of class-based strikes are part of the explanation why unions often only resort to them to defend existing configurations of class relations against attacks from capital, and why they are often symbolic.

In the age of neoliberalism, class-based strikes represent a response to the ability of capitalists to put pressure on governments. The latter has been magnified by governments deciding to remove tariffs and capital controls, which has intensified international competition, and has enabled investors to move their assets abroad. Under these conditions, the simple threat of relocating can be used by capital to influence government policy (Crotty and Epstein, 1996: 121; DeMartino, 1999: 346). Indeed, it acts a self-reinforcing mechanism strengthening capital vis-à-vis labour. This has also crystallized at the levels of the national state and of international institutions in a range of regulations and legal constructs that protect the interests of capital against demands from the side of labour: from central bank independence to international trade agreements (which are legally binding and usually cannot be revoked without the consent of all contracting parties); from the repressive features of trade union law to the institutions of transnational and global governance like the EU or the WTO (which are shielded from popular demands but impose binding regulations) (Scherrer, 2000; 2014; Harvey, 2005: 66; Gallas, 2016: *passim*; Oberndorfer, 2019: 34–7; Palley, 2019). Furthermore, the vast increases in economic inequality produced by neoliberalization enables the side of capital to use its material resources to influence political decision-making (Gallas et al, 2014: 147–8; see also Harvey, 2005: 78).

Correspondingly, neoliberalism can be defined as a class political project in favour of capital that is attempting to insulate market results from popular interventions – no matter whether they were based on street protests, strikes or on formal democratic procedures (see Harvey, 2005: 66–7; Šumonja, 2021 220; Watkins, 2021: 6; see also Chapter 2). All of this suggests that the side of labour has little chance to influence political decision-making without resorting to forceful instruments of struggle such as strikes – and among them, class-based strikes play an important role.

There is a number of strikes that stand out in the context of resistance to the dominant, neoliberal mode of crisis management. The general strikes in India are relevant due to their sheer size, culminating in the huge strike in November 2020 that allegedly mobilized up to 250 million people. The eight-week public-sector strike in Botswana in May and June 2011 was noteworthy because it started out as a pay dispute and, inspired by the Arab Spring, then escalated into a full-on revolt against the authoritarian government in the country that was supported by the political opposition. It was unsuccessful, but it showed that organic strikes can be offensive and can pose a threat to governments. A similar point can be made about the one-day general strike in Chile in October 2019. It may have been symbolic, but it was an offensive strike demanding changes to the pension system as well as fundamental political and economic reforms including a new constitution. The strike formed part of the larger movement against the neoliberal order in the country, which triggered a negotiation process for a new constitution and culminated in the election of a new left-leaning president, Gabriel Boric, who assumed office in March 2022.

Another important set of strikes in the conjuncture of crisis showing links across national boundaries were the large-scale feminist mobilizations in Argentina, Poland, Spain and Switzerland. The wave was triggered in Poland and Argentina in October 2016, where the strikes focused on a government decision to ban abortions and on femicide, respectively. These stoppages fell under the 'strikes for political aims' category, which are explained in the next section. But the more feminist protests and strikes spread out around the world, the more those involved started to highlight that they were both women and workers – and thus faced with a distinct articulation of class and gender domination reflected in earning lower wages than their male counterparts plus carrying the double burden of waged work and unpaid reproductive work. Here, to paraphrase Stuart Hall et al (2013: 394), gender was the modality in which class was lived. An expansive form of solidarity emerged, which involved both trade unions and feminist groups (Tejada, 2019; Zengerling, 2019; Santoro, 2020; Köhler, 2021: 21). In other words, the feminist strikes became organic strikes (see Chapter 8).[6]

---

[6] This underscores Luxemburg's point that during strike waves, the aims of the actions can shift (2008: 121–2). The important methodological implication of this observation is that it would be wrong to see one's codes as referring to clearly demarcated objects. There is a degree of fuzziness and ambiguity and thus some space for interpreting the aims of strikes in different ways.

Last but not least, there was a wave of general strikes in Western Europe after austerity measures were rolled out in the wake of the financial and economic crisis. These strikes affected a range of countries – and were a standard means of protest in the wake of cuts to public expenditure. They took place in Belgium, France, Greece, Portugal and Spain (including a separate strike in the autonomous Basque country). There were also public sector strikes in Britain that had a similar dynamic but – due to the repressive strike law in the country – did not involve privately employed workers. Notably, in one instance, there was a 'genuine transnational strike' (Helle, 2015: 240) – the one-day Transiberian general strike against austerity in November 2012 that affected all of Portugal and Spain. In Greece, the strikes formed an important part of the resistance to the austerity regime imposed by the Troika of the European Central Bank, the European Commission and the IMF. They culminated in the election victory of SYRIZA in January 2015 and the όχι referendum in July of the same year and continued after that point. In France, general strikes have also been very frequent over the investigation period, and have mostly been attempts to defend the pensions system against encroachments by the government.[7]

Some commentators have been critical of the mostly defensive, symbolic strikes described here, highlighting that they did not lead to material concessions in many cases, and that they did little more than allowing workers to vent their anger (Karyoti, 2012: 168–9; Stevens, 2018). Arguably, however, the critique that this form of the strike constitutes a 'safety valve' stabilizing the status quo misses the point because they took place against the backdrop of unfavourable relations of forces (see Volume 1, Chapter 7). The symbolic mobilization of workers' power can disrupt the dominant, neoliberal discourses around social, economic, monetary and fiscal policy somewhat, and can serve as a reminder that organized labour is still a factor to be reckoned with. In the cases of Greece, Portugal and Spain as well as Argentina (where there were also five general strikes against austerity between April 2017 and May 2019), the stoppages contributed to political pushbacks against the governments of Mauricio Macri, Antonis Samaras, Pedro Passos Coelho and Mariano Rajoy, which resulted in election victories of centre-left or left-of-centre forces. And in the case of Britain, the public sector strikes were a factor in the leftwards shift of the Labour Party under the leadership of Jeremy Corbyn, who ran a comparably successful election campaign in 2017.

None of these political projects managed to derail neoliberalism, and some did not even intend to do so. But what they attempted was to alleviate some of the hardship caused by the politics of austerity. And even more importantly,

---

[7] For detailed accounts of the political strikes against austerity in Western Europe, see Gallas and Nowak (2012) as well as Nowak and Gallas (2014).

they contributed – due to being based on broad mobilizations – to creating alliances between the comparably narrow constituency of the unions and other parts of the population (see Engelhardt, 2017: 418; Huke and Tietje, 2018: 262; Katsaroumpas and Koukiadi, 2019: 276), which suggests that they facilitated processes of class adsorption.

Strikes for political aims: mobilizing workers' power for non-work issues

Last but not least, there are two strikes that stand out from all the others in the sample as regards the character of their aims. These were about airing genuinely political grievances and had only indirect links to work-related issues. In Honduras, there was a one-day public sector strike in June 2009 against the *coup d'état* of the military and right-wing political forces, which had toppled the democratically elected president Manuel Zelaya (*Página 12*, 2009; Público, 2009). In Catalonia, there was a one-day general strike for independence with a strong backing in education, transport and retail in October 2019 (Ferrero, 2019). Furthermore, there was also a strike wave in the second half of 2020 in Belarus against the Lukashenko regime. Despite falling into the period under research, it was not included in the sample because it was mostly based in manufacturing (Walker, 2020; Shuntov, 2021).

In all three cases, the power that workers can exercise by disrupting economic processes as well as everyday life was used to advance towards genuinely political goals. These were shared by large groups in the respective population, but they were not primarily economic or work-related. In the cases of Belarus and Honduras, the strikes were about who should govern the country, and in the case of Catalonia, the stoppage demanded the foundation of a new national state.

Consequently, strikes for political aims are of secondary importance for my research project: first because of their very low frequency, and second because they have limited significance for my research question. By definition, they are strikes that do not directly address class relations because they are not about how work is organized in society. As such, little can be read off from them concerning class formation – at least on the grounds of the limited information on them contained in the articles examined for the sample. Of course, this is not to say that they are irrelevant for class politics. But assessing their potential relevance requires more detailed, case-by-case analyses.

Collective action of workers in the age of crisis and austerity

If different strike patterns are compared, one can observe, first of all, that national settings diverge in terms of prevalence. For example, the sample does not contain a single organic strike in Germany; this is different in neighbouring France, where there have been 19 such stoppages. In the first instance, this reflects different legal conditions. Whereas general strikes around socioeconomic issues are legal in France, they are banned across the Rhine, at least under the dominant interpretation of strike law. Furthermore, labour relations in France are characterized by a more openly political form of unionism. Union confederations with distinct political agendas compete with one another for members. This is different in Germany. Here, the principle of industrial unionism predominates, which means that unions operate in different branches of the economy, and only unofficial ties between some union leaders and officials and political parties exist (see Gallas and Nowak, 2012: 44). Unsurprisingly, the diverging strike patterns across countries reflect how labour relations have been institutionalized at the national level.

This also raises the question of whether communalities exist between countries. What they share is that strikes take place against the backdrop of the dominance of a global neoliberal regime, a multifaceted, organic crisis and the emergence of novel, non-industrial economic branches across the globe. Many of the strikes in the sample amount to attempts to mobilize workers in those branches. This applies to extension strikes in particular, but also to strikes protesting against neoliberalization and neoliberal crisis management, among them most of the expansive-politicized and class-based strikes. These three strike patterns show that there are indeed indications of working-class formation taking place across the globe – and, notably, in public sectors faced with austerity, there are also signs of processes of adsorption that draw workers in contradictory class locations who are negatively affected closer to the working-class forces in formation. In some cases, there is evidence of transnational links between striking workers, and the sample also contains transnational strikes. In Kim Moody's words, 'a new terrain of class struggle' has emerged (2017: 69), and the prospects for organized labour are not all bleak under the new conditions.

Generally speaking, it should follow from Castells that there is little evidence of collective action by workers in the non-industrial sectors, and even less of expansive moves connected to their mobilizations. Conversely, Panitch's line suggests such action is widespread, and that workers create ties with one another along class lines. The sample indeed suggests that there are a significant number of non-industrial strikes in the conjuncture of crisis, and a variety have a mass basis involving large numbers of workers across sectors. From a global vantage point – which, admittedly, produces a somewhat patchy picture because my map exhibits a few white spots – it appears that there is little evidence for Castells' claim, and that Panitch's counterclaim is more plausible. In the last part of the book, I discuss whether my observations concerning specific strike waves in Western Europe confirm this assessment.

PART II

Strike Research from a Western European Angle: Class Formation in Non-Industrial Settings

5

Deindustrialization and Dwindling Union Density: Labour in Western Europe

As I argued in Chapter 1, it makes sense, in the context of an incorporated comparison focusing on deindustrialization, to zoom in on Western Europe and examine different national cases that reflect different aspects of the variegation of global capitalism. After all, Western Europe was the first macroregion in the world to industrialize, and it has been witnessing sustained processes of deindustrialization in recent decades, which is at odds with the global trend (see Figure 5.1).

Against this backdrop, I have three chosen country cases that represent political and economic hubs in Western Europe, and that each reflect the characteristic varieties of capitalism in the region: Britain as a 'liberal market economy', Germany as a 'coordinated market economy' and Spain as a 'Mediterranean mixed type'. In line with the general development of industrial employment in the region, all three countries have been experiencing sustained processes of deindustrialization. In 2019, industrial workers constituted 18.1, 27.2 and 20.4 per cent of the overall workforce in Britain, Germany and Spain, respectively, and 22.7 per cent across the macroregion. This is a decline of 11.8, 10.2 and 11.4 percentage points if compared to the figures for 1992 – all roughly in line with each other and above the Western European average of 8.7 percentage points. Clearly, industrial workers are a minority in the overall workforce, and their sector does not heavily dominate the economy in any of the three countries or in Western Europe as a whole (see Figure 5.1).

With reference to Castells, one could hypothesize that trade union density should be decreasing significantly in countries where there has been industrial decline. After all, union demise could be interpreted as a sign of worker fragmentation. To a degree, this is borne out by the numbers, as Figure 5.2 demonstrates. Between 1977 and 2019, union density fell by

Figure 5.1: Share of industrial employment (in per cent)

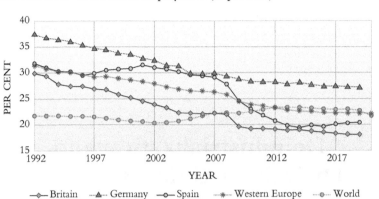

Source: ILO, Trends Econometric Models (Employment by Sector), https://www.ilo.org/wesodata/chart/s4sZKt3gV [Accessed 9 October 2022]

24.8 percentage points in Britain and 19.4 percentage points in Germany, which, in both cases, is a significant decline. Union density has consistently been higher in Britain than in Germany, even if it declined steeply in the Thatcher era (see Gallas, 2016). Importantly, both countries have been developing more or less in tandem since 1991, which was the year after the German reunification. For Spain, the picture is fuzzier. Union density has been lower than in the other two countries, and the number for union decline is 5.6 percentage points, which is considerably smaller.[1] Furthermore, union density during the opening stages of *la Transición* was roughly the same as it was on the eve of the Eurozone crisis in the late 2000s. This suggests that the decline of trade unionism either came considerably later than in the other two countries, or that it is a mere conjunctural trend reflecting the effects of the Great Crisis. All in all, the numbers from Britain and Germany are roughly in line with the hypothesis that there is a sustained decline in trade unionism, even if unionization rates of 23.5 and 16.3 per cent in 2019 mean that millions of workers in both countries are still union members. For Spain, this is not the case; here, the jury is still out on whether the decline in recent year constitutes a longer-term trend (see Figure 5.2).

---

[1] The volatility in the figures for Spain in the late 1970s reflect the specific circumstances of *la Transición*, the transition of the country to representative democracy after the death of dictator Francisco Franco in 1975. The numbers for Germany refer to West Germany before 1991 and then to the united country, which explains the sudden hike in union density in 1991.

Figure 5.2: Trade union density

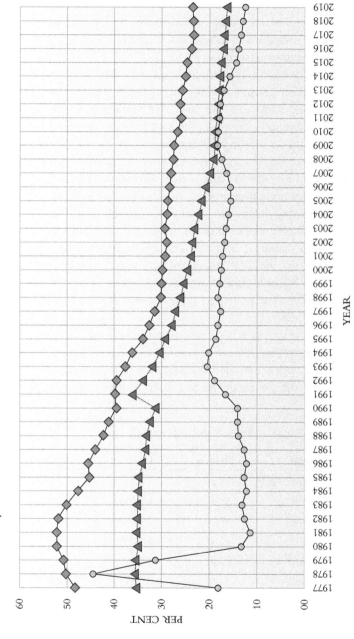

Source: ICTWSS database (OECD-AIAS), https://www.oecd.org/employment/ictwss-database.htm [Accessed 9 October 2022]

It may be worth breaking the down the numbers according to sectors. This way, it is possible to obtain a more fine-grained picture. In line with the Castellsian claim, one could hypothesize that if industrial decline is the driver of union decline, one cannot expect a strong or even increasing presence of unions in non-industrial sectors. Conversely, the counterclaim suggests that the decline of unionism in industry does not translate into a decline in unionism in non-industrial sectors.

The data offering a sectoral breakdown are not as comprehensive as the ones capturing union density overall, but they are nevertheless relevant. For Britain and Germany, one can infer that industrial decline is indeed accompanied by a drastic weakening of industrial trade unionism: in Britain, the unionization rate in industry fell by more than 70 per cent within the space of three-and-a-half decades; in Germany, the number was more than 55 per cent. Does this mean the case is closed? Not quite, because in Spain, the unionization rate grew slightly over the same period – despite a sustained fall in industrial employment and a fall in unionization in the context of the Great Crisis. Indeed, the decline in the overall unionization rate in the country is down to a steep fall of the union density in the agricultural sector, which dropped by 60 per cent, as a consequence of which trade unionism is almost absent in Spanish agriculture today. Besides, union density in the British agricultural sector increased slightly between 1997 and 2018 (see Table 5.1).

In this context, it is also relevant to compare unionization rates in the private and public sectors. What is visible here is that public sector unions are significantly stronger than their counterparts in the private sector across countries and during the entire period under consideration. Against the

Table 5.1: Union density across sectors (in per cent)

Year	Sector	Britain	Germany	Spain
1980	Agriculture	22.3	19.3	4.9*
	Industry	59.5	43.2	10.9*
	Services	47.5	27.7	13.4*
2000	Agriculture	10.4	12.4**	5.7***
	Industry	27.8	41.3**	15.1***
	Services	30.6	21.9**	19.0***
2016	Agriculture	8.5	6.5	2.0
	Industry	17.2	18.8	12.1
	Services	24.9	15.3	15.4

Notes: Numbers for 1981 (*), 1998 (**) and 2002 (***)

Source: https://www.ictwss.org/downloads [Accessed 12 October 2022]

Castellsian hypothesis, I contend that the public sector was, and remains to be, a stronghold of organized labour. It follows that deindustrialization hits unions, but not to such a degree that it ceases to be a relevant factor everywhere. Importantly, there has been a sustained rise in Spain in union density across the public sector in recent years. In Germany and Britain, unionization rates in the public sector have dropped quite drastically – by more than 60 and 30 per cent, respectively, in three-and-a-half decades. But in comparison to the other figures cited, they are still high: 54.3 and 23.3 per cent (see Table 5.2). All in all, one can argue that unionization rates support the Castellsian claim in certain ways, but that the overall picture is more complicated: if we go by the numbers, public sector unions are still comparably strong, and an unambiguous process of trade union decline is absent in Spain.

If one takes seriously the refusal to equate workers' power and union capacities (see Volume 1, Chapter 4), simply looking at unionization rates is not enough. Consequently, it is also worth considering data on strike incidence. Again, one can hypothesize, following Castells, that labour struggles should fizzle out, or, following Panitch, that there should be a resurgence of labour militancy in non-industrial sectors. The available data show that there was a significant drop in strike activity in Spain in the last two decades, with average days not worked due to strikes declining by more than 75 per cent if 2000–9 and 2010–19 are compared; a sustained decrease of more than 35 per cent in Britain (see Figure 5.3 and Table 5.3); but also an increase of more than 35 per cent in Germany, in which service sector strikes played an important part (see Bewernitz and Dribbusch, 2014; Bispinck, 2016).

All in all, the picture that emerges confirms what I said about union density: There is a decline that can be interpreted as a sustained weakening of organized labour, and as a shift in the relations of forces between labour and capital in favour of the latter. This is in line with Marcel van der Linden's

Table 5.2: Union density in the private and public sectors (in per cent)

Year	Sector	Britain	Germany	Spain
1979	Private	45.6	28.8*	n/a
	Public	81.5	59.4*	n/a
1998	Private	19.5	21.1	15.0**
	Public	60.4	40.0	31.2**
2015	Private	13.9	15.4	14.0***
	Public	54.3	23.3	38.0***

Notes: Numbers for 1980 (*), 1999 (**) and 2013 (***)

Source: https://www.ictwss.org/downloads [Accessed 12 October 2022]

Figure 5.3: Days not worked due to strikes (per 1,000 employees)

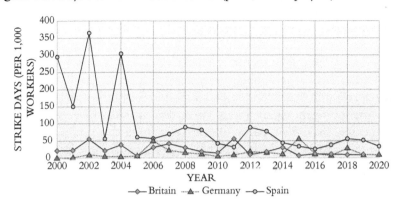

Source: ETUI Strike Map, https://www.etui.org/strikes-map/germany, https://www.etui.org/stri
kes-map/spain, https://www.etui.org/strikes-map/united-kingdom [Accessed 9 October 2022]

Table 5.3: Average days not worked due to strikes (per 1,000 employees)

Country	Years	Days
Britain	2000–9	28.4
	2010–19	17.9
Germany	2000–9	12.6
	2010–19	17.3
Spain	2000–9	152.9
	2010–19	49.1

Source: https://www.etui.org/strikes-map/germany, https://www.etui.org/strikes-map/spain,
https://www.etui.org/strikes-map/united-kingdom [Accessed 9 October 2022]

claims about global labour relations, according to which '[t]raditional labour
movements are in trouble almost everywhere' (2016: 201). The developments
reflect the offensives of capital against labour in the age of neoliberalism and
the collapse of settled capitalism.

But this is not the whole story, which is why this decline cannot be seen
as a full confirmation of the Castellsian claim: There are still significant
union organizations and strikes in Western Europe, and even subtle signs
of a resurgence that comes from non-industrial sectors, as is evidenced by
the increase in strike incidence in Germany. To announce the death of
organized labour would be premature; what is needed are more detailed
case studies of non-industrial strikes, which assess whether or not they have
expansive effects.

6

Union Competition and Militancy: The Railway Strikes in Germany

'Social partnership' and 'competitive corporatism': labour relations in Germany

An industrial base and non-industrial strikes

Considering my findings so far, it is only plausible to assume that there is a broader trend towards or against class formation if it also possible to show, with the help of more fine-grained case studies at the national level, that strikes have expansive effects. If this does not turn out to be the case, one can indeed argue that the Castellsian claim holds. I start my case studies with Germany, which is still a country with a comparably strong industrial base: More than a quarter of the workforce is employed in the sector. It is not just that industrial employment is significantly higher than in Britain and Spain, but it exceeds the European and the global averages, which were 22.1 and 21.7 per cent, respectively, in 2020 (see Figure 5.1).

If one presumes that there is a strong link between the prevalence of industrial work and strike activity, Germany should be at the forefront of labour struggles. But this is not borne out by the numbers. Indeed, the country has the lowest figures of the three countries, Britain is in the middle, and Spain comes out on top (see Figure 5.3 and Table 5.3). And in recent years, strike activity has been more pronounced in the service and public sectors than in industry in Germany, at least in terms of the absolute numbers of strikes (Frindert et al, 2022: 4). It is more plausible to assume that the figures for strike incidence reflect the dominant regimes of labour relations in the three countries, which corresponds to the three varieties of capitalism (see Behrens et al, 2004: 19). After all, coordinated market economies are known for the prevalence of corporatism, a regime type designed to prevent confrontations through consultation and negotiation.

The fact that Germany combines a comparably lower strike incidence and a comparably higher share of industrial employment suggests that the country is an interesting test case for Castells' claim and Panitch's counterclaim: Contrary to the Castellsian scenario, Germany has been witnessing a slight decline in industrial employment combined with an increase in strike activity in recent years. But in the defence of the Castellsian claim one could argue that the level of strike activities is not very high overall, which is visible in particular if it is compared to the strike activities in Spain before 2010 (see Figure 5.3 and Table 5.3; see also Birke, 2018: 225).

The strikes in the German railway sector are particularly interesting because of their disruptive effects, which are felt by economic actors and the broader population, and the inter-union competition that drives it, which is a rare scenario in the German context. This is revealed by a closer look at the German system of labour relations.

The class effects of 'social partnership'

The labour regime predominating in Germany today came into being with the emergence of the West German state, the Federal Republic of Germany, after the Second World War. In political and academic discourses, it is often referred to with the expression 'social partnership' (Streeck and Hassel, 2003; Kädtler, 2012). This term invokes the image of a harmonious relationship between capital and labour. It suggests that both sides operate on a level playing field, avoid open confrontations and act in concert to resolve problems. In so doing, it conceals class domination and antagonism – as well as the fact that worker militancy does indeed exist in a country where leading politicians have been promoting the idea of 'social peace' for decades (Offe, 2018a: 161).[1] 'Social partnership' is an ideologically loaded term, and West German trade unionists were, on the whole, hostile to using it up until the 1980s (Kädtler, 2012: 357–8).

The institutional backbone of the labour regime is collective bargaining. In the mid-1990s, more than 75 per cent of people in employment in West Germany were covered by collective bargaining agreements. Thanks to neoliberal restructuring, precarious work has been proliferating from the turn of the century, which meant that by 2018, this number had decreased to 54 per cent for the entire country. Admittedly, this is more a middling rather than a high figure if compared to other EU countries; the EU average is 60 per cent.[2] Nevertheless, the fact that roughly every second worker is

---

[1] For historical accounts of militant trade unionism in West Germany, see Birke (2007) and Redler (2012).

[2] https://www.oecd.org/employment/ictwss-database.htm and https://www.eurofound. europa.eu/topic/collective-bargaining [Accessed 8 October 2022].

covered by an agreement shows that collective bargaining continues to play a significant role (see Offe, 2018a: 162).

Economically, the regime is underpinned by an accumulation strategy that focuses on export-oriented manufacturing cores, for example in the machine tools and car industries (Lucarelli, 2012; Haas, 2021: 663–4). According to estimates of the Institute of the German Economy, around a quarter of jobs in the country depend on exports (IDW, 2020). These cores are usually characterized by high levels of trade union density, even if the unionized core workforces have been shrinking in recent years and union membership is not equally spread across branches (Dribbusch and Birke, 2019: 12–13).

At the level of the state, the executive branch secures the regime, for example through welfare legislation and the legal regulation of labour relations. Among them are statutory floors (a minimum wage and a minimum annual leave) and ceilings (maximum daily work hours). Outside the provisions of a legal framework, there is limited direct state involvement in collective bargaining. A principle that figures heavily in the dominant discourses on labour relations in the country is 'freedom of collective bargaining'. It is enshrined in the German constitution, the Basic Law, and emphasizes bipartism: labour and capital are responsible for negotiating wages and working condition without direct state interference. Accordingly, compulsory arbitration does not exist in the country. Extension mechanisms exist, but they only cover specific branches, and they do not enter into force unless both unions or employers' associations agree (Dribbusch and Birke, 2012: 7; 2019: 17; Aranea and Kraemer, 2015).

The German state has institutionalized corporatism, on the side of labour, through a four-tier mode of representation, which first emerged in the interwar period and was revived after the Nazi era in West Germany. Accordingly, workers are represented, at the economic level, through unions and works councils. At the political level, governments, organized labour and representatives of capital have been engaging in tripartite forms of concertation at various points in the history of Federal Republic. Apart from that, centre-right, centre-left and far left parties have been claiming to represent workers' interests and have been enjoying close connections with organized labour (see Offe, 2018b: 350).[3]

Representation through unions is brought to bear particularly in the area of collective bargaining. The latter is carried out by unions and employers' associations at the firm, branch or sectoral level and mostly concerns wages

---

[3] The Federal Republic of Germany is the present-day German state. It was established in 1949 and initially only comprised the territory that was also referred to as West Germany. After the collapse of authoritarian socialism in Eastern Europe, it came to incorporate East Germany in 1990.

and working times. It is secured through a legal framework guaranteed by the state. The German Basic Law contains a provision on the freedom of association at work, which means that workers have the right to unionize, and unions act in the collective bargaining process on behalf of their members. Famously, the federal labour court has ruled at various points since the beginning of the 1980 that collective bargaining without the right to strike amounts to 'collective begging' (see Volume 1, Chapter 7). Consequently, freedom of association, under the dominant interpretation of the law, also entails a right to strike.

However, there is a range of legally enshrined obstacles to exercising this right. Under the dominant interpretation of the law, only unions are allowed to call strikes; stoppages for purposes other than collective bargaining, for example, political or general strikes are banned; and two large groups of workers do not enjoy the right to advance their interests through collectively stopping work: public employees with *Beamten* status, who enjoy tenure for life, and people employed by the Catholic or the Protestant Church, who are mostly care and education workers.[4] Furthermore, the law imposes a 'peace obligation' on workers as long as a valid collective bargaining agreement exists and has not expired yet. And finally, 'pilot agreements' are often extended beyond the region where they were made (Dribbusch and Birke, 2012: 12; Schmid, 2014: 380; Nowak, 2015; Raehlmann, 2017: 13, 44–5).

All of this means that it is difficult for workers to take strike action – not just because they lose pay and face adverse consequences from management, but also because they need to meet a range of preconditions to be protected by the law. Correspondingly – and in line with both the idea of social partnership and the data on strike incidence – German unions often prioritize negotiations. They either refrain from going on strike altogether or stage short, symbolic 'warning' strikes, which usually do not last for longer than a day (Dribbusch and Birke, 2012: 12–13; Boll and Kalass, 2014: 535). As a result, the course and results of disputes often follow routines and thus are fairly predictable. This is why Germans speak of the '*Tarifritual*' – or the ritual of collective bargaining.

In a nutshell, 'freedom of collective bargaining' under conditions of 'social partnership' fosters particularization – the object of bargaining is

---

[4] In 2019, 1.7 million out of the 4.9 million people working the public sector in Germany – among them civil servants, teachers and police officers – had *Beamten* status (https://tinyurl.com/bdcvspe8 [Accessed 9 October 2022]). In 2018, there were 837,000 people employed by the Protestant Church in Germany and its social service, Diakonie (EKD, 2020). The social service of the Catholic Church, Caritas, had 693,000 employees in the same year (DBK, 2022: 39). The existence of these groups creates significant divisions among workers and is a serious impediment for broad mobilizations for strikes.

limited to wages and hour hours – as well as segmentation – groups of workers of a significant size are exempted from the right to strike. In other words, it leads to the formalization, regularization, deceleration and pacification of class conflict and the separation of economic and political class struggle. Consequently, the German regime of labour relations is a good illustration of my theoretical point that the existence of the capitalist state tends to bestow upon workers certain collective rights, but also renders class conflict controllable and thus stabilizes class domination (see Volume 1, Chapter 7).

The stabilizing effects of 'collective bargaining autonomy' are reinforced by 'co-determination', which consists in employees of a company unit setting up a works council. Its members are responsible for consulting and negotiating with management on issues concerning work that are not covered by collective bargaining agreements, for example, recruitment and health and safety. Works councillors are elected by the whole workforce, not just by union members, which means that in certain cases, they are against unions or at least sceptical. Nevertheless, many are union members and see themselves as active trade unionists, so that works councils are indeed an important site of union activity. But the effects of trade union work that is channelled through works councils is ambiguous, in much the same way that representative democracy has ambiguous effects on popular initiatives: On the one hand, their existence creates legitimacy for activities of organized labour and allows elected activists to speak on behalf of all members of the workforce; on the other hand, it separates activists from workers, which contributes to turning the latter into passive bystanders of institutionalized negotiations and confrontations and can serve as an obstacle to their organization and mobilization. Apart from that, there is a danger of works councillors getting co-opted into management strategies. By law, both management and the works council are obliged to cooperate with good faith. This creates obstacles for works councillors who take a confrontational stance towards management. The boards of large corporations also have members who are workers' representatives, which means that they are involved, to a degree, in corporate strategizing (Dribbusch and Birke, 2012: 10–11; 2019: 14–15; Müller-Jentsch, 2014: 516; Schroeder and Greef, 2014: 132; Sperling, 2014: 489).

Last but not least, it is important to note that tripartism is not wholly absent from the system of labour relations in Germany – despite the strong focus on 'collective bargaining autonomy'. In times of economic crises, there have been tripartite negotiations over political-economic crisis management, which were chaired by the government (see Esser, 1982; Esser et al, 1983). These negotiations usually result in agreements between the three sides. Governments have tended to force through arrangements that benefit workers in certain ways, but that also oblige them to make 'sacrifices'.

This has led to co-optation and has fortified capitalist class domination in conjunctures marked by instability.

With a view to class formation, the prevalence of 'social partnership' as an ideology reflects a certain strength of the side of labour. It recognizes that unionization is a valid response by workers to the power imbalance inscribed in the capitalist relations of production and a legitimate avenue for making economic demands. In this sense, it legitimizes the collectivization of workers along class lines, which is an important precondition for class formation. Its emergence is a reaction to the advances of the working classes in Western Europe after the Second World War (see Crouch, 2004: 6–11; Canfora, 2006: 174–84). And yet, the institutionalized strength of labour is countered by an array of mechanisms of class partition: organized labour is constituted at the level of the national state ('nationalization'); unions are locked into a political-economic framework of institutions with strong rules and regulations, which does not give them a mandate to advance demands through strike action that are political in nature ('particularization'); and they are not allowed to criticize the foundations of this framework ('co-optation'). Unsurprisingly, the Confederation of German Employers' Associations (BDA), the umbrella organization of the employers' association facing unions in processes of collective bargaining, sees social partnership in a very positive light: 'The principle of social partnership – the will to mutually agreed solutions – secures stability and social peace, and contributes significantly to growth, employment and prosperity' (BDA, nd).

Unions and the politics of non-partisanship

On the side of labour, the labour regime is institutionalized through the existence of large union federations, whose member organizations are heavily involved in the process of collective bargaining. The dominant force is the DGB, which has 6 million members and represents 77 per cent of all unionized workers in the country. It has eight member unions, among them the two biggest unions in the country. These are the industrial workers' union IG Metall and the service and public sector union ver.di. They have 2.3 and 2 million members, respectively (Dribbusch and Birke, 2019: 6–9). Officially, the DGB and its member are unions are non-partisan organizations committed to the principles of trade union unity and industrial unionism. The former says that unions are open to all workers irrespective of their political allegiances, the latter that there should only be one trade union per business unit (Dribbusch and Birke, 2012: 6–7). In other words, DGB unions are supposed to operate at a distance to parties, and they should not compete against one another.

In practice, competition happens, for example, on campuses, where both ver.di and the Education and Science Workers' Union (GEW) are active, which are both affiliated with the DGB. And likewise, DGB unions are by no means neutral when it comes to party politics. Indeed, trade unionists are also members of parties, no matter whether they belong to the union leaderships, the intermediate stratum of full-time officials or the rank-and-file. Some trade unionists in leading positions are aligned with the left-liberal Green Party or the centre-right bloc constituted by the Christian Democratic Union of Germany (CDU) and its Bavarian sister party Christian Social Union (CSU), which has a faction that aims to represent Christian and Conservative workers and trade unionists. And in some cases, it is unknown whether they are in a party or not. But the majority enjoy close ties with the SPD (Dribbusch and Birke, 2019: 6).[5] At the time of writing, two out of four members of the national executive of the DGB were members of the SPD, among them Reiner Hoffmann, the president of the confederation, and at least five out of the eight leaders of its member unions. The close ties of the heads of DGB-affiliated unions to the SPD (and other centrist parties) underpins the settlement between capital and labour in Germany: It commits them to a moderate political course. There are significant political differences between the member unions of the DGB, but the latter converge in that they usually refrain from questioning the notion of 'social partnership' or capitalist class domination. In this sense, the non-partisanship of trade unionism in Germany is a highly political principle.

A comprehensive restructuring of the welfare state and the labour market took place under the SPD-led governments headed by Gerhard Schröder between 1998 and 2005. Some leading trade unionists colluded in this push for neoliberalization, in particular during its initial stages. But voices of discontent have also been audible ever since (see Volume 1, Chapter 4; Heinrich, 2004). Notably, many medium-level officials of IG Metall and ver.di have aligned themselves in recent years with the Left Party (Dribbusch and Birke, 2019: 6), a left-socialist political formation founded in 2007. This has introduced a new political option for trade unionism that goes beyond administering the status quo, at the least at the level of discourse. In practice, however, the type of radical political unionism with a mass base that can be found in some of the other large Western European countries – among them Britain, France and Spain – is mostly absent in Germany (see Connolly and Darlington, 2012; del Bado, 2012).[6]

---

[5]   The party is the main centre-left party-political formation in the country and has had, for decades, a reputation of promoting a very moderate version of social democracy. It is the party of the current chancellor Olaf Scholz and has been in government (in coalitions with a variety of partners) from 1966 to 1982, from 1998 to 2009 and from 2013 until today.

[6]   There are, of course, exceptions, for example the anarcho-syndicalist Free Workers' Union and the higher education union Unterbau [Base], which both have played a role in recent, locally based disputes. However, on a national scale, they are marginal. Unterbau confine

A number of unions are not part of the DGB, some of which have been very active in terms of going on strike in the conjuncture of crisis. Among are occupational unions such as the GDL, the pilots' union VC, and Marburger Bund, a union of medical doctors. There are also two more union federations, which are considerably smaller than the DGB: The first is the German Civil Service Federation (DBB), a non-partisan umbrella organization that traditionally has strong informal ties to the CDU and the CSU. The DBB consists mostly of small professional unions active in the public sector. Among them is not just the GDL, the protagonist of the railway strikes, but also a host of organizations that are opposed to militancy or represent mostly *Beamte*. The other confederation is the Christian Trade Union Federation of Germany, whose member organization have a reputation for 'yellow' unionism, that is, for consenting to collective agreements that undercut standards negotiated by the DGB unions (Dribbusch and Birke, 2019: 8–10).

The existence of alternative unions with occupational and potentially centrist or even right-wing leanings suggests that there is an institutional base for sectionalism, which can be seen as a strategy for unions that is working against class formation. I will discuss in detail, in the course of this chapter, whether the railway strikes can be seen in this light. What can be said at this point is that the strikes by occupational unions in recent years, among them those of the GDL, have often had a significant disruptive effect on everyday life. Indeed, the unions involved have sometimes been more militant than some of their counterparts in the DGB, and they have made effective use of their leverage as occupational groups that are of crucial importance for the day-to-day operation of the socioeconomic infrastructure of the country (Dörre et al, 2016: 161; Keller, 2016a; 2016b; Lesch, 2016; Raehlmann, 2017: 2; Dribbusch and Birke, 2019: 9–10).

'Agenda 2010' as an attack on labour

For several decades after the Second World War, the West German labour regime rested on a corporatist-welfarist arrangement. Like similar configurations existing at the time in Western Europe, for example the postwar settlement in Britain, labour and capital traded consent to class domination for material concessions to large groups of workers across society in the form of employment security, 'decent', increasing wages as

---

their activities to the University of Frankfurt. According to the Federal Office for the Protection of Constitution, the controversial domestic secret service, the Free Workers' Union has only about 1,200 members in the entire country; media coverage speaks of 500 to 1,000 members in Berlin alone (Nowak, 2018; Shaller, 2021; Verfassungsschutz, 2022: 169).

well as benefits and services provided by a welfare state. The arrangement was underpinned by productivist cycles based on the production of relative surplus value. The relative strength of organized labour forced capitalists to compete with one another via productivity gains, and the latter were partly translated into wage increases (see Jessop, 1989: 271; Offe, 2018a: 162). Importantly, the arrangement by no means benefited all workers to the same degree. The migrant workers that had entered the country under so-called hiring schemes for 'guest workers' were in a significantly weaker position than ethnic German workers – and likewise, many women did jobs at the margins of the labour market (see Birke, 2007: 45–6, 296–304).

Despite the fact that the rhetoric of 'social partnership' is still intact, the corporatist-welfarist arrangement has been eroding from the 1980s. In cooperation with the German power bloc, governments have been making 'neoliberal policy adjustments' (Jessop, 2013: 71) time and again, and with growing intensity. This process culminated in the wholesale restructuring of labour relations along neoliberal lines under the Schröder governments, which were in power from 1998 to 2005. It led to a rise in precarious employment. Precarious workers either operate on the grounds of comparably weak collective agreements or are not covered at all.

After German reunification, intellectuals aligned with the power bloc had started pushing for neoliberalization. In 1999, *The Economist* portrayed the country as the 'sick man of ... Europe' (*The Economist*, 1999: 21), and other voices from the media and politics chimed in. A neoliberal discourse emerged that blamed the existing regulations of labour relations and the German welfare regime for stagnating economic growth as well as a level of unemployment that was significantly higher than in West Germany in the 1960s and 1970s, and that painted the 'neoliberal regime shifts' in the Anglophone world in a positive light (Jessop, 2013: 71).[7] Contributors to this discourse – among them leading representatives of capital, politicians and scholars – saw labour market liberalization and cuts to benefits as a restructuring strategy that would decrease unemployment and drive up economic growth. There was a push for extending the precarious labour relations that had emerged in East Germany during the transition to capitalism to the country in its entirety (see Brinkmann and Nachtwey, 2013: 7).

The culmination point of neoliberalization was Agenda 2010, a push for labour market liberalization and welfare state restructuring launched in 2003 by Gerhard Schröder's government, the so-called red-green coalition

---

[7] For example, the influential economist Hans-Werner Sinn took up the theme in a speech from 2003 that was broadcast on public radio. He emphasized that the German economy was facing 'great dangers', in particular high unemployment, and that 'we have to act' (Sinn, 2003: 1).

between the SPD and the Green Party. The Agenda was met with massive popular protests and created a deep rift in the political scene, which persists until today: some left-leaning representatives of the SPD, first and foremost its former leader Oskar Lafontaine, decided to leave the party. Four years later, they would join forces with the Party of Democratic Socialism, the successor organization of the East German Socialist Unity Party (SED), to form the Left Party.

The Agenda had the effect of massively increasing the number of people working in temporary jobs, which shot up from 282,000 in 2003 on the eve of the Agenda to 834,000 in 2021 (BfA, 2022: 7). Furthermore, the low-wage sector expanded. The share of workers employed in it has increased from 17.1 per cent in 1998 to 21.7 in 2018 (Grabka and Göbler, 2020: 20). This makes Germany the country in the EU-15 with the largest share of low-wage workers.[8] Against this backdrop, it is not surprising that there has been a substantial decrease in collective bargaining coverage. All in all, since German reunification, there has been a massive extension of zones of precarious work where unions struggle to make an impact.

In sum, the Schröder government launched interventions aimed at strengthening the German power bloc at the expense of labour, most importantly by removing safeguards against the proliferation of temporary work, cutting pension entitlements and unemployment benefits as well as introducing welfare-to-work schemes and a repressive system of administering unemployment. In class-analytical terms, the adjustments constituted attempts to increase profitability by changing the conditions of the extraction of surplus labour in favour of capital and shifting class relations of forces in favour of the power bloc.

The emergence of competitive corporatism

The changes in the labour market, which can be seen as resulting from a successful offensive of the German power bloc, had drastic effects on workers' incomes. Germany was the OECD country with the highest decrease of real wages from 2000 to 2009 (Brinkmann and Nachtwey, 2013: 23). Considering the generally high level of productivity, this created a significant competitive advantage for German manufacturers vis-à-vis their foreign competitors. The export-oriented accumulation strategy dominating the German economy benefited from a substantial drop in labour unit cost. This was bad news in particular for countries that were also in the Eurozone. They no longer

---

[8] 'EU-15' refers to the member states of the EU before its expansion to former Eastern Bloc countries in 2004. https://ec.europa.eu/eurostat/statistics-explained/index.php?title= Earnings_statistics [Accessed 9 October 2022].

had a currency of their own, which they could have devalued to boost their position vis-à-vis Germany (see Lucarelli, 2012: 218).

The flipside of this development was that the productivist cycles underpinning the corporatist-welfarist arrangement of the postwar decades had been broken for good. German workers were dealing with heavy pressures on wages and a significant expansion of precarious work, and organized labour started to acknowledge that the relations of forces with the power bloc had shifted. In particular, the unions representing industrial workers were prepared to enter company pacts that traded wage restraint for job security, which, however, only applied to core workforces (Hübner, 2015).

When the Great Crisis hit the country, a tripartite mode of political crisis management emerged that was based on such pacts. Industrial unions became part and parcel of tripartite negotiations over a government strategy aiming to alleviate the impact of the recession on the industrial cores, which was achieved through short-time working, a car scrappage scheme and public investment in infrastructure. This revival of tripartism came after a period of estrangement between the political mainstream and the unions, which was characteristic, in particular, of the last years of the Schröder government (see Dribbusch and Birke, 2012: 3; Brinkmann and Nachtwey, 2013: 41; Dörre, 2016: 349).

What emerged was a new arrangement that can be called 'competitive corporatism' (Rhodes, 2001), which was based on co-opting unions to the world market strategies of leading industrial companies through concessions, most importantly job security for core workforces. It was consistent with 'social partnership' as it was based on collective negotiations, and it also can be seen as a form of tripartite crisis management. In contrast to corporatism-welfarism, the strong strategic focus on export-orientated industries by much of the political scene and many representatives of labour and capital meant, on the one hand, that there were competitive pressures that kept wages from growing and, on the other hand, that an increasing number of workers fell outside the realm of protected, permanent employment. What resulted was a segmented labour market with a deep division between shrinking core workforces with protected and comparably well-paid jobs that were strongly unionized and an expanding contingent of 'peripheral' workers, who often earned low wages, were on fixed-term contracts and remained outside unions because they kept changing jobs. It is understandable that unions chose to fight for existing jobs in a situation where they were pushed on the defensive. But competitive corporatism deepened divisions between core workforces and other 'peripheral' workers and was thus based on exclusive solidarity. At the same time, it did not change the fortunes of trade unionism in Germany. The collective bargaining coverage declined, and so did the membership of DGB unions.

In 2000, 7.77 million were members; in 2021, the number was 5.73 million (Brinkmann and Nachtwey, 2013: 23; Dörre, 2016: 350–6).[9]

The railway system in the neoliberal age

From the 1980s onwards, successive governments in Germany have been taking steps to liberalize the German political economy. Part of the process was the privatization of state-owned companies, which happened from the mid-1990s onwards. This affected the national airline Lufthansa, the telecommunications sector, the postal service, public transport, hospitals and public utilities at the local level as well as the railway system. The 'social partnership' model soon started to show signs of strain, in particular in the public and service sectors.

The East and West German railway services, Deutsche Reichsbahn and Deutsche Bundesbahn, merged in 1994 to become a state-owned, joint-stock company under private law called Deutsche Bahn. Significantly, however, the stock was not traded; even today, the state is still the sole owner of the corporation, which is why labour scholar Stefanie Hürtgen speaks of a 'quasi-privatisation' (2016: 61). The government justified this move by invoking free-market thinking. It assumed that transforming the German railways into a 'proper' business and inviting competitors to offer regional services would address the three critical problems: The West German service had accrued a significant level of debt in the postwar decades, the East German railway infrastructure in particular was in a bad state, and both services were loss-making (see Kalass, 2012: 76–85; Hürtgen, 2016: 61).

The new corporation operated on the grounds of the principle of internal flexibilization. Initially, it was composed of four sub-divisions, which were supposed to become stand-alone stockholding companies; after various modifications, the corporation covered eight 'fields of business' and has, at the time of writing, 521 subsidiary companies or investments in companies in Germany and abroad (Cleven, 2021; Deutsche Bahn, 2022: 39). These are responsible for different tasks linked to the operation of the German railway network and other services in the field of transport and logistics (Kalass, 2012: 81; Hürtgen, 2016: 61). Notably, the 'quasi-privatisation' of the German railway system and the transformation of Deutsche Bahn into a multinational transport company has not made it profitable. In 2021, more than 25 years after the reform, the state still subsidized it with €7.85 billion.[10] In the same year, it accrued losses of €911 million – and its debt stood at €29.1 billion (Deutsche Bahn, 2022: U4).

---

[9] https://www.dgb.de/uber-uns/dgb-heute/mitgliederzahlen [Accessed 9 April 2022].
[10] https://tinyurl.com/3kadev2p [Accessed 9 April 2022].

The new corporate structure of Deutsche Bahn had far-reaching effects on labour relations in the railway system. Four aspects stand out.

First, a substantial number of jobs has been cut. In 1989, the number of people employed by both the East and the West German services taken together was 489,000 people (Kalass, 2012: 81). In 2021, the corporation employed 209,763 people in Germany (Deutsche Bahn, 2022: 192).

Second, management has adopted techniques such as 'lean production' and 'lean administration', which means that the status of Bahn employees has changed significantly (Keller and Seifert, 2014; Raehlmann, 2017: 43). As a result, precarious and temporary work have become more widespread, and new recruits are no longer offered *Beamten* status. The number of *Beamten* has dropped from 116,885 at the time of the merger to 14,705 in 2021 (Kalass, 2012: 96; Deutsche Bahn, 2022: 265). With the merger, new employees also were no longer offered a number of bonuses available to both *Beamte* and the old employees without *Beamten* status, which meant that wages decreased (Kalass, 2012: 95; Lesch, 2016: 158). Furthermore, wages of train drivers are low: In 2021, they earned between €2,800 and 3,700 a month before tax, depending on their qualifications, responsibilities and experience. The average gross wage in the country was €4,100 (Milankovic, 2021; Liedke and Buske, 2022). At the same time, a workforce at Deutsche Bahn has emerged step-by-step due to the elimination of the *Beamten* status whose right to strike is officially recognized, and which, in the case of train drivers and on-board staff, finds itself in a consistent class location.[11] In the process, the GDL has transformed itself from an organization advocating on behalf of *Beamten* with means of persuasion and lobbying into a militant force that is prepared to call strikes (see Kalass, 2012: 173).

Third, the patterns of collective bargaining have shifted significantly. Before the establishment of Deutsche Bahn AG, public sector bargaining agreements were simply extended to the railway sector. From 1994, a fragmentation of collective bargaining took place, which reflected the internal reorganization of the corporation. As a result, different sub-divisions and occupational groups have different agreements. The fragmentation plus the emergence

---

[11] It can be argued that *Beamte* are, by default, in a contradictory class position because their employers are stripped of the option of cancelling the labour contract. Tenure for life amounts to a suspension of wage dependency because the threat of unemployment no longer exists. In other words, labour power is transferred continuously, but no longer sold. This is reflected in German legalese: *Beamte* find themselves not a in a relationship of 'employment' but of 'service'. They are 'appointed' [*ernannt*], not 'employed' [*eingestellt*] and have a 'service master' [*Dienstherr*], not an 'employer' [*Arbeitgeber*]. Obviously, they receive a monthly salary for their service, but this is also referred to with a specific, technical term not used in other contexts [*Besoldung*] (see GEW Sachsen, nd).

of privately owned competitors has translated into additional pressure on workers (Brandt and Schulten, 2008: 573).

Last but not least, the changes in the working conditions and wages of the workforce and its composition have shaken up the dynamics of trade unionism in the sector, which merits a more detailed description. In postwar West Germany, three large unions were active in the sector: the Union of Railway Workers of Germany (GdED), which operated in the entire industry and was open all workers, was affiliated with the DGB and close to the SPD; the Union of *Beamten* and *Beamten* Candidates at Deutsche Bundesbahn (GDBA), which was Christian-conservative in its outlook and catered only for this one status group; and the GDL – one of the oldest unions in the country, which was committed to an occupational unionism with conservative political leanings and focused on drivers. There were deep divisions between the unions – initially between the GdED on one side, which saw itself as part of the social democratic, main current in the German labour movement, and the GDBA and GDL on the other side, which committed themselves to defending *Beamte* and entered a collective bargaining alliance in 1963 (Kalass, 2012: 109–13, 117; 134; Hürtgen, 2016: 59).

The restructuring of the sector, and the political machinations taking place to secure change, drastically altered the labour relations in the sector, which deeply affected the three unions. For the 'railway reform' to go ahead, a constitutional amendment was required. As constitutional amendments require a two-thirds majority in parliament, the centre-right government of Helmut Kohl needed the votes of the SPD, which decided to externalize responsibility. It announced that it would only agree to the amendment if the GdED did, too. This meant that the union was in a good position to halt the 'reform', but it chose to refrain from stopping it. It did not have a specific interest in protecting *Beamte*. Adopting a business unionism approach (see Hoffmann and Schmidt, 2008: 309), it quickly accepted the 'railway reform', vowing to pull its weight by negotiating modifications on behalf of its members. In a nutshell, the GdED played an active role in pushing through the quasi-privatization. In the following years, it committed itself to a defensive strategy. It aimed to protect jobs through negotiations with management and a cooperative attitude – an approach that can be seen as 'concession bargaining' (Hoffmann and Schmidt, 2008: 330; Kalass, 2012: 124). This had limited success: it prevented enforced redundancies, but not job cuts altogether. In addition, the discontent of the remaining workers grew thanks to the intensification and precarization that followed on the heels of the job cuts. An internal opposition to 'quasi-privatization' emerged within the GdED, which questioned the cooperative stance of the union leadership (Kalass, 2012: 119–24, 127, 133; Müller and Wilke, 2014: 165–7).

In contrast, the GDBA and the GDL opposed the 'reform' because they were committed to defending the *Beamten* status. Once it was no longer possible to derail it, the two unions chose diverging paths. For the GDBA, 'quasi-privatization' posed an existential threat because it was an organization exclusively for *Beamte*. It opted for broadening its constituency and chose to present itself as a union open for anyone working in the sector. Furthermore, it chose to seek cooperation with the other unions. It envisaged merging with the GDL and working more closely with the GdED. On the side of the GDL, internal disagreements emerged over the merger question, and in 2002, it decided against it. Furthermore, it abandoned the collective bargaining alliance that had existed for decades. Consequently, the GDBA decided to align itself more closely with Transnet, as the GdED had renamed itself in 2000. In 2005, the two unions entered a collective bargaining alliance; in 2010, they merged and became the DGB-affiliated EVG (Kalass, 2012: 118–24, 134–53, 321; Müller and Wilke, 2014: 165–7). Based on membership numbers, the EVG dominates the sector today: In 2021, it had 186,301 members; the figure for the GDL was approximately 40,000.[12] The difference reflects the EVG's broad constituency. Like the GdED – and in contrast to the GDL – it caters to everyone working in the railway system.

The GDL decided to deal with the changes in a different manner. It committed itself to building its strength not through creating a larger organization, but through staying independent and opting for a more conflict-oriented strategy. In other words, it embraced a militant form of occupational unionism that used strikes as a bargaining tool and rejected both the 'reform' and the collusion with management. There were internal debates as to whether this was the right way forward or whether a closer alignment with the more moderate railway unions should be sought. But by 2002, the split with the GDBA had become a reality. Furthermore, the GDL expanded its constituency, which now included everyone who worked on board, not just drivers but also conductors and catering staff (Kalass, 2012: 236–46, 241; Dörre et al, 2016: 158–62).

All in all, neoliberalization shook up inter-union relations in the railway sector. A moderate camp emerged committed to business unionism and cooperating with management, which was represented first by the GdED or Transnet plus the GDBA, and then by the EVG, and a camp committed to a militant occupational unionism, represented by the GDL.

Importantly, the new-found militancy of the GDL did not amount to a full rupture with its fundamental orientation. It did not embrace the 'radical political unionism' (Connolly and Darlington, 2012) of other Western

---

[12] https://www.dgb.de/uber-uns/dgb-heute/mitgliederzahlen/2020-2029 and https://www.gdl.de/UeberUns/Startseite [Accessed 20 April 2022].

European railways union such as the RMT in Britain or SUD-Rail in France. And it still operated on the grounds of a strong occupational identity and an anti-egalitarian, status-based approach to pay. Furthermore, it demanded that private, capital-based pension schemes are rolled out for employees of Deutsche Bahn, and it accepted the principle of competition in the railway system, at least as long as it was not detrimental to employees (see Kalass, 2012: 267; Hürtgen, 2016: 59–62). Notably, its president Claus Weselsky is a self-professed social conservative and a member of the CDU. He has criticized the EVG for passing a resolution declaring that being a member of the far-right Alternative for Germany party is incompatible with being a member of the union. His predecessor, Manfred Schell, even sat in parliament for the Christian Democrats (Gutschker, 2014; Kowalla, 2021).

The positions of the unions make the German railway system an interesting case from the perspective of class formation. In their fundamental orientations, both the EVG and GDL exhibit expansive and exclusive tendencies, but in an inverted manner: Whereas the EVG has a broad constituency and an expansive approach as a DGB-affiliated union, it has been cooperating closely with management; in contrast, the GDL has a narrow constituency and a strong occupational identity, but has been taking a confrontational stance towards management and has taken strike action time and again. This merits a closer inspection – and it underscores the importance of using a class-analytical framework and refraining from equating union activities with the exercise of class power (see Volume 1, Chapter 3). The German railway system is an excellent test case for Castells and Panitch because it exhibits the ambiguities that are needed to avoid subsumptionism.

The railway strikes in Germany and the question of class formation

Controversies and hostility
In the conjuncture of crisis, there were frequent strikes in the railway system. The GDL was behind three large-scale strike waves, which occurred in 2007–8, 2014–15 and 2021. The EVG staged a four-hour, national strike in December 2018 and made strike threats on several occasions. Both unions have been organizing smaller, regional or localized strikes at Deutsche Bahn subsidiaries or other railway and transport companies.

In my analysis, I chart the entire period, but my focus is on the 2014–15 strike wave. It was remarkable in various ways: its long duration; the fact that it turned into a political statement concerning the right to strike; the economic cost that it incurred; the disruption in public and freight transport that it caused; the public attention that it attracted; and the fact that the union was, on the whole, successful. Most of all, however, it stands out because a contradiction emerged that is indicative of the obstacles faced by organized labour in present-day Germany. Despite bringing gains for workers, the strike wave was met with hostility – not just from representatives of the right, but also from centre-left political leaders, commentators and trade unionists. They alleged that it deepened division among workers because it was an instance of inter-union competition.

The strikes in the German railway sector are well-suited to serve as a case study in this monograph because the challenges of assessing the class effects of strikes discussed in the preceding parts become very clear. Was the action by the GDL conducive to class partition because it fuelled union competition and sectionalism, as some of the presidents of the DGB-affiliated unions suggested? Or is this outweighed by the fact that workers embraced militancy and learned that they can win against management if they are prepared to use confrontational tactics? In other words, did the strikes in the railway exhibit signs of exclusive or inclusive solidarity?

To answer these questions, it is necessary, as I have argued in Chapter 4, to examine the *constituency*, *demands* and the *mobilizing dynamic* of the strikes. And to identify the latter, one needs to take a broader historical perspective that considers their pre-history and their aftermath. Operating this way will also allow me to discuss the continuity and change visible in the German configuration of labour relations. Accordingly, I present, in what follows, a periodization of the railway strikes starting with the process of German reunification and ending in the present.

The prehistory: rank-and-file unionism in the East

The prehistory of the strikes wave goes back to the fall of the Berlin Wall in November 1989. Like all DGB-affiliated unions, the GdED took over its East German counterpart Industrial Union Transport and Communications, an organization that was integrated into the authoritarian socialist regime of the German Democratic Republic and thus refrained from questioning the East German authorities or organizing strikes. In contrast, the GDL started organizing train drivers in the East a few weeks after the Wall had come down by reaching out to workers and providing direct support. As a result, the GDL was quickly seen, in the East, as an independent trade union whose leadership was responsive to the rank-and-file. In contrast to the GdED, it demanded that the employees of the East German railway service should be afforded *Beamten* status, which contributed to its popularity. Furthermore, it used to its successes in organizing East German train drivers to test its capacity for industrial action. In July 1990 and July 1991, it conducted two warning strikes over pay and pension entitlements, which were successful insofar as the demands were met shortly after (Kuba, 2009; Kalass, 2012: 150–1).

The successful recruitment of new members in East Germany reinvigorated the union – and the absence of *Beamten* in the East contributed to it

113

experimenting with industrial action and militant interventions (see Kalass, 2012: 152; Dörre et al, 2016: 159–60). The 'reform' and the decision of the GdED to cooperate closely with management also played a key role in changing the identity and strategy of the GDL. Not only did it create the opportunity of broad-based strikes in the sector; the business unionism of the GdED also created a vacuum in terms of worker representation, which the GDL chose to fill through embracing militant occupational unionism and expanding its base to all members of train staff. The emergence of this strategic option can be explained with neoliberalization, in particular the loss of the *Beamten* status, the organizational history of the GDL and the response of the other railway unions to the reunification process.

The option of militancy: the 2007–8 strike wave

In 2007–8, the GDL organized a wave of stoppages, which consolidated its new role as a force prepared to use the strike weapon. It demanded a hefty wage increase of 31 per cent on average and a new, separate collective bargaining agreement covering the GDL members who were train staff (see Hoffmann and Schmidt, 2008: 332–3; Hürtgen, 2016: 59). At first sight, this appears to have been a strike based on exclusive solidarity. Its *constituency* was narrow because it excluded the large number of workers employed by Deutsche Bahn who did not work on trains. Furthermore, the EVG, up to that point, had been the sole union negotiating on behalf of on-board staff who were not train drivers. In this sense, the GDL strategy fostered inter-union competition. And yet, it also needs to be considered that it reflected the need to forcefully stand up for the interests of workers instead of colluding with management.

The strike was met with sympathy in the German population. Jürgen Hoffmann and Rudi Schmidt argue that it reflected the fact that workers in Germany had been faced with stagnating real wages for ten years, so that the GDL acted as a 'proxy' for them (2008: 334); Viktoria Kalass agrees and states that the generally positive image of train drivers and the attempt by Deutsche Bahn to seek a strike ban in court also contributed to the positive perception of the strike (2012: 246, 255). All of this suggests that the *demands* for an agreement for train staff and a sizeable wage increase had expansive aspects.

What followed was a dispute that almost lasted for a year and involved six strikes ranging from one to four days and affecting different parts of the railway system (Kalass, 2012: 254). In the end, Wolfgang Tiefensee, Minister of Transport and a member of the SPD, intervened and forced Deutsche Bahn to settle. All in all, the union achieved two things: a collective bargaining agreement exclusively for train drivers (but not for all members of the train staff), and a wage increase by 11 per cent on average. This reveals the strategic significance of the strike: it vindicated the GDL's decision to go it alone and opt for a confrontational strategy. Significantly, the wage increase was extended to a large number of employees and *Beamte* at Deutsche Bahn (Hoffmann and Schmidt, 2008: 335–6).

The GDL pursued a strategy that was both status-oriented and militant. Initially, it was based on a narrow *constituency*. And yet, it can be seen as triggering a *mobilizing dynamic* that went beyond exclusive solidarity. The GDL contested not just the collusion of GDBA and Transnet with the management of Deutsche Bahn and thus created pressure for them to move beyond business unionism, but also competitive corporatism more generally. It responded to wage pressures not with concession bargaining, but with expandable *demands* for a substantial wage increase – and importantly, it won, and the agreement was extended to railway workers who were not part of the union. All in all, the mobilizing dynamic worked against the exclusive nature of the constituency and the demands for a separate collective bargaining agreement. On balance, the strike contributed to class formation and not partition.

The strike wave in 2007–8 also had serious class political consequences. For decades, labour relations in Germany had been characterized by industrial unionism. The legal principle of 'unity of collective bargaining' emerged as a product of case law, which prescribed that there should only be one collective bargaining agreement per firm. In the 2000s, this principle was challenged by occupational unions such as VC and the GDL, which started to use the strike weapon to bargain on behalf of smaller groups of workers defined through their occupation. As has been discussed with reference to the GDL, this was a reaction to the privatization of the transport infrastructure, which created considerable pressure on jobs, wages and working conditions in the railway and aviation sectors.

Responding to this new challenge, representatives of the German power bloc demanded a government intervention aimed at protecting the principle. As a reaction to 2007–8 railway strike, Reinhard Göhner, executive director of the BDA and a former MP for the CDU, started lobbying for a parliamentary bill reinstating it. His efforts gained traction in 2010 when the federal labour court decided that the principle of 'collective bargaining unity' did not conform with the principle of 'freedom of coalition' enshrined in the German constitution, and that there was the possibility of more than one collective bargaining agreement existing in a firm. The BDA now gained the support of the DGB for a legal initiative reinstating the principle of 'unity of collective bargaining'. As part of the coalition negotiations after the 2013 election, Chancellor Angela Merkel, the future Minister of Labour Andrea Nahles, an SPD member, and the heads of some of the unions met in order to strike a deal: There would be a minimum wage and an improvement for pensions entitlements if unions accepted the need for a bill for 'collective bargaining unity', which would make the principle of 'one firm, one collective bargaining agreement' legally binding again. The implication was not just that minority unions would struggle to make themselves heard and reach enough strength to bargain on behalf of its members, but also that the right to strike of their members was restricted through the 'peace obligation' linked to the agreement struck by the majority union. Unsurprisingly, the GDL was hostile towards the initiative for a new law, and Weselsky suggested in an interview that going on strike would be a suitable response (Dribbusch and Birke, 2012: 2; Weselsky, 2013; Frese, 2014a; 2014b; GDL, 2014a; Bachmann, 2015; Nowak, 2015; Keller, 2016a: 254, 262).

The preparedness of the GDL to embrace a militant strategy that included a non-cooperative stance towards the EVG and hostility towards 'collective bargaining in unity' put it on collision course not just with Deutsche Bahn and the DGB, but also with the federal government, which tried to prevent smaller occupational unions from negotiating their own collective bargaining agreements. As a result, the GDL strikes were not exclusively about wages and working conditions. They concerned the shape of labour relations in Germany and, in particular, the right to strike. In other words, the fact that the GDL embraced militancy politicized the activities of the union. They fall under the category of an expansive-politicized strike.

From a class-analytical perspective, this means the GDL strikes did not just concern train staff or the railway sector, but the German configuration of labour relations in its entirety. The GDL defended the right to strike – but importantly, an aspect thereof that is ambiguous in its class effects. The right of different unions in a workplace to go on strike independently of each other creates opportunities for inter-union competition, and it is by no means clear, at the conceptual level, whether such competition deepens or reduces divisions among workers. Two diverging scenarios are plausible: Competition can create hostilities between different unions, which creates opportunities for management to play them off against each other. In this scenario, it weakens the side of labour. However, it can also create pressure on unions to deliver for their members, which may result in their strengthening. It remains to be seen which of the two scenarios more adequately captures the strikes in the German railway system.

The class politics of labour disputes: the 2014–15 strike wave

In 2015, Germany experienced a hike in strike incidence. About two million working days were lost due to strikes, which is significantly more than the average for the country and the highest number in the last two decades (see Figure 5.2). Importantly, 90 per cent of the strike activity took place in the service and public sectors (WSI-Tarifarchiv, 2016), which led commentators to speak of 'a tertiarization of strikes' (Lesch, 2015: 3; see

Table 6.1: The 2014–15 strike wave in the German railway system

#	Dates	Length (goods traffic, hours)	Length (passenger traffic, hours)
1	1 September 2014	3	3
2	6 September 2014	3	3
3	7/8 October 2014	9	9
4	15/16 October 2014	14	14
5	17–20 October 2014	51	50
6	6–8 November 2014	75	64
7	21–23 April 2015	66	43
8	4–10 May 2015	138	127
9	19–21 May 2015	52	41
	Overall	411	354

Source: https://tinyurl.com/3des2t8a [Accessed 15 April 2022]

also Rehder, 2016: 367).[13] Due to their sectoral location, the strikes had a disruptive effect and directly affected people's everyday lives. And the shift to the service sector is obviously in line with developments elsewhere in the world (see Chapter 3). It shows that Germany is a well-suited case for testing Castells' claim and Panitch's counterclaim.

The hike in strike activity reflected how weakly wages had been developing in preceding years, and how the pressure on workers had increased in the wake of the 'Agenda' politics of the Schröder era. Furthermore, there were specific grievances in the public sector caused by neoliberalization. These were caused by privatization, as is illustrated by Deutsche Bahn, and well as by efforts to limit public expenditure. Since 2011, a so-called 'debt brake' is in operation in Germany, which is enshrined in the constitution and forces governments to limit borrowing. This has created sustained pressure on the wages of public sector workers (see Birke, 2018: 224; Ege and Gallas, 2019: 119–25).

Among the stoppages and conflicts in various sectors, one dispute stood out. Once more, the GDL and Deutsche Bahn entered a confrontation. This time, it brought nine time-limited stoppages all in all, among them a six-day strike in May 2015, which was the lengthiest in the history of the corporation (see Table 6.1; FAZ, 2015a). The new strike wave in the railway

---

[13] It is important to note that 81 per cent of people on strike in 2015 still came from the industrial sector (including construction) (WSI-Tarifarchiv, 2015; 2016). This suggests that whereas industrial workers mostly resorted to short warning strikes involving a lot of people, the strikes in public and service sectors were longer and carried by fewer people.

system was longer than the ones preceding and succeeding it (in 2007–8 and 2021, respectively). Even more importantly, it became heavily politicized: It triggered a lot of hostility in the media, contributed to dividing the DGB and created tensions in the political scene over how to regulate strike activities by minority unions – and it still had significant popular support.

Indeed, the 2014–15 strike wave polarized organized labour because the GDL insisted once more on going it alone and demanding the right to bargain on behalf of on-board staff. The presidents of the three largest unions in the country, which are all DGB-affiliated, made it very clear in public statements that they fundamentally disagreed with this strategy. Frank Bsirske, the leader of ver.di, openly criticized the GDL for not cooperating with the EVG (*Der Spiegel*, 2014a); the head of the mining, chemicals and energy workers' union, Industriegewerkschaft Bergbau, Chemie, Energie (Industrial Union Mining, Chemicals, Energy, Germany) (IG BCE), Michael Vassiliadis, charged the GDL with being a clientelist organization that misunderstood the nature of trade unionism (*Neues Deutschland*, 2015); and the president of IG Metall, Detlef Wetzel, went even further when he stated that the GDL's claim to represent non-driving workers amounted to 'the death of the union movement' (cited in *Der Spiegel*, 2014b). In a nutshell, leading representatives of the DGB unions charged the GDL with stoking inter-union competition and thus deepening divisions among railway workers and organized labour more broadly.

The *warm-up phase* of the 2014–15 strike wave commenced when the collective bargaining agreement expired that had been struck to settle the 2007–8 dispute. Talks about a new agreement started in July 2014. The GDL made several demands: a wage increase of 5 per cent; a reduction of the working week to 37 hours; restrictions on the flexibilization of working times and the recognition of the right of GDL to negotiate collective bargaining agreements for all its members operating on trains and not just train drivers. In August, the negotiations stopped without a result; in September, the union walked out twice for short warning strikes and shortly afterwards held a strike ballot. In early October, it announced that 91 of participants in the ballot had voted for strike action in support of the demands (GDL, 2014b; 2014c; 2014d; *taz*, 2014a).

What followed was a *phase of escalation and polarization*. There were four strikes of increasing length in October and November, which affected both goods and passenger traffic across the country and led to significant disruption in the railway system. Support for it among train drivers was solid. For the second October strike, Deutsche Bahn announced that two thirds of long-distance passenger trains would be cancelled; during the much longer November strike, the share of cancelled long-distance trains was still a third (*Die Welt*, 2014; *Die Zeit*, 2014a). According to an estimate of the Cologne Institute of Economic Research, the cost for

German industry of the strikes in the same month was between €50 and 100 million.[14]

An Emnid poll in October indicates that the strike activities enjoyed broad popular support during its initial stages: 55 per cent of respondents agreed with the statement that they had 'sympathy' for the striking workers, but this number dropped to 31 per cent in November (N24, 2014). This is not surprising considering that numerous journalists, politicians and even trade unionist reacted with outright hostility to the strike wave. The leader of the SPD and Minister for Economic Affairs, Sigmar Gabriel, said in an interview with Germany's most important tabloid *Bild-Zeitung* that it amounted to an 'abuse of the right to strike' (*Bild-Zeitung*, 2014). The president of the DGB, Reiner Hoffmann, stated that he was 'very sceptical' about the confrontational stance of the GDL (cited in *Der Spiegel*, 2014c). And even the leader of the Left Party, Bernd Riexinger, a former trade union official, was quoted as saying that the strike was 'wrong' (cited in *Rheinische Post*, 2014).

Certain quarters of the mainstream media were even sharper in their condemnation. The online edition of news magazine *Der Spiegel* published an opinion piece with the title 'Germany's most stupid union' (El-Sharif, 2014). Some news outlets also launched ad hominem attacks on Weselsky, the union president. Tabloid *Bild* used a heading in bold, capital letters that referred to him as 'Größenbahnsinniger', a pun on the words *Größenwahnsinniger* [megalomaniac] and *Bahn* [railway] (cited in Martens, 2014). *Bild* and *BZ*, also a tabloid, published the phone number of his office, inviting readers to vent their anger caused by the disruption by calling Weselsky. News magazine *Focus* included in an article a photo of the façade of the building where he lived (Martens, 2014). Klaus Dörre et al attribute the one-sidedness of many of the mainstream media during the initial stages of the strike to a successful public relations campaign of Deutsche Bahn (2016: 161). Considering the breadth of the condemnation of the strike and the fact that the population increasingly turned against it, it is justified to speak of a 'moral panic' (Hall et al, 2013: 3).

On top of the discursive interventions directed against the strike, the government pressed ahead with the bill for 'unity of collective bargaining'. The first draft was presented in October 2014 by Nahles. According to it, only collective bargaining agreements struck between employers and the union with most members in a business unit was supposed to be valid. This caused a deep split inside the DGB: IG Metall and IG BCE welcomed Nahles' initiative; in contrast, ver.di, the EVG, the education union GEW and the Food, Beverages and Catering Union (NGG) were opposed because they

---

[14] https://de.statista.com/statistik/daten/studie/351963/umfrage/streiktage-gdl-kosten-industrie/ [Accessed 10 October 2022].

saw it as a threat to the right to strike (*Die Zeit*, 2014b; Wisdorff, 2014). The GDL was hostile to the bill from the start and created a clear link to its industrial action, underscoring the political nature of the dispute. It posted on its website a link to the *Streikzeitung* [strike newspaper], a publication edited by supporters of the GDL. On its title page, it carried the slogan 'Yes to the GDL strike! No to the bill for unity of collective bargaining!'. Furthermore, the main headline of the paper's first edition from November 2014 was 'Defending the right to strike!' (*Streikzeitung*, 2014).

Around the same time, Deutsche Bahn sought an injunction against the union. It attempted to end the strike by force, but the responsible labour court declared the injunction void and also rejected an appeal by Deutsche Bahn. The GDL responded to the verdict by announcing that it saw it as a boost to morale, but that it would shorten the November stoppage as a gesture of goodwill and return to the negotiating table (*Der Spiegel*, 2014d; *taz*, 2014b).

What followed was a *phase of new negotiations*. All in all, there were 16, on the whole unsuccessful, rounds of talks before the seventh strike started, which took place in late April 2015. At the time, journalist Alfons Frese suspected that Deutsche Bahn stalled the negotiations because the 'unity of collective bargaining' bill was about to be passed (Frese, 2015a). According to him, Deutsche Bahn wanted to turn the new legislation against the GDL. The GDL seems to have shared this view because it accused Deutsche Bahn of 'stonewalling' and 'blockading' (GDL, 2015a; 2015b; 2015c) when it announced that the negotiations had failed.

As a result, the next phase of the dispute was characterized by a new escalation. There were three more strikes. Among them was the comparably lengthy stoppage in early May that almost lasted for a week and contributed to more than a third of the overall work hours lost during the strike wave. According to the GDL, there was considerable support for the strike among train drivers: 50 per cent of freight trains, 70 per cent of long-distance passenger trains and 90 per cent of regional passenger traffic did not run (GDL, 2015d; see Hürtgen, 2016: 66). Again, the GDL was attacked – both by journalists and leading politicians (Augstein, 2015; Steltzner, 2015). A short-lived attempt to restart negotiations in mid-May came to nothing (*Der Stern*, 2015); what followed was another three-day strike.

Subsequently, a phase marked by a *push for a new settlement* followed. A turning point was reached on 21 May 2015, when Deutsche Bahn finally accepted that the GDL could negotiate collective agreements on behalf of all its members among train staff, not just among train drivers. Both sides agreed to an arbitration process under the guidance of the prime minister of the federal state of Thuringia, Bodo Ramelow, a member of the Left Party, and the former prime minister of the federal state of Brandenburg and former leader of the SPD, Matthias Platzeck. Only one day later, the bill for 'collective bargaining unity' was passed in parliament. It was supported by the 'grand coalition' of the CDU, its Bavarian sister party CSU and the SPD, and opposed by the Green Party and the Left Party. The new law became effective on 10 July 2015. Importantly, the GDL and Deutsche Bahn had come to an agreement before this happened. On 1 July 2015, both sides agreed that the remit of the GDL would be expanded; wages would be increased by 3.5 per cent straight away plus another 1.7 per cent in May 2016; there would be a one-off payment of €350; and the working week would be reduced to 38 hours in 2018 (DLF, 2015; FAZ, 2015b; *Die Zeit*, 2015b). Furthermore, a procedure for arbitration was introduced to avoid future conflicts (Raehlmann, 2017: 32). The fact that the agreement was struck before the law became effective meant that the latter could not be applied to it. This meant that the GDL was protected from having the agreement declared null and void.

All in all, the settlement amounted to a success for the GDL. Some of its key demands were met, in particular its claim to negotiate on behalf of all members of the train staff. This was important not just because it extended the union constituency and showed that it was serious about its expansive demands. The agreement was also significant because it meant that as long as it was valid, the GDL was able to bypass the new law (see Dörre et al, 2016: 162; Hürtgen, 2016: 57; Birke, 2018: 229). Since it had connected its strike action to the legal initiative directed against strikes of minority unions, this can be seen as a partially successful act of political resistance. Of course, the likelihood of preventing the passage of the bill had been slim considering that the grand coalition, with its substantial parliamentary majority, supported it. But the GDL managed to undermine its effectiveness somewhat – which mattered also because its activities were portrayed as a primary example for the 'problem' addressed by the law, for example by Hoffmann and Nahles (see Frese, 2015b; Aue, 2021). Conversely, the dispute was expensive for Deutsche Bahn. According to its own calculations, it accrued a cost of €500 million (*Die Welt*, 2015), which shows that there was a strong financial incentive for it to accept a settlement. Since representatives of Deutsche Bahn had rejected the demand of the GDL to negotiate on behalf all train staff throughout the strike and gave in on that front in the end, the agreement can be seen as a defeat for the corporation.

The *immediate aftermath* of the strike wave was characterized by political arguments about 'collective bargaining unity'. The bill passed parliament during the final stage of the dispute; the recriminations around the law have been continuing ever since. A number of unions brought complaints before the constitutional court, among them ver.di, the GDL, the public servants' federation DBB, the physicians' union Marburger Bund and the pilots' union VC. Apart from ver.di, none of these unions are affiliated with the DGB. Their hope was that the court would declare the law unconstitutional (*Die*

Zeit, 2017), which did not materialize in the end. In July 2017, it decreed that the law is 'largely compatible with the Basic Law'. Nevertheless, it required the legislative to revise the law and ensure that 'the interests of specific occupational groups or sectors must not be neglected, in a one-sided manner, if existing collective bargaining agreements are supplanted' (BVerfG, 2017; DBB, 2019). In 2018, the Bundestag passed an amendment that changed the law accordingly. Jakob Schäfer, a rank-and-file activist from IG Metall, highlighted in a comment to the verdict that its provisions were 'vague', and that they would not remove the threat to the right to strike of minority unions (2017). Wolfgang Däubler, a labour lawyer, went as far as calling it a 'law without force' (2017; see also Sell, 2017). In his opinion, the provisions restricted the ability of employers to completely undermine minority unions.

The split among the DGB-affiliated unions resurfaced in their responses to the ruling. In a press release, ver.di criticized it and argued that its ambiguities would create legal insecurity and overburden labour courts. In contrast, the IG BCE and the EVG – both organizations committed to 'social partnership' – welcomed the ruling. According to the IG BCE, it amounted to 'a clear signal against group egotisms and the division of the labour force'; the EVG saw it as a confirmation of its view that 'a collective bargaining policy based on solidarity, which is applicable for all workers, can only be administered by those unions that represent the majority of workers' (cited in *Express*, 2017).

Notably, Hoffmann, the president of the DGB, qualified his position on the law somewhat – possibly a reflection of the divisions among the DGB-affiliated unions. In 2015, he had come out in favour by saying that it did not restrict the freedom of smaller organizations and offered 'an opportunity for strengthening the cooperation of the unions' (Bundestag, 2015; NTV, 2015). In January 2017, he was cited as stating that the principle of a 'collective bargaining unity' is desirable, but that it should be based on agreements between unions, and not be enforced by law (WAZ, 2017). After the verdict, he said that he found it 'somewhat reasonable' that the court required the law to be amended and added that any future legislation 'must not ... allow the cancellation of collective bargaining agreements' (cited in *Express*, 2017). Of course, Hoffmann's wavering can be seen as an attempt to manage the tensions inside his confederation. Through giving qualified support to the law, he signalled that he found the arguments of both sides worth considering.

All in all, the strike wave was based on a narrow *constituency*. The GDL only represented a minority of railway workers. Of course, it sought to broaden its base, but this did not go beyond on-board staff. Accordingly, it chose to shun the EVG. In contrast, many of the GDL's *demands* – higher wages, a working time reduction and flexibilization – were expandable, which is also reflected in the fact that the strike was seen with sympathy by a significant part of the population, in particular during its initial stages. It follows that there were exclusive and inclusive aspects to the activities of the GDL.

This also becomes clear when one looks at the *mobilizing dynamic* triggered by the strike wave. It was met with hostility by certain quarters – in particular, trade union officials, politicians and journalists. For working-class formation to occur, support from the latter two groups is not crucial. Matters are more complicated when it comes to trade unionists. At first sight, the disunity among representatives of organized labour could be interpreted as reflecting divisive effects of the strike wave. But on closer inspection, ambiguities and contradictions emerge that need to be factored into the equation. Arguably, competitive corporatism is a divisive strategy because it is based on defending (nationally defined) core workforces, which in turn means neglecting the needs and interests of other workers. If, as is the case in Germany, it is institutionalized and deeply embedded in labour relations and organizations, it is next to impossible to move against this divisive strategy without triggering hostile reactions. In this sense, the militant occupational trade unionism of the GDL deepened existing divisions, but it was not responsible for their existence. And importantly, it offered an alternative to the strategy that had caused them in the first place. Indeed, by showing that it was possible to make gains with the help of militancy, its activities were of relevance for all workers in the country, not just for railway workers. In this sense, there was an inclusive aspect to what it did.

Importantly, the GDL actions occurred in the context of, and were connected to, the broader 2015 strike wave in Germany. Workers from different branches of the economy – significant stoppages took place in the railways, social care and education as well as the postal service – inspired one another (see Birke, 2018: 226–32). This was captured in headlines from the news media, which detected 'The new German lust for strikes' (Steiner, 2016) and 'The new culture of struggle of the trade unions' (Kessen, 2017) and also said that a 'Lust for strikes [has been] awoken' (Müller, 2016). Against this backdrop, Dörre et al asserted that there was a 'new tendency towards conflict in labour relations' (2016: 185).

The emerging connections came to the fore in solidarity actions between railway and care workers, whose stoppages took place at roughly the same time. And this was despite the fact that their unions, the GDL and ver.di, belong to different confederations. In three of the background interviews I conducted for this book, striking railway workers from North Hessen, independently from one another, relayed how solidarity from below emerged between the two groups.[15] Sven Baumgartner, a train driver, and Bianca Schröder, a conductor, referred to an event in Kassel near the main station,

---

[15] For a list of people interviewed for this book, see Appendix B. I have changed the names of the interviewees from the GDL to ensure anonymity. The federal state of Hessen is located in the centre of Germany.

where they and their fellow unionists visited a strike assembly of social care and education workers. According to Schröder, some of the latter had already visited a GDL picket line to show their support; following Baumgartner, social care and education workers were also present at a later GDL assembly in Frankfurt. An article in a small socialist newspaper called *SoZ* confirms that there was rank-and-file solidarity between railway and social care workers (Kuhn, 2015). It discusses a strike assembly of the latter that also took place in Kassel. According to the article, a ver.di official used a speech at the assembly to point to a poster pledging support for the GDL and to highlight the need to protest against the unity of collective bargaining bill. This comment earned him a round of applause by those present. The events in Kassel can be seen as instances where 'class feeling' – a notion of being together in one's struggles and facing the same antagonist – was in evidence.

It follows that the GDL's clear stance on the unity of collective bargaining bill meant that it led the resistance against an authoritarian government move that amounted to restricting the right to strike, and that one of the most powerful unions in the country, ver.di, protested against. In this sense, its interventions were expansive-politicized strikes and constituted proxy struggles, that is, sectoral struggles with a great significance for the side of labour in general. On balance, I contend that the 2014–15 strike wave in the railway system contributed to class formation because it was connected to the bill, a political issue that concerned all workers, and because there are some indications that rank-and-file solidarity between workers across branches and union confederations emerged – or 'class feeling', to quote Luxemburg.

An expansive dynamic across the railway system: the warning strikes of the EVG and the reactions of the GDL

If one wants to gauge the effects of the 2014–15 strike wave, one also needs to consider how railway trade unionism evolved outside the GDL after the events – and how the EVG fared, the other main union representing employees of Deutsche Bahn. Transnet, one of the EVG's two predecessor organizations, had closely collaborated with the management of Deutsche Bahn, and its leadership had consistently supported privatization. At first sight, it appears that the EVG continued this course. During the 2014–15 dispute, it publicly denounced the belligerent stance of the GDL. At its 2014 congress, it passed a resolution that described 'social partnership' as a 'success model' and emphasized the need for 'collective bargaining unity' (cited in Behruzi, 2014). However, it also criticized the bill promoted by the governments and parts of the DGB, arguing that it would obstruct solidarity among railway workers. After all, Deutsche Bahn had more than 300 sub-companies, and the bill stipulated that in each of these business units, only the majority union would be allowed to engage in collective bargaining (Behruzi, 2014). In other words, the EVG was worried that the bill would hamper its efforts to negotiate on behalf of workers across the entire railway system.

Despite its endorsement of 'social partnership', the EVG also reacted to the GDL's frequent use of the strike weapon by hesitantly shifting away from Transnet's focus on cooperation and concession bargaining. On 16 March 2013, after demanding a wage increase of 6.5 per cent, hundreds of workers organized with the union went on strike for two hours in selected areas across the country. At the same time – and in marked contrast to the GDL – the EVG used conciliatory rhetoric when it explained its intervention: 'We don't want to upset the travellers more than is necessary', said union spokesman Uwe Reitz, adding that the short stoppage would be carried out 'with a sense of proportion' (cited in *SZ*, 2013; see also *Die Zeit*, 2013a). The union agreed a settlement soon after, which brought a wage increase of 3 per cent (*Die Zeit*, 2013b).

In May 2015, briefly before the GDL dispute was settled, its competitor again took a confrontational stance towards Deutsche Bahn. The EVG threatened to go on strike once more and thus played with fears that the entire railway sector would grind to a halt. In line with its conciliatory stance, however, it soon after entered an agreement with the corporation, which brought a staggered wage increase of 5.1 per cent overall (*Der Spiegel*, 2015; Wacket, 2015). This result was similar to what the GDL would eventually settle on. As the timing of its intervention shows, the EVG had been freeriding on its rival's campaign. It exploited, for its purposes, the decision of the GDL to go on the attack against Deutsche Bahn and make expandable wage demands. And it benefited from the fact that it would have been risky for Deutsche Bahn to open a second front. This shows that the intervention by the GDL had strengthened the hands of both railway unions in their negotiations with the corporation.

When the next round of collective bargaining negotiations came in 2016, the EVG again uttered strike threats. In December of that year, it once more settled on a staggered wage increase. This time, however, workers obtained an option to convert the second of two raises into longer holidays. After again entering the compulsory arbitration procedure that was part of the 2015 agreement, the GDL agreed a settlement with the corporation that resembled the one the EVG had negotiated (*Die Zeit*, 2016; Bispinck, 2017: 19–21; *Der Spiegel*, 2017).

In 2018, the pattern of 2015 was reversed. This time, the EVG went on a nationwide strike, even if was just for four hours in the morning of 9 December, a Monday. In contrast to 2013, the stoppage extended beyond regional areas or specific branches of the railway system. According to labour scholar Heiner Dribbusch, the union managed to bring 'rail traffic in Germany to full standstill' and demonstrate 'effectively its capacity to engage in labour struggles' (2018: 8). This was a step away from social partnership, albeit a hesitant one. Shortly after, the union agreed a settlement that resembled the one struck in the preceding round. Again, it brought a staggered wage increase – and the option for workers to forego the second raise for additional free time. In contrast, the GDL, which was still bound by compulsory arbitration, refrained from stopping work and negotiated until early 2019. Again, it reached a settlement with Deutsche Bahn that resembled the one struck by the EVG: a staggered wage increase plus an option for additional time off (*Die Zeit*, 2018; 2019; *Junge Welt*, 2018; NDR, 2018).

If the EVG had benefited from the GDL being prepared to go on strike in 2014–15, it was now the other way round. Despite the open hostilities between the two unions, union competition, in the scenario that emerged, benefited railway workers overall. It forced the EVG to move beyond concession bargaining and embrace more forceful forms of interest representation. This confirms my assessment that on the whole, the railway strikes facilitated class formation because they caused workers to act collectively across the entire railway system – and make similar demands, albeit through different organizations. In other words, they had a constituency that was broad in the case of the EVG and widening in the case of the GDL, were characterized by transferable *demands* concerning wages and working conditions and, through their combination, triggered an expansive *dynamic*. The collective bargaining agreements won by the two unions active brought improvements for workers.

Unresolved tensions and new militancy: the 2021 strike wave

Labour relations in the German railway system have been characterized by strife ever since the government embarked on its privatization in the 1990s. Things once again reached boiling point in the spring of 2021. The existing collective bargaining agreement between Deutsche Bahn and the GDL from early 2019 was about to expire, and the GDL was no longer bound by a compulsory arbitration clause. Unsurprisingly, new strikes were to follow.

A year earlier, Deutsche Bahn had attempted to use the COVID-19 pandemic to co-opt the unions into a pact and force them onto the path of concession bargaining, the *Bündnis für unsere Bahn* [alliance for our railways]. Next to securing financial support from the state to make up for the losses accrued due to the pandemic, the rationale behind the alliance was to get the unions to trade wage restraint for job security. In May 2020, five parties signed the pact: the management of Deutsche Bahn, the Federal Ministry of Transport, AGV MoVe (an employers' association for transport services), the works council of Deutsche Bahn and the EVG (Bündnis für unsere Bahn, 2020). The GDL refused to join, citing its concern over how Deutsche Bahn was acting as a for-profit corporation that had heavily invested in transport services outside Germany. It suggested that the Federal Parliament create a commission of experts tasked with critically assessing the state of the railway system, and that the rail infrastructure should become a not-for-profit, state-owned entity detached from the corporation (GDL, 2020). This amounted to proposing that Deutsche Bahn should be broken up.

In contrast to the GDL, the EVG accepted a proposal by Deutsche Bahn to bring forward collective bargaining negotiations and talk about a new settlement well in advance of the expiry date of the existing one. In line with the pact, it secured a jobs guarantee, but also accepted that there would be no wage increase in 2021 and a very moderate raise of 1.5 per cent for 2022. The agreement forced the hand of the GDL because its rejection of the pact meant that accepting similar terms would have amounted to a loss of face. Importantly, the EVG agreement contained a clause that allowed it to reopen negotiations should the GDL secure more substantial gains (*Handelsblatt*, 2020; Schwarz, 2021). This was a clever strategic move that allowed the EVG to have its cake and eat it: It would be able to reap the benefits of a potential strike wave, but did not have to take the risks attached to getting involved; and it was able to present itself as a force of moderation, which is why it was unlikely to draw the ire of members of public or political decision-makers. In other words, it created conditions for freeriding once more in case there were militant interventions of the GDL.

The GDL reacted to EVG's strategy with attacks on the latter. Weselsky had already rejected the latter's invitation to join the alliance in a harshly worded open letter (Weselsky, 2020). Then, in an interview in March 2021, he went as far as suggesting that administrative staff should be cut to safeguard the future of the railway system (Frese, 2021a). This was a divisive move and an open attack on a part of the constituency of the EVG – even if he targeted workers in contradictory rather than in consistent class locations.

Against the backdrop of the agreement with the EVG, it is unsurprising that Deutsche Bahn offered very little in the way of wage increases to the GDL once negotiations over a new agreement got underway in the spring of 2021. Furthermore, it had already begun to apply the Unity of Collective Bargaining Act in its management of labour relations, and it had renounced the demand by the GDL to collectively negotiate on behalf of members who did not work on-board. Negotiations over a new agreement broke down after four rounds of meetings. Officially, the bone of contention was pay. Management was not prepared to make an offer that amounted to an increase in real wages and pointed to the dire financial situation of the corporation. It also alleged that the GDL disregarded the difficult economic circumstances, and that its main motive for taking a confrontational stance was trying to improve its position under the Unity of Collective Bargaining Act (Erhardt, 2019; RBB24, 2021; Schwarz, 2021; Tagesschau, 2021a). The GDL started balloting for a strike. In August 2021, the result was announced: turnout

Table 6.2: The 2021 strike wave in the German railway system

#	Dates	Length (goods traffic, hours)	Length (passenger traffic, hours)
1	10–13 August 2021	55	48
2	21–25 August 2021	81	48
3	1–7 September 2021	129	120
	Overall	265	216

Source: Own calculation via gdl.de and tagesschau.de [Accessed 29 April 2022]

was 70 per cent, and 95 per cent were in favour of walking out (GDL, 2021). This shows that there was huge discontent among the GDL rank-and-file, and that the decision to refuse the pay offer was not just a strategic consideration in reaction to the Act.

What followed was a strike wave that disrupted train travel and goods transport to a significant degree. Its magnitude was not quite as big as in 2014–15, but it still hit the operation of the railway system (see Tables 6.1 and 6.2). Deutsche Bahn sought to the stop the strikes by seeking an injunction against the third strike in September, but was unsuccessful (Gefken, 2021; Frindert et al, 2022: 13).

As in 2014–15, the strike wave triggered hostile reactions from journalists, politicians and the DGB. The leader of the SPD, Norbert-Walther Borjans, criticized the union for dividing 'different groups of staff at the railway service' (cited in *Der Spiegel*, 2021a). A well-known Green politician, Oliver Krischer, charged the GDL with acting without consideration for the 'customers' of Deutsche Bahn and showing a lack of proportion in how it chose its interventions (cited in Tagesschau, 2021b). Enak Ferlemann, a CDU MP and secretary of state in the Ministry of Transport, tried to delegitimize the activities of the GDL by claiming that the latter was pursuing 'political goals' (cited in *Der Spiegel*, 2021b). The leader of the DGB, Reiner Hoffmann, criticized the union for being unwilling to cooperate with the EVG and instrumentalizing the dispute for the purpose of securing its survival under the Unity of Collective Bargaining Act (Frese, 2021b). *Bild* published an opinion piece in which one its journalists charged the GDL with 'showing a lack of solidarity' with holidaymakers and commuters and putting the health of the passengers at risk because the latter would have to rely, in a pandemic, on the few, crowded trains that were still running (Uhlenbroich, 2021). Franz Josef Wagner, a well-known columnist of *Bild*, called Weselsky the 'railway Rambo' (2021), a trope that already been in use in 2014–15 (see *Börse am Sonntag*, 2014; Riedler, 2014). A commentator for *taz*, Gunnar Hinck, echoed the critique of *Bild* about infection risks and went as far as suggesting that the GDL was endangering the continued existence of the railway system, adding that it was a key means of transportation needed to address the climate crisis (2021).

Despite the support for the strike among GDL members, commentators said that the GDL was not transparent about its motives, which they believed to be about defending its room for manoeuvre under the Act. Some added a critical note by arguing that the dispute showed how the latter failed to pacify labour relations (Aue, 2021; Dettmer, 2021; Frese, 2021c; Peters, 2021). Notably, these observations were based on two surprising implicit assumptions: the idea that militancy pays off; and the idea that it is somehow objectionable for unions to use strikes to win new members and grow in strength. What none of the critical commentators mentioned was the fact that the confrontational course of the GDL was, once again, connected to the concession bargaining of the EVG, and how the former justified its activities. It reacted to the risky and on the whole unsuccessful management strategy of Deutsche Bahn, whose losses had not just been caused by the COVID-19 pandemic, but also by its decision to venture abroad and invest in transport services outside of Germany (*Manager Magazin*, 2020; GDL, 2021; Budras and Heeg, 2022). Importantly, the general public seems to have been more receptive to this line than the commentariat. There appears to have been significant support for the strike, which is also something that was not discussed much in the news media. According to a nation-wide opinion poll by public broadcaster ZDF, respondents were evenly split at the end of August 2021 when asked whether they supported or opposed the strikes (ZDF, 2021).

In mid-September, and with the help of two mediators, Deutsche Bahn and the GDL reached an agreement. According to it, there would be wage increases in stages, first 1.5 per cent in December in 2021, then another 1.8 per cent in March 2023, plus two one-off payments, so-called 'Corona bonuses'. Importantly, the GDL accepted that the Unity of Collective Bargaining Act would be applied. On the grounds of this agreement and the aforementioned clause, the EVG negotiated improvements to its own agreement with Deutsche Bahn and secured extra payments. Its strategy of avoiding confrontation while benefiting from the GDL's militancy paid off (Frindert et al, 2022: 13; Lesch and Winter, 2022: 13–14).

This last dispute demonstrates once more that union competition in the German railway system, on the whole, benefited workers rather than allowing Deutsche Bahn to play off the two unions against each other. Of course, one could imagine a scenario where unity would strengthen workers even more. But this is a counterfactual consideration – and it is not likely to emerge given that the EVG organizes a wide range of workers, among them groups in contradictory class locations. The militancy of the GDL has forced the EVG to move away somewhat from its conciliatory stance, and the latter has profited from the former, which was revealed when it was able to renegotiate its collective agreement. Despite the recriminations between the two unions, what emerged implicitly was a division of labour where the GDL sought full-on confrontation, and the EVG attempted to achieve improvements via negotiations. This reflected the different social bases of the unions: the focus of the GDL on on-board staff allowed it to build on a well-organized rank-and-file that was prepared to take strike action; the breadth of the EVG's constituency meant that it was able to bring together workers representing different professions and inhabiting both consistent and contradictory class locations. What emerges is a 'bad cop, good cop' scenario, albeit one where the two cops do not openly collaborate and publicly dismiss each other's approach. From a class-analytical point of view, what matters most in this context is the *dynamic* of the labour disputes – there were strikes across the entire railway system that fed into one another because many of the *demands* voiced in the strikes were transferable and expansive – in the sense that it was possible to overcome concession bargaining on behalf of the core workforce. This also means that the *constituency* of the strikes, if taken together, was expanding and, in the end, broad. In a nutshell, the EVG supplied the breadth and the GDL the militancy; and the expansive outweighed the divisive effects of the strikes because the two unions were forced to respond to each other in a manner benefiting workers.

Class formation in the railway system

The GDL episode illuminates a shift in German labour relations: Neoliberalization brought an end to the corporatist-welfarist arrangement of the postwar decades. The reactions of the DGB-affiliated unions to this development diverged somewhat. Big unions operating mainly in manufacturing like the IG BCE and the IG Metall responded by embracing competitive corporatism. This was rational from an organizational point of view because it protected, to a degree, core workforces in situations of fierce transnational competition. But it came at a price: It deepened the divides between core workforces, or insiders, and temporary workers, or outsiders, and did not address the resulting representational gap. In this sense, it contributed to class partition. To be fair, IG Metall and other unions were aware of this issue and responded to it with organizing drives, and there have been some success stories (Dörre et al, 2016: 226–34; Rehder, 2016). But their results all in all vary – and union density has reached a low point. All in all, the German unions have been struggling to find adequate responses to the proliferation of precarious work, and the economic pressures created by the Great Crisis have weakened them even more.

By embracing business unionism, first Transnet and then the EVG went further than its allies in the DGB when it came to responding to neoliberalization. They engaged in concession bargaining, acted against the interests of those workers badly affected by privatization and embraced the introduction of market mechanisms in the railway sector. As a result, a representational gap emerged in a branch of the economy that was formerly known for job security – an instance of fragmentation and class partition that could be used to back up the Castellsian claim.

But the story did not stop here. The GDL offered an alternative strategy, namely, militant occupational unionism. To a degree, this addressed the gap because it constituted a forceful form of interest representation that rejected concession bargaining. However, it did not address all employees of Deutsche Bahn. The emergence of a union strategy in the railway system diametrically opposed to business unionism reiterates the Marxian point that a full pacification of labour relations is impossible, and that conflict is always present in capitalist relations of production.

The class effects of this alternative strategy are difficult to assess. Due to its narrow constituency, the 'moderate' wing of the DGB portrayed the GDL's activities as divisive and sectionalist. This suggests that they contributed to class partition. But the broader context of the GDL strikes shows that things are more complicated. There are three expansive aspects. First, the GDL has attempted, in a situation characterized by a representational gap, to broaden its constituency, initially to everyone working on trains, and once this had been achieved in 2015, to other groups of railway workers. In this sense, its reaction can be seen as an expansive move made in response to a divisive strategy from a competing union. It is difficult to call inter-union competition divisive if it constitutes an attempt to broaden one's constituency and a response to a competitor refusing to represent workers' interests forcefully.

Second, the privatization of the German railway system has created new opportunities for militant interventions, which the GDL has used. In fact, it managed to bat above its average and bypass the EVG in its negotiations with Deutsche Bahn on several occasions despite the fact that it is a much smaller union. In embracing militancy, it managed to turn a feeling of degradation that was linked to privatization into mobilization, and it also delivered in terms of securing improvements to wages and working conditions (see Kalass, 2012: 97–8, 153). This shows that militancy and a confrontational strategy can pay off. Indeed, the GDL forced the EVG to shift away from business unionism and towards militancy, and the concessions won by it benefited the latter's constituency by being extended to other workers. Put differently, the GDL triggered an activating dynamic that was to the advantage workers across the railway system and even created links to striking workers in other branches of the economy.

Third, it must be noted that the confrontational approach hit service users, which is why it was comparably easy for the government and the media to campaign against the GDL, criticize its strikes and advocate for laws against minority unions. At first sight, the strikes may thus be interpreted as causing division. But as the union decided not to give in, the 2014–15 strike wave in particular obtained a general class political significance: It became a mobilization in defence of the right to strike, which is also visible in the fact that some DGB unions, among them the EVG, protested against the Act. If we take Marx's argument seriously that workers' struggles precede class formation, defending this right, which ensures the legality of such struggles, must be seen as a move with a great class political significance.

The jury is still out on what the effects of the new law will be. It has only been applied recently in the railway sector. The fact that the constitutional court declared it, by and large, as being in line with the Basic Law, and that legislators had to amend to it where it was not, poses a serious threat to the rights of minority unions and also creates a space for future debates on restricting the right to strike further. At the same time, there have been commentators, in the context of the third GDL strike wave of 2021, who pointed out that the law does not work as intended: it has not led to a pacification of labour relations.

To conclude, it should be clear that some of the GDL's interventions, for example, Weselsky's demand to cut administrative staff at Deutsche Bahn, have been divisive. And yet, its strikes triggered a dynamic that was favourable for workers across the railway system and even for workers in other branches of the economy who started to embrace militancy. On balance, the activities of the GDL contributed to class formation rather than class partition. Despite complications, the picture that emerges is closer to Panitch's than to Castells' claim about how labour relations in the non-industrial sectors evolve: Workers outside of industry organize, strike and make gains – and they create links with other workers in the process.

7

Adsorption and the Struggle against Austerity: The Junior Doctors' Dispute in Britain

From liberal collectivism to neoliberal individualism: labour relations in Britain

Britain as a stronghold of economic liberalism

As I argued in the preceding chapter, it makes sense, in the context of an incorporated comparison concerned with processes of deindustrialization, to zoom in on Western Europe and examine different national cases that reflect the variegation of global capitalism. Britain bears hallmarks of a liberal market economy. Accordingly, the institutions characterizing the British political economy reflect the assumption that the market mechanism allocates resources efficiently: the regulation of the financial sector is comparably 'light' (see Gallas, 2010; Tooze, 2018); for-profit, private sector companies and public–private partnerships play an important role in delivering public services (Flinders, 2005; Gallas, 2016: 241–2); and economic inequality is higher than in the other Western European countries.[1]

Indeed, economic liberalism has deep roots in the country. Paired with colonialism and imperialism, it was a prominent feature of government policy in the age of the British empire in the 19th century. Back then, leading politicians had been promoting the erection of a 'world market' based on 'free trade' (Arrighi, 1994: 47–58; Gallas, 2008: 283; 2016: 76, 134–5). After the Second World War, economic and social policy shifted. Under the postwar settlement between capital and labour, full employment and benefits were traded for union acquiescence. A welfare state was erected, and successive governments started to experiment with Keynesianism and corporatism. But

---

[1]   https://ec.europa.eu/eurostat/databrowser/view/ilc_di12/default/table?lang=en [Accessed 9 October 2022].

in reaction to a deep crisis of the British political economy and a wave of rank-and-file militancy on the side of organized labour, leading politicians re-embraced, from the mid-1970s onwards, 'free market' ideas. Ever since, the country has been at the forefront of efforts to promote neoliberalism. Governments have been fostering financialization, competition, private ownership of corporations and transnationalization – and have attempted to insulate the economy from interventions from popular, subaltern forces. Today, the country is deeply integrated in global financial networks; indeed, the City of London is not just the centre of the national economy but also one of the hubs of global finance (see Gallas, 2010; 2013; 2016).

Importantly, Britain was also the first country in the world to industrialize and the first where strikes and workers' movements based on industrial work emerged – as well as the first to witness a demise of manufacturing. During the second wave of industrialization in the late 19th century, the country already fell behind other countries in the Global North, among them Germany and the US, and it continued to lose ground during the 20th century. Neoliberalization accelerated the decline. In particular, the Thatcher government, formed in 1979, pursued economic policies that hit the industrial sector hard. It removed capital controls, increased interest rates, privatized state-owned firms and liberalized financial markets. And in so doing, it created an environment characterized by fierce, in part international, competition and the emergence of new investment opportunities in finance. This drove a large number of industrial firms into bankruptcy. In 1973, close to every second British worker had still worked in industry (Tomlinson, 2021: 622). Between 1980 and 1983, industrial employment decreased by 7 per cent per annum (Gallas, 2016: 134). Today, its share (18.1 per cent in 2019) is lower than in Spain (20.4 per cent) and considerably lower than in Germany (27.2 per cent; see Figure 5.1).

The co-existence of a highly financialized, transnationalized economy and a well-organized labour movement makes Britain a very well-suited case for testing whether or not there are signs of class formation in the context of deindustrialization. The first part of the Castellsian scenario, the transnationalization and financialization of capital, is clearly in evidence in Britain. An open question remains whether organized labour is fragmenting in the process, or whether new forms of solidarity among workers emerge outside industry.

Liberal collectivism and the two arms of organized labour

Against the backdrop of industrialization, labour relations in Britain evolved in a manner broadly compatible with liberalism. State interventions remained limited. What emerged was a regime that has been termed 'liberal collectivism' (Crouch, 1977: 155–6; see Howell, 2005: 46–7; Gallas,

2016: 60, 77). It was informed by the assumption that labour relations and class conflict could be regularized and stabilized through capital and labour resorting to negotiations and finding agreement on how to resolve critical issues. The belief in the power of collective negotiations did not just extend to wages and working conditions, but also to identifying suitable mechanisms for dispute resolution. Organized labour enjoyed protection through the existence of immunities from legal prosecution, and it was accepted by capital and the various apparatuses of the state that workers acted collectively and sometimes went on strike. While state apparatuses took a back seat, capital and organized labour took it upon themselves, to a significant degree, to organize the day-to-day operation of the labour regime.

In this context, a monist system of worker representation emerged at the economic level, which is still in place today. If the workers are represented collectively at all, shop stewards and unions negotiate on their behalf. This happens at the level of the business unit, the company or an industry. It also means that in contrast to Germany, Spain and various other countries, works councils are usually absent in Britain (Gallas and Nowak, 2012: 66; Fulton, 2021).

To ensure that worker representation also existed at the political level, trade unions set up the Labour Party – a process that commenced in the late 19th century and was completed when the party first appeared under this name in 1906 (Morton and Tate, 1956: 206–24; Pelling, 1981: 126). Today, 12 unions are still affiliated with the party, among them the three largest unions in the country – the GMB, a general union; Unite, a union active in construction, manufacturing and other branches of the private sector; and Unison, the biggest public sector union. Conversely, the Labour Party continues to portray itself as a force operating on behalf of workers or 'working people' (see Labour Party, nd). Consequently, organized labour in Britain has often been seen as a movement with an economic and a political arm, that is, a joint endeavour of the unions and the party – not least by Lenin, who referred to the newly founded Labour Party as the 'parliamentary representative of the trade unions' (2004; see also Hobsbawm, 1984: 194). And yet, and in line with a materialist understanding of party politics, the latter also acted as a force claiming to represent the 'national interest'. Accordingly, there have been strong tensions, time and again, between Labour governments and certain sections of organized labour. However, other political forces have never seriously posed a threat to the dominant position of the Labour Party in this area. The 'first-past-the-post' voting system discriminates against smaller parties because it prevents voters from 'spoiling' their ballot by voting for outsider candidates. Nevertheless, it needs to be considered that the main union confederation in the country, the Trades Union Congress (TUC), has 48 member unions, and of course, some unions remain outside the TUC. Accordingly, some significant organizations of workers in Britain operate at a distance to party politics in general or the Labour Party in particular (see Panitch, 1976: 1, 33; Gallas, 2013; 2016: 77–8, 280–8; 2018: 240–5).

Neoliberalization and the individualization of labour relations

The commitment of successive British governments from the mid-1970s onwards to neoliberalization was accompanied by a hostility to collective action by workers. The conservative governments of Margaret Thatcher (1979–90), John Major (1990–7) and David Cameron (2010–16) mobilized the state to actively weaken organized labour. They implemented trade union legislation that created obstacles for unions to go on strike legally and thus undermined liberal collectivism. The 'New Labour' governments of Tony Blair (1997–2007) and Gordon Brown (2007–10) did not outrightly attack unions and also strengthened some individual rights of workers, but they chose not to repeal any of the restrictive legislation installed by their predecessors (Gallas, 2016).

The Thatcher government in particular fought against militant trade unions. It instituted changes to trade union law, making it harder for unions to strike legally, and fortified the repressive state apparatus to make it easier for the police to crack down on striking workers and pickets. Most importantly, Thatcher decided to phase out coalmining, a state-owned industry. This decision was also motivated by the fact that the NUM acted as a spearhead of militant trade unionism in the country. The Great Strike of 1984–5, which resulted in a fierce confrontation between the government and the repressive state apparatus on one side and the NUM and its supporters on the other – and the eventual defeat of the union – was the direct consequence of this move (Cohen, 2006: 53–100; Gallas, 2016: 166–99).

The Thatcher and Major governments weakened the unions profoundly. Both union density and strike incidence fell considerably. The former had peaked at 50.7 per cent in 1979, the year when Thatcher took office, and then declined to 31.4 per cent in 1997, the year when Labour under Tony Blair won the general election and formed its first government after Thatcher and Major (see Figure 5.2); over the same period, the latter fell from 29,747,000 to 235,000 working days lost, the third lowest number on record.[2] The ferocity of the Thatcherite attack becomes clear if these numbers are compared to those from Germany and Spain: Union density dropped by only roughly two percentage points over the same period in Germany, and – after falling drastically between 1978 and 1980, in the very

---

[2] https://www.ons.gov.uk/employmentandlabourmarket/peopleinwork/employmenta ndemployeetypes/timeseries/bbfw/lms [Accessed 9 October 2022].

specific situation of *la Transición* – remained stable in Spain (see Figure 5.2; see Köhler, 2021: 7).

In the same spirit, the Cameron government enacted a trade union bill in 2016, which limited the unions' room for manoeuvre further when it came to going on strike. Most importantly, it stipulated that for a stoppage to be legal, it had to be based on a secret ballot with 50 per cent turnout, and in key public services, at least 40 per cent of potential voters had to vote 'yes' (Bogg, 2016; Dukes and Kountouris, 2016). The 'Hard Brexit' governments of Theresa May (2016–19) and Boris Johnson (2019–22) have moved the country out of the immediate reach of EU law, which potentially has dramatic repercussions for workers. Despite the existence of a non-regression clause concerning labour and social rights in the post-Brexit trade deal between Britain and the EU, the TUC has voiced worries that future governments could repeal laws protecting workers that historically derive from regulation at the European level (Strauss, 2021; Morris, 2022).

Public sector trade unionism and the politics of austerity

Union decline, novel sites of struggle and the adsorption of public sector workers

At first sight, the developments in Britain appear to back up Castells' claim. The transition to a deindustrialized, financialized economy undermined and marginalized organized labour in the country, and neither the consumer debt- and public spending-driven boom of the 'New Labour' era nor the Great Crisis led to a turnaround concerning strike incidence. Numbers of hours lost have been oscillating somewhat in recent years but have not recovered significantly since 1997 (see Figure 5.3). In addition, the decline in trade union density has continued, from 31.4 per cent in 1997 to 23.5 in 2019, even if it has levelled off in recent years (see Figure 5.2).

And yet, the actions contained in my sample show that the matter may be more complicated. There has been a significant number of extension strikes in unorganized areas of the public and the service sector involving precarious workers and workers from the gig economy, namely stoppages by outsourced support staff and cleaners at the Ministry of Justice (2016; 2019), of riders at Deliveroo (2016), of workers at McDonald's (2017; 2018) and of outsourced service and cleaning workers at four London hospitals (2016). These actions do not make up for the decline in hours lost, but they reiterate the Marxian point that capitalist relations of productions entail conflict, struggle and forms of collective agency on the side of workers – and Panitch's version of this general point: novel areas of waged work tend to produce novel forms of struggle and solidarity. Put differently, the sample shows that there are new constituencies for organized labour in Britain.

And notably, there is a development in the data on union density that goes against the Castellsian narrative. In 2020, 51.9 per cent of public sector workers belonged to a union, as opposed to 12.9 per cent in the private sector.[3] In the neoliberal era, trade unionism has been declining drastically across in both sectors – in 1979, the numbers were 81.5 and 45.6 per cent, respectively (see Table 5.2). But this does not change the fact that the public sector is still a union stronghold, and that it matters for the overall economy. In 2022, it employed 5.7 million people. This is significantly less than the 27 million people employed in the private sector, but still 17.5 per cent of all people in employment.[4] It follows that it is too simple to argue that deindustrialization leads to fragmentation and individualization across the board. It can be said that deindustrialization is weakening trade unionism because it affects strongholds of organized labour, and that it is shifting class relations of forces in favour of capital by facilitating union decline. But in defence of Panitch' claim, it needs to be considered that this does not preclude the emergence of unionism in other parts of the economy – and that it also does not rule out that non-industrial branches of the economy exist where workers continue to be organized and prepared for mobilization. The British public sector is a case in point, all the more since there have been several large-scale class-based and expansive-politicized strikes in the era of the Great Crisis (see Gallas and Nowak, 2012; Gallas, 2018).

However, there are two complications concerning the class effects of strikes in the public sector. First, public sector workers are not employed by capital but the state, which raises the question of whether labour relations in the public sector can be seen as being based on capitalist relations of production. As I have argued in Chapter 3, this is a critical problem for a class theoretical account of labour relations only at first sight. Thanks to the ecological dominance of the capitalist relations of production, there is a tendency for labour relations in the public sector to be modelled on those of the private sector. The main mechanism for this to happen is the existence of an integrated labour market where public sector entities compete with private sector firms over recruiting workers. If wages and working conditions in the public sector were significantly better than in the private sector, this would pose a threat to the supply of capital with

[3] https://www.gov.uk/government/statistics/trade-union-statistics-2020 [Accessed 9 October 2022].

[4] https://www.ons.gov.uk/employmentandlabourmarket/peopleinwork/employmentandemployeetypes/datasets/publicandprivatesectoremploymenttemp02 [Accessed 9 October 2022].

labour power, which would create a barrier to capital accumulation and, in consequence, to the tax base of the state. Consequently, there is a strong incentive for political decision-makers to keep a balance between the private and the public sector in terms of recruitment. It follows that surplus labour is extracted not just in the private, but also in the public sector. Consequently, class domination and antagonism exists in the public sector – and public sector workers are potentially involved in processes of class formation. The fact that many organic strikes in my sample have taken place in the public sector confirms that it is a site where solidarity along class lines emerges.

A second complication lies in the fact that many of public sector workers inhabit contradictory class locations. In Britain, civil servants, teachers, academics and medical doctors have been on strike in recent years – and they are highly qualified workers conducting conceptive work and enjoying a degree of autonomy. This raises the question of whether collective mobilizations in these areas contribute to working-class formation. For it to happen, there should be indications of adsorption, processes whereby workers in contradictory locations become allied with workers in consistent locations, and of configurations of struggle that facilitate adsorption. A suitable test case is the 2016 junior doctors' strike in England. The workers carrying the strike were highly qualified professionals, and the political context was the politics of austerity pursued by the Cameron government.

The politics of austerity and the reaction of organized labour

To trace the strike dynamic in the field of healthcare, it is worth looking at its context. It became clear that Britain was experiencing a deep crisis when there was a run on the mortgage bank Northern Rock in September 2007. The crisis affected the entire banking sector, and the Brown government reacted by nationalizing institutions that were struggling. This did not just concern Northern Rock, but also the Royal Bank of Scotland, Lloyds and Bradford & Bingley. All in all, the government brought half of the retail banking sector in the country under its control. Due to the economic slump and the bailouts, the GDP/public debt ratio shot up from 52.9 per cent in 2007 to 89.1 per cent in 2010.[5]

In response, the Brown government announced cuts to public expenditure. But it was David Cameron's coalition government with the Liberal Democrats, which succeeded 'New Labour' in May 2010, that embarked on an austerity agenda and used the explosion of public debt to justify it. Briefly after its formation, the new Chancellor of the Exchequer,

---

[5]   https://data.oecd.org/gga/general-government-debt.htm [Accessed 9 October 2022].

George Osborne, announced that Britain was on the 'brink of bankruptcy' (cited in Inman, 2010). He blamed the Labour governments of Tony Blair and Gordon Brown for the state of public finances. The coalition used this narrative to justify swingeing cuts to public expenditure, which reached a level unparalleled since the interwar period. Its Conservative successor governments, first led by Cameron (2015–16) and then by Theresa May (2016–19), continued the austerity strategy. While financial capital enjoyed the support of the governments, subaltern groups had to deal with reduced benefits, stripped down public services and increased service charges. An example is higher education in England, where tuition fees for undergraduate programmes trebled in 2012 from £3,225 to £9,000. Just like their predecessors in the Thatcher era, the Cameron and May governments engaged in acts of 'crisis exploitation' and orchestrated an offensive on behalf of the power bloc (Boin et al, 2008; see Gallas, 2010; 2011; 2013; 2016).

Notably, the cuts agenda translated into an all-out attack on the British public sector, which was legitimized not just with reference to the public purse but also with the need to move from state provision towards a 'big society' capable of addressing social problems with the help of the voluntary sector and charities. Public sector jobs had decreased by roughly one million between 2010 and 2016 from 6.4 to 5.5 million, and there was constant pressure on the pay and conditions of the remaining public sector workers (see Tailby, 2012: 449, 456).[6] The attacks led to a broad wave of protests carried by a movement that included unions and other civil organizations (Gallas and Nowak, 2012: 73–86). However, the protests did not derail the cuts agenda.

When the government announced that it would limit, as part of the austerity agenda, pension entitlements in the entire public sector, this created the opportunity for the unions to strike legally across its different branches. The unions made use of the opportunity and responded with a wave of organic strikes, which were not just about public sector pensions, but about the cuts agenda in general. The pensions issue initially led to three one-day strikes, which took place on 30 June 2011, 30 November 2011 and 10 May 2012, respectively. The number of participants ranged from hundreds of thousands to millions; the highest number was recorded in November. Despite the high turnout, the stoppages did not thwart the government plans, to which most of the unions agreed in the end. Significantly, however, they were political interventions from the start: the participants consistently

---

[6]   https://www.ons.gov.uk/employmentandlabourmarket/peopleinwork/employmenta
      ndemployeetypes/datasets/publicandprivatesectoremploymenttemp02 [Accessed 9
      October 2022].

talked about cuts and government attacks on the public sector (Gallas and Nowak, 2012: 80–6).

The first wave of mass strikes was followed by a second one in 2014, which was based on ballots that had taken place, in part, in 2012. Apart from pensions, this new round of stoppages was mostly about the decision of the government to freeze public sector wages. The strikes took place on 10 July and in October 2014 of the same year, and participation was roughly the same as in 2011–12. The protests culminated in a big demonstration in London that was attended, according to union officials, by approximately 90,000 people (Campbell and Johnson, 2014; Johnston, 2014). Again, the striking workers protested against the government's agenda, but they were not able to force a U-turn. There is no doubt about the political motivations behind the strikes; they amounted to public sector unions attacking the austerity agenda of the coalition. As such, the stoppages constituted organic strikes. They were the focal point of workers' protests against austerity during the crisis.[7]

On strike for the National Health Service (NHS)

The attack on public healthcare

The NHS is the largest employer in Europe and one of the largest in the world. It provides healthcare accessible to everyone considered a legal resident of Britain, which is state-funded and free at the point of access. The NHS was established in 1948 by the Labour government of Clement Attlee. Thanks to its universal character, it constituted one of the institutional pillars of the postwar settlement between labour and capital after the Second World War. At the time of the junior doctors' strike, the NHS enjoyed significant support in the population. In a YouGov poll from 2015, 74 per cent of respondents in England and 61 per cent of respondents in Wales stated that they trusted the NHS 'to provide a high quality service' either 'a great deal' or 'a fair amount' (Scully, 2015).

At this point, the Conservative governments of the Thatcherite era were criticized heavily for having neglected the NHS (Tailby, 2012: 458). In line with their free-market orientation, some of the leading representatives of Thatcherism had already flirted with replacing the NHS by a privately owned healthcare sector, but these plans never came to fruition (Gallas, 2016: 241). Against this backdrop, Cameron and his cabinet pursued what seemed at first sight like a contradictory strategy in the healthcare sector, which reflects the history of the NHS and its standing in the population. On the one hand, they shielded the NHS from the substantial spending cuts made elsewhere in the budget. On the other hand, they demanded from the

---

[7] This is also the interpretation of the five trade unionists active in Britain that I interviewed.

NHS 'efficiency savings' to the tune of £20 billion in order to meet rising 'demand'. Consequently, healthcare spending increased in absolute terms in the Cameron era, albeit at a very low level in historical comparison (Toynbee et al, 2016: 167). It also increased somewhat per capita, but fell slightly as a percentage of GDP.[8] Nevertheless, the NHS came under serious pressure and close to breaking point because the spending increases did not make up for the increasing strains caused by an ageing population (*The Lancet*, 2015). In the 2015–16 financial year, English NHS hospitals accumulated a record deficit of £2.45 billion – a number unprecedented at the time (Campbell, 2016a).

Furthermore, there have been consistent attempts to establish market mechanisms inside the NHS. In 1991, an internal market was created by setting up NHS funding bodies with a budget 'buying' services from NHS service providers, which was subsequently opened up for external, private sector providers. The 2012 Health and Social Care Act stipulated that 'any qualified provider' should deliver treatment within the NHS (Tailby, 2012: 459). As a result, the private sector has taken over an increasing share of the services that are part of the NHS. Public healthcare funds that went 'private' more than doubled in the Cameron era – from £4.1 billion or 4 per cent of the overall budget in 2009–10 to £8.7 billion and 8 per cent in 2015–16 (Campbell, 2016b). All in all, what is visible is an attempt by the Cameron governments to instigate 'privatisation by the back door' (Tailby, 2012: 460).

The response of the junior doctors

The quality of healthcare, funding issues and creeping privatization form the background to the 2016 junior doctors' strikes in England, which were the first stoppages among this group of workers in 40 years.[9] Generally, the dispute can be divided into four stages: a run–up; a stage of strike action; a stage marked by arguments over how to settle; and a stage of a renewed negotiations, which ended in an agreement. All in all, the dispute spanned six years, stretching from October 2013 until June 2019.

The *run-up* to the strike consisted in negotiations between NHS employers and the British Medical Association (BMA) – the main doctors' association in the country, an occupational union outside the TUC – over a new contract.

---

[8] https://www.ons.gov.uk/peoplepopulationandcommunity/healthandsocialcare/healthcar esystem/datasets/healthaccountsreferencetables [Accessed 9 October 2022].

[9] The dispute did not affect Northern Ireland, Scotland and Wales. There are separate healthcare bodies in the four nations constituting the United Kingdom with different labour relations. Together, they constitute the NHS.

Negotiations had started in October 2013 and broke off a year later because fundamental disagreements emerged over safeguards protecting junior doctors from working excessive hours (Rimmer, 2014). The background to the disagreements was that the health secretary was intent on introducing a full service in the NHS for seven days a week. His aim was to address the problem that the mortality of patients admitted to hospitals at the weekend was higher. There were serious doubts, however, over whether the cause of increased weekend mortality were the lower staffing levels (O'Brien, 2015a; 2015b) – and obviously, junior doctors were already working weekends.

Next to the grievances about work hours, the healthcare specialist Steve Iliffe lists, in a detailed study of the trajectory of the junior doctors' strike (Iliffe, 2017), a range of issues faced by them that caused discontent. Following him, junior doctors 'were beginning to look like members of a high-end precariat' (Iliffe, 2017: 132) due to insecurities surrounding their jobs. Their income was unstable because work hours were already variable and diverged significantly in pay according to time of the day and week; they faced increasing levels of student debt thanks to the hike in tuition fees; the cost of housing, in particular in the Southeast of England, had increased significantly; and, reflecting the budget pressures faced by the NHS, there were too many applicants for too few jobs, which increased the threat of unemployment. Added to this, junior doctors experienced a high degree of stress thanks to the organization of work, which limited contact with senior colleagues and required them to work in constantly changing teams drawn from a large pool of people. Furthermore, deeply ingrained, general doubts played a role about how the NHS had been managed by successive governments, and by Cameron and Jeremy Hunt, the Health Secretary, in particular. This created the conviction on the side of junior doctors that they had to protect the NHS against encroachments (Iliffe, 2017: 131–6).

As a result of the break-down of the talks, the government commissioned a report from the Review Body on Doctors' and Dentists' Remuneration. This was published in July 2015. Subsequently, Hunt called for new negotiations on the grounds of the recommendations, which the union rejected (Hunt, 2015; Rimmer, 2015).

The stage of *strike action* began when Hunt resorted, in August 2015, to threatening to impose a new contract based on the report (Billingsley and Gillett, 2015). Now a point of no return was reached; a phase of open conflict began. The union condemned Hunt's move on the grounds that the proposed contract did not contain financial incentives for employers to refrain from asking junior doctors to work excessive hours. It limited the times during which junior doctors were entitled to out-of-hours premiums and consequently created concerns about overwork and patient safety. Furthermore, it shifted from a system of automatic, annual pay rises reflecting increased experience to a system based on training and level of responsibility (BMA, 2015: 3–4). Andrew Collier, co-chair of the BMA's junior doctors committee, summarized the union's stance at the time: 'We urge the government not to impose a contract that is unsafe and unfair. We will resist a contract that is bad for patients, bad for junior doctors and bad for the NHS' (cited in Campbell, 2015).

Correspondingly, the BMA announced that it was going to hold a strike ballot. Furthermore, it staged demonstrations in London, Nottingham and Belfast, which took place on 17 October 2015 and were joined by tens of thousands of people. At the rally in London, Shadow Health Secretary Heidi Alexander of the Labour Party spoke, attacking Hunt for his plans, which shows that the dispute from the start was as much about the working conditions of a specific group of professionals as about the future of the NHS. It can be categorized as an expansive-politicized strike. The result of the strike ballot, which was held a few weeks later, was unanimous: 98 per cent of those casting their vote supported strike action; the turnout was approximately 76 per cent (Elgot, 2015; Sippitt, 2015).

As a result, the junior doctors held five brief strikes in January to April 2016. For the first four dates, around 40 per cent of junior doctors still turned up for work, but this reflected the fact that the strike was restricted to doctors not doing emergency services or intensive care. Only the last date was an all-out strike, and roughly 80 per cent of junior workers walked out (see Figure 7.1). Considering that this number also roughly represents the share of BMA members among junior doctors (Sippitt, 2015), one can conclude that support for the strikes among the union rank-and-file was solid. In a collection of short statements by striking junior doctors, NHS staff and patients in the *British Medical Journal* (Cassidy et al, 2016), an important theme was the conviction that the government's plan would endanger patient safety.

The BMA made it clear that this was a politically charged dispute: 'The government is threatening the future of the NHS' was the starting line of a leaflet addressed at the general public that was distributed during the days of action (BMA, 2016a). This framing seems to have reached the population, at least initially, because support for the strike was sizeable. Five YouGov polls between November 2015 and April 2016 indicated that around 50 per cent or more of respondents stated that junior doctors are 'right' to go on strike, and about 30 per cent that they are 'wrong' (Smith, 2016). Furthermore, other groups of medical professionals declared their solidarity. The presidents of 11 Royal Colleges, responsible for training specialisms in the medical profession, had already written a letter to Hunt in September 2015, in which they expressed their opposition to his plans. They saw the latter as 'a real and immediate threat to the current stated priorities of the NHS' (Khomami, 2015). In April 2016, ten presidents wrote a second letter confirming their support for the strike by stressing that it was the

Figure 7.1: Turnout for the 2016 junior doctors' strikes in England

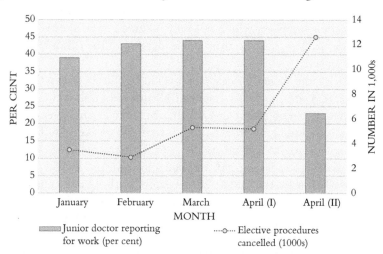

Source: NHS England, https://www.england.nhs.uk/?s=%22NHS+England+update+on+ind ustrial+action+by+junior+doctors%22 [Accessed 9 October 2022]. Months refer to the days of action on 12–13 January, 10–11 February, 9–11 March, 6–8 April and 26–27 April 2016. The figures for junior doctor reporting for work include junior doctors performing emergency services, who were exempt from strike calls on all days of action except 26–27 April. The figures for elective procedures cancelled includes inpatient and day care procedures, but not cancelled appointments.

government's task to restart negotiations through withdrawing the threat of an imposed contract (BBC, 2016a).

Importantly, there were also declarations of support from organized labour. The general secretary of the TUC, Frances O' Grady, announced that she backed the junior doctors' 'right to strike' right after the ballot and laid the blame for the conflict on the government's approach to the NHS (TUC, 2015). Similarly, the largest public sector union, Unison, and the doctors organized in Unite announced that they were behind the strike (Unison, 2015; Singer, 2015). In February 2016, Unite the Resistance, an organization linked with the Socialist Workers' Party, a small Trotskyite organization, launched a petition in support of the junior doctors, which was signed by a number of trade union leaders, among them Mark Serwotka from the Public and Commercial Services Union (PCS) (Change.org, 2016). In April, the PCS, together with the Fire Brigades Union, called for the TUC to organize a day of action in support of the junior doctors, but this did not come to fruition. According to Serwotka, the idea was met with hostility by representatives of other TUC unions (*Salford Star*, 2016). In May, BMA representatives at a meeting in London called for a joint national demonstration and strike action together with the TUC in defence of the NHS, but a BMA spokesperson refrained from endorsing the idea and suggested that it was better not to escalate the conflict (Iacobucci, 2016). Despite these tensions, the junior doctors managed to create broad support for their stoppage, which not only included important voices from the union movement, but also from the leadership of the Labour Party and the general public.

In May 2016, the stage of *negotiations* began. In talks between the BMA, NHS employers and the Department of Health held under the guidance of the Advisory, Conciliation and Arbitration Service, an agreement was found, which included a new premium system for weekend work: junior doctors' pay was to be topped up by 3 to 10 per cent if they worked more than six weekends a year (Campbell and Johnson, 2016). The offer was put to a ballot by the BMA, but rejected, with 42 per cent of votes in favour and 58 per cent of votes against. The turnout was 68 per cent (BMA, 2016b). In response, Hunt stated that he would impose the new contract from October (Campbell, 2016a), and the BMA announced that it would call for five-day, all-out strikes taking place once a month from September with the aim of thwarting the contract imposition. This led to protests from the Patient Association and an umbrella group of health and social care charities who saw these strikes as a risk to patient safety (Boseley and Weaver, 2016). In early September 2016, the BMA responded first with calling off the first strike, and then announcing that it would refrain from contesting the contract imposition through stoppages, citing safety concerns. The strike announcement was detrimental to the cause of the junior doctors because public support dropped significantly: 42 per cent of respondents to a YouGov published just after the September strike had been cancelled said they were in favour of the strikes, while 38 per cent were now opposed (Smith, 2016). Notably, many members of the rank-and-file also shared the concern for patient safety (Tapper and Campbell, 2016).[10]

A few days later, the TUC Congress 2016 passed an emergency motion in support of the BMA and the junior doctors, which underscored that there was still support from broader forces representing organized labour for strike action (NSSN, 2016; TUC, 2016). Nevertheless, the BMA decided for good, at the end of the same month, to call off the strike action and announced that it would no longer contest the imposed contract (Milne,

---

[10] A later study by David Furnivall et al (2018) showed that the strikes did indeed result in a significant decrease in admissions, outpatient appointments and A&E attendances, but that there was no increase in mortality. This in line with an earlier study of strikes of medical doctors by David Metcalfe et al (2015), which suggests that they disrupt medical procedures but have no negative effect in terms of mortality. In the case of the strike in England, consultants covered for junior doctors (Goddard, 2016), which meant that some patients received treatment from far more experienced staff.

2016; Pym, 2016). The handling of the third phase of the dispute caused anger and frustration among the rank-and-file (Campbell, 2016c).

The final stage, a phase of *new negotiations*, started with junior doctors working under the imposed contract. The BMA and the government had agreed to review it, which happened in August 2018. This brought a new round of talks and a settlement, which was put to a ballot in June 2019. Eighty-two per cent of participants voted in favour. Provisions included changes to rest periods and limits on work hours, an 8.2 per cent pay rise over four years and increased rates for night and weekend shifts. Importantly, the settlement led to recriminations with Unite, one of three largest unions in the country, which has a healthcare section with a sub-group called 'Doctors in Unite'. Representatives of Unite criticized the new agreement for not sufficiently recognizing the value of overtime and weekend work as well as offering too little in terms of pay. They lamented that only BMA members would be allowed to take part in the ballot (Unite, 2019). The critique of the deal was also echoed by the Doctors' Association UK, a professional body (Campbell, 2019).

Dilemmas of striking in the public healthcare system

The *constituency* of the junior doctors' strike initially was narrow: it consisted in a group of young healthcare professionals who were in training. But in a conjuncture characterized by a deep crisis and austerity, the junior doctors exploited a number of opportunities that sustained their strike action, and that allowed them to build a broad coalition of supporters. The air of respectability surrounding their job made it hard to portray them as mindless troublemakers, in particular since they found the support of 'reputable' professional bodies like the Royal Colleges. The publicly held worries about the future of the NHS made the general public sympathetic to their cause. And the fact that most of the unions and the Labour leadership under Jeremy Corbyn were opposed to austerity and saw a need to defend the public sector against the government made coalition building comparatively easy. Against this backdrop, the junior doctors temporarily managed to garner broad popular support for their strike, and to use it to advance a political, expansive *demand*: the protection of a free, universal healthcare system of a high standard.

But likewise, the strikers faced constraints. They managed to deal with the legal restrictions on strike action, in particular the ban on political strikes, comparably easily – in particular because strikes in the public sector are, by definition, addressed to the state, which makes it harder for legislators to distinguish 'economic' from 'political' demands. This worked despite the Under-Secretary of State for Health, Ben Gummer, claiming in March 2016 in parliament that England was 'held for ransom' by the BMA, and that 'a democratically elected Government must be able to proceed to fulfil the promises they have made to the people' (Hansard, 2016). This was echoed by an intervention from an unnamed 'government source' claiming just before the second strike in April 2016 in a conversation with the BBC that the strike leaders are 'trying to topple the government' (BBC, 2016a). These claims implied that a minority of radical workers was obstructing the decisions of a democratically elected government, neglecting the fact that the strategic selectivity of the capitalist state creates far more direct opportunities for capital to put democratically elected governments under pressure (see Hensche, 2012: 221; Pike, 2012: 255). The source employed a discursive pattern that has been used by British government for decades to delegitimize strikes (Hain, 1986: 11–16), but it did not appear to stick: According to an ORB opinion poll, public support for the strike was still high after the claim was made and the strike in late April was over (see Grice, 2016).

The more serious constraint was the effect of the strike on British society broadly understood. The junior doctors were dealing with two connected dilemmas that are characteristic of strike action in the public sector. The first one can be called the public purse dilemma. Public sector strikes tend not to hit employers in an economic sense unless they concern for-profit, state-owned corporations like Deutsche Bahn. In fact, such stoppages leave public coffers untouched because striking workers cannot expect to be paid. In other words, the state saves money when public sector workers go on strike. The pressure they put on the authorities results from the disruption they create, which gives rise to a second dilemma. This can be called the interrupted services dilemma: Public sector strikes indeed create (potentially massive) disruption, but they do so at the expense of the service users. Indeed, a split between service providers and users may emerge. A standard way to address this dilemma is to create alliances with service users and the wider public by turning them against the government. But this requires workers to be able to lay the blame for their predicament on the government and convince the public that the latter is responsible for the disruption caused by the strike (see Dörre et al, 2016: 247).

Notably, this approach is a double-edged sword. It can easily be turned against strikers. As a result, they have to be careful to show that their action is justified or unavoidable – in particular in the healthcare sector, where service users are patients who are dependent on getting treatment. There is not a lot of evidence concerning the effects of doctors' strikes on mortality, but the existing data do not back up claims that they put the lives of patients at risk. It appears that effective forms of emergency coverage exist. In fact, if senior doctors stand in for junior doctors temporarily, mortality outcomes may even improve. Nevertheless, doctors' strikes obviously have a disruptive effect on the delivery of healthcare because procedures that are not urgent are cancelled – and patients may be in pain and distress (Metcalfe et al, 2015;

see Toynbee et al, 2016: 169). There is no denying that strikes in healthcare have negative short-term effects on patients because they are denied care and treatment. As a result, it can be difficult to hold alliances behind public sector strikes together, and moods can shift depending on how they evolve.

The handling of the dispute by the BMA after the second strike in April 2016 shows this. The union was not capable of addressing the dilemmas in a manner that led to satisfactory outcomes. It first misjudged the mood among the rank-and-file when it agreed to a contract that then was rejected in a ballot; it then escalated the situation by announcing monthly five-day all-out strikes. This would have created massive disruption, but the announcement of the strike plans was enough to undermine the alliances with patients and members of the public. In other words, they were seen as a threat to patient safety. Despite the expansive demands and the ability to build a broad coalition behind the strike, its *dynamic* shifted. Initially, the strike was inclusive, but over time, divisions emerged.

Class formation in the healthcare system

The junior doctors' strikes were motivated by an economic issue, the opposition to the new contract that the government was trying to impose. But this was aligned with a political message. The strikes were directed against the government's health policy, which formed part of a bigger agenda of shrinking the public sector and cutting public expenditure. As such, it linked a narrow economic demand with the general political issues of austerity and its impact on the public infrastructure in Britain. Furthermore, it connected with the unsuccessful attempt by the public sector unions to undermine the cuts agenda by going on strike against the restructuring of pensions. Importantly, the stoppages mobilized labour as a social force, which was visible in declarations of support from other unions; it was marked by a high degree of participation from a group of workers of a significant size (approximately 55,000) (BBC, 2016b); and it turned into a general confrontation between two camps with two fundamentally different visions of British society: those in favour of a big public sector with universal services benefiting workers against those in favour of a business-friendly, free-market national economy.

Consequently, the junior doctors' interventions constituted expansive-politicized strikes and a proxy struggle that was facilitating working-class formation. It formed part of attempts by organized labour to start a defensive against the Cameronite offensive, which was orchestrated by the government on behalf of the power bloc in an act of 'crisis exploitation'. In a politically charged situation, the decision to stand up collectively for public healthcare represented a form of working-class politics. After all, free public healthcare forms part of the social wage of most workers in Britain (the exception being undocumented workers). This defensive, however, was not successful: The junior doctors did not manage to derail the restructuring plans of the Health Secretary and the implementation of a new, repressive trade union act.

Notably, in this confrontation a group of workers acted collectively that challenge the traditional perception of trade unionists. Junior doctors are professionals from the public sector with a high level of formal education and comparably well-paid jobs: wages vary greatly according to experience and level of training, but the average total annual wage at the time of the strike was £37,000 (Briggs, 2015). In a conjuncture marked by an onslaught of the power bloc on the public sector, these workers rallied round a pro-labour, anti-capital course: the defence of the NHS against cuts and privatization. Accordingly, it is justified to speak to a process of class adsorption, which was triggered by the political circumstances of the strike, and of instances of class feeling flaring up.

Despite the optimistic overtones, some qualifications are in order. The coalescence between the junior doctors and working-class forces in Britain appears to have been brittle, that is, a reflection of the conjuncture of crisis. No permanent organizational alignment between the BMA and the broader workers' movement emerged because it remains outside the TUC, the biggest British union umbrella, which underscores the contradictory class location of its members. In this respect, it is a classical occupational union. That said, there were some temporary, tentative links brought about through the political context, the attack on the public sector. The TUC leader came out in support of the strike, leading trade unionists signed a petition supporting the junior doctors, and there was the unsuccessful attempt to organize a national day of action. Labour activists and trade unionists from other branches of the economy joined demonstrations of junior doctors. But this did not result in sustained efforts for coordinated action from the side of the TUC, which is also a reflection of the fact that secondary action is banned under the dominant interpretation of the law. The fact that the BMA leadership mishandled the service provider–user dilemma in particular had divisive results, and meant that it proved difficult to sustain the coalition behind the strike.

All of this suggests that political circumstances can indeed facilitate the alignment of doctors with workers in consistent class locations. After the pensions strikes had ceased, the interventions of the junior doctors revived the idea of a worker-led popular coalition in defence of public services. This did not trigger a profound shift in the class relations of forces, but served as an inspiration (and a warning) for other trade unionists in the public sector. Jo Grady, today General Secretary of the University and College Union (UCU), discussed, on social media, the lessons from the junior doctors' strike just after her union had walked out in 2018 (Grady, 2018). Likewise, Steven Parfitt, a historian, stressed how important it had been for him and his fellow UCU strikers to reflect on the lessons of the junior doctors' strike, in the particular how the arbitration through the Advisory, Conciliation and Arbitration Service had enabled the employers to win because there was no longer a strike threat (Parfitt, 2018).

Unsurprisingly, the COVID-19 pandemic has turned out to be another instance of preparing the ground for alliances, with the BMA campaigning against unequal access to healthcare (BMA, 2021). But due to the instability of the political circumstances and the lack of institutionalized links, it is also the case that divisive strategies have been emerging. In conclusion, adsorption, in the case of the junior doctors, was a reality, but it also turned out to be a conjunctural phenomenon because it has not led to the emergence of strong, permanent links between junior doctors and other workers. In a nutshell, their strike contributed to class formation, but did so only temporarily. Put differently, it followed, on the whole, Panitch's playbook, but the jury is still out on how much of a lasting impact it had.

8

Changing Terrains: The General and Feminist General Strikes in Spain

General strikes against austerity in the Great Crisis

The general strike stands out as a form of labour unrest because of its openly visible class dimension. It calls the entire labour force across a society to stop work. By definition, stoppages only count as general strikes if they are based on cross-sectional, inclusive solidarity. Sometimes this is done exclusively for political aims, for example when people protest against an authoritarian government. But often, general strikes are organic strikes: They articulate economic and political demands and formulate a general, class-based agenda. In so doing, they usually concern the organization of work across the whole of society and create a divide between workers on one side and capital and the government on the other. Consequently, they are of particular interest when one examines working-class formation.

The Spanish state is a useful test case for examining the demands, constituencies and dynamics of general strikes. Since *la Transición*, there have been ten union-led, national, general strikes (1985, 1988, 1992, 1994, 2002, 2003, 2010, 2012 [March] and 2012 [November]); two general national strikes with mass participation led by feminist organizations (2018 and 2019); and a number of regional mobilizations.[1] In what follows, I will focus on the two most recent cycles of struggle and explore their connection: the cycle spanning the beginning of the Great Crisis and the sovereign debt crisis from

---

[1]   The two main unions in the country are the General Union of Workers of Spain (UGT) and the Workers' Commissions (CC.OO, see below). The strike in 1985 was only called by CC.OO, but not by the UGT. In contrast, the UGT, but not the CC.OO, called for a two-hour national general strike in 2003 against the Iraq War. The latter also found the support of some of the smaller unions, but its impact was limited. See Luque Balbona (2010: 203, 236).

2008 until 2014, which includes three general strikes against austerity, and the subsequent cycle encompassing the two feminist general strikes against violence against women, the precarity of women workers, the disregard for care work and the effects of austerity on the social infrastructure. I will discuss what accounts for how the terrains have changed on which these strikes have taken place, and to what extent they have contributed to class formation.

In the context of my overall line of argument, one may object that general strikes are not purely non-industrial strikes because by definition, manufacturing workers are also participating in them. But importantly, they always also mobilize workers from non-industrial branches of the economy, and their constituencies extend beyond the confines of the workplace. And in many cases, general strikes are accompanied by demonstrations, which can be joined by non-waged people – and by people whose work hours do not overlap with the timing of the strike. Indeed, they constitute a form of intervention with very broad constituencies. Even if a significant number of manufacturing workers are involved, it would be a mischaracterization to refer to them as 'industrial strikes'. In the Spanish case, workers from a range of non-industrial branches of the economy were involved – as well as people who were unemployed. This underscores that looking at the general strikes in Spain is highly useful for examining Castells' claim and Panitch's counterclaim.

The recent general strikes in Spain have a clearly defined historical context – the recession caused by the Great Crisis and the sovereign debt crisis in the Eurozone that followed on its heels. The country was badly hit, and the fundamentals of the economy turned out to be weak. Between 2008 and 2013, there was a double-dip recession, which was accompanied by the loss of a great number of jobs (Rocha, 2012; Köhler, 2021: 14–16). The unemployment rate more than tripled between 2007 and 2013 and, at the time of writing, is highest in all of the EU-15 countries (14.8 per cent) – and youth unemployment is also very high (34.8 per cent).[2] Unsurprisingly, the slump shook labour relations and the political system to the core.

The first dip was a product of the bursting of two bubbles: a 'big' bubble affecting the entire global financial system and a smaller real estate bubble (Gowan, 2009: 18). Whereas the bursting of the 'big' bubble had a profound impact on banks all over the world, the degree to which to collapse of real estate markets shook different economic zones depended on national conditions, most importantly the regulation of the mortgage market (Martin, 2011: 592–3). The Spanish state is particularly significant in this context because it is a model case of an economy heavily reliant on real estate. In the

---

[2]   The number refers to 2021. https://ec.europa.eu/eurostat/databrowser/view/UNE_RT_ A__custom_3592178/default/table?lang=en [Accessed 9 October 2022].

1990 and early 2000s, it had witnessed a significant increase in the overall number of households and a strong demand for vacation homes – the country is among the most popular tourist destinations in Europe – which was facilitated by the easy access to mortgages. The contribution of construction to overall GDP increased from 6.7 per cent in 1998 to 10.8 per cent in 2005, with annual nominal house price increases ranging from 7.7 to 18.5 per cent over the same period and an overall gain of 184 per cent between 1997 and 2007. This contributed to a massive rise of employment in the country – from 12 to 22 million people between 1993 and 2007. Correspondingly, unemployment went up significantly when the bubble burst: In construction, 41 per cent of jobs were lost between 2008 and 2012, which amounted to 1.4 million jobs in total (Bernados Domínguez, 2009: 24, 29; Alonso Pérez and Furió Blanco, 2010: 47–8, 50; Rocha, 2012: 72; Köhler, 2021: 14).

The second dip followed on from a pro-cyclical reaction by the government, at later stages in cooperation with the Troika, to the first dip (Gil Calvo, 2014: 40). Initially, political leaders assumed that Spain would be able to weather the storm comparably well (Calvo González, 2016: 69). After all, public debt was comparably low: it stood at 35.8 per cent of GDP on the eve of the crisis in 2007.[3] In summer 2008, Prime Minister José Luis Rodríguez Zapatero, who had just been re-elected, announced that 'we have to prepare ourselves for governing with austerity' (quoted in Díez, 2008), which at this stage, however, remained limited to cutting job offers in the public sector by 70 per cent and freezing the income of high-ranking officials (Segovia, 2008). Correspondingly, the government not only provided bailouts for struggling banks, but also 'pseudo-Keynesian' economic stimuli aimed at containing the slump (Calvo González, 2016: 69), which consisted in substantially raised spending and interventions to stabilize demand. They included, among other measures, investment in public infrastructure, subsidies for the car industry, a deferment of mortgage payments for unemployed people, plus increases of pensions and the minimum wage (Burnett, 2008; El País, 2008; Lifona and Sánchez, 2008). By design, these measures neither addressed the deep crisis of the global financial system nor the lopsided nature of the Spanish economy, which was heavily dependent on the construction and tourism industries. On the whole, they remained ineffective in terms of averting a slump and resulted in a significant increase in public debt (Calvo González, 2016: 79–80; Zelik, 2018: 70; Köhler, 2021: 14).

In 2009, it became clearer to the government that it was dealing with grave problems in the financial sector, and it reacted with the creation of the Fund for Orderly Banking Restructuring (Fondo de Reestructuración Ordenada Bancaria), a bailout programme for ailing institutions (Calvo González,

---

[3]   https://tinyurl.com/yperzawj [Accessed 9 October 2022].

2016: 79). A year later, public debt had gone up by almost 25 percentage points compared to 2007.[4] This increase took place against the backdrop of a sovereign debt crisis unfolding in the Eurozone. The Greek government had sought the help of the EU and the IMF in May 2010, the Irish government followed in November 2010, and there were speculations that Spain would be next. Under pressure from the Troika to change course, the Zapatero government responded by fully embracing austerity.

In reaction to this change of course, the first cycle of protest started. It pitted the trade unions and other subaltern forces against the government. This cycle consisted in a run-up – the government embracing austerity; a first, hesitant response, with the majoritarian unions calling for a general strike; a second, unstable intermittent phase, with new forms of protests in the form of the square occupations; a third phase characterized by expansive moves, which consisted (a) in the *mareas* [waves], that is, linked-up demonstrations, strikes and protests in different branches of the public sector and (b) two more general strikes, which took place in 2012; and, finally, a process of erosion from 2014 onwards, in which the resistance against austerity lost steam.[5]

Importantly, none of the dominant institutional and strategic configurations changed fundamentally in the process. This explains why a second cycle of resistance commenced from 2017 onwards, albeit in a shifted shape. The focus was now on gender relations. There were two feminist general strikes with mass support in 2018 and 2019, which formed part of a transnational wave of protests for women's rights.

The first cycle: The Eurozone crisis and resistance to austerity

Labour relations and trade unionism in the Spanish state

The trade unions took a leading role in the first cycle of struggle. Consequently, if one wants to understand how it evolved, it is necessary to have a closer look at the Spanish regime of labour relations. From this vantage point, it becomes possible to make sense of the strategic choices of organized labour in the context of crisis and austerity.

If one follows the varieties of capitalism literature, Spain is an economy of the Mediterranean type, which mixes elements of liberal and coordinated

---

[4] https://tinyurl.com/yperzawj [Accessed 9 October 2022].
[5] I depart somewhat from the periodization offered by Luque Balbona and González Begega (2016: 55; 2017: 104), which neither includes the prehistory of the protests nor highlights the important expansive moves that happened during the third phase. The latter is simply called 'plateau' [*meseta*], which suggests consolidation and not expansion.

market economies. State intervention plays a role, but its reach is somewhat limited. The regime of labour relations reflects this. On the one hand, it is characterized by corporatist mechanisms that are mediated by state apparatuses and settlements aiming to stabilize class relations. On the other hand, concertation does not always work and does not result in permanent pacification (González Begega and Luque Balbona, 2014; Köhler, 2021: 4, 12). Since the fall of the Franco regime, the country has been alternating between phases marked by large-scale disputes between organized labour on one side, and the government and capital on the other side, and less confrontational phases characterized by tripartite social pacts (González Begega and Luque Balbona, 2014; Huke and Tietje, 2014b). Strike incidence is considerably higher than in Britain and Germany (see Figure 5.3 and Table 5.3), even if it has fallen in recent years. Contributing factors are a 'liberal' understanding of the right to strike; the existence of a multiplicity of scales at which collective bargaining takes place, which creates numerous avenues for interventions of organized labour; and a fragmented union landscape inviting union competition. In other words, strikes are an oft-used instrument that unions in the Spanish state resort to when there are grievances (see Gorosarri and Sauviat, 2016: 42). Furthermore, there are effective extension mechanisms: collective bargaining agreements are automatically binding for workers and companies no matter whether they are members of organizations involved in bargaining or not (the 'erga omnes' principle). This creates incentives for 'free riding' among workers, which explains the seemingly paradoxical fact that Spain is a country where a comparably high collective bargaining coverage co-exists with a comparably low union density: In 2018, the figures were 80.1 and 13 per cent, respectively (Campos Lima and Martín Antiles, 2011: 391; Köhler, 2021: 7–12; Molina, 2021).[6]

In contrast to Germany, trade unionism in Spain is more openly political; and in contrast to Britain, the politics of trade unions are not necessarily based on a strong institutional link to social democracy. In fact, it is dominantly based on political, cross-sectoral union umbrella organizations – a model that is commonly referred to as 'class trade unionism' [*sindicalismo de clase*], and that is distinguished from free, independent or occupational unionism [*sindicalismo libre, independiente o profesional*] (Martín Valverde and García Murcia, 1998: 229–30). Politically, most of the important unions are on the left in a broad sense, but there is a wide variety of positions, among them social democracy, democratic socialism, party communism, left radicalism,

---

[6] https://stats.oecd.org/Index.aspx?DataSetCode=TUD [Accessed 9 October 2022]. The data on collective bargaining may have fallen significantly in recent years due to legal changes that concern the hierarchy of agreements at different scales (further information can be found in the next sections of this chapter). But at the time of writing, there were no newer figures available.

anarcho-syndicalism, left regionalism and nationalism, moderate pragmatism, Catholicism and, in some cases, conservatism. This contributes to a certain degree of fragmentation and weakening of organized labour. An important unifying factor is the existence of two large, left-of-centre confederations that are seen as 'class unions', and that collaborate closely:

- The General Union of Workers of Spain (Unión General de Trabajadores y Trabajadoras de España, UGT) has approximately 900,000 members. It was founded in 1888 and had strong ties, historically, with the Spanish Socialist Workers' Party (Partido Socialista Obrero Español, PSOE), the main force of social democracy in the country. The UGT was weakened significantly in the Franco era, but was revitalized during *la Transición*.
- The Workers' Commissions (Comisiones Obreras, CC.OO) are about the same size. This confederation has emerged out of rank-and-file organizations founded in the 1950s, which became the most important oppositional force against the Franco regime in 1960s. It cooperated closely with the Communist Party of Spain (Partido Comunista de España) and soon became the latter's main ally in the union landscape.

Today, both UGT and CC.OO operate at a distance to their traditional allies on the party political level, even though they still occupy a broad, left-of-centre political space between social democracy and democratic socialism (Montoya, 2012: 162–3; Huke and Tietje, 2014a: 532; 2014b: 377; Gómez, 2016; Köhler, 2021: 6).

Notably, there is a host of other organizations operating outside the two main federations. Among them are the Christian federation Workers' Trade Union (Unión Sindical Obrera, USO) with 100,000 members; two smaller formations that build on the long tradition of anarcho-syndicalism in the country, the General Confederation of Work (Confederación General del Trabajo, CGT) and the National Confederation of Work (Confederación Nacional del Trabajo, CNT); and regionalist formations like the left-Catholic union Solidarity of Basque Workers (Eusko Langileen Alkartasuna, ELA), the radical-left Nationalist Workers' Commissions (Langile Abertzaleen Batzordea, LAB), also from the Basque Country, and the Galician Unions Confederacy (Confederación Intersindical Galega, CIG). Furthermore, there is a number of professional and sectoral unions, which vary in political allegiances and size. In the education sector, for example, there is a left-wing confederation called Unions of Education Workers (Sindicatos de Trabajadores de la Enseñanza), as well as two conservative unions, the Independent and Civil Servants' Union Centre (Central Sindical Independiente y de Funcionarios, CSIF) and the National Association of Education Professionals (Asociación Nacional de Profesionales de la Enseñanza) (Gómez, 2016; Huke, 2016: 75; Köhler, 2021: 6).

Similar to Germany, worker representation at the economic level is based on two tiers: Next to the workplace committees elected by all employees in a workplace, there may also be union sections comprising all union members in a place of work if there are no less than 250 employees overall. Both entities are entitled to negotiate collective bargaining agreements or call strikes – a clear difference to the German system of co-determination. And yet – again in contrast to Germany – the workplace committees only have consultation and information rights, which means that their capacities are somewhat limited when it comes to decision-making at the level of the business unit. Since all workers may vote in the election of the workplace committees, and the union federations stand in them, the election results give an indication of popular support for different union federations that is based on a more comprehensive sample than membership statistics. They show that the two large confederations predominate and enjoy widespread (if somewhat lukewarm) support (see Table 8.1). Importantly, there is a legally enshrined principle of 'representativeness', which says that unions gain a general right to negotiate binding collective bargaining agreements, represent workers in public institutions and get access to subsidies if they gain more than 10 per cent of delegates nationally or more than 15 per cent in one of the autonomous communities (regions) of Spain, or 10 and 15 per cent in a sector. The importance of committee elections creates a 'voters trade unionism', whose dynamics of negotiation and action diverge from a British-style 'members trade unionism' (Köhler, 2021: 10; Molina, 2021).

Political and administrative procedures in Spain contain various corporatist mechanisms, which are both bipartite and tripartite. Through them, unions are involved in consultation across various scales and in numerous institutions that concern labour relations. Among them are job centres; job training programmes; universities; the Economic and Social Council, a body

Table 8.1: The 2019 workplace committee elections

Union	Per cent of total
CC.OO	35.07
UGT	32.07
USO	4.01
ELA	3.01
CIG	1.07
LAB	1.06
Others	23.71
Total	100.00

Source: Köhler (2021: 10)

tasked with consulting the government; and the Inter-confederal Service of Mediation and Arbitration (Servicio Interconfederal de Mediación y Arbitraje) (Huke and Tietje, 2014b: 378; Köhler, 2021: 11; Molina, 2021). There is a tradition of 'concertation', which refers to tripartite 'social pacts' in the areas of economic and employment policy, social welfare and healthcare. It goes back to the period of *la Transición* and has served to fortify not just representative democracy, but also capitalist class domination by facilitating temporary settlements between capital and labour (see Pérez Domínguez, 1994: 280; Martín Valverde and García Murcia, 1998: 67–8; González Begega and Luque Balbona, 2014: 85).

Importantly, the 'social pacts' were not just used to institutionalize collective bargaining, but also to promote the flexibilization of the labour market. They were an instrument for negotiating and implementing neoliberalization and the pressures imposed by European monetary integration and became part and parcel of a 'competitiveness' agenda. From the fall of the Franco regime onwards, there have been various steps towards flexibilizing the labour market – with the result of creating an economy characterized by low wages compared to other Western European countries, permanent wage stagnation and a segmented, 'dual' labour market where secure, permanent positions co-exist with precarious jobs based on fixed-term contracts (Ruiz Galacho, 2011a: 10–14; Gago, 2013: 1079–80). After the 1988 general strike, concertation showed strains, and unions increasingly resorted to militancy to make political demands. But from the mid-1990s, corporatism was revitalized to a degree. This changed again when the Great Crisis hit; at this point, the government more or less abandoned tripartite mechanisms, and the large union federations eventually responded with general strikes and new forms of militancy as means of opposing government policy. There was a last social pact over pensions in 2011, but the Conservative governments from 2012 to 2018 under the leadership of Mariano Rajoy mostly imposed their social and economic policies in a unilateral manner. With reference to the class political strategy pursued by the power bloc, one can speak of a 'generalized shift from negotiation to imposition' (Luque Balbona and González Begega, 2017: 103; see also Hamann, 2013: 125, 133–5; González Begega and Luque Balbona, 2014: 86–90, 93–4; Huke and Tietje, 2014b: 378; 2016: 1–4; Köhler, 2021: 11; Molina, 2021).

As Sergio González Begega and David Luque Balbona correctly predicted in 2014 (2014: 98), this did not signal that corporatism had come to an end. Bipartite negotiations continued to take place, and the large union confederations never renounced the idea of negotiated settlements. The formation of the Sánchez government in 2018, first a minority government of the PSOE on its own, then a minority government of the PSOE in coalition with the left-of-centre formation Unidas Podemos, has resulted in a revitalization of the idea of tripartite settlements. In July 2021, the government, the CC.OO, the UGT and the employers' associations CEOE and CEPYME signed a social pact over pensions (Riveiro, 2021; see Köhler, 2021: 22). This demonstrates that corporatist arrangements are still part of the repertoire of class politics in the Spanish context, but that their importance varies greatly depending on the conjuncture and the strategies and tactics of governments (see Hamann, 2013: 126–7; González Begega and Luque Balbona, 2014). The Spanish case illustrates Esser's general point that unions, under capitalist conditions, oscillate between exercising class power and facilitating mass integration (see Gago, 2013: 1075 and Volume 1, Chapters 3 and 7), and that shifts in the class relations of forces as well as events at the conjunctural level influence the role they play in the reproduction of capitalist class domination.

The run-up: a frontal attack by the government

The run-up to the first protest cycle began when Prime Minister Zapatero announced in January 2010 that the pension age would be raised from 65 to 67, and that there would be significant public spending cuts. In May 2010, the government published plans to decrease public expenditure by €15 billion over the next two years. Again, these measures did nothing to address the root causes of the sovereign debt crisis. But they directly affected labour relations. Among other things, they included a wage cut of 5 per cent for public sector workers – a first in the history of the Spanish state post transition – and a pensions freeze. A few weeks later, the government revealed that it would pass a law aimed at countering unemployment with labour market flexibilization. The bill amounted to facilitating competition between capitals via depressing wages and allowing working conditions to worsen. It contained provisions for reducing severance payments for businesses and made it easier for business owners to dismiss workers for economic reasons. Importantly, it also attacked existing collective bargaining agreements by allowing struggling firms to opt out from higher-level deals. In a nutshell, the bill seemed 'to be giving companies the opportunity to promote individualized industrial relations, decentralize collective bargaining and undermine the protective character of labour legislation' (Campos Lima and Martín Antiles, 2011: 399). Considering the pressure from the EU to address the crisis with austerity and further neoliberalization, one can speak of a 'transfer of sovereignty from the national to the European level' with the aim of insulating the dominant, finance-driven accumulation strategy from popular resistance (Luque Balboa and González Begega, 2016: 45; see also Cruz, 2010; *El Mundo*, 2010; Wandler, 2010; Ruiz Galacho, 2011a: 20; Hamann, 2013: 131; Jiménez Diaz, 2013: 126–7; Calvo González, 2016: 79; Zelik, 2018: 70–1; Köhler, 2021: 14–17). In a nutshell, the Zapatero government had begun to orchestrate an 'anti-worker' offensive of the

Spanish power bloc, which amounted to offloading the costs of the crisis onto workers and subaltern groups (Sanz Alcántara, 2013; see also Gago, 2012).

Notably, the large union federations struggled to find a response to this attack. They were faced with a dilemma: They had the option to defend core workforces through the existing corporate channels, that is, through negotiations, which left them at the mercy of a government that was under pressure from the Troika and intent on embarking on an austerity agenda. Or they could have sought confrontation with the government by building a mass movement against austerity, which was difficult in the light of the fact that their social base was narrow. On the eve of the crisis, 86 per cent of union members had permanent positions and only 14 per cent fixed-term contracts – despite the fact that 40 per cent of workers had precarious jobs. Indeed, the large union confederations in Spain had been struggling to organize precarious workers and had been focussing on the public sector and core workforces in manufacturing (Cortavitarte Carral, 2011: 14; Ruiz Galacho, 2011b: 29). Reaching out to new groups of workers came with the risk of not winning them over and losing ground elsewhere (see Gago, 2013: 1079–80; Köhler and Calleja Jiménez, 2014: 755–6).

When the crisis hit, the mechanisms of concertation were still in operation, and the PSOE was in power. The slump coincided with a fall in strike incidence at the firm level (Luque Balbona and González Begega, 2016: 56). This was in line with the predictions of business–cycle explanations for labour struggles, which suggest that in weak labour markets, workers are more hesitant to organize and take action because being made redundant comes at a high cost.[7] Furthermore, the decline also matched the identified organizational weaknesses – a low union density and limitations to the constituency of unions. If one also factors in the political orientation of the government and the importance of corporatist mechanisms since *la Transición*, it is unsurprising that the large union federations initially reacted to the crisis by seeking negotiations at the political level. Even after the government had announced swingeing public sector cuts and a restructuring of the labour market in favour of capital, union leaders held on to the belief that negotiated compromises were possible (Cortavitarte Carral, 2011: 14; Huke and Tietje, 2014b: 383). Again, this illustrates Esser's point that large union apparatuses oscillate between mobilizing workers and co-opting them to the status quo (see Volume 1, Chapters 3 and 7).

Accordingly, the unions reacted slowly and hesitantly to the measures announced, in a unilateral fashion, by the government, which is why I contend that at this point, they still found themselves in the run-up to the

---

[7] For a detailed debate on business cycle models (and their limitations), see Franzosi (1995: 30–55).

cycle of protest. They responded to the increase in the pension age with a demonstration, which was organized by the CC.OO and the UGT in February 2010 (Mitchell et al, 2010). In response to the cuts announced in May, the CC.OO, the UGT and the CSIF called a national public sector strike on 8 June 2010. It amounted to an act of protest against a government intervention concerning labour relations, with the majoritarian unions calling on the government to ditch the cuts and instead increase public revenue through taxing wealth and inheritances and fighting the black economy. This shows that it was an organic strike articulating economic and political *demands*, and it had a fairly broad *constituency*. According to the unions, 75 per cent of the 2.5 million public sector workers in the country participated; the government put the number at 12 per cent. And yet, these numbers are significantly lower than those for general strikes in the preceding decades (Minder, 2010; *Público*, 2010a; Luque Balbona and González Begega, 2017: 103).

Critics stated that the strike call came too late. They argued that the government had made its intentions clear months earlier, that the focus on the public sector was too narrow to pose a threat to the austerity plans, and that the unions were harbouring illusions concerning the government's willingness to compromise (Cortavitarte Carral, 2011: 13; Ruiz Galacho, 2011a: 20). Despite the limited turnout and the hesitancy betrayed by the leaderships of the main unions, the strike was an important event because it signalled the start of a new cycle of class struggle where strikes became heavily politicized (see Luque Balbona and González Begega, 2016: 56, 60). Just like in the case of the German train drivers and the junior doctors in England, they amounted to a confrontation between workers and a government guarding the interests of capital, and in this sense, they were instances of class feeling and organic strikes. The direct politicization of strikes during the Great Crisis can be seen as an expression of the need for working-class forces to operate outside party politics (see Gallas, 2018).

A hesitant response: the general strike of 2010

A few days after the public sector strike, the Zapatero government showed that it was not prepared to change course. It escalated the situation further by publishing a labour bill whose aim was to flexibilize labour relations. The bill contained provisions for making redundancies easier and less costly for capital; facilitating the creation of fixed-term, low-wage and precarious employment; allowing firms to withdraw from collective bargaining agreements in cases where their 'economic perspective' was difficult (cited in Ruiz Galacho, 2011a: 20–9); and setting up private employment agencies. In other words, the government had embarked on a thorough restructuring of labour relations that was detrimental to labour.

In reaction, the first proper phase of the protest cycle started – the majoritarian unions now responded in a more forceful manner, that is, by expanding the constituency of its interventions. They called for a general strike on 29 September, which pitted workers across the country against the government. This amounted to a *dynamic* of escalation and expansion. The key *demand* was that the government should change course and withdraw the labour law reform (*El País*, 2010). Despite the escalation, this reaction was not as strong as it could have been. The late strike date gave the government enough time to fast-track the enactment of the bill. It made sure that the latter had come into force before the day of action (Ruiz Galacho, 2011a: 20–2; 2011b: 30–1), which turned the protest into an act of ex-post, symbolic dissent.

Pronouncements of union leaders suggest that the large union federations were still hesitant to seek a confrontation with the government. They were banking on a government U-turn and new negotiations. In a radio interview, Ignacio Toxo, the general secretary of the CC.OO, stated: 'The general strike is a great cock-up [*putada*]. It's rarely the case that people applaud us for calling it. It is a declaration of the failure of social dialogue' (cited in Ruiz Galacho, 2011b: 28). Cándido Mendez, his counterpart at the UGT, said: 'After 29 September, the executive will have to repair the damage it has inflicted on the labour regulations and renounce that it will continue with its attack on the public pension system' (cited in Ruiz Galacho, 2011b: 28). The hesitancy of the large unions can be seen as a strategic miscalculation, which had demoralizing effects on workers. The Basque nationalist unions and the occupational unions representing public sector workers in the administration, the healthcare sector and education decided to refrain from supporting the strike, which narrowed its *constituency* (see Ruiz Galacho, 2011b: 31; Zelik, 2018: 71).

According to union numbers, 70 per cent of workers or 10 million workers participated in the strike (Ayuso, 2010; *El País*, 2010). Official data from the authorities are much lower – 14 per cent and 2 million participants, down from 29 per cent and 4 million during the preceding general strike in 2002 (cited in Luque Balbona and González Begega, 2017: 103). Nevertheless, there were large demonstrations with 95,000 participants in Madrid, 75,000 in Barcelona and up to 30,000 in Valencia. Notably, strike support in manufacturing, in particular the car industry, was very strong. But this does not mean that the general strike was an industrial strike. Transport workers also stopped working, which had significant effects. Only 40 per cent of flights took place, and long-distance bus travel and long-distance trains in Northern Spain were affected significantly (Ayuso, 2010; *El País*, 2010; *Público*, 2010b). The strike was aimed at mobilizing workers across the country and depended on both industrial and non-industrial workers – and it happened against the backdrop of an overall tertiarization of labour conflict, that is an increase in the strike incidence in the service and public sectors, which reflected their sizeable economic weight (Köhler and Calleja Jiménez, 2014: 753; see Lacalle, 2015: 106–7).

It follows that the strike had an expansive character. It mobilized workers across the different branches and sectors of the economy and across the entire country. In other words, it contributed to class formation insofar as it involved a large number of workers and pitted them against capital and its allies on the government benches. Nevertheless, two qualifications are in order: The large union federations struggled to reach people outside of their core constituencies, and the timing of the action was unsuited for derailing the plans of the government.

Unsurprisingly, there were no concessions from the government concerning the new labour law. It had no reasons to seek a compromise after the successful enactment of its bill. Instead, the large union federation returned to the negotiation table over the pensions issue. They agreed a social pact on the matter in early 2011 and accepted that the pension age would increase from 65 to 67, but also managed to negotiate some exemptions. Notably, the Basque unions, which had refrained from joining the strike action in September, now staged their own general strike, which directly concerned the increase (El País, 2011; Ruiz Galacho, 2011b: 33–4; González Begega and Luque Balbona, 2014: 93–4).

The failure of CC.OO and UGT to create broad unity and achieve far-reaching concessions contributed to them being perceived in a negative manner by a sizeable part of the population. Many people held the belief that the large union confederations were integrated into an objectionable political system characterized by endemic corruption, which had brought about the deep economic crisis and did not protect workers, in particular those outside the core workforces. According to opinion polls from the autumn of 2010, it was a widely held belief that the general strike had failed. This can be seen as a representational gap for working people at the national level or a 'legitimacy crisis' caused by the 'incorporation of the majoritarian unions into the state', as labour sociologists Holm-Detlev Köhler and José Pablo Calleja Jiménez put it (2014: 756; see also Gago, 2013: 1077, 1082; Hamann, 2013: 135; Huke and Tietje, 2014a: 531; 2014b: 376; Zelik, 2018: 71; Köhler, 2021: 23). In this respect, Spain is similar to many countries around the world dealing with the rejection of corporatism and the proliferation of precarious work that tends to follow on the heels of neoliberalization. The loss in credibility of Transnet in Germany, which facilitated the rise of the GDL, was also premised on the fact that the union sought close ties with the management of Deutsche Bahn and politicians intent on privatizing the railways.

The decision of the unions to cling on to negotiations with the government is understandable in the light of the strategic relevance of social pacts in the 1990s and 2000s, but it contributed to deepening divisions. It came at the price of damaging their reputation among large groups of workers. Likewise, observers speak of the demoralizing effect of the 2010 general strike (Sanz Alcántara, 2013; Zelik, 2018: 71). With the benefit of hindsight, however, the strike can be seen, as defensive and hesitant as it was, as facilitating working-class formation. It did not just mobilize workers along class lines, but also constituted the first signpost in a cycle of struggle that brought a wave of mobilizations against austerity and pitted workers against the government.

An unstable intermittent phase: 15-M

The slow reaction of the unions to the plans of the Zapatero government and their preparedness to reopen talks fuelled popular protest movements outside the existing system of labour relations. In the third phase of the cycle, networks of resistance to austerity sprung up that filled the representational gap left by the unions. On 15 May 2011, demonstrations took place in 50 Spanish cities against the politics of austerity and the politicians of the PSOE and the People's Party (Partido Popular, PP) – a nationalist and conservative force that is the other large party in the Spanish political system. In Madrid, tens of thousands of people participated – 25,000 according to the police and 60,000 according to the organizers. The motto was 'We are not a commodity in the hands of politicians and bankers'; the participants referred to themselves as 'the outraged' [indignados or indignadas]. Behind the protests was a small alliance of political groups called Real Democracy Now [Democracia Real Ya].

Notably, this protest was inspired by the Arab Spring, which had been rocking North Africa and the Middle East since 2010. Some of the protestors took to occupying city squares – a form of protest that was important in the Arab world, with the occupation of Tahrir Square in Cairo becoming a symbol for dissent (Antentas, 2015: 137; Huke, 2016: 9; Romanos, 2016: 107–9; Galdón Corbella, 2018: 8). Resistance against austerity and difficult working and living conditions was by no means an exclusively national issue, and people paid close attention to what was going on elsewhere.

In the following weeks, the emerging protest movement used the occupied squares as fora for assemblies and political discussions, which often started from the everyday experiences of those present and used an open form of debate. This approach made for a certain ideological fuzziness; the movement did not formulate a clear-cut agenda. It rejected austerity and traditional party politics and demanded a democratic reawakening from the grassroots. With this stance, the movement produced a rupture with the political settlement that had emerged with la Transición and aligned this rupture with a demand that it had inherited from the general strikes against austerity. The square occupations only lasted for a few weeks, but participants continued to hold assemblies and demonstrations and got involved in other protests (Alcaide, 2011; Antentas, 2015: 142; Huke, 2016: 8–38; Machuca, 2016; Galdón Corbella, 2018: 8).

The movement was mostly carried by what the British journalist Paul Mason called, at the time, 'graduates without a future', that is, young people with university degrees and precarious jobs or university students with dire job prospects (2013: 46; see also Martínez Iglesias, 2011: 41; Antentas, 2015: 147; Huke, 2016: 20–2; Galdón Corbella, 2018: 5). Unsurprisingly, this created a distance between the movement and the majoritarian unions, which the *indignados* and *indignadas* saw as part of the political system that needed to be rejected. Mistrust existed on both sides. Nevertheless, many trade unionists got involved in the protests in a personal capacity (Antentas, 2015: 149; Huke, 2016: 20–3; Pérez de Guzmán et al, 2016: 467–9). Consequently, 15-M, as the movement was also called with reference to its founding date, played an important role in facilitating class formation. It showed that there was an alternative to social dialogue – and that it was possible to build mass support for a platform that took a confrontational stance towards the politics of austerity of the Zapatero government (see Montoya, 2012: 159). The fact that much of the discontent concerned austerity and work paved the way for a convergence of the core workforces, represented through the unions, and precarious and unemployed workers, which emerged in subsequent months (see Pérez de Guzman et al, 2016: 467). In a nutshell, 15-M took up the main *demand* of the general strikes, the rejection of austerity, aligned it with a call for fundamental political change, and triggered an expansive *mobilizing dynamic* that shifted and somewhat broadened the *constituency* of the protests.

Expansive moves: the emergence of the mareas *and a new round of general strikes*

The convergence started with the *mareas* [waves] – protests that united public sector workers with the users of the services they offered, and workers organized in trade unions with those with a penchant for grassroots activism. They were named after different colours marking the branch of the public sector where they took place. The most important mobilizations took place in education (*marea verde* [green wave]) and healthcare (*marea blanca* [white wave]). The waves were an innovative, expansive practice of protest that addressed the representational gap and an important obstacle that strikes of workers offering public services always face – the 'interrupted services' dilemma (see Chapter 7). At the same time, their defensive character contributed to increasing the cohesion between the participating groups

Figure 8.1: Workers in public health institutions according to gender (in per cent)

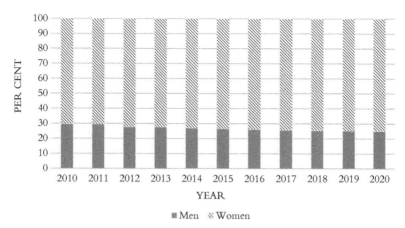

Source: Ministry of Territorial Policy (*Ministerio de Politica Territorial*), public sector of the autonomous communities (health institutions), https://tinyurl.com/4zyuvpak [Accessed 15 October 2022]. Own calculation and visualization.

because it allowed people with a range of political views to get involved (González Begega and Luque Balbona, 2014: 96–7; Köhler and Calleja Jiminez, 2014: 751–2; Helle, 2015: 239; Luque Balbona and González Begega, 2017: 105–6).

Importantly, the two main waves affected branches of the public sector with a very high and increasing share of women workers: In public healthcare, approximately three-quarters of all workers are women; in public education, the number is about 70 per cent (see Figures 8.1 and 8.2). Consequently, the fact that education and healthcare became hotspots of workers' resistance against austerity can be seen as a feminization of labour struggle, which matters because it created important preconditions for the second cycle, the feminist general strikes in 2018 and 2019.

The green wave started in Madrid in the summer of 2011 as a protest against the municipality, which demanded two extra hours of teaching in the classroom for teachers and announced that it would not renew the contracts of 3,000 teaching assistants. It attracted both trade unionists from the majoritarian and the minority unions (some of which were radical and others sectoral or occupational), as well as networks from the 15-M movement, and parents' and students' associations. The demands veered between protesting against the fact that working conditions were deteriorating, and that the students' right of access to public education needed to be defended. There were regular assemblies, some of which were held in offices of the CC.OO and the UGT, that brought people

Figure 8.2: Workers in public education according to gender (in per cent)

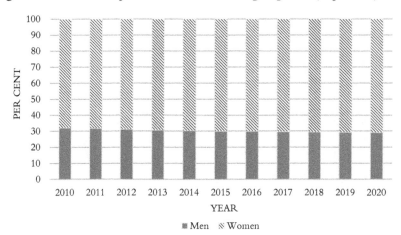

Source: Ministry of Territorial Policy (*Ministerio de Política Territorial*), public sector of the autonomous communities (non-academic teaching), https://tinyurl.com/4zyuvpak [Accessed 15 October 2022]. Own calculation and visualization.

together – as well as several days of action and strikes from September to November 2011 (Huke and Tiedje, 2014a: 536–9; Köhler and Calleja Jiménez, 2014: 751; Rogero-García et al, 2014: 569–75; Huke, 2016: 74–7). This shows that expansive tendencies followed on from the 2010 general strike, and that the first steps towards a convergence among workers had been taken.

In the general elections of November 2011, the PP obtained a 44.6 per cent share of the vote, which amounted to an absolute majority of seats in the Congress of Deputies. Mariano Rajoy became prime minister. The new government vowed to continue and deepen the politics of austerity and to restructure the labour market. It presented a bill, in February 2012, which made it easier and cheaper to lay off workers. Furthermore, it allowed firms to withdraw from existing collective bargaining agreements if the economic situation, technological change or competition required it, and to negotiate enterprise-based deals even if there were industry-wide settlements. The bill amounted to a 'direct assault on free collective bargaining' (Köhler, 2021: 17; see also Gago, 2013: 1079, 1087–90; Zelik, 2018: 80). Importantly, the Rajoy government had decided to act in unilateral manner and thus suspended the mechanisms of social dialogue (Köhler, 2021: 17). Under these circumstances, the unions had few options but to re-embrace militancy.

The CC.OO and the UGT responded by mobilizing for a nationwide day of action. On 19 February 2012, demonstrations against the government plans concerning the labour market took place in 57 cities. According to the unions, 500,000 people participated in Madrid and 450,000 in Barcelona; according to the police, the numbers were 50,000 and 30,000. Despite mass participation in the demonstrations, the government was not moved to change course when the majoritarian unions demanded negotiations. This resulted in the latter supporting a call for a general strike on 29 March that the Basque unions had issued already (Gómez, 2012; Gago, 2013: 1089; Pérez de Guzmán et al, 2016: 470; Zelik, 2018: 81). On the strike day, more people stopped work than in 2010. According to the unions, 10.4 million people participated, and 900,000 people joined a demonstration in Madrid. The authorities announced that 3.4 million people had participated, and that the participation rate had been 23.4 per cent. This was a lot higher than in 2010 (14 per cent) and closer to the number for 2002 (28.7 per cent). According to the unions, strike support was more than 95 per cent not just in manufacturing, construction and stock farming but also in transport – and still over 70 per cent in the service sector. This reiterates my earlier point that industrial workers continued to play an important role in the general strikes in Spain, but that the stoppages were not simply industrial strikes (Krakowiak, 2012; *Público*, 2012).

With the strike, the confrontation between the unions and the government over the labour market and austerity continued. Again, its *demands* were class-based, political and economic, which why it is justified to speak of an organic strike: It was directed against austerity and the restructuring of the labour market, and it mobilized subaltern forces across society against a political agenda that clearly prioritized the needs of capital. Accordingly, it had a very broad *constituency*. The Basque unions took part, and it facilitated, to a degree, the convergence between the milieus of precarious workers that had been behind 15-M and the core workforces (Krakowiak, 2012; *Público*, 2012; Gago, 2013: 1090; Luque Balbona and González Begega, 2017: 103). According to Nuria Montoya, the general secretary of the CC.OO in the Barcelona region, '[f]or the first time since long ago we have cooperated with the social movements and the neighbourhood and workplace associations in a solid and trusting manner. It appears as if a united movement has emerged with the strike – with a prospect of future cooperation' (2012: 156). The fact that grassroots protesters adopted the slogan *toma la huelga* [take the strike] – a direct reference to the slogan *toma la plaza* [take the square] of the *indignados* and *indignadas* – and demanded an 'inclusive strike' also underscores that people dissatisfied with the politics of austerity and involved with the 15-M movement veered away from their scepticism towards the modes of interventions propagated by the majoritarian unions. Now, they got involved in the general strike, most of the time by joining actions organized by smaller, radical grassroots unions. Notably, the activists of the green wave were very visible in the demonstrations accompanying the strikes because they wore green shirts (Cerrillo Vidal, 2013: 43; Rogero-García et al., 2014: 57; Antentas, 2015: 151; Pérez de Guzmán et al, 2016: 470). All of this demonstrates that the strike triggered an *expansive* dynamic – and did so much more than the stoppage in 2010, which is reflected in the stronger and broader mobilization of workers.

Nevertheless, the protestors did not manage to derail the plans of the government; the labour market bill was enacted in July 2012. Furthermore, Rajoy and his cabinet continued with the austerity agenda. Immediately after the strike day, it presented its budget for 2012, which contained swingeing cuts of €29 billion heavily affecting education, health, social services, employment support and social security. Importantly, financial support for the unions, an important pillar of concertation, was also going to be cut drastically. Rajoy and his ministers signalled, once again, their intention to replace corporatism and social pacts with unilateralism.

A few weeks after the strike, the government announced additional cuts in education, which amounted to job losses in the high five figures and an increase in class sizes by 20 per cent. In response, all the unions active in education, the CC.OO and the UGT plus smaller occupational and sectoral unions, called for a strike day on 22 May 2012 for the entire sector, including higher education. Importantly, the action still formed part of the green wave: It was supported by parents and students, and it was preceded by a students' strike and followed by demonstrations. According to the unions, 80 per cent of workers participated; the Ministry of Education put the number at 22.7 per cent. Across the country, demonstrations were held; in Madrid, 40,000 people congregated according to the newspaper *El País* and 100,000 according to the unions (*El País*, 2012a; Gago, 2013: 1091–2; Rogero-García et al, 2014: 569). Again, this can count as an organic strike because it was expansive and was clearly linked to the mobilizations against austerity.

Already in May 2011, the CC.OO and UGT had propagated the idea of coordinated strikes at the European level or even a general strike at the congress of the European Trade Union Confederation (ETUC) (Pedrina, 2012). Toxo, in his candidate speech before being elected president of the ETUC, had also emphasized the need for a 'European strike' against austerity (*El País*, 2011). In October 2012, the Portuguese union confederation, the General Confederation of Portuguese Workers (CGTP), announced that it was calling a general strike against austerity on 14 November. It did not mention the European dimension of the issue beyond general statements and did not explicitly ask other European unions to join. Nevertheless, the executive council of the ETUC took up the ball by announcing a Europe-wide day of action on the same day. In reaction, the CC.OO and UGT announced that they would follow the CGTP's lead and turn the stoppage into an 'Iberian' general strike.[8] A little later, some of the smaller, rank-and-file unions in Spain decided to join. The main *demand* in the country was for a referendum over economic policy – with a view to derailing austerity (Navarro, 2012; Pedrina, 2012; Estanque et al, 2013: 37; Gago, 2013: 1095; Dias and Fernandes, 2016: 31–2; Gorosarri and Sauviat, 2016: 51–2).

On 14 November, there was broad support for the strike across the Iberian Peninsula. In Portugal, it was supported across sectors, which meant that the number of workers participating in strikes per year shot up to the level of the mid-1990s – and turnout was particularly high in public transport. In Spain, the strike participation rate was 21 per cent – slightly lower than in March 2012, but higher than in September 2010. At the end of the strike day, there were demonstrations in the provincial capitals of Spain attended by tens of thousands of people, which also enabled people who were not organized in the unions to participate in the protest. In Madrid, there was an overnight vigil organized by a network that had emerged out of 15-M (*El País*, 2012b; Rodríguez and González, 2012; Dias and Fernandes, 2016: 34; Luque Balbona and González Begega, 2016: 57). This shows how broad the *constituency* of the strike was. There was also a three-hour stoppage in Greece and a four-hour stoppage in Italy plus strikes in Cyprus and Malta and some smaller protests in other European countries (Navarro, 2012; Pedrina, 2012; Estanque et al, 2013: 37).

Luque Balbona and González Begega (2016: 57–8) argue that the strike was distinctive for two reasons: the action was supported not just by the unions, but also by other organizations involved in the resistance against austerity, and it was a truly transnational mobilization, even if the strike calls still referred to the respective national levels (Gorosarri and Sauviat, 2016: 52). Thanks to the breadth of the mobilization, one can argue that the processes of class formation resulting from workers resisting austerity culminated in 14-N, as the Transiberian general strike came to be known in Spain.

Importantly, 14-N fortified the protest *dynamic* that had already existed insofar as it was a large-scale demonstration of discontent. After the two general strikes in 2012, the resistance against austerity decentralized again. The green wave continued and brought two more national education strikes not just involving education workers but also students and parents – on 9 May 2013 and 24 October 2013. They had a mass following, but their success, in terms of averting cuts in the education sector, was limited (*El País*, 2013; *La Vanguardia*, 2013; Rogero-García et al., 2014: 582; Huke, 2016: 78).

---

[8]   Once the strike effort had become transnational, the other large, more moderate confederation in Portugal, the General Union of Workers (União Geral de Trabalhadores), also joined – but only after some soul-searching (Dias and Fernandes, 2016: 32–3; Engelhardt, 2017: 427).

The white wave had more positive results. In 2012, the regional government of the PP in Madrid announced that it would privatize six hospitals and 27 health centres. In response, the majoritarian unions and their smaller, sectoral and occupational counterparts agreed to work together closely and across professions – an unprecedented development. The networks inspired by 15-M and the green wave also got involved, which meant that the movement enjoyed broad support from the public. There was a wave of occupations involving 20 hospitals in November 2011, as well as strikes engulfing the entire public healthcare sector in the Spanish capital on 26 and 27 November as well as 5 and 6 December. Furthermore, there was a range of other interventions: doctors went on an open-ended strike against the privatization plans for five weeks in November and December 2012, which points to processes of adsorption similar to those visible in the case of the junior doctors in Britain. Furthermore, there was juridical activism in the form of lawsuits against privatization but also street mobilizations in the form of monthly demonstrations. The expansive character of the protests is also reflected in the fact that they had an anti-racist dimension. The cutbacks in the healthcare sector meant that some groups lost their public health insurance, and this affected, in particular, undocumented migrants. Support groups emerged that protested against this effect of austerity and facilitated access to healthcare of those excluded. In January 2014, the regional government of Madrid abandoned its plan for the healthcare sector, which can be seen as a great success for the white wave and the resistance to austerity more broadly (Muriel, 2012; Gago, 2013: 1097–8; Huke, 2016: 88–90, 93–6, 100–4; Zelik, 2018: 84).

A process of erosion: the decline of mass mobilizations and the return of party politics

From 2014 onwards, there were no large-scale general strikes, and the street-level mobilizations against austerity ran out of steam (Zelik, 2018: 103). According to Luque Balbona and González Begega (2017: 104–5; see also Luque Balbona and González Begega, 2016: 55), three factors contributed to this development: the fact that the European Central Bank had relaxed its monetary policy somewhat in July 2012; the fact that the restructuring of labour relations and pensions had been completed; and the prospect of local and general elections in 2015, which raised the question of whether to institutionalize the protest against austerity at the level of the political scene. Likewise, Zelik observes that there was a widespread feeling that it was no longer possible to stop the plans of the PP government (2018: 87). With the exception of the privatization of hospitals in Madrid, the movement against austerity had neither managed to stop the cuts nor the changes to labour law.

Against this backdrop, an important shift in the party politics took place in 2014. In January, a group of intellectuals published a manifesto calling for an electoral platform representing the protest movements at the European elections in May, which proved to be a success. Under the name Podemos [we can], it gained a share of almost 8 per cent of the vote, which was surprising given that it was only a few months old and had next to no funds. In November of the same year, the founding congress of Podemos as a party took place (*Público*, 2014; Zelik, 2018: 87–110). The cycle of struggles ended with a forum shift – the foundation of a party, which amounted to the transfer of the resistance against austerity from street mobilizations to the political scene.

Class formation in the protest against austerity

On the whole, the general strikes responded to an offensive of the power bloc orchestrated by the Zapatero and Rajoy governments and were defensive in character (see Gago, 2012). They hit serious obstacles in the mobilization and organization of precarious workers and the unemployed and did not succeed in derailing austerity. Nevertheless, they demonstrate how class agency can shift under conditions of deindustrialization. Köhler and Calleja Jiménez (2014: 753; see also Luque Balbona and González Begega, 2016: 56) describe the evolution of labour relations in Spain as a 'tertiarization', turning workers in the service and public sectors into 'frequent protagonists of strikes and demonstrations'. They add that these processes compensate for the decline of industrial labour and the decreasing strike incidence in the country:

> While the frequency of strikes in absolute terms has been diminishing since decades, the contents, forms and motives of strikes are changing. The classic industrial conflict in the private sector between entrepreneurs and workers is losing relevance. ... On the other hand, strikes with political motives against unjust political measures are increasing. (Köhler and Calleja Jiménez, 214: 753)

Notably, demonstrations concerning labour issues were also on the rise (Luque Balbona and González Begega, 2017: 105).

In a nutshell, the general strikes amounted to a politicization of labour unrest. This is reflected in the political nature of their *demands* and the fact that the public sector became the primary site of protest (Sanz Alcántara, 2013: 9). In so doing, they show how strikes can extend beyond their original *constituency* and expand. Importantly – and thanks to the increasingly closer links between trade unionists and other protestors – they helped produce what in the Spanish political discourse is called a *confluencia* [confluence] of mobilizations, that is, the emergence of broad networks of solidarity that extended beyond core workforces: 'The incorporation of the unions in citizen platforms and waves has facilitated the combination of classic registers of labour protest such as the strike with other forms of protests such as the occupation of public squares' (González Begega and Luque Balbona, 2014: 96–7; see also Cortavitarte Carral, 2014: 9).

Reflecting the broad base of the protest and the fact that they left corporatist co-optation mechanisms behind, Köhler speaks of the unions being forced 'into the role of an extra-parliamentary opposition' (2021: 16). Thanks to the fact that they teamed up with grassroots activists, sociologist Josep Maria Antentas (2015: 151) refers to 'a kind of social movement unionism soaked in the spirit of 15-M' and suggests that the protests during the second and the third stage of the protest cycle enabled people to leave behind the resigned mood that characterized the first stage (2015: 155). Zelik goes as far as saying that there had been a 'mobilization of millions of people since 15 May 2011, which had blown up the political consensus and had undermined neoliberal hegemony' (2018: 83). One may argue that the unions in Spain, teaming up with grassroots networks, engaged in what is called, in the US context, 'bargaining for the common good' (McCartin, 2016; McCartin et al, 2020; 2021): They defended public goods against the encroachment of capital in the name of subaltern classes – and did so by creating broad alliances between organized labour and community-based grassroots networks. This way, they ensured that there was broad support for their demands. It follows that processes of class formation were indeed in evidence – even if they occurred against the backdrop of an offensive of the power bloc – and that deindustrialization did not stop them, but shifted the terrain on which they took place. Idar Helle captures this – and describes what I call adsorption with reference to the Spanish case:

> From the local struggle alliances that are forged against a political and economic accumulation regime in systemic crisis, there are signs of a re-composition of social class, bringing together public service workers, precarious workers, battle-hardened activists and huge parts of local civil society. Losing their jobs, losing their wages, losing their pensions, together they are fighting in the hope of a better future by defending public services and the idea of a common good. Possibly shaped by political battles and similar events described by Thompson during the industrialization era, these social groups could lose their middle-class features and appear more as a proletariat with collective self-interest in direct opposition to those of the political elites and the capitalist classes. (Helle, 2015: 240)

In other words, the expansive *dynamic* connected to the general strikes in Spain lends credence to Panitch and speaks against Castells.

The second cycle: the feminist general strikes

Class domination and struggles against patriarchy

The terrain of the mass strikes in Spain changed quite drastically after 2014. A relatively quiet period without large-scale mobilizations of the type visible in 2010 and 2012 terminated by the end of the decade; the general strike made a comeback in a novel form. In 2018 and 2019, feminist strikes took place on International Women's Day that mobilized hundreds of thousands of people across the entire country. They demanded an end to male-chauvinist violence and femicide as well as the gender pay gap, precarious work, cuts to the welfare state and the unequal care burden. In the context of this book, this raises two questions: First, to what extent is there a continuity between the general strikes against austerity and the feminist strikes, which would suggest that the two cycles in Spain are closely connected; and, second, to what extent can the feminist strikes be seen as reflecting processes of class formation?

I will address these questions in this second section of the chapter, and I will do so by charting the feminist strike wave in Spain with the help of a periodization. In the next section, I will discuss the run-up to the first push for a strike in 2017. In the section after that, I will focus on the mobilization in 2017 plus the main strikes, which took place in 2018 and 2019. In the last-but-one section, I will look at feminist activities and protests during the COVID-19 pandemic. I will end the chapter with a strategic assessment of the strikes and the prospects for interventions after the pandemic.

But before I turn to the strikes in the Spanish state, I address a theoretical issue that is of key importance to the subject matter. I have argued that stoppages of wage workers tend to facilitate class formation because they make demands concerning the conditions of the extraction of surplus labour vis-à-vis capital or governments imposing capital-friendly agendas. But does this equally apply to strikes that primarily address, in their *demands*, gender relations? How are struggles challenging patriarchal domination linked with struggles challenging class domination?

I start from two assumptions: Historically speaking, patriarchal domination has been in existence long before capitalist class domination, and it has been reproduced continuously in and through gender divisions of labour (see Hartmann, 1979: 11–14; Fraad et al, 1994: 6–7). Put differently, the capitalist mode of production emerged against the backdrop of already existing patriarchal gender relations. At the same time, I presume that it has achieved a state of ecological dominance over social formations across the globe (see Chapter 3). This suggests that under capitalist conditions, patriarchal gender relations and divisions of labour are likely to become articulated with capitalist relations of production and transformed in the process.

Marx did not discuss the articulation of class and patriarchal domination systematically. But there are two lines of reasoning that give us hints how this articulation can be conceptualized. The first line is connected to his presumption that 'capital by its nature is a leveller' (Marx, 1976: 520). Famously, Marx and Engels argued in the *Manifesto of the Communist Party* (1959: 465) that '[a]ll that is ... solid melts into air'. With this phrase, they suggested that capitalist development results in capitalist social relations marginalizing, breaking up and replacing the existing, traditional social configurations. The implication is that the days of patriarchy are numbered because it is a remnant of pre-capitalist times. This is an evolutionist claim, which is not convincing (see Volume 1, Chapter 6): It does not explain why traditional ways of life, organizations and institutions continue to exist in capitalism. For example, more than 40 countries around the world are currently monarchies – and in many parts of the globe, religious organizations keep on influencing politics. And crucially, the argument does not account for the extant presence of patriarchy in contemporary capitalism, which is visible, for example, in the gender pay gap, the ubiquity of violence against women and the existing inequalities concerning care work as well as political and cultural representation. Consequently, I contend that the evolutionist line of reasoning is of little help when one tries to make sense of how different relations of social domination are articulated in capitalism.

In defence of Marx and Engels, one can argue that it is possible to salvage the notion of capital as a leveller if it is understood in a less totalizing manner. Capital may not be a leveller to the degree that it melts everything; it may be more usefully characterized as a force that transforms all other social relations, and whose all-encompassing nature results from the ecological dominance of the capitalist mode of production and the key relevance of work for the organization of societies. Put differently, if one accepts that capital leaves certain traditional social relations (or aspects thereof) intact, it is still possible to say that it can potentially have levelling effects if barriers to capital accumulation emerge. For example, patriarchal domination can, under certain circumstances, prevent capitalists from tapping into reservoirs of female labour power if women are prevented from gaining formal qualifications needed for labour market entry or face other obstacles when they want to take up waged work, for example, cultural assumptions about what kind of activities are 'suitable' for them. Accordingly, political interventions with the aim of driving back patriarchal configurations that hold back prospective female wage labourers may find support from the side of the capital (or certain fractions thereof) from time to time.

A particularly pertinent example are traditional barriers to schooling faced by girls. Many of these barriers have been contested and removed across the globe in recent decades, albeit in an uneven manner. In the first instance, this is down to the work of activists and political decision-makers committed to gender equality. But importantly, demands for access to schooling have found the support of pro-capitalist forces, most importantly the World Economic Forum and the World Bank (see World Bank, 2021; World Economic Forum, 2022), which reflects the importance of a steady supply of educated workers for capital around the world. Today, there are reports of a 'gender gap reversal' when it comes the educational attainment of male and female students, with the latter on average outperforming the former on a global scale (Esteve et al, 2016: 616–17; Bossavie and Kannine, 2018). In the area of schooling, one can conclude that global capitalist development has indeed contributed to marginalizing patriarchal domination.

In the light of the evidence of the persistence of patriarchy in other areas, this is of course only one part of the story. There are at least three key characteristics of work in capitalist social formations – no matter whether we are talking about present-day Spain or Britain in the era of industrialization – that reflect patriarchal domination. First, there are gender biases in the recognition of qualifications, experience and performance. This leads to wage differences even if men and women are compared who carry out similar work. Second, waged work is gendered in the sense that there are dominant expectations about whether certain types of work are suited better for men or for women, and types of work carried out by more women than men often come with lower wages and worse conditions. Third, unpaid reproductive work is a condition of existence for the capitalist mode of production and its characteristic relations of production. After all, it secures the reproduction of labour power as a commodity – and this work has been, since the inception of capitalism up until today, mostly carried out by women. This work is not just an unequally shared burden in itself, but also tends to weaken the position of women in labour markets. It gives rise to patriarchal ideas such as the perception that women are less committed to waged work due to their care responsibilities, or that they are naturally inclined to prioritize care work (see Fraad et al, 1994: 6–7; Weeks, 2011: 9–10, 27; Arruzza, 2013: 89, 126–7; Buckel, 2015: 36–9; Bhattacharya, 2017a: 2–3; 2017b: 73; Arruzza et al, 2019: 20–1; Carreras García, 2020: 65).

In the light of the persistence of patriarchy in capitalism, it is worth paying heed to a second line of reasoning in Marx's works. This line is centred on the idea that the side of capital uses social difference to its advantage. It is implicit in his considerations on the production of relative surplus value in *Capital* volume one. Here, he describes how competition fosters technological development (see Volume 1, Chapter 5), and how the emergence of machinofacture creates incentives for capitalists to hire female and child labourers because work becomes less physically straining, and because their labour power is cheaper than that of their male counterparts. Accordingly, he suggests that the side of capital in 19th-century England used these pools of labour to depress wages. Eventually, all members of workers' families who had reached a certain age had to sell their labour power to ensure the survival of the family unit. But contrary to the line of argument pursued in the *Manifesto*, the facts that women workers were included in the labour market, and that the existing gender division of labour was being transformed, did not lead to patriarchal domination vanishing. The opposite is the case:

> Machinery also revolutionizes, and quite fundamentally, the agency through which the capital-relation is formally mediated, i.e. the contract between the worker and the capitalist. ... Previously the worker sold his own labour-power, which he disposed of as a free agent, formally speaking. Now he sells wife and child. He has become a slave-dealer. (Marx, 1976: 519)

This is a reference to the common law principle of 'coverture', which denied married women a legal existence independent of their husbands. Accordingly, any of their earnings were the latter's property (Lyndon Shanley, 1989: 8, 68; see also Pateman, 1988: 90–1). Following Marx, capitalists turned married, male workers into people who controlled and brokered the sale of the labour power of their wives and children. In other words, male workers became intermediaries who were forced, due their poverty, to supply capital with additional, cheaper labour power. The result of the fact that women and children entered the industrial workforce was not just that the pressure on the existing wage levels of men increased, but also that it became divided along gender lines, as Sonya O. Rose, a historian working on gender relations in England, observes:

> In the industrial period when employers hired women for a trade in which men had been working, men's jobs and wages were threatened. The struggle between women and men for jobs resulted in open expressions of antagonism between them in addition to demonstrations of hostility between workers and employers. Frequently the men went on strike or initiated other kinds of actions to preserve their jobs for men only. Whenever the men could figure out a way of maintaining or creating sex-typed jobs, they succeeded in staving off the threat posed by women. (Rose, 1992: 6)

Importantly, the legal vulnerability of married female workers is by no means exclusive to the era of industrialization or to the Anglophone world with its common law tradition. In France, married women were not allowed to take up waged work without their husband's permission until 1965 (Effose, 2021: 117); in West Germany, it took another 12 years for a restriction of this type to be lifted (Lembke, 2019: 137). And today, at least 18 countries around the globe still have similar legal regulations in place (World Bank, 2021: 22).[9]

Marx's second line of reasoning convincingly shows that capital accumulation tends to reproduce non-class relations of social domination. Indeed, the three mechanisms behind gender divisions of labour discussed above are all functional for capital accumulation in the way described: Their existence allows the side of capital to play off different groups of workers against one another, obstruct the emergence of solidarity and strengthen its control over workforces. Consequently, there are strong incentives for capitalists to use such differences against workers rather than working to eradicate them, for example by using patriarchal assumptions about women's roles as mothers to justify the existence of precarious, fixed-term and part-time positions – and then hiring women to these positions. As a result, class and non-class relations of domination, among them patriarchal relations, are closely linked in 'really existing' capitalist social formations, and processes of accumulation tend to reproduce them (see Arruzza, 2013: 126; Bhattacharya, 2017b: 87–9; Arruzza et al, 2019: 84).

All in all, the accumulation of capital has contradictory effects on patriarchal and other non-class relations of social domination. If the latter pose an obstacle to it, capitalists and political forces allied with them may actively seek to undermine them, and this may have significant effects, as the example of schooling demonstrates. But it is highly likely, due to the functionality for capital accumulation of divisions between workers, that non-class relations are used by capitalists to their advantage and thus are reproduced in the course of capitalist development. This has important class political implications. If one wants to foster working-class formation and drive back class domination, one needs to remove obstacles to unity – and divisions along the lines of non-class relations of domination are such obstacles. Consequently, the struggle against social domination in all its facets is not just a normative commitment reflecting the Marxian categorical imperative (see Volume 1, Chapter 1). It is also a strategic exigency for a successful class politics from below. In other words, it is self-defeating to suspend struggles against patriarchy, racism and other forms of social domination for the sake of class unity. If one wants to facilitate working-class formation, one needs to fight social domination in its all its forms *simultaneously*. Marx is clear on this matter when he discusses slavery in the US:

---

[9] The number is in all likelihood higher because the World Bank surveyed only 120 countries for its inquiry.

In the United States of America, every independent workers' movement was paralysed as long as slavery disfigured a part of the republic. *Labour in a white skin cannot emancipate itself where it is branded in a black skin.* However, a new life immediately arose from the death of slavery. The first fruit of the American Civil War was the eight hours' agitation, which ran from the Atlantic to the Pacific, from New England to California, with the seven-league boots of the locomotive. (Marx, 1976: 414; own emphasis)

Following Marx, neither male nor female labour will be free as long as patriarchy persists. From this vantage point, it is obvious that feminist strikes do not just concern gender relations, but also class relations – and that they have both gender and class effects.

The run-up: a transnational wave of protests

The roots of the feminist strikes extend far beyond the borders of the Spanish state. They emerged, in their current form, in the context of a global resurgence of feminism. There was a wave of protests by women against patriarchy, which started in the mid-2010s in Latin America, the US and Europe.

One of the first visible signs was the *Ni una menos* [not one less] movement against patriarchal violence and femicide in Argentina. It began with a protest on 26 March 2015 in Buenos Aires when a 19-year-old woman called Daiana García was killed. On 3 June 2015 – after the murder of 14-year-old Chiara Páez – the protests spread to all the major cities in the country. Within the space of a year, they proliferated in Latin America, with mass demonstrations in Brazil, Mexico and Peru. In October 2016, after it was reported that 16-year-old Lucía Pérez had been murdered, the Argentine branch of the movement went on to organize several national general strikes. The first was a one-hour stoppage on 19 October, which was dubbed 'Black Wednesday' by the protestors, who wore dark outfits. This strike was supported by the large independent union confederation, Central de Trabajadores de la Argentina (Argentine Central Workers' Union) (Cué and Rebossio, 2015; Centenara, 2016; Cué et al, 2016; Lorey, 2019; Varela, 2020: 136–9).

The dark clothes were a reference to a second string of important events, which had occurred in Poland in the autumn of 2016. In July, the Sejm, the Polish parliament, had accepted to discuss a petition for a total ban on abortions by a far-right organization that 500,000 people had signed. In September, the legislative process started. As a response, a protest movement emerged that was coordinated by an organization called Ogólnopolski Strajk Kobiet [All Polish Women's Strike]. Again, people sported black outfits when they demonstrated. On 'Black Monday', 3 October 2016, a general strike was called against the abortion ban. According to the police, almost 100,000 people participated; according to the organizers, there were gatherings and demonstrations in 118 cities across the country and 50 solidarity actions abroad (BBC, 2016c; Druciarek, 2016; DW, 2016; Borraz, 2017; Varela, 2020: 135–6).

A third important instance of feminist mass protest emerged in the US during the first stages of Donald Trump's presidency in 2017. On 21 January, the day after his inauguration, the Women's March took place, a worldwide protest against the new president and encroachments on human and women's rights. According to estimates by political scientists, between 3.6 and 4.6 million people participated in the US alone, which turned the march into the largest single-day protest in the history of the country (Hartocollis and Alcindor, 2017; Waddell, 2017; Varela, 2020: 142).

In Spain, the issue of violence against women led to mass mobilizations around the same time. There was a demonstration in Madrid on 7 November 2015, which was attended by tens of thousands of people. A few months earlier, on 19 May, feminist networks had already called for a feminist general strike (*Vaga de Totes*, Catalan for 'strike of all') that took place in Catalonia, the Balearic Isles and Valencia. Two thousand people demonstrated in Barcelona against the invisibility of care work and the 'feminization' of poverty (Bengoa and Serrato, 2015; Borraz and Domenech, 2015; Congostrina, 2015; García Grenzner, 2017: 7, 10).

These are just a few instances of a wave of mobilizations concerning gender relations that have been happening across the globe in recent years. What stands out are two things: First, the mobilizations were transnational in character from the start, and, second, they used a pattern of intervention associated with labour movements, the general strike, but were focusing heavily – and justifiably – on violence against women and attacks on their reproductive rights. The first point underscores the need for a globally informed perspective, the second point returns us to the questions posed at the beginning of this section – the issues of continuity and of the connection between strikes and class formation.

8M: the comeback of the mass strike

At first sight, labour issues were not at the forefront of the feminist mobilizations that took place in the mid-2010s. The one exception was the May 2015 strike in the three autonomous communities belonging to the Spanish state, which only mobilized a limited number of people. Correspondingly, it was mostly feminist networks, not unions or groups of labour activists, that led the mobilizations. Following Paula Varela, 'the epicentre' of the protests in Latin American was 'male-chauvinist violence' [*violencia machista*] (2020: 138).

Against this backdrop, my claim that there is a connection between the two cycles of protest could be called into question. But the issue of whether feminist strikes are labour strikes is fairly straightforward. From an historical vantage point, it is obvious that they are. Women's strikes originated in the 19th century in factories in Europe and the US and were about the wages and working conditions of female workers. And importantly, the 2016 strike call in Argentina was not just about femicide or violence against women. It also criticized the precarity and joblessness of female workers, the fact that most domestic work remained unpaid and the persistence of a sizeable gender pay gap (Varela, 2020: 133–5; see also Koller, 2011). Consequently, it would be plain wrong to separate feminist movements from labour movements and assume that they are 'borrowing' the strike weapon from the latter – and do so to advance a cause that is detached from labour and, by implication, class. What remains to be seen, in the remainder of this chapter, is whether, and to what extent, they facilitate class formation. In what follows, I will assess the class effects of the feminist strikes in Spain by tracing their emergence and examining their demands, constituency and mobilization dynamics.

From October 2016, the feminist mass protests had started spreading geographically, had reached Italy and then the US, and the feminist networks involved had started to create transnational networks with the aim of coordinating their actions. They now decided to mobilize across the globe for an International Women's Strike, which took place on 8 March 2017 and became a turning point: There were mobilizations on the same day on all six continents (Borraz, 2017; Varela, 2020: 143).

In Argentina, the date marked the beginning of recurring, annual general strikes that attracted mass support (*Página12*, 2018; 2019; 2020; Palomino et al, 2021). In the US, a number of public intellectuals and activists, among them Angela Davis and Nancy Fraser, had promoted the idea of a general strike on 8 March. Notably, they had issued an expansive strike call, in which they not only protested against misogyny and racism, but additionally stressed that it was necessary 'to target the ongoing neoliberal attack on social provision and labor rights', adding that there had been 'an attack on women (and all working people)' long before Trump became president. The 'Day without a Woman', as it was later called, led to demonstrations across the country, even if participation was significantly lower than in January 2017 after Trump's inauguration (Ax and Fernandez, 2017; Chira et al, 2017).

In Spain, a loose network of feminist groups issued a strike call inviting women to interrupt their everyday routines on International Women's Day, no matter whether they concerned production, reproduction or consumption. The call invited them to do so for half an hour (between 12 noon and 12.30) and to join demonstrations. Importantly, it made a link between violence against women and austerity and labour issues. It concerned both productive and reproductive work, mentioned a strike of female textile workers in the US and contained references to 'capitalism', 'exploitation' and the precarious status of women workers.

Due to the short duration of the action, one can ask to what extent it constituted a strike, that is, a collective disruption of work with the aim of advancing a cause. Nevertheless, participation across the country was significant. Demonstrations took place in 49 cities across Spain. According to the authorities, 40,000 people demonstrated in Madrid, and 7,000 in Barcelona. Unions and labour activists were involved – for example, the strike call was adopted by the CGT-A, the Andalusian branch of the anarcho-syndicalist union CGT, and the public sector union Intersindical – but they were not at the forefront of the protests overall. The majoritarian unions supported the action but did not call a strike (Álvarez and Sahuquillo, 2017; Borraz, 2017; Coordinadora Feminista, 2017; *Crónica Global*, 2017; *El País*, 2017; López, 2017; Quelart, 2017; *La Vanguardia*, 2017; Vázquez, 2017; Campillo, 2019: 253).

Even if it was in the background initially, the labour dimension of the strike pointed to deep divisions among workers along gender lines, which can be illustrated with the help of statistical data. According to a small union of civil servants called Gestha, the gender wage gap in Spain in 2020 was €4.593 or 25.5 per cent per annum on average. Furthermore, women were far more likely than men to face precarity and poverty.[10] The non-governmental organization Oxfam says in a report that roughly two-thirds of the Spanish workers belonging to the 30 per cent of the population with the lowest wages in the 2010s were women (Oxfam, 2018: 17). Likewise, the share of women in two important sectors of the economy known for widespread precarity – hospitality and care – were 55.8 and 87.9 per cent, respectively (Oxfam, 2018: 5). At the same time, women in Spain tended to do 'double shifts'. According to the National Institute of Statistics, they did, on average, 26½ hours of unpaid domestic work per week in 2015 – 12½ hours more than men.[11] Such divisions reflect vastly different working and living conditions and are obstacles to creating solidarity. Following Marx's second line of reasoning, they can be used by the side of capital to play off male and female workers against one another.

Straight after 8 March 2017, a platform called, initially, Coordinación Estatal de la Huelga Feminista [National Coordination of the Feminist Strike] and then Comisión 8 Marzo Estatal [National Commission '8 March'] was established, which connected regional and local assemblies

---

[10] https://www.gestha.es/archivos/actualidad/2022/22-02-2022AnexoVIInformeBrechaSalarial.pdf [Accessed 9 October 2022].

[11] https://tinyurl.com/bdzcykyy [Accessed 9 October 2022].

and collectives from across the country. In continuity with the 15-M movement, it was based on a bottom-up model of organization that bypassed existing political institutions as well as organizations integrated in the state. Under the slogan *¡Hacia la huelga feminista!* [Towards the feminist strike!], it began organizing, and mobilizing for, a large-scale strike on the same day a year later. An oft-used slogan in the mobilization was *Si nosotras paramos, se para el mundo* [If we go on strike, the world stops]. This was a reference to the fact that the work carried out by women is indispensable for the continued existence of the social world; that this work is not remunerated and recognized in the same way as men's work; and that it is often invisible. After all, invisibility tends to affect work that is relegated to the private sphere of the household or is carried out in sectors of the economy unjustifiably regarded as ephemeral like cleaning or retail (Comisión 8M, 2017; Álvarez, 2018a; García et al, 2018; Alabao, 2020; Montero et al, 2021).

Three national assemblies took place in preparation of the 2018 strike – one in Madrid in June 2017 (officially a local meeting, de facto a national gathering), one in Elche in September of the same year, and another one in Zaragoza in January 2018. A journalistic report on the latter described the objective of the strike as 'making visible the labour, remunerated or not, which they [women] shoulder every day' (S. Montero, 2018a). In a manifesto adopted by the participants of the Zaragoza meeting, the network did not just call for an end to male-chauvinist violence, but also condemned labour-related aspects of patriarchy – the precarity of women workers, the effects on women of processes of neoliberalization and the swingeing cuts to state expenditure imposed by the Spanish government in reaction to the sovereign debt crisis. It called for '[a] strike against the glass ceilings and labour-related precarity, because the jobs that we can access are marked by their fixed-term character, insecurity, low wages and unwanted part-time work' (Comisión 8M, 2018; see also Álvarez, 2018a). The manifesto contained a commitment to staging an expansive feminist strike on 8 March 2018, which was supposed to reach all areas of society. Accordingly, the stoppage was not just going to be a labour strike, but also a care, consumption and education strike – a strike type that is often referred to by activists and academics as a 'transversal strike' because it crosses and connects production and reproduction, brings women together across different social divides and is transnational in character (Arruzza, 2018; CNT, 2018; Navarro, 2018, cited in Ferragut, 2018; Gago, 2018: 668; Lorey, 2019). It follows that the strike was not just about contesting and resisting patriarchy, but also about attacking different forms of social domination, among them class, in their articulation (J. Montero, 2018: 23). Importantly, popular support for the idea of a strike appears to have been strong. In an opinion poll from February 2018, 88 per cent of female and 77 per cent of male respondents agreed that there were 'sufficient reasons' to call a strike (Blanco, 2018; Campillo, 2019: 255).

A separate, more detailed text published by the network in December 2017 provides some hints on how the network saw its activities in relation to class and other forms of social domination. As befits a document that reflects a discussion process between many different groups and individuals, tensions are visible. For example, it highlights the need for cross-class alliances:

> We practice an intersectional feminism because we know that we are affected by inequalities and precarities that situate us in very diverse places ..., by the differences that affect some of us in terms of provenance, *class*, age, sexual orientation, gender identity and ability. But our strike is for everyone, there is a place for each and every one of us in our feminist strike on 8 March. (Comisión 8M, 2017: 2; own emphasis)

One could interpret this passage as leaving room for an encompassing, liberal-feminist vision of bringing together women from both sides of the capital–labour divide and recognizing how diverse women are. Such a stance would create tensions with the Marxian normative commitment to be 'on the side of workers'. However, this interpretation is incompatible with other passages that openly criticize class domination and signal a commitment to class struggle. The section on the economy contains the following sentence, which does not explicitly mention class, but points to the structure-based inequalities that arise from the accumulation of capital and the need to overcome them: 'Patriarchy and capitalism with their logic of profit and of capitalist accumulation go against what we propose, give rise to sharp inequalities, relations of power and the destruction of the resources and conditions necessary for a life in dignity' (Comisión 8M, 2017: 14). In a section discussing how the strike is an intervention in anti-racist and border struggles, the document contains an explicit reference to class domination and class struggle – as part of a broader struggle articulating a range of practices of resistance against different forms of social domination: 'We practice an intersectional feminism that recognizes the differences that characterize everyone's situations, and that seeks a joint struggle against the violence of patriarchy, of racism, of *class* and of the border, but we engage in a politics with a focus on the resistance of migrants and/or racialized people' (Comisión 8M, 2017; own emphasis). These passages are paired with a commitment to deep social transformation consisting in the shift from a profit-based to a needs-based economy: 'We put live at the centre, which is why we defend lives in dignity where every person, in different parts of the world, can access the resources necessary to cover our needs – under conditions of equality and environmental sustainability.' The document ends with a call for a 'feminist revolution' (Comisión 8M, 2017). It is impossible to construe any of this as taking a pro-capitalist, liberal-feminist stance.[12]

Eventually, 300 feminist organizations backed the strike. The unions also supported it, but in different ways, which reflected divergences in their strategies as well as tensions between them and activist networks. The anarcho-syndicalist unions CNT and CGT, as well as the Intersindical and the rank-and-file union Comisiones de Base (Base Commissions), declared that people should stop work for a full 24 hours, which was in line with the strike call of the Comisión 8M and provided legal coverage for the latter. Much to the chagrin of many feminist activists, the majoritarian unions mobilized people to strike for just two hours, which was criticized by the smaller unions for causing confusion and having a demobilizing effect. The reasoning of the majoritarian unions was that a shorter strike would make it easier for precarious workers to take part who could not afford to lose a day's wage. In their view, this was a way to secure a wider social base for the strike. In any case, the fact that unions were more directly involved in the mobilization than in 2017 demonstrates that labour issues became more pronounced in the strike movement (Álvarez, 2018a; García et al, 2018: 36; J. Montero, 2018; S. Montero, 2018b; Campillo, 2019: 254; González Rodriguez, 2019).

Notably, the strike calls also found support at the party-political level. Podemos and Izquierda Unida (United Left, a federation of parties around the Communist Party of Spain that has been operating in an electoral alliance with Podemos since 2016) were fully behind the 24-hour strike, and so were the left-leaning mayors of Madrid and Barcelona, Manuela Carmena and Ada Colau. The PSOE chose to only back the two-hour stoppage. Unsurprisingly, the party-political right, represented by the centre-right Ciudadanos party and the PP, criticized the strike (Álvarez, 2018a; Campillo, 2019: 254–5). Even before the date, the strike calls had a political impact because a debate in the media and the political scene ensued about gender relations.

Reflecting the breadth of support, the strike mobilized a great number of people. There were demonstrations and assemblies in 120 cities; the majoritarian unions announced that six million people had heeded their call for a two-hour strike. Likewise, hundreds of thousands of people took to the streets, with the unions announcing that one million people had marched in Madrid, a figure which the authorities put at 170,000 people. The numbers for Barcelona

---

[12] A reaction of Patricia Reyes, an MP of the right-wing liberal party Ciudadanos [Citizens], to the manifesto confirms this interpretation. She announced that she would not support the strike due its anti-capitalist leanings and added: 'Some of us are feminists, but [we are] not communists' (cited in Álvarez, 2018a). Similarly, the party leader in Catalonia, Inés Arrimadas, stated that she was against the strike because it 'appeals to anti-capitalism' (cited in Blanco, 2018).

were 600,000 and 200,000. The high turnout exceeded the expectations of the people involved in organizing the strike; 8M was the biggest feminist mobilization in the history of the country (Gómez and Marcos, 2018; Dias, 2018; García et al, 2018: 37; J. Montero, 2018: 21; Campillo, 2019: 253–5).

Unsurprisingly, tensions similar to those described with reference to the longer document published in advance of the strike – and the increasing weight of labour activism in the movement – were also palpable for those involved. In June 2018, a national assembly of the Comisión 8M took place in Mérida, which was dedicated to evaluating the mobilization three months earlier and exploring whether there should be another strike in 2019. A participant described the discussion thus:

> Part of the activists at Mérida understood that the strike axes of care and consumption neither found as much support nor were as impactful as expected; at the same time, a labor strike is not an instrument [*repertorio*] recognizable or available to all women living in Spain. The contradictory nature of the intersections of the oppressive structures of patriarchy, capitalism and colonialism poses a strategic and symbolic challenge when it comes to building congruent and encompassing feminist political paradigms. (Dias, 2018)

Around the same time, the Rajoy government fell, and Pedro Sánchez took over – first forming a PSOE minority government, and then, from January 2020 onwards, a minority coalition with Unidas Podemos. The Comisión 8M held two more national assemblies, which took place in October 2018 in Gijón and in January 2019 in Valencia. At the Gijón meeting, the participants decided that there should be a strike on 8 March 2019 (Álvarez, 2018b; Vázquez, 2019), which was going revolve around the same 'axes' as in the preceding year – a labour strike, a care strike, a consumption strike and an education strike. In line with the 'transversal' character of the action, the motto was *Tenemos 1.000 motivos* [We have 1,000 reasons]. Again, the smaller unions and the Comisión 8M called a 24-hour strike, and the majoritarian unions a two-hour stoppage, and again, participation was similar: The CC.OO and the UGT announced that between 5.3 and 6 million people had followed their strike call, and some of the demonstrations held across the country were even bigger than in the year before. The authorities announced that there had been between 350,000 and 370,000 people demonstrating in Madrid and 200,000 in Barcelona (Comisión 8M; *El Salto*, 2019; Gómez and Aunión, 2019; Grodira, 2019).

The Madrid branch of the commission published a manifesto in 2019. Next to condemning male-chauvinist violence and patriarchal biases of the legal system, it contained a range of demands concerning work. It called for an end to the gender division of labour, which was identified as the cause of unequal pay, discrimination in the labour market, the relegation of women to precarious jobs and the expectation that they do unpaid reproductive work; an increase of the social wage through a strengthening of social and public services; and an economic order that prioritizes 'human needs', not 'capitalist profit', and is 'just, sustainable and based on solidarity' (Comisión 8M Madrid, 2019). Furthermore, it contained references to precarity and social and public services and also highlighted the need to fight 'cuts'.

This demonstrates that the feminist strikes 'inherited' demands from the general strikes in the early 2010s – but also transformed them by inserting them into a new context, which started from the presumption that there are divides between workers along gender lines, but also along the lines of other relations of social domination, for example, race and sexual orientation. Besides, the unions were actively involved in the strikes, even if the Comisión 8M played the leading role. Against this backdrop, my answer to the question I posed about the continuity between the two cycles at the beginning of the chapter is that it was significant – in terms of the pattern of intervention (a general strike) and the organizations involved (the unions). If the large presence of female workers in the strikes against austerity and the *mareas* is considered, one can argue that the *constituency* was similar. The same can be said be about the *demands*, in particular those concerning cuts and the social wage as well as the opposition to the proliferation of precarious work, and the fact that the organizers were successful in triggering an *expansive* dynamic.

Instability and crisis: mobilizing workers during the COVID-19 pandemic

The strikes in 2018 and 2019 had been successes in terms of mobilizing hundreds of thousands of people across the country and attracting significant attention from the media and the political scene. This changed somewhat in the next two years. Mass protests still happened on 8 March 2020 and 2021, but strike activity was limited.

For 2020, the commission did not reach a consensus over whether to stage a strike at all. The tensions reflected the breadth that characterized the feminist movement in Spain. Activists argued over its constituency, political strategy and aims; like in many other countries sex work and the rights of trans people were contentious issues. A spokesperson of the Madrid branch of the commission argued that the strikes had been successful in mobilizing a lot of people, but not in transporting equally its range of demands in different areas. She added that this was why the Madrid branch had decided to refrain from calling a strike but was organizing a string of actions and interventions under the heading 'feminist revolt' over the space of a whole month – from 8 February to 8 March. Again, it published a manifesto (Comisión 8M Madrid, 2020), which took up many of themes of the preceding years – the need to oppose male-chauvinist violence and the gender division of labour, to protest against neoliberalism and exploitation, and to embark on a 'radical transformation of society' towards an economy and a politics based on the 'defence of life'. Other groups took diverging positions on what to plan for; what resulted was a decentralization of protest. Unions and regional assemblies did indeed call for strikes, but this only happened in five of out the 17 autonomous communities that constitute the Spanish state, among them Catalonia (Comisión 8M Madrid, 2020; *El Confidencial*, 2020; *Europa Press*, 2020; Poyo, 2020; *Público*, 2020a; 2020b; Sanmartín, 2020).

By March 2020, COVID-19 had started to spread in Europe, which certainly impacted on how people turned out for the demonstrations on International Women's Day. Nevertheless, around 800 collective interventions took place across Spain, according to the news media. If official numbers are to be believed, 120,000 and 50,000 people took the streets in Madrid and Barcelona, respectively – fewer than in the preceding years, but still a broad mobilization. The strike in Catalonia had the support of some trade unions, namely the CGT and the left-nationalist unions Intersindical – Confederació Sindical Catalana (Catalan Union Confederation), a general union, and Intersindical Alternativa de Catalunya (Alternative Union Confederation of Catalonia), a union active in the public sector. In contrast, the majoritarian unions did not support the strike. They justified their refusal to get behind the mobilization with reference to the fact that in 2020, 8 March fell on a Sunday. Afterwards, the authorities stated that turnout for the stoppage was limited compared to other general strikes due to the date; in contrast, the CGT announced that 50 per cent of workers at Barcelona metro had heeded the strike call (Collell, 2020; Goméz and Quesada, 2020; *Público*, 2020b; *La Vanguardia*, 2020a; 2020b).

Notably, the World Health Organization announced, three days after the mobilization, that a global pandemic had started, and another three days after that, the Spanish government declared a state of emergency. In this situation, representatives of the political right, most prominently of the PP and the far-right Vox party, peddled a conspiracy myth. Without any medical evidence, they claimed that 8M, and the fact that the Sánchez government did not step in, were to blame for the fact that Spain was badly hit by the virus (González, 2020; Monforte, 2020).

Over the next year, the health crisis in the country compounded its social and economic woes, and the tensions inside the feminist movement persisted. For 2021, the latter switched to a fully decentralized form of protest, which was based on small gatherings that conformed to social distancing measures. Notably, the pandemic was reflected not just in the form of interventions, but also in the demands. 8M Madrid mobilized under the slogan *Ante la emergencia social, el feminismo es esencial* [Facing the social emergency, feminism is essential]. Its manifesto highlighted how the pandemic had compounded the already existing economic and political crisis; how capitalism was to blame for precarity, which required an anti-capitalist feminist reaction, and – in the clearest possible manner – how the current predicament was linked with the politics of austerity: 'During this year, we have seen a public health system beaten to death by neoliberalism. The cuts and austericide endanger our health and have left us at hands of the health workers, 80 percent of whom are women' (Comisión 8M Madrid, 2021). In Madrid, a ban on demonstrations – upheld by the constitutional court – came into effect, to which protestors reacted by resorting to small, symbolic acts of protest, for example, taking to their balconies across the city at the same time. Elsewhere, there were small gatherings, but no strikes (Álvarez, 2021; J. Montero et al, 2021; Polo et al, 2021).

All in all, the developments after 2019 show that the demands of the movement still had purchase, and that there was a significant degree of continuity with the strikes in the early 2010, as the reference to 'austericide' in the 2021 manifesto makes clear. At the same time, the feminist activists were faced with shifted conditions and a certain degree of instability in terms of their capacity to mobilize people. On the one hand, there was the organizational challenge of keeping together an array of different groups and individuals with partly diverging needs and demands. On the other hand, the pandemic, and the restrictions to public assembly following on its heels, constrained the room for manoeuvre of social movements across the globe.

It is an open question whether the feminist strike movement will resurface after the pandemic has ended. There are two reasons why this could be case: The magnitude of the crowds that gathered in 2019 and 2020 suggests that people still might be prepared to invest themselves in mobilizations, and the pandemic has compounded the crisis tendencies concerning care, precarious work and a weak social infrastructure that contributed to the waves of protests and strikes in the first place and has brought them into sharp relief.

Class formation in the feminist strikes

My account of the feminist strikes shows that there was continuity with the general strikes in the early 2010s in five different ways. First, the fundamental political-economic conditions were the same – the regime of austerity had not been abandoned in the late 2010s, the effects of the cuts were still widely felt, and until June 2018, the Rajoy government was still in power (see Cámara, 2019; Sales Gelabert, 2019: 87).

Second, the two strike waves also shared the same patterns of intervention. They were symbolic, one-day, political, general strikes. And they constituted a low-threshold form of political intervention that mobilized large numbers of people.

Third, 15-M served as an important stimulus for both cycles of protests. Indeed, a new generation of activists had emerged when the occupations of squares took place. Many of them first got involved in the general strikes against austerity and then in the feminist strikes. But the forms of mobilization can also be said to have been *quincemayista* in inspiration. Both protest waves were premised on the ideas that there should mass mobilizations from 'below' – and that people should make their presence felt in public spaces by turning up en masse and demanding fundamental change. The strikes and interventions were about disrupting everyday life and economic processes and bypassing the channels of representative democracy (see Cerrillo Vidal, 2013; Arruzza, 2018; Galdón Corbella, 2018; Campillo, 2019: 255–7; Montero et al, 2021).

Fourth, the networks behind the strikes consisted of similar organizations – networks of grassroots activists; the whole spectrum of unions from the majoritarian giants to the smaller rank-and-file syndicates; and left-wing political parties and organizations. The bottom-up form of mobilization also meant that important channels of feminist and class politics from 'below' were established, which were located at a distance to the procedures of corporatism and representative democracy enshrined in the Spanish state. Importantly, women had already played a crucial role in the first cycle – the *mareas* concerned areas of the public sector where the vast majority of workers were female.

And, fifth, demands overlapped to a degree in both strike waves. One of the common themes was that the protestors rejected the politics of austerity and called for an end to precarious work. In fact, they took a highly critical stance on how processes of neoliberalization had undermined the social infrastructure and argued that it was deficient and in need of expansion and transformation.

All of this demonstrates that even if the framing of the mobilizations had shifted from being protests of workers against austerity to protests of women against patriarchy, there was a lot that the strikes had in common. In a nutshell, the feminist strike movement inherited the demands of the strikes against austerity and gave them a new lease of life by shifting them to a new terrain and putting them in a new, global political context (see Arruzza, 2018; Campillo, 2019: 255–7).

This raises the issue of class formation again. One of the premises of working-class solidarity is that workers perceive themselves as having something in common with other workers – and that they have a common adversary, which is capital (as well as governments and political forces acting in favour of capital). The anti-neoliberal and anti-capitalist stance of the feminist strikes, visible in the official pronouncements of the networks behind them, demonstrates that there was indeed this common adversary.[13] The more complicated question is whether the other component of working-class solidarity – the existence of practices and ideas that create connections between workers located in different sectors and working under different conditions – was present in the strikes. What was of course in evidence was solidarity between women. But since not all women are necessarily workers in terms of their class location, and not all workers are women, the mere fact that this solidarity is in evidence does not mean, by default, that this emergence of collective agency can be seen as an instance of class formation. In other words, feminist struggles can be as ambiguous in terms of their class effects as class struggles can be in terms of their gender effects, which is why a more detailed examination of the strikes from a class-analytical angle is needed.

The question boils down to what the class horizon of the interventions was, that is, whether the effects on working-class formation of the feminist strikes in Spain can be described as absent, divisive or expansive. In line with my anti-identitarian conception of class, this is not a question about class identity or class consciousness. Rather, it is a question that refers to the emergence of collective practices that have consequences on the class relations of forces and class as a form of social domination.

The first horizon, the absence of direct class effects, concerns strikes with political aims.[14] By definition, these refrain from addressing questions of waged work and focus on other issues (see Chapter 4). In other words, the strike weapon is transferred to arenas of struggle where waged work is of secondary importance – in terms of their *demands, constituency* and *dynamic*. Recent stoppages of this type are the public sector strike in Honduras against the military coup in 2009, the general strike in Catalonia for independence in 2019 or the strikes against the Lukashenko regime in 2020 (see Chapter 3). But the feminist strikes in Spain followed a completely different pattern: Waged work figured heavily in them from the start, which rules out subsuming them under this category.

---

[13] This is not to claim that each and every striker was fully behind anti-neoliberal and anti-capitalist demands, only that the latter were loudly and clearly articulated in the manifestos and by strike leaders. As the politicians criticizing the anti-capitalist stance of the networks behind the strikes did not prevent people from turning up for the demonstrations in large numbers, it is plausible to assume that most of them did not fundamentally object to the radical messages voiced in the context of the mobilizations. Consequently, the latter need to be considered when the class effects of the strikes are gauged.

[14] I speak of 'direct class effects' because it is hard to think of practical interventions and social processes, in social formations characterized by class domination, that are completely neutral in class terms. In this context, 'directness' refers to whether the aims of a strike address the capitalist relations of production or not.

The second horizon, divisive class effects, refers to strikes based on exclusive solidarity. An action is characterized by exclusive solidarity if the *demands* are particularistic, which means that they are aimed at creating relative advantages for the workers involved and cannot be transferred easily to other contexts; the *constituency* is limited and closed because it consists of a clearly defined group of workers, which is difficult to expand; and there is little in the way of an expansive *dynamic* environment creating links to other groups of workers. In a nutshell, strikes of this type deepen divides between an in-group and other workers and – if specific advantages are won – make it harder for inter-group solidarity to emerge. As such, they are detrimental to class formation. Some commentators have suggested that the strikes of Lufthansa pilots were based on exclusive solidarity because of the simple fact that their action concerned their highly specific pension entitlements, which were fundamentally different from those of people finding themselves in working-class locations (see Chapter 4). The Spanish strikes diverged significantly from this scenario as well because they were not about relative advantages for a clearly defined, specific group of workers. They were about reducing *disadvantages* for women workers, and about opposing austerity, neoliberalism and capitalism in general.

Consequently, one also needs to consider the third horizon, expansive class effects. They are in evidence if strikes concern waged work and are based on expansive solidarity. This form of solidarity has three distinctive characteristics:

1. expandable demands, which are transferable and do not just concern particular needs and interests, but can be taken up by other groups of workers;
2. a broad and open constituency in the sense that different groups of workers come together and there are signs of class feeling and mobilizations along class lines; and
3. a mobilization dynamic where connections to other strikes and interventions emerge.

There are three types of *demands* voiced in the feminist strikes in Spain. The first type address conditions that just concern women workers, for example, the gender pay gap, but still have beneficial effects on class relations overall. Attacking the gap is about achieving equality in the labour market and the workplace with male workers, that is, about eradicating disadvantages. It is not about defending, consolidating or achieving positions of relative advantage, which would indicate the prevalence of exclusive solidarity.

This leads on to Marx's more general point about the articulation of different relations of social domination in capitalist social formations. The existence of non-class relations of social domination, among them patriarchy, tend to create obstacles for workers connecting with one another (see Arruzza, 2013: 89, 126–7; Bhattacharya, 2017b: 87–9; Arruzza et al, 2019: 84; Williams and Davis-Faulkner, 2021: 124). Differences between workers can contribute to making the accumulation of capital easier, which is why accumulation strategies often leave them intact or even deepen them. It follows that struggles aimed at eradicating disadvantages and attacking non-class relations of social domination are not, per se, divisive or an impediment to solidarity, quite the contrary. They remove obstacles to the emergence of expansive solidarity. Consequently, stoppages of women workers against disadvantages in the workplace or the labour market more generally are not just important in their own right, that is, because they contest patriarchal domination. They also make it harder for representatives of capital to play off different groups of workers against one another, which is why they create more favourable conditions for working-class formation. For solidarity among workers to expand, it is necessary that differences between them are reduced. And yet, there is a serious limitation to the first set of demands, at least from a class angle, if they are voiced in isolation: '[F]or poor and working class women, wage equality can only mean equality in misery' (Arruzza et al, 2019: 14).

This points to the second type, which concerns specific groups that include both male and female workers. The call to end precarious work falls under this category because it does not concern all people in working-class locations, but a specific group. This group contains a large number of workers across sectors, which is why, in my understanding, it is not particularistic. Similar to the point advanced with reference to the gender pay gap, driving back precarity means reducing obstacles to solidarity, which is why such struggles are crucial for class formation.

The third type concerns all workers, that is, all people who find themselves in working-class locations. The demands for strengthening the social infrastructure and ending austerity are cases in point, and the same can be said for the most radical and far-reaching demand made in the context of the feminist strikes – the call for a radical transformation of the economy, which means redirecting it from being driven by profit to being based on human need. The profit motive is based on the capitalist mode of production, in which human needs are of secondary importance because they are subsumed to money-mediated demand. Consequently, the call amounts to an anti-capitalist agenda committed to abolishing this mode of production and, by implication, capitalist class domination. The mobilization of women workers on the grounds of this call can be seen as not just producing conditions that are favourable to class formation, but as an expression of class feeling and an active contribution creating links between workers along class lines. This reveals that the strikes were organic strikes because they articulated economic and political demands that were class-relevant. They challenged the neoliberal as well as the capitalist status quo. In the words of Arruzza (2018), they contributed to 'blurring the boundaries (real and imaginary) between class struggle and feminist movement'.

Concerning the *constituency*, the strikes had to deal with the dilemma of, on the one hand, needing to highlight the specific contribution of female work for the reproduction of human life and society, and, on the other hand, of demanding an end to neoliberalism and capitalism, which obviously concerned male workers as well. This tension is captured in the 2019 manifesto. It contained the slogan *si paramos nosotras, se para el mundo* [if we strike, the world stops] – a reference to the general significance of work carried out by women and the fact that it is often hidden. But there is also a commitment to universalism: '*Tenemos una propuesta positiva para que todas y todos, desde nuestra diversidad, tengamos una vida digna*' [We have a positive proposal, which is about everyone, in our diversity, living a life in dignity]. Notably, the authors use '*todas y todos*' here, which is the female and the male form of 'all' or 'everyone' in Spanish. This reveals that the strikes had a universal character – in the sense that the striking women had the 'capacity to speak for the whole' (Arruzza, 2018; see also Arruzza et al, 2019: 14–5; Varela, 2020: 147). Combining gender-specific with general demands on how society should be organized, they were aimed at driving back all forms of social domination including class and transforming society as a whole and for everyone. This was fully in line with the Marxian categorical imperative. In other words, the strikes demonstrated the extent to which the interests of women converged with those of all workers. But for this universal project to be viable, it was also necessary to recognize difference, which is why there was a need to articulate specific demands of women with those universal demands (see Arruzza and Henwood, 2017; Arruzza et al, 2019: 83; Cámara, 2019).

The practical-organizational question of how male workers could support the stoppage was dealt with in a variety of ways, with different networks and organizations taking different views. At a most basic level, the intention behind the strike was to push men to reflect on 'what each and everyone of them can do to change a situation that they should already should have demonstrated against', as a statement published by the Comisión 8M in December 2017 put it. As for more direct forms of involvement, there were diverging positions. The commission argued that its aim was to make visible the work carried out by women – and that this would be impossible if men went on strike as well. The suggestion was for them to turn up at their workplace, but also take over the care work carried out by women to enable the latter to participate. If it was not possible to do both, the alternative was to take a day off (Vázquez, 2018; Cuéllar, 2019; *Público*, 2019). In contrast, both the majoritarian and the anarcho-syndicalist unions called women and men to go on strike. In 2018, Cristina Antoñanzas, the vice secretary general of the UGT, stated that 'we call out men and women because we see equality as a question concerning everyone' (cited in S. Montero, 2018b). Importantly, both positions – despite being diametrically opposed concerning the details – demonstrated that there was a broad and open constituency behind the strikes because they were aimed at including men in the mobilization in direct or indirect ways. This was also reflected in the fact that the commission invited men to join most of the demonstrations linked to the strike – as long as they did not march at the front and respected that there were women-only sections (see Álvarez, 2018a; Vázquez, 2018; Larriu, 2019). This demonstrates that the networks behind the strikes successfully articulated the interests of women and the interests of all workers, not just at the level of discourse, but also in terms of organizational practices.

Concerning the mobilization *dynamic*, an important point to note is the continuity with the general strikes and protests against austerity, and the strong involvement of women in the latter. Furthermore, a significant number of strikes and mobilizations have been taking place in Spain in recent years whose protagonists have been female, and that have been concerning the precarity of women workers. Noteworthy examples are a 370-day strike of carers for the elderly in Biscay in 2016–17, who won a collective agreement, increased wages and a working time reduction; Las Kellys, an organization of housekeeping staff in hotels, which has been campaigning against precarious work in the sector since 2014[15]; and a nine-day strike at the end of 2017 at a branch of fashion retailer Bershka in Galicia, in which the workers won reduced and more flexible work hours as well as higher wages (J. Montero, 2018: 23; García Grenzner, 2018: 17–8; Carreras García, 2020: 63–4). In all of these struggles, there is a clear overlap with the demands and the constituency of the feminist strikes.

All of this demonstrates that the feminist strikes followed the third scenario: they had a number of demands that were conducive to class formation; they had a fuzzy and open constituency; and they were linked to other, smaller labour disputes that resembled them in terms of their demands and constituency. It may be too early to say that they have changed gender or class relations profoundly in a material sense. They have yet to translate into an expansive government agenda addressing issues such as precarity and care work, just like the general strikes did not derail the politics of austerity. But of course, the feminist strikes waves have contributed to creating a different political environment, in which a government has formed that is supportive, at the level of rhetoric, of some of its demands. The feminist strikes have contributed to shaking the discursive supports of patriarchy and

[15] The name of the organization originates out of a pun. La Kelly is short for '*la que limpia*', which means 'she who cleans'.

neoliberalism – and considering how deeply entrenched both are, this is no mean feat. Taking up the Marxian argument about removing obstacles, the strikes can be said to have created an environment that is conducive to class formation.

It follows that the strikes promoted what could be called a feminist-socialist agenda that, similar to the mobilization for International Women's Day in the US in 2017, was deeply critical of institutionalized, liberal feminism and, in contrast to it, highlighted the need for a rupture with neoliberalism and capitalism (Martín Alcoff et al, 2018; see also Arruzza et al, 2019; Cámara, 2019). The political demands made in the strikes were aligned with economic demands to the benefit of all workers. Consequently, the strikes can be seen as organic strikes, in which class feeling and solidarity along class lines emerged. In a nutshell, they were, at the same time, struggles against patriarchy and class struggles, or an instance of *'feminist class struggle'*, as Arruzza puts it (2018; emphasis in the original; see also Varela, 2020: 135).

All in all, the feminist stoppages – and the way they inherited demands of the general strikes against austerity – demonstrate how class struggles are changing their terrain and keep on fomenting processes of class formation. Arruzza has a very optimistic assessment of what they mean: 'Far from expressing a particularism ... through women's strikes the feminist movement is increasingly placing itself as *the* international process of class formation of this phase' (2018; own emphasis).

I agree insofar as the Spanish feminist strikes are an important instance showing how struggles produce collective agency along class lines. They demonstrate that gender is a modality in which class is lived (which in no way is meant to suggest that patriarchy can be reduced to class domination or is simply an extension thereof). My only qualification is that they are not the only instance of class formation. Indeed, as I have argued in my case studies, there is a variety of struggles taking place that can be categorized this way. But the struggles in Spain show how class struggle is being revitalized in the current conjuncture, and how feminist strikes safely belong in the repertoire of worker resistance to class domination. They matter greatly because of their breadth and the sheer force of numbers of people that they have been mobilizing (see Arruzza, 2017; Arruzza et al, 2019: 9; Campillo, 2019: 253). Of course, the pandemic emerged as an obstacle to continuing with the mobilizations. But the successes of 2018 and 2019 show that feminist movements are a force to be reckoned with – and that they are of vital importance for organized labour and class struggles.

Conclusion

Sitting at my desk and composing this last section of my book, I revert to looking at images of work, this time two pictures on my wall. Up in front of me is a reproduction of a painting by Mancunian artist L.S. Lowry from the mid-20th century.[1] It depicts a football match on a bleak, grey day in what is presumably the Northwest of England. We see a goal and two teams battling it out on pitch. Two of the players, one representing each side, are jumping towards the ball, probably with the aim of heading it. They are surrounded by their respective teammates. In the foreground, there is a perimeter, and a few people watching who are positioned in front of it, mostly with their backs turned towards the observer. In the back, an industrial cityscape is visible: smoking chimneys, factory buildings and a gasometer.

In Lowry's painting, we glimpse what philosopher Bertrand Russell called, with dismissive overtones, the 'industrial civilisation' (2010). He referred to a way of life centred on industrial work and the factory, which was prevalent, in the 19th and 20th century, in many parts of Britain, Western Europe and the wider world. Lowry's imagery indicates that this civilization is characterized by strenuous, manual labour and a popular culture that celebrates comradery and confrontational physical activity (see Gramsci, 1971: 277–320; Hobsbawm, 1984: 182). And arguably, he depicts a male-dominated world. In the picture, there are only two females – a woman and a girl watching from outside the perimeter.[2]

Importantly – and as both Silver's observations and the ILO numbers presented in Chapter 3 suggest (Silver, 2003; Figure 3.1) – it would be plain wrong to presume that the industrial civilization has vanished. Indeed, there is no evidence of deindustrialization as a general trend. The share of industrial workers in the global workforce has been constant in the last three decades. Manufacturing may have declined in many of its former hubs, be

---

[1] A reproduction of the picture can be found here: https://tinyurl.com/3ekawmmx [Accessed 10 November 2023].

[2] This, of course, does not mean that the industrial civilization has existed or exists without female labour. In fact, it is heavily dependent upon it, both inside the factory and the home.

it the North of England, the 'Rust Belt' in the US or the Ruhr Valley in Germany. But it has been emerging and rising in others, for example in the Pearl River Delta in China, in the Southern hinterlands of the border between the US and Mexico, or, on a smaller scale, on the outskirts of the city of Hawassa in Ethiopia. And as Silver shows (2003), the emergence of industry also means the emergence of labour unrest.

And yet, the ILO numbers also reveal that there is a significant expansion of the service sector – and the figures on OECD countries presented in Chapter 5 suggest that the public sector continues to be highly relevant. As I have shown in this volume, both are zones of union activity and militancy. This is captured in the poster to my right, which was created, on the occasion of Mayday 2022, by Bay Area artist Christen Alqueza.[3] It shows a young-looking woman of colour standing on a green meadow with white flowers. The woman is a barista, and in keeping with the colour theme of the overall poster, she is dressed in a white shirt, a green apron and cap, black trousers and white shoes. With spread arms, she stands in front of a green wreath adorned with flowers as well as banners carrying slogans like 'production for use not for profit', 'art & enjoyment for all' and 'the cause of labor is the hope of the world'. The colouring of the picture and its content are unsurprising given that it is a poster is promoting and celebrating the unionization of workers at Starbucks, the global chain of coffeehouses.

Just like the book and the newspaper cover I discussed in the introduction, the two pictures show some similarities, but also profound differences. On the one hand they are both representations of the world of labour, and they depict the people inhabiting it in a manner that shows respect and, perhaps, affection. On the other hand, these people are captured in different ways, and the same goes for the atmosphere created. In Lowry's picture, the comradery of the football match is framed by a rather bleak cityscape, and the smoke and grey sky add to what is maybe a sense of fatalism. The scenery reminds one of the despotism of the factory regime – as well as the difficult living conditions of workers and the damage to the environment and public health that industrialization brought. Looking from this angle, the contrast to Alqueza's picture is stark. The latter is of course not just simply a work of art, but also a campaign instrument. Accordingly, the stance of the barista and the colouring convey a sense of optimism, much as is the case with the old union banners that it was inspired by. It was created at a time when there was talk of a resurgence of US labour and a number successful unionization drives among people working in cafés had taken place (Prasad Philbrick, 2022; Sainato, 2022). If Lowry depicted the

---

[3]   A reproduction of the poster can be found here (on the right-hand side): https://tinyurl. com/4yd8m89w [Accessed 10 November 2023].

industrial civilization, in its 20th century British manifestation, Alqueza portrays the 'service work civilization' in its contemporary form in the US. The latter is characterized by the fact that workers, on a day-to-day basis, have to see to the needs of their customers and clients – and the fact that many of them are non-White and female. Besides, people in many service-work settings have to put up with bad pay, harsh working conditions and precarity.

I have chosen to emphasize the differences between the two civilizations because they illustrate some of my key observations: Silver's analysis of global labour unrest is, on the whole, convincing. But the picture emerging from her work needs to be complemented. As I have demonstrated in this volume of my book, it would be plain wrong to link labour unrest exclusively with industrial work. In Chapter 4, I showed that it has been proliferating, in the conjuncture of crisis, in the service and public sectors around the globe. Indeed, there is ample evidence that collective interventions of non-industrial workers take place frequently, and that many of them are based on inclusive solidarity. They establish links along class lines and across business units as well as branches and sectors of the economy. This tends to get overlooked if one focuses on manufacturing.

A similar picture emerges if one compares the strikes waves in different Western European settings that I discussed in Part II (see Table C.1). The systems of labour relations in Britain, Germany and Spain differ significantly, with the first representing repression and individualization, the second corporatism, and the third a mixture. The same can be said about the three strikes waves examined. Each of them had specific features that set them apart – from one another, from other strike waves in the respective country and from standard presumptions about labour relations.

This latter point becomes clearer if we revisit what I have called, in Chapter 1, 'methodological Fordism'. This concept refers to a flawed process of universalization: Presumptions concerning labour and class that are derived from 20th-century Western Europe are taken as general features of capitalism. In a stylized fashion, one can describe some of these presumptions thus: Industrial workforces serve as the core constituencies of unions. Through strikes and labour disputes, a mobilizing dynamic ensues that constitutes organized labour as a collective actor at the national level. It takes the form of a union movement characterized, despite tensions, by a significant degree of unity. Thanks to its existence, industrial workforces are unified into a working class. At the same time, a division of labour emerges between unions and worker parties, with the former focusing on economic, and the latter on political issues (see Hobsbawm, 1984: 182; Gallas, 2019: 136).

The three strike waves diverge from the presumptions of methodological Fordism in one important respect each. This shows how little such

Table C.1: Strike waves in Western Europe in comparison

	Railways (Germany)	Junior doctors (England)	General strikes (Spain)
Labour relations	Corporatism	Repression and individualization	Corporatism and repression
Specific features of strike wave	Inter-union competition	Contradictory class location of workers	Openly political demands
Demands	Rupture with concession bargaining	Broad resonance	Concern with society as a whole
Constituency	Narrow but expansive	Narrow but expansive	Broad and class-based
Mobilizing dynamic	Proxy struggle (GDL, for the right to strike); mutual reinforcement (GDL and EVG)	Proxy struggle (for the NHS)	Broad, continuous struggle against austerity; struggle for removing obstacles to unity (feminist general strikes)
Class effects	→ Inclusive solidarity and working-class formation		

presumptions have to do with the real, concrete labour struggles in contemporary capitalism. Furthermore, it demonstrates that I have refrained from picking low-hanging fruit when I selected my cases, that is, from following the logic of subsumptionism. My cases concern strikes led by organizations that cannot be easily presumed to commit themselves to militancy, class struggle and working-class unity (see Chapter 1). And most importantly, it reveals how each of the strike waves has a defining feature that is specific and sets it apart from the other two.

In the case of the railway strikes in Germany, this defining feature was *inter-union competition*. Despite the fact that workers were not unified, their strikes still contributed to working-class formation: The interventions of the GDL put a stop to concession bargaining and led the EVG, the more acquiescent union, to embrace militancy. The competition between the two unions created a race to the top that improved wages and working conditions; links with other groups of workers emerged in the process.

In the British case, the defining feature was the *contradictory class location* of the junior doctors as young professionals. Thanks to the dispute, they were pushed to the forefront of the resistance against cuts to the NHS and were adsorbed to worker struggles against austerity. Despite their class location, they stood up for workers in Britain across branches and sectors.

And in Spain, what stood out about the general and feminist general strikes was that they were *outrightly political* from the start. They were directed against neoliberalism and austerity – and, during the second cycle, patriarchy. Importantly, they attacked both governments from the centre-right and the centre-left. This underscores the important political role played by organized labour in the struggles against cuts.

Next to the differences concerning the systems of labour relations and defining features, there were also communalities. This becomes clear if we focus on the demands, constituencies and dynamics of the strike waves. In none of the three cases, the *demands* were exclusively about issues pertaining to a business unit, branch or sector. They had a wider significance for, and a resonance among, workers in general. In the case of the GDL, the preparedness to make robust demands forced a rupture with concession bargaining and acquiescence. Furthermore, its interventions amounted to acts of resistance against government plans to restrict the right to strike. In the case of the BMA, the demands resonated insofar as they facilitated a broad debate on the state of the NHS as a public service and a social infrastructure available to most people in Britain. And in Spain, they concerned, from the inception, the handling of the Eurozone crisis and the way society was organized.

Similar points can be made about the *constituencies* of the strike waves. In the case of the German railways and the English hospitals, they concerned clearly defined groups of workers (railway workers and junior doctors), but links to other struggles and other groups of workers emerged in the course of the disputes. The Spanish general and feminist general strikes called upon workers in general to get involved.

And finally, an expansive *mobilizing dynamic* was in evidence in all three cases: the GDL pushed the EVG into action, and links to other strikes emerged. The GDL strikes showed that militancy can pay off and amounted to acts of resistance to restrictions to the right to strike. Similarly, the stoppages of the BMA were about defending the NHS and became linked with the broader movement against austerity. In both cases, one can speak of proxy struggles on behalf of workers in general. In Spain, the strikes were linked to protests against austerity and had political aims from the start. But even here, the dynamic was expansive because, over time, they created links between trade unionists with activists operating outside the unions. During the second cycle, the feminist character of the demands strengthened the internal cohesion of the strike and the protest movement behind it because it reduced hierarchies and divisions between workers.

The demands, constituencies and dynamics resembled one another in the three cases – and can be interpreted as showing signs of inclusive solidarity and class feeling. Following the logic of a most-different research design, the communalities in those highly different settings suggest that the three strike waves were not isolated events, but reflective of a broader trend. This observation fits with what I found at the global level: there are non-industrial strike everywhere in the world, and many of them exhibit signs of inclusive solidarity.

Consequently, I contend that it is justified to presume that there is a global trend for working-class formation outside the industrial sector. My response to the research question is that there is ample evidence for non-industrial strikes that create links between workers, and that there are numerous settings in which workers in the service and public sectors take the lead in interventions aimed to strengthen the side of labour. Strikes are still a go-to form of struggle that workers resort to when they respond collectively to capitalist class domination, no matter in which sector they are located. More prosaically, the industrial civilization is by no means capitalism's normalcy, and it coexists with a service-sector civilization that creates its own struggles.

Against this backdrop, it becomes possible to assess Castells' claim and Panitch's counterclaim. Macroregional or regional processes of deindustrialization can indeed lead to working-class partition, as Castells claimed. An obvious example is Britain in the Thatcherite era, where government interventions contributed significantly to industrial decline and the demise of organized labour (Gallas, 2016). Furthermore, a degree of fragmentation to workers' struggles is visible in the conjuncture of crisis. My case studies revealed tensions among organized workers and unions in Germany and Spain, and also the sober fact that neither the British nor the Spanish strikes managed to derail the austerity agendas of their respective governments. But what Castells did not see at the time was the rise of trade unions and labour activism in the service sector and their continued relevance in the public sector – as well as the ample evidence that working-class formation is indeed taking place in those sectors. In light of the evidence I found for class formation, I contend that Castells' claim is difficult to defend as a general observation, and that Panitch is, all in all, right.

To prevent misunderstandings, a few additional remarks are needed. If I stress the importance of non-industrial labour struggles, this should not be interpreted as an attempt to revive a teleological understanding of class formation. My point is not that capitalist development by necessity leads to the formation of a unified working class, now located in the service and public sectors. Put differently, I am not arguing that a new proletariat of non-industrial workers has emerged – at least not in the Bukharian understanding of the term, which presumes that the working class is a single collective actor on a historical mission. What I am capturing is the existence of opportunities for working-class formation outside manufacturing, and the emergence of class feeling and collective agency when these opportunities are taken. Anything else would be at odds with my Luxemburgian, conjunctural take on class formation, which I have described in Volume 1, Chapter 6.

Furthermore, it is important to stress that the division between industrial and non-industrial work, in my framework, is a heuristic, that is, an assumption used to shed light on a research problem that emerges out of existing, and in some ways problematic, academic discourses about work, class and strikes. If one wants to criticize methodological Fordism and the strong focus, in some areas of critical political economy and labour studies, on industrial work, one needs to test claims that rest on the division – and this also means operating with it for research purposes.

When I discuss industrial and non-industrial work, I do not attach strong ontological claims to the distinction, which would suggest that there are two (or more) clearly delimited, separate spheres in the world of work (see Piketty, 2014: 90). I contend that there are indeed some differences, for example, the fact that many service workers encounter clients in their work on a day-to-day basis. But there is also an important communality: Work in the industrial, service and public sectors in capitalist social formations rests on the capitalist relations of production, which give rise to specific forms of exploitation, despotism, alienation – and conflict between labour and capital. Besides, industrial and non-industrial work are linked in processes of production and service provision – and the workers involved encounter one another, interact and collaborate. It follows that class formation bridges the existing divides between industrial and non-industrial work all the time. The general and feminist general strikes in Spain are testament to this: They successfully mobilized workers across sectors and, in so doing, gained strength.

The analytical and political relevance of this point cannot be stressed enough. It would be wrong to replace methodological Fordism with a position that entirely disregards struggles around industrial work. This is not just because industrial work retains its economic weight globally, and because it still exists and matters in many of the economic zones experiencing processes of deindustrialization. It is also politically important. An over-emphasis on non-industrial work in zones of deindustrialization could have the consequence of further marginalizing the remaining industrial or post-industrial milieus of workers and adding insult to injury. It could add to existing barriers for expansive solidarity and obstruct working-class formation. And this would work against my Bourdieuan intention, stated in the Preface to Volume 1, of contributing to working-class formation by making it visible. Therefore, I emphasize that the division has served me as a heuristic, and that it only has strategic relevance insofar as it suggests that non-industrial workers are important for organized labour – from which it follows by no means that industrial workers do not matter. This is all the more relevant in light of attempts by right-wing political forces across North America and Western Europe to rally a mysterious 'White working class', often presumed to be located in manufacturing, behind their agendas. As it always has been the case, trade unionists and labour activists face the challenge of bringing workers together for the cause of labour – and do so across divisions. Of course, this involves overcoming divides between industrial and non-industrial workers.

In the Preface I also stated that it was my intention to search for the working class in contemporary capitalism. What I found was working classes, in the plural, around the globe that were in formation. These classes emerge and transform themselves through collective actions by workers that trigger expansive mobilizations. Working class formation is in evidence in public sector strikes in South Africa and teachers' strikes in the US; in the strikes of Amazon workers in Europe and North America; in general strikes and feminist general strikes in Western Europe and South America; and in the strikes of healthcare workers that take place in various places – my database contains stoppages in Barbados, Britain, Costa Rica, Denmark, France, Germany, Greece, India, Kenya, South Africa, Spain, the US and Zimbabwe.

Interestingly, there is a lot of talk about labour shortages in recent days. This is not just visible in North America and Western Europe, but also China and numerous other countries (see Causa et al, 2021; Wildcat, 2021). If the demographic trends detected gain weight, this problem will continue to act as a barrier to capital accumulation in many parts of the world and will, in all likelihood, alter the conditions of struggles for workers. With optimism of the will, one could argue that the shortages will make it easier for workers to exercise class power and for working classes to form. This would indicate that my book has only mapped the beginning of a new global cycle of intensifying workers' struggle. But whether this really turns out to be the case will be the subject of the next chapter in the long-winded and complicated history of global labour – and that chapter still needs to be written.

APPENDIX A

Mapping

Dataset creation

Part of my research was a mapping exercise that was dedicated to capturing non-industrial strikes around the globe in the conjuncture of crisis. I have discussed the results and their implications for my research question in Chapter 4. In this Appendix, I explain how I proceeded when I conducted my actual research, which was influenced methodologically by an approach to mapping used by colleagues in a project that was about transitions to renewable energy in 34 countries in Africa (Müller et al, 2020). This section is dedicated to how I created my dataset; in the next one, I discuss how I coded the data. Since my approach to data analysis is contained in Chapter 4, I do not repeat the different steps in detail here.

Inspired by Silver's *Forces of Labor* (2003), my starting point was a search for the coverage of non-industrial strikes in online archives of well-known quality papers, that is, *The Mail & Guardian* (Johannesburg), *The Times of India* (Mumbai), *The New York Times*, *Página 12* (Buenos Aires), *The Guardian* (London), *Die Tageszeitung* (*taz*, Berlin) and *Público* (Madrid). I chose those papers to ensure that there was geographical balance; that they were written in languages that I understood; that their archives were accessible online; that they had reputation for good journalism with a sound factual basis; and that they were interested in labour issues.

I conducted online searches for each paper. The search terms were 'public sector' or 'service sector' and 'strike' (or the respective terms in German and Spanish).[1] They ensured that I was able to pick up a wide range of stoppages, but the number of hits was always significantly higher for 'public sector' and

---

[1] The German terms were '*Öffentlicher Dienst*' (which is more common than '*öffentlicher Sektor*'), '*Dienstleistungssektor*' and '*Streik*'; the Spanish words were '*sector público*', '*sector servicios*' and '*huelga*'. I decided against using '*paro*', which is synonymous with '*huelga*' but also means 'unemployment' and thus creates a lot of false hits.

'strike' than for 'service sector' and 'strike'. The reason is, in all likelihood, that in contrast to stoppages in the public sector, service sector strikes often take place at a specific company or in a specific sub-sector, which is why journalists writing about them do not necessarily have to refer to the 'service sector' when they cover them.

With the help of the articles found through my online searches, I created a simple database in the form of a spreadsheet. It contained detailed information on 244 strikes in the public and service sectors from January 2007 to October 2020 from 33 countries and autonomous territories. To order the information at this initial stage, I used a range of simple, descriptive categories: country; type of country (home country, neighbouring country or other country in relation to the place of publication of the newspapers selected); city or region; sector; duration; date; number of participants; participating unions; as well as reasons, demands and outcomes.

Inspired by the 'snowball' approach often used for selecting interviewees (see Auerbach and Silverstein, 2003: 18; Ritchie et al, 2003: 94), I also used the articles found through online searches to click on linked additional coverage from the same newspaper. This helped fill in my categories and check the accuracy of the data that I included. In several cases, I could not fill the 'duration', 'numbers of participants' and 'unions' categories; if so, I left them blank. I excluded opinion pieces because they are, by definition, not about presenting factual information but making a political point. Furthermore, I left out most articles that referred to strike announcements because stoppages are often called off at the last minute. I only included them if the strike in question was to be held on the same day, and if the newspaper in question contained other articles that allowed me to verify that it indeed had happened, or if I found such articles through an online search. In other words, I complemented the dataset through targeted searches. Finally, I also attempted to draw different manifestations of the same strike together where coverage focused on local actions, for example, picketing or demonstrations. Importantly, some disputes are long-winded and sometimes run over several years. Consequently, I decided to list strikes individually that formed part of one and the same dispute but were clearly separated in time. Moreover, I included general strikes if there was proof that service or public sector workers were involved. As it turned out, publicly employed workers often played a leading role in them.

Due to the fact that various G20 countries were missing in the initial dataset, I expanded the sample by also using two online platforms for my searches, labourstart.org and labournet.de. Furthermore, I added news media coverage of strikes that I found through researching my three cases covered in Part II. This way, I created my final sample of 387 strikes, which were located, all in all, in 56 countries and autonomous territories (see Figure 4.1).

Importantly, the resulting dataset is incomplete and not representative. The map included shows that the sample covers Australia, East Asia, North and South America, Southern Africa and Western Europe, but there are large gaps in Central America, Africa, the Middle East and Southeast Asia (see Figure 4.1). This reflects the biases created through the geographical location of the papers covered and possibly some additional issues such as language barriers, differences in the availability of online resources, the vagaries of search engine algorithms, different degrees of labour organization, diverging political conditions and, last but not least, the biases of the news media included. Obviously, strike coverage is influenced by editorial policies, the choices of individual journalists concerning what is newsworthy and the diverging visibility of labour struggles in different social contexts. This, combined with the pragmatic limitations of research (limited time and language barriers), means that my sample is not even in terms of its geographical spread. All of the initially selected papers covered fewer strikes abroad than at home. Accordingly, the sample contains 224 stoppages in the home countries of the seven newspapers, as opposed to 168 in other countries.[2] Nevertheless, there were significant differences between the papers. Whereas some covered strikes abroad in detail, others focused mostly on domestic strikes. *The Times of India* search, for example, produced just one hit for an article on a strike outside the country. In contrast, the *Página 12* search led to numerous articles on labour disputes in Latin America and Europe and on at least one strike in the US. A certain imbalance is also caused by the fact that three Western European newspapers were included, which was a conscious decision because it helped me prepare for the more detailed case studies in Part II. Finally, it is also noteworthy that the country with the largest number of strikes in the sample is Germany (70 in total, followed by Greece [43], Britain [31], Spain [30], India [29], France [26] and Argentina [25]). This is not because the country is particularly strike-prone (see Chapter 5), but because both *Die Tageszeitung* (taz) and labournet.de cover strikes in the country in great detail, including local or regional strikes that involve small numbers of workers. A similar point can be made with reference to *The Times of India*, which covers local strikes extensively in its city sections. Conversely, South Africa has the image of being a particularly strike-prone country (see Nicolson, 2013; Van der Walt, 2015), but the sample only contains 14 items from it. This suggests that many of the stoppages that take place are either in the industrial sector or are not covered in the media.[3]

---

[2] The numbers do not add up to 387, the overall figure for items in the sample, because it contains five transnational strikes, all of which count as strikes in several countries.

[3] Besides, there are doubts over whether the image of South Africa as being a country with a very high number of strikes is justified. With reference to ILO data, Haroon Bhorat and David Tseng (2014) contest it. They argue that strike incidence is not vastly different

Due to the organization of the sample – one strike is one item – it covers a huge variety of actions in a large number of sectors and countries. This also means that there is a significant variation in number of participants. The lowest number on record is approximately 25 – a strike of rail food supply workers in Edinburgh in December 2016 – and the highest 250 million – the general strike [*Bharat Bandh*] in India in November 2020.[4] It also needs to be considered, in this context, that not all sources included figures on the people involved.

Coding

As my research is based on strong theoretical assumptions, I started the coding process with a deductive move. I identified a range of provisional categories – and mutually exclusive codes falling under those categories – before I started analysing my first sample. I derived the first category from my research question and complemented this with four categories that came out of earlier work in the field of strike research that my colleague Jörg Nowak and I had carried out over the past decade. In this work, we identified a number of key characteristics of mass strikes under capitalist conditions (Nowak and Gallas, 2014: 311–12; Gallas, 2018: 239–40; 2020: 184; Nowak, 2019: 49–50).

I used the categories and codes in question both to record and arrange the information in the articles that I had collected for my first sample. My aim in this first round of coding was to check whether the codes were applicable in the sense that they could indeed be used to classify the existing information. My guiding assumption was that codes worked well if there were no (or only a few) doubtful cases that were hard to categorize.

The first category, 'class effects', directly spoke to my research problem. It referred to the question of whether the unifying effects of a strike in class terms outweigh its divisive consequences, or whether the contrary is the case. Correspondingly, my codes were 'exclusive solidarity' and 'inclusive solidarity', with the former referring to strikes whose divisive effects outweigh their unifying consequences, and the latter to stoppages where the opposite applies. I imagined that there would be two scenarios of how I would identify class effects: for one, through establishing how workers inside or outside the constituency of the strike in question saw it,

---

if the country is compared to other middle- and high-income countries. But even so, strike incidence should not necessarily be less than a fourth of those in Germany, which is why it is plausible that media bias also plays a role.

[4]   By definition, general strikes aim to mobilize workers both inside and outside manufacturing. They have been included in the sample if there was significant participation of non-industrial workers so that they could not be seen as industrial strikes.

and two, by showing that mobilizations were so broad that they could be seen as operating along class lines, or so exclusive or so disruptive for other groups of workers that the latter were likely to turn against them. There was indeed evidence of solidarity action – for example, a strike in the Finnish postal sector in November and December 2019 led to secondary action by workers at national carrier Finnair and, in the end, to resignation of the Finnish prime minister (Kauranen, 2019; Tanner, 2019) – and also of broad mobilizations in the form of general strikes. And there were strikes that were described as being divisive, for example, the pilots' strikes in various European countries, which were construed as instances of stoppages carried by highly privileged workers, or the strike in the German railway sector, which were discussed as an instance of inter-union competition. But it proved impossible in the vast majority of cases, on the grounds of the limited information to be found in short newspaper articles, to decide whether an individual strike could be seen as having unifying or divisive effects or whether the former outweighed the latter or vice versa. As a consequence, I decided to drop the category, which was consistent with my aim to avoid a subsumptionist research design.

In line with the literature, I also employed four other categories and the corresponding codes that were less clearly connected with the research problem. My expectation was that systematizing strikes this way would allow me to find patterns that spoke to my research question in an indirect fashion, or that it would at least generate observations that enhanced my understanding of the role of strikes in contemporary capitalism.

Accordingly, my second category was 'mode of confrontation', which was about contextualizing the demands of the workers and deciding whether they attempted to fend off worsening conditions of work (broadly understood) and threats to existing arrangements, or whether they fought for improvements. Accordingly, the two codes I used were 'offensive' and 'defensive'. These codes proved to be straightforward in their application. There was only one strike in my sample, the general strike in India in February 2012, which did not quite fit because there was a mix of offensive and defensive demands: The striking workers campaigned for an increase in the minimum wage and efforts to contain inflation, which can be seen as offensive demands, as well an end to privatization plans of the government, which is a defensive demand (Krishnan, 2012; Shah Singh, 2012; TOI, 2012). Consequently, I created a third code ('offensive and defensive') to leave room for such contradictory scenarios, but left the basic distinction intact because it appeared to be working in terms of classifying the existing information.

The third category was 'character of aims', which was referring primarily to the constituency of a strike and the instance addressed through its demands. The codes were 'mostly economic', 'economic and politicized', 'organic' and 'political in a narrow sense'. The first code, 'dominantly economic', referred to strikes that occurred in a clearly defined workplace, business or sector and were targeting a clearly defined group of workers by making demands vis-à-vis their employer. In other words, these stoppages concerned remuneration or conditions of work and employment. The classic case of a collective bargaining strike over wages and conditions falls under this category, but also strikes for union recognition, a collective bargaining agreement or against job cuts – provided they remain outside the realm of political debate altogether or are only debated by political 'insiders'. The second code applied to strikes based on economic demands that became heavily politicized and led to debates about work in the respective sector and beyond – either because the employer was a state body, or because they were particularly disruptive. The strikes in the German railway sector and the junior doctors' strike discussed in Volume 2, Part II are cases in point. The third code, 'organic', concerned strikes with a large extension along class lines and an articulation of economic and political demands. They differ from 'economic and politicized' strikes insofar as they are broad and attempt to mobilize workers as a class. An example are the frequent general strikes in India, which target the labour, social and economic policies of the respective government in power. These strikes bring millions of people to the streets so that they possibly are the largest strikes in human history. According to union estimates, the numbers for the strike in January 2019 are 150–200 million people, and 250 million each for the strikes in January and November 2020 (see Crowley, 2020; Gallas, 2020: 182). But similar stoppages are occurring all over the world. The sample contains general strikes against governments and their social and economic policies in Argentina, Brazil, Chile, France (including French Polynesia), Greece, Israel, Italy, Portugal, South Africa, Spain and Turkey and large-scale feminist general strikes in Argentina, Poland, Spain and Switzerland, which protested against violence against women as well as restrictions to women's reproductive rights, but also against the inequalities faced by women workers. Furthermore, there were public sector stoppages in a wide array of countries that qualified as 'organic' strikes because they were based on a broad mobilization; demands were made on behalf of workers as a class. Here, the Finnish case is particularly relevant because it led to solidarity action and to the resignation of the prime minister. Last but not least, there was also a fourth code, 'mostly political', which referred to strikes for political aims that were not directly related to economic issues or issues of work, for example, strikes against *coups d'état*. All in all, the distinction between the different codes was fuzzier than in the case of the third category. Differentiating between 'narrowly political' and 'economic and politicized' strikes was not always straightforward. However, there were no cases where it was impossible, on the grounds of the existing information, to decide how a certain strike should be classified.

The fourth category was 'mode of intervention' and referred to the question of whether a strike was 'symbolic' – the first code – in the sense that it was about demonstrating the potential power of workers through creating limited disruption, or whether it was about 'enforcement' – the second code – that is, about stopping work until the instance addressed in the demands chooses to negotiate or settle. Whereas the general strikes mentioned are typical examples of symbolic strikes because they usually end after one or two days, the latter can be quite drawn-out affairs. What is noteworthy in this context is that the disruption created through symbolic strikes varies considerably. In the cases where there were recurring (and sometimes rolling) strikes, their effects were felt in the everyday lives of people fairly frequently over a certain time span. If they were a one-off event, this was of course not the case. But since even short symbolic mass strikes had quite disruptive effects for a day or two and discernible consequences for the economy and everyday routines, it did not make sense to further break down symbolic strikes.

The fifth category, geographical extension, referred to the question of whether strikes were 'local', 'regional', 'national' or 'transnational'. It is noteworthy in this context that there are indeed some transnational strikes. There was a general strike against austerity in Portugal and Spain in November 2012, plus various strikes of people employed with online retailer Amazon as well as stoppages of pilots and flight attendants working for the Irish budget airline Ryanair. The application of the codes for this category was unproblematic because the articles usually contained the information in question.

Finally, I added a category called 'type of country'. This was not directly or indirectly connected with the research question; the aim was to gauge the breadth of the sample. It referred to the countries where strikes took place. The codes 'home country', 'neighbouring country' and 'other country' highlighted where the nearest of the seven newspapers discussed was located in relation to the country in question. These codes proved easy to apply; the numbers on the geographical spread of items in the sample were produced with their help.

The five categories emerged out of my theorization of class relations and strikes. But sticking exclusively to a deductive approach creates the risk of falling into the trap of subsumption. I drew inspiration from an approach to qualitative empirical research developed by Claes Axel Belfrage and Felix Hauf called 'Critical Grounded Theory' (Belfrage and Hauf, 2015). This proved to be fitting insofar as it was based on critical realist ontological assumptions, and I found the way in which this approach connects conceptualization with empirical analysis in the research process particularly relevant. According to

Belfrage and Hauf, research passes through a 'deductive' and an 'inductive moment' (2015: 335), which allows one to combine strong theoretical assumptions with an open-ended research process. Accordingly, I added, after the first of round of coding, an inductive element by adding three new categories plus codes that I derived from examining my sample and identifying aspects that were not captured by the existing categories. I used them, together with the existing categories (with the exception of class effects) in my second round of coding, for which I examined the expanded, second sample. Whenever the existing articles in the sample did not contain enough information to apply codes, I again resorted to snowballing and added newspaper coverage that I found through online searches relating to specific strikes.

The first new category was 'economic extension', with the codes 'single branch' and 'multiple branches' capturing the issue of whether strikes remained within the confines of a specific branch of the economy or not. It is important to note that not just the private sector comprises multiple branches but also the public sector: the work of teachers is fundamentally different from that of civil servants or sanitation workers. My hunch was that information on the economic extension of strikes could be relevant for my research question because strikes involving multiple branches bring together different groups of workers, which could, potentially, be seen as an expansive move. The codes proved straightforward in their application. It was possible to apply them to every single strike in the sample.

The second category referred to the 'ownership of means of production' in order to get an understanding of whether the strikes concerned publicly or privately owned entities. This was of relevance for my research question because, first, class relations in the public sector are somewhat different from those in the private sector – the employer is a state body, and not a direct representative of capital – and, second, because it was also important to leave room for different strike dynamics playing out in the different sectors. Accordingly, there were three codes: 'public', 'private' and 'public and private'. I introduced the latter code to do justice to the fact that broad mobilizations in particular, for example general strikes, cross the public/private divide.

And finally, I added an open category called 'branch of the economy', which allowed me to classify strikes according to where in the topography of the economy they are located. By going through the sample, I created 17 codes including 'sanitation', 'media', 'postal services' and 'healthcare', and complemented them with three codes for strikes involving multiple branches ('public', 'private', 'general').

To enhance the reliability of my codes, I started coding from a 'clean' version of my second sample and left a few weeks between the two coding exercises. Operating this way, I checked the reliability of my coding.

I compared the results of the two rounds to check whether my coding was consistent, and examined items again where there was a divergence (see Elliott, 2018: 2858). In a third round of coding, I settled on final results.

My last step, an inductive move, was to identify different strike patterns, again with the help of three rounds of coding. I found five patterns – the collective bargaining strike, the extension strike, the expansive-politicized strike, the class-based strike, the strike for political aims – and then related them to the 'character of aims' category (see Figure 4.2). This allowed me to zoom in on the class question, as is explained in Chapter 4.

APPENDIX B

Background Interviews

I did three rounds of background interviews with active trade unionists, which I used both as a source of general information on the subject matter of strikes, and to learn about specific disputes. The first round took place in May 2012 and formed part of a research project I carried out with my colleague Jörg Nowak on political strikes against austerity, which was funded by the Rosa Luxemburg Foundation. Edited versions of the interviews were published in the book *Politische Streiks im Europa der Krise* [*Political Strikes in the European Crisis*, Hamburg, 2012] that I co-edited with Jörg Nowak and Florian Wilde. This project constituted the starting point of my research on strikes. Since these interviews are in the public domain anyway, there is no need for me to use pseudonyms. The interviewees were:

- Sabin del Bado, LAB, Basque Country, Spain
- Felipe Van Keirsbilck, National Centre of Employees [Centrale Nationale des Employés], Belgium
- Olga Karyoti, Association of Translators, Editors, Copy-Editors [Σωματείο Μεταφραστών, Επιμελητών Διορθωτών], Greece
- Christine Lafont, Solidaires Union, France
- Deolinda Martin, CGTP, Portugal
- Nuria Montoya, CC.OO, Catalonia, Spain
- Michael Pieber, Union of Private-Sector Employees Print Journalism Paper [Gewerkschaft der Privatangestellten Druck Journalismus Papier], Austria
- Sean Vernell, UCU, Britain

In a second round, I discussed the state of unionism, the resistance against austerity and the social and political relevance of strikes in Britain with four trade unionists active in the country. At this point, I had not decided yet that I would zoom in on non-industrial strikes, which explains why one of my interviewees is active in the chemical industry. This second round took place in September and October 2015. These interviews have not been published and were not led with the intention of fully publishing them. To protect my sources, I use pseudonyms and do not disclose the exact geographical location of their workplaces and places of residence:

- Ricardo Jameson, community organizer, Unite, Southeast of England
- Thomas Hunter, shop steward in the chemical industry, Unite, Northwest of England
- Timothy Mackenzie, head of a branch of the PCS, Scotland
- Laura Wilson, full-time official, Chartered Society of Physiotherapy, Midlands

In a third round, I interviewed four trade unionists representing the GDL in July 2018, who were actively involved in the strikes of 2014–15. My aims were to learn about their motivations, their take on the political effects of the stoppages and the way in which the strike was received by their colleagues and the customers of Deutsche Bahn. Again, I use pseudonyms and do not disclose the exact location of their workplaces and places of residence:

- Sven Baumgartner, train driver employed with Deutsche Bahn, head of a GDL branch, Hessen
- Peter Obentraut, train driver employed with Deutsche Bahn, head of a GDL branch, Hessen
- Christoph Wartenberg, former train driver, full-time works councillor at a subsidiary of Deutsche Bahn, Hessen
- Bianca Schröder, conductor employed with Deutsche Bahn, deputy head of a GDL branch, Hessen

References

Aalbers, M.B. (2013) 'Debate on neoliberalism in and after the neoliberal crisis', *International Journal of Urban and Regional Research*, 37(3): 1053–7.

Abendroth, W. (1954) 'Der politische Streik', in W. Abendroth (1975) *Arbeiterklasse, Staat und Verfassung: Materialien zur Verfassungsgeschichte und Verfassungstheorie der Bundesrepublik*, edited by J. Perels, Frankfurt am Main: EVA, pp 54–63.

Aborisade, F. and Povey, D. (2018) 'Mass strikes in Nigeria, 2000–2015: struggling against neoliberal hegemony', in J. Nowak, M. Dutta and P. Birke (eds) *Workers Movements and Strikes in the Twenty-First Century: A Global Perspective*, London: Rowman & Littlefield, pp 185–202.

Aglietta, M. (2000) *A Theory of Capitalist Regulation: The US Experience*, new edn, London: Verso, original work published in 1979.

AKSU (Arbeitskreis Strategic Unionism) (2013) 'Jenaer Machtressourcenansatz 2.0', in S. Schmalz and K. Dörre (eds) *Comeback der Gewerkschaften? Machtressourcen, innovative Praktiken, internationale Perspektiven*, Frankfurt am Main: Campus, pp 345–75.

Alabao, N. (2020) 'Feminismo 2020: avances y desuniones', *CTXT*, 9 March. Available from: https://ctxt.es/es/20200302/Politica/31286/8m-feminismo-psoe-podemos-nuria-alabao.htm [Accessed 9 October 2022].

Alcaide, S. (2011) 'Movimiento 15-M: los ciudadanos exigen reconstruir la política', *El País*, 17 May. Available from: https://elpais.com/politica/2011/05/16/actualidad/1305578500_751064.html [Accessed 9 October 2022].

Alonso Pérez, M. and Furió Blanco, E. (2010) 'La economía española: Del crecimiento a la crisis pasando por la burbuja immobiliaria', *Cahiers de civilisation espagnole contemporaine*, 6. Available from: https://journals.open edition.org/ccec/3212 [Accessed 19 January 2024].

Althusser, L. (1969) *For Marx*, London: Allen Lane, original work published in 1965.

Álvarez, P. (2018a) 'Qué es la huelga feminista y más claves de la protesta del 8 de marzo', *El País*, 14 November. Available from: https://elpais.com/politica/2018/02/13/actualidad/1518533587_229354.html [Accessed 9 October 2022].

Álvarez, P. (2018b) 'El movimiento feminista prepara una huelga para el 8 de Marzo de 2019', *El País*, 7 October. Available from: https://elpais.com/ sociedad/2018/10/06/actualidad/1538862263_827951.html [Accessed 9 October 2022].

Álvarez, P. (2021) 'El feminismo cambia las marchas masivas por símbolos y homenajes en el 8-M de la pandemia', *El País*, 8 March. Available from: https://elpais.com/sociedad/2021-03-08/el-feminismo-cambia-las-marchas-masivas-por-simbolos-y-homenajes-en-el-8-m-de-la-pandemia. html?rel=listapoyo [Accessed 9 October 2022].

Álvarez, P. and Sahuquillo, M.R. (2017) 'Miles de mujeres marchan en España por la igualdad de derechos', *El País*, 9 March. Available from: https://elpais.com/politica/2017/03/08/actualidad/1488980420_ 408460.html?event_log=oklogin [Accessed 9 October 2022].

Álvarez Vallejos, R. (2010) '¿Represión o integración? La política sindical del regimen militar, 1973–1980', *Historia*, 43(2): 325–55.

Antentas, J.M. (2015) 'Spain: the indignados rebellion of 2011 in perspective', *Labor History*, 56(2): 136–60.

Ap, S. (2014) 'Zim cricketers to return after wage strike', *Mail & Guardian*, 3 February. Available from: www.mg.co.za/article/2014-02-03-zim-cri cketers-to-return-after-wage-strike/ [Accessed 23 February 2022].

Apicella, S. and Hildebrandt, H. (2019) 'Divided we stand: reasons for and against strike participation in Amazon's German distribution centres', *Work Organisation, Labour & Globalisation*, 13(1): 172–89.

Aranea, M. and Kraemer, B. (2021) 'Working life in Germany: collective bargaining', *Eurofound*, 6 August. Available from: https://www.eurofound.eur opa.eu/country/germany#collective-bargaining [Accessed 10 October 2022].

Armanski, G. (1974) 'Staatliche Lohnarbeiter im Kapitalismus', *PROKLA. Zeitschrift für kritische Sozialwissenschaft*, 4(16): 1–16.

Arrighi, G. (1994) *The Long Twentieth Century: Money, Power and the Origins of Our Times*, London: Verso.

Arruzza, C. (2013) *Dangerous Liaisons: The Marriages and Divorces of Marxism and Feminism*, Pontypool: Merlin.

Arruzza, C. (2017) 'From social reproduction feminism to the women's strike', in T. Bhattacharya (ed) *Social Reproduction Theory: Remapping Class, Recentering Oppression*, London: Pluto, pp 192–6.

Arruzza, C. (2018) 'From women's strikes to a new class movement: the third feminist wave', *International Viewpoint*, December. Available from: https:// viewpointmag.com/2018/12/03/from-womens-strikes-to-a-new-class-movement-the-third-feminist-wave/ [Accessed 6 October 2022].

Arruzza, C. and Henwood, D. (2017) 'The first strike: March's women's strike was an electric first step towards forging a new feminist movement', *International Viewpoint*, 16 April. Available from: https://internationalvi ewpoint.org/spip.php?article4929 [Accessed 9 October 2022].

Arruzza, C., Bhattacharya, T. and Fraser, N. (2019) *Feminism for the 99 Percent: A Manifesto*, London: Verso.

Ärzteblatt (2015) 'Rund 500 Charité-Mitarbeiter legen Arbeit nieder', 27 April. Available from: www.aerzteblatt.de/nachrichten/62625 [Accessed 23 February 2022].

Ärzteblatt (2017a) 'Warnstreik an der Charité: Fronten verhärtet', 8 August. Available from: www.aerzteblatt.de/nachrichten/77474/Warnstreik-an-der-Charite-Fronten-verhaertet [Accessed 23 February 2022].

Ärzteblatt (2017b) 'Charité richtet sich auf Pfleger-Streik ein', 13 September. Available from: www.aerzteblatt.de/nachrichten/79260/Charite-richtet-sich-auf-Pfleger-Streik-ein [Accessed 23 February 2022].

Ärzteblatt (2017c) 'Vorerst kein weiterer Streik an der Charité', 4 October. Available from: www.aerzteblatt.de/nachrichten/80692/Vorerst-kein-weiterer-Streik-an-der-Charite [Accessed 23 February 2022].

Ärztezeitung (2017a) 'Verdi fordert Streichung von Betten und OPs', 9 August. Available from: www.aerztezeitung.de/Nachrichten/Pflegekraefte-beenden-Streik-an-der-Charite-310860.html [Accessed 23 February 2022].

Ärztezeitung (2017b) 'Pflegekräfte beenden Streik an der Charité', 5 October. Available from: www.aerztezeitung.de/Nachrichten/Pflegekraefte-beenden-Streik-an-der-Charite-310860.html [Accessed 23 February 2022].

Aue, K. (2021) 'GDL-Streik: Versagt das Tarifeinheitsgesetz?', *Tagesschau*, 12 August. Available from: https://www.tagesschau.de/wirtschaft/unternehmen/tarifeinheitsgesetz-119.html [Accessed 9 October 2022].

Auerbach, C.F. and Silverstein, L.B. (2003) *Qualitative Data: An Introduction to Coding and Analysis*, New York: New York University Press.

Augstein, J. (2015) 'Danke, Herr Weselsky!', *Der Spiegel*, 7 May. Available from: https://www.spiegel.de/politik/deutschland/bahn-streik-danke-claus-weselsky-augstein-kolumne-a-1032521.html [Accessed 19 January 2024].

Avarena Carasco, A. and Muñoz, M. (2018) 'Conflicts around subcontracted workers in Chile's copper mining sector', in J. Nowak, M. Dutta and P. Birke (eds) *Workers Movements and Strikes in the Twenty-First Century: A Global Perspective*, London: Rowman & Littlefield, pp 133–50.

Ax, J. and Fernandez, L. (2017) 'Women worldwide rally for equality, and against Trump in U.S.', *Reuters*, 8 March. Available from: https://www.reuters.com/article/us-womens-day-usa-idUSKBN16F19D [Accessed 9 October 2022].

Ayuso, G. (2010) 'La industria sí para en todas partes', *Público*, 30 September. Available from: https://www.publico.es/espana/industria-partes.html [Accessed 9 October 2022].

Baca, G. (2004) 'Legends of fordism: between myth, history and foregone conclusions', *Social Analysis*, 48(3): 169–78.

Baccaro, L. and Pontusson, J. (2016) 'Rethinking comparative political economy: the growth model perspective', *Politics & Society*, 44(2): 175–207.

Bachmann, A. (2015) 'Wer andern eine Grube … Oder: Wer fällt der Tarifeinheit zum Opfer?', *Express*, January. Available from: https://express-afp.info/wp-content/uploads/2016/01/2015-01_Bachmann_Wer-andern_Tarifeinheit.pdf [Accessed 9 October 2022].

Banwart, J. (2013) 'Jerry Falwell, the rise of the moral majority, and the 1980 election', *Western Illinois Historical Review*, 5: 133–57.

Bardertscher, C. and Kurz, N. (2017) 'Genfer Uber-Fahrer treten in den Streik', *SRF News*, 6 December. Available from: www.srf.ch/news/schweiz/loehne-von-650-franken-genfer-uber-fahrer-treten-in-den-streik [Accessed 23 February 2022].

Bar-On, T. (2008) 'Fascism to the Nouvelle Droite: the dream of pan-European empire', *Journal of Contemporary European Studies*, 16(3): 327–45.

BBC (2016a) 'Junior doctors' leaders "trying to topple the government"', 25 April. Available from: https://www.bbc.com/news/health-36126740 [Accessed 9 October 2022].

BBC (2016b) 'Junior doctors' row: the dispute explained', 6 April. Available from: https://www.bbc.com/news/health-34775980 [Accessed 9 October 2022].

BBC (2016c) 'Black Monday: Polish women strike against abortion ban', 3 October. Available from: https://www.bbc.com/news/world-europe-37540139 [Accessed 9 October 2022].

BDA (nd) 'Soziale Marktwirtschaft'. Available from: https://arbeitgeber.de/themen/wirtschaft-gesellschaft/soziale-marktwirtschaft/ [Accessed 10 May 2022].

Behrens, M., Frege, C.M. and Hurd, R. (2004) 'Conceptualizing labour union revitalization', in C.M. Frege and J. Kelly (eds) *Varieties of Unionism: Strategies for Union Revitalization in a Globalizing Economy*, Oxford: University Press, pp 11–30.

Behruzi, D. (2014) 'Nur die Form stört', *Junge Welt*, 5 November. Available from: https://www.jungewelt.de/loginFailed.php?ref=/artikel/251177.nur-die-form-st%C3%B6rt.html [Accessed 9 October 2022].

Belfrage, C.A. and Hauf, F. (2015) 'Operationalizing cultural political economy: towards critical grounded theory', *Journal of Organizational Ethnography*, 4(3): 324–40.

Bell, S. and Hindmoor, A. (2018) 'Are the major global banks now safer? Structural continuities and change in banking and finance since the 2008 crisis', *Review of International Political Economy*, 25(1): 1–27.

Bengoa, A. and Serrato, F. (2015) 'Una multitud participa en la marcha contra la violencia machista', *El País*, 7 November. Available from: https://elpais.com/politica/2015/11/07/actualidad/1446888439_982462.html [Accessed 9 October 2022].

Bergmann, J., Bürckmann, E. and Dabrowski, H. (2002) *Krise und Krisenerfahrungen: Einschätzungen und Deutungen von Betriebsräten und Vertrauensleuten*, Hamburg: VSA.

Bernados Domínguez, G. (2009) 'Creación y Destrucción de la Burbuja Inmobiliaria en España', *Información Comercial Española, ICE: Revista de economía*, 850: 23–40.

Berry, C. (2016) 'UK manufacturing decline since the crisis in historical perspective', SPERI British Political Economy Brief, 25 October. Available from: http://speri.dept.shef.ac.uk/wp-content/uploads/2018/11/Brief-25-UK-manufacturing-decline-since-the-crisis.pdf [Accessed 7 October 2022].

Bewernitz, T. and Dribbusch, H. (2014) '"Kein Tag ohne Streik": Arbeitskampfentwicklung im Dienstleistungssektor', *WSI-Mitteilungen*, 5: 393–401.

BfA (2022) 'Entwicklungen in der Zeitarbeit', January. Available from: https://statistik.arbeitsagentur.de/DE/Statischer-Content/Statistiken/Themen-im-Fokus/Zeitarbeit/generische-Publikation/Arbeitsmarkt-Deutschland-Zeitarbeit-Aktuelle-Entwicklung.pdf;jsessionid=5F507213B6E9A2051D7041E781E2A919?__blob=publicationFile&v=12 [Accessed 9 October 2022]

Bhaskar, R. (1979) *The Possibility of Naturalism: A Philosophical Critique of the Contemporary Human Sciences*, London: Routledge.

Bhattacharya, T. (2017a) 'Introduction: mapping social reproduction theory', in T. Bhattacharya (ed) *Social Reproduction Theory: Remapping Class, Recentering Oppression* , London: Pluto, pp 1–20.

Bhattacharya, T. (2017b) 'How not to skip class: social reproduction of labor and the global working class', in T. Bhattacharya (ed) *Social Reproduction Theory: Remapping Class, Recentering Oppression*, London: Pluto, pp 68–93.

Bhorat, H. and Tseng, D. (2014) 'South Africa's strike data revisited', 2 April. Available from: https://www.brookings.edu/blog/africa-in-focus/2014/04/02/south-africas-strike-data-revisited/ [Accessed 26 June 2021].

Bidgood, J. (2018) 'West Virginia raises teachers' pay to end statewide strike', *New York Times*, 6 March. Available from: www.nytimes.com/2018/03/06/us/west-virginia-teachers-strike-deal.html [Accessed 23 March 2022].

Bidgood, J. and Robertson, C. (2018) 'West Virginia walkouts a lesson in the power of a crowd-sourced strike', *New York Times*, 8 March. Available from: www.nytimes.com/2018/03/08/us/west-virginia-teachers-strike.html?searchResultPosition=62 [Accessed 23 March 2022].

Bieler, A. and Morton, A. (2018) *Global Capitalism, Global War, Global Crisis*, Cambridge: Cambridge University Press.

Bieling, H.-J. (2011) *Internationale Politische Ökonomie: Eine Einführung*, 2nd edn, Wiesbaden: VS.

Bieling, H.-J. (2018) 'Jenseits der (neo-)liberal-kosmopolitischen Hegemonie? Die "Doppelkrise" der transatlantischen Globalisierungspolitik', *Zeitschrift für Internationale Beziehungen*, 25(2): 164–80.

Bild-Zeitung (2014) 'Wie kann ich rausfinden, ob mein Zug doch fährt?', 13 November. Available from: https://www.bild.de/geld/wirtschaft/bah nstreik/bild-erklaert-den-ersatzfahrplan-38435918.bild.html [Accessed 9 October 2022].

Billingsley, M. and Gillett, G. (2015) 'Timeline of the junior doctors contract dispute', *BMJ*, 18 December. Available from: https://www.bmj.com/cont ent/351/sbmj.h6669 [Accessed 9 October 2022].

Birke, P. (2007) *Wilde Streiks im Wirtschaftswunder: Arbeitskämpfe, Gewerkschaften und soziale Bewegungen in der Bundesrepublik und Dänemark*, Frankfurt am Main: Campus.

Birke, P. (2018) 'The strike wave of 2015 in Germany', in J. Nowak, M. Dutta and P. Birke (eds) *Workers Movements and Strikes in the Twenty-First Century: A Global Perspective*, London: Rowman & Littlefield, pp 221–36.

Bispinck, R. (2016) 'Tarifpolitischer Jahresbericht 2015: Harte Arbeitskämpfe und kräftige Reallohnsteigerungen', WSI Informationen zur Tarifpolitik, January. Available from: https://www.boeckler.de/pdf/p_ta_jb_2015.pdf [Accessed 8 October 2022].

Bispinck, R. (2017) 'Tarifpolitischer Jahresbericht 2016: Deutliche Reallohnsteigerung und Anhebung der Mindestlöhne', *WSI Informationen zur Tarifpolitik*, January. Available from: https://www.boeckler.de/pdf/p_ ta_jb_2016.pdf [Accessed 9 October 2022].

Blaikie, N. and Priest, J. (2017) *Social Research: Paradigms in Action*, Cambridge: Polity.

Blaikie, N. and Priest, J. (2019) *Designing Social Research*, Cambridge: Polity.

Blair, A. and Schröder, G. (1998) 'Europe: The Third Way/Die Neue Mitte', Friedrich Ebert Foundation, South Africa Office, Working Documents, 2, June. Available from: https://library.fes.de/pdf-files/bueros/suedafrika/ 02828.pdf [Accessed 30 May 2022].

Blanc, E. (2019) *Red State Revolt: The Teachers' Strike Wave and Working-Class Politics*, London: Verso.

Blanc, E. (2020) 'Breaking the law: strike bans and labour revitalization in the red state revolt', *Labour Studies Journal*, 45(1): 74–96.

Blanco, S. (2018) 'El 82% de los españoles cree que hay motivos para la huelga del 8 de marzo', *El País*, 6 March. Available from: https://elpais.com/ politica/2018/03/05/actualidad/1520245089_636623.html [Accessed 9 October 2022].

BMA (2015) 'BMA briefing: junior doctors' contract'. Available from: https:// web.archive.org/web/20151024002021/http://bma.org.uk/-/media/files/ pdfs/working%20for%20change/policy%20and%20lobbying/pa-briefjunio rdoctorscontractoct-23-10-2015.pdf [Accessed 9 October 2022].

BMA (2016a) 'The truth about the junior doctors' contract dispute'. Available from: https://www.central-surgery.co.uk/mf.ashx?ID=331599e2-edae-400b-874e-95c7306de05a [Accessed 9 October 2022].

BMA (2016b) 'Junior doctors reject proposed contract', press release, 5 July. Available from: https://web.archive.org/web/20161107231150/https://www.bma.org.uk/news/media-centre/press-releases/2016/july/junior-doctors-reject-proposed-contract [Accessed 9 October 2022].

BMA (2021) 'Mitigating the impact of Covid-19 on health inequalities'. Available from: https://www.bma.org.uk/media/3944/bma-mitigating-the-impact-of-covid-19-on-health-inequalities-report-march-2021.pdf [Accessed 9 October 2022].

Bock, V. (2018) 'Neues von Amazon', *SoZ. Sozialistische Zeitung*. Available from: www.sozonline.de/2018/07/neues-von-amazon/ [Accessed 23 March 2022].

Boewe, J. and Schulten, J. (2019) *Der lange Kampf der Amazon-Beschäftigten. Labor des Widerstands: Globale Gewerkschaftliche Organisierung im Onlinehandel*, Berlin: Rosa Luxemburg Stiftung.

Bogg, A. (2016) 'Beyond neo-liberalism: the Trade Union Act 2016 and the authoritarian state', *Industrial Law Journal*, 45(3): 299–336.

Boin, A., t'Hart, P. and McCowell, A. (2008) 'Conclusions: the politics of crisis exploitation', in A. Boin, P. t'Hart and A. McCowell (eds) *Governing after Crisis: The Politics of Investigation, Accountability and Learning*, Cambridge: Cambridge University Press, pp 285–316.

Boll, F. and Kalass, V. (2014) 'Streik und Aussperrung', in W. Schroeder (ed) *Handbuch Gewerkschaften in Deutschland*, 2nd edn, Wiesbaden: Springer VS, pp 535–80.

Boltanski, L. and Chiapello, È. (2005) *The New Spirit of Capitalism*, London: Verso.

Book, C., Huke, N., Tiedemann, N. and Tietje, O. (2020) 'Konservative Mobilmachung: Liberale Demokratie als fragile Herrschaftsordnung und der Aufstieg des Populismus', in C. Book, N. Huke, N. Tiedemann and O. Tietje (eds) *Autoritärer Populismus*, Münster: Westfälisches Dampfboot, pp 8–27.

Booth, R. (2020) 'University of London cleaners win 10-year outsourcing battle', *The Guardian*, 3 November. Available from: www.theguardian.com/education/2020/nov/03/university-of-london-cleaners-win-10-year-outsourcing-battle [Accessed 22 March 2022].

Bordogna, L. and Cella, G.P. (2002) 'Decline or transformation? Change in industrial conflict and its challenges', *Transfer*, 4: 485–507.

Borraz, M. (2017) 'El movimiento feminista prepara una huelga internacional de mujeres para el 8 de marzo', *El Diario*, 17 February. Available from: https://www.eldiario.es/sociedad/movimiento-feminista-prepara-internacional-mujeres_1_3577306.html [Accessed 9 October 2022].

Borraz, M. and Domenech, M. (2015) 'Una marcha histórica y multitudinaria toma la calle contra la violencia machista', *El Diario*, 7 November. Available from: https://www.eldiario.es/sociedad/feminismo-exigir-violencia-machista-cuestion_1_2391918.html [Accessed 9 October 2022].

Börse am Sonntag (2014) 'Viel Feind, viel Ärger', 25 October. Available from: https://www.boerse-am-sonntag.de/spezial/artikel/weselsky.html [Accessed 9 October 2022].

Boseley, S. and Weaver, M. (2016) 'Junior doctors' row: BMA announces three more five-day strikes', *The Guardian*, 1 September. Available from: https://www.theguardian.com/society/2016/sep/01/patients-association-national-voices-condemn-planned-five-day-junior-doctors-strike [Accessed 9 October 2022].

Bossavie, L. and Kannine, O. (2018) 'What explains the gender gap reversal in educational attainment?', World Bank, Policy Research Working Paper 8303, January 2018. Available from: https://documents1.worldbank.org/curated/en/659501516200427470/pdf/What-Explains-the-Gender-Gap-Reversal-in-Educational-Attainment.pdf [Accessed 9 October 2022].

Boukalas, C. and Müller, J. (2015) 'Un-doing labour in Greece: memoranda, workfare and Eurozone "competitiveness"', *Global Labour Journal*, 6(3): 390–405.

Brand, U. and Wissen, J. (2013) 'Crisis and continuity of capitalist society-nature relationships: the imperial mode of living and the limits to environmental governance', *Review of International Political Economy*, 20(4): 687–711.

Brandt, T. and Schulten, T. (2008) 'Liberalisierung und Privatisierung öffentlicher Dienstleistungen und die Erosion des Flächentarifvertrags', *WSI-Mitteilungen*, 10: 570–6.

Brie, M. (2009) 'Ways out of the crisis of neoliberalism', *Development Dialogue*, 51: 15–32.

Briggs, H. (2015) 'Junior doctors' pay: how does your job compare?', *BBC*, 15 October. Available at: https://www.bbc.com/news/health-34475955 [Accessed 9 October 2022].

Brinkmann, U. and Nachtwey, O. (2013) 'Industrial relations, trade unions and social conflict in German capitalism', *La Nouvelle Revue de Travail*, 3. Available from: https://journals.openedition.org/nrt/1382 [Accessed 8 October 2022].

Brookes, B. (2018) 'Bartlett, Patricia Maureen', *Dictionary of New Zealand Biography*, Te Ara – the Encyclopedia of New Zealand. Available from: https://teara.govt.nz/en/biographies/6b4/bartlett-patricia-maureen [Accessed 12 February 2022].

Brooks, M. and McCallum, J. (2017) 'The new global labour studies: a critical review', *Global Labour Journal*, 8(3): 201–18.

Bruff, I. (2021) 'The politics of comparing capitalisms', *Economy and Space*, 53(6): 1273–92.

Buckel, S. (2015) 'Dirty capitalism', in D. Martin, D. Martin and J. Wissel (eds) *Perspektiven und Konstellationen kritischer Theorie*, Münster: Westfälisches Dampfboot, pp 29–48.

Budras, C. and Heeg, T. (2022) 'Deutsche Bahn riskiert zu viel im Ausland', *FAZ*, 4 March. Available from: https://www.faz.net/aktuell/wirtschaft/deutsche-bahn-riskiert-zu-viel-im-ausland-bahnreform-17852991.html [Accessed 9 October 2022].

Bundestag (2015) 'Kontroverse Expertisen zum Tarifeinheitsgesetz'. Available from: https://www.bundestag.de/webarchiv/textarchiv/2015/kw19_pa_arbeit_soziales-367818 [Accessed 9 October 2022].

Bündnis für unsere Bahn (2020) 'Bündnis für unsere Bahn', 26 May. Available from: https://www.deutschebahn.com/resource/blob/6860154/c3e705558b18550c9c97745c1eb2e1fb/Buendnis-Bahn-data.pdf [Accessed 9 October 2022].

Burnett, V. (2008) 'Spain unveils €11 billion economic stimulus package', *New York Times*, 27 October. Available from: https://www.nytimes.com/2008/11/27/business/worldbusiness/27iht-peseta.4.18215053.html [Accessed 9 October 2022].

Burnham, P. (2004) 'Comparative methodology', in P. Burnham, K. Gilland, W. Grant and Z. Layton-Henry (eds) *Research Methods in Politics*, Houndmills: Palgrave Macmillan, pp 58–79.

BVerfG (2017) 'Das Tarifeinheitsgesetz ist weitgehend mit dem Grundgesetz vereinbar', press release, 57, 11 July. Available from: https://www.bundesverfassungsgericht.de/SharedDocs/Pressemitteilungen/DE/2017/bvg17-057.html [Accessed 9 October 2022].

Calvo González, J.L. (2016) 'La Gran Recesión en Irlanda y España: Un análisis comparative', *Revista Universitaria Europea*, 25: 59–88.

Cámara, J. (2019) 'Change everything: foundations and challenges of the feminist strike in Spain', *Viewpoint Magazine*, 13 May. Available from: https://viewpointmag.com/2019/05/13/change-everything-foundations-and-challenges-of-the-feminist-strike-in-spain/ [Accessed 9 October 2022].

Campbell, D. (2015) 'Junior doctors condemn new contract they say could cut pay by 40%', *The Guardian*, 18 September. Available from: https://www.theguardian.com/society/2015/sep/18/junior-doctors-new-contract-cut-pay-40-per-cent [Accessed 9 October 2022].

Campbell, D. (2016a) 'Jeremy Hunt to impose new contract on junior doctors', *The Guardian*, 6 July. Available from: https://www.theguardian.com/society/2016/jul/06/jeremy-hunt-to-impose-new-contract-on-junior-doctors [Accessed 9 October 2022].

Campbell, D. (2016b) 'How much is the government really privatising the NHS?', *The Guardian*, 15 August. Available from: https://www.theguardian.com/society/2016/aug/15/creeping-privatisation-nhs-official-data-owen-smith-outsourcing [Accessed 15 January 2024].

Campbell, D. (2016c) 'BMA facing backlash from members over handling of contract dispute', *The Guardian*, 26 September. Available from: https://www.theguardian.com/uk-news/2016/sep/26/bma-facing-backlash-from-members-over-handling-of-contract-dispute [Accessed 9 October 2022].

Campbell, D. (2019) 'Junior doctors agree new contract to end four-year dispute', *The Guardian*, 26 June. Available from: https://www.theguardian.com/society/2019/jun/26/junior-doctors-agree-to-82-pay-rise-ending-four-year-dispute [Accessed 9 October 2022].

Campbell, D. and Johnson, S. (2014) 'NHS strike: clinics close and operations cancelled in dispute over pay', *The Guardian*, 13 October. Available from: http://www.theguardian.com/society/2014/oct/13/nhs-strike-dispute-pay-walkout [Accessed 9 October 2022].

Campbell, D. and Johnson, S. (2016) 'Junior doctors split over deal with Jeremy Hunt to end contract dispute', *The Guardian*, 18 May. Available from: https://www.theguardian.com/society/2016/may/18/junior-doctors-bma-jeremy-hunt-agree-deal-end-contract-dispute [Accessed 9 October 2022].

Campillo, I. (2019) '"If we stop, the world stops": the 2018 feminist strike in Spain', *Social Movement Studies*, 18(2): 252–58.

Campos Lima, M.P. and Martín Antiles, A. (2011) 'Crisis and trade union challenges in Portugal and Spain: between general strikes and social pacts', *Transfer*, 17(3): 387–402.

Candeias, M. (2004) *Neoliberalismus – Hochtechnologie – Hegemonie: Grundrisse einer transnationalen kapitalistischen Produktions- und Lebensweise – Eine Kritik*, Hamburg: Argument.

Canfora, L. (2006) *Democracy in Europe: A History of an Ideology*, Oxford: Blackwell.

Carchedi, G. (1977) *On the Economic Identification of Social Classes*, London: Routledge and Kegan Paul.

Carreras García, J. (2020) '¿Puede el feminism ser un revulsive sindical?', *Laborem*, 22: 59–70.

Carter, D.T. (1996) 'Legacy of rage: George Wallace and the transformation of American politics', *The Journal of Southern History*, 62(1): 3–26.

Carver, T. (1998) *The Postmodern Marx*, Manchester: Manchester University Press.

Cassidy, T., Macauly, T. and Soltan, M. (2016) 'Junior doctors' all-out strike: voices from the picket lines', *The BMJ*, 27 April. Available from: https://www.bmj.com/content/353/bmj.i2409 [Accessed 9 October 2022].

Castells, M. (2010) *The Rise of the Network Society*, 2nd edn, Hoboken: Wiley, original work published in 1996.

Causa, O., Abendschein, M., Luu, N., Soldani, E. and Soriolo, C. (2021) 'The post-COVID-19 rise in labour shortages', OECD Economics Department Working Papers, 1721, 7 July. Available from: https://www. oecd-ilibrary.org/deliver/e60c2d1c-en.pdf?itemId=%2Fcontent%2Fpa per%2Fe60c2d1c-en&mimeType=pdf [Accessed 9 October 2022].

Centenara, M. (2016) 'Una mujer es asesinada cada 30 horas en Argentina por violencia machista', *El País*, 31 March. Available from: https://elpais. com/internacional/2016/03/31/argentina/1459457396_981225.html [Accessed 9 October 2022].

Cerrillo Vidal, J.A. (2013) 'From general strike to social strike: movement alliances and innovative actions in the November 2012 Spanish general strike', *Interface*, 5(2): 39–46.

Change.org (2016) 'Solidarity with junior doctors – no imposition of contracts'. Available from: https://www.change.org/p/jeremy-hunt-mp-we-oppose-jeremy-hunt-s-decision-to-impose-the-junior-contract-on-jun ior-doctors [Accessed 9 October 2022].

Chapman, B. (2019) 'UCL strike: hundreds of outsourced cleaners, porters and security guards protest to demand better conditions', *The Independent*, 19 November. Available from: www.independent.co.uk/news/business/ news/ucl-strike-cleaners-security-guards-porters-outsourced-workers-sod exo-axis-a9209296.html [Accessed 20 September 2022].

Chira, S., Abrams, R. and Rogers, K. (2017) ' "Day without a woman" protest tests a movement's staying power', *New York Times*, 8 March. Available from: https://www.nytimes.com/2017/03/08/us/a-day-with out-a-woman.html [Accessed 9 October 2022].

Choudhury, S. (2017) 'Workers' resistances in the Indian railways and the general strike of May 1974', *Journal of Political Studies*, 13: 98–116.

Christophers, B. (2016) 'Geographies of finance III: regulation and after-crisis financial features', *Progress in Human Geography*, 40(1): 138–48.

CIA (2022) *The World Fact Book*. Available from: https://www.cia.gov/ the-world-factbook/ [Accessed 9 October 2022].

Cleaver, H. (1995) 'The subversion of money-as-command in the current crisis', in W. Bonefeld and J. Holloway (eds) *Global Capital, National State and Politics of Money*, Houndmills: Palgrave, pp 141–77.

Cleven, T. (2021) 'Bahn auf Shoppingtour: 2020 waren 521 Töchter und Beteiligungen im Portfolio', *RND*, 30 October. Available from: https:// www.rnd.de/wirtschaft/deutsche-bahn-auf-shoppingtour-521-toechter-und-beteiligungen-im-portfolio-von-2020-K4J3HM4KNZBPFCVIULS P4Q7KCE.html [Accessed 9 October2022]

CNT (2018) '#8M: la huelga que liberó al feminismo'. Available from: https://nosotras.cnt.es/huelga-8m-2018/8m-la-huelga-que-libero-al-feminismo/ [Accessed 9 October 2022].

Cohen, S. (2006) *Ramparts of Resistance: Why Workers Lost Their Power and How to Get It Back*, London: Pluto.

Collell, E. (2020) 'La calle mantiene el pulso contra el machismo en el 8-M'. Available from: https://www.elperiodico.com/es/sociedad/20200 308/la-calle-mantiene-el-pulso-contra-el-machismo-7880973 [Accessed 9 October 2022].

Collier, A. (1994) *Critical Realism: An Introduction to Roy Bhaskar's Philosophy*, London: Verso.

Comisión 8M (2017) 'Argumentario: 8 Marzo 2018', December. Available from: https://www.feministas.org/IMG/pdf/contenidos_8m-2.pdf [Accessed 9 October 2022].

Comisión 8M (2018) 'Manifiesto 8M: Hacia la Huelga Feminista'. Available from: https://hacialahuelgafeminista.org/manifiesto-8m/ [Accessed 9 October 2022].

Comisión 8M Madrid (2019) 'Manifiesto comisión feminista 8 de Marzo Madrid', 4 March. Available from: https://hacialahuelgafeminista.org/wp-content/uploads/2019/03/Manifiesto-8M-2019.pdf [Accessed 9 October 2022].

Comisión 8M Madrid (2020) 'Manifiesto comisión feminista 8 de Marzo Madrid: Revuelta feminista – con derechos, sin barreras – feministas sin fronteras', 2 March. Available from: https://hacialahuelgafeminista.org/wp-content/uploads/2020/03/Revuelta-feminista.-Manifiesto.pdf [Accessed 9 October 2022].

Comisión 8M Madrid (2021) 'Ante la emergencia social, el feminismo es essencial'. Available from: https://amecopress.net/IMG/pdf/manifiesto_8m_madrid_2021.pdf [Accessed 15 January 2024].

Congostrina, A.L. (2015) '2.000 mujeres marchan por Barcelona contra el machismo', *El País*, 19 May. Available from: https://elpais.com/ccaa/201w5/05/19/catalunya/1432063053_612717.html?prm=copy_link [Accessed 9 October 2022].

Connolly, H. and Darlington, R. (2012) 'Radical political unionism in France and Britain: a comparative study of SUD-Rail and the RMT', *European Journal of Industrial Relations*, 18(3): 235–50.

Cook, M.L., Dutta, M., Gallas, A., Nowak, J. and Scully, B. (2020) 'Global labour studies in the pandemic: notes for an emerging agenda', *Global Labour Journal*, 11(2): 74–88.

Coordinadora Feminista (2017) 'Convocatorias 8 de marzo 2017: Día Internacional de las Mujeres', 23 February. Available from: https://www.feministas.org/convocatorias-8-de-marzo-2017-dia.html [Accessed 9 October 2022].

Cortavitarte Carral, E. (2011) 'El movimiento obrero en 2010: El agridulce sabor de la derrota, a pesar de la huelga general del 29 S', *Anuario de Movimientos Sociales*. Available from: http://fundacionbetiko.org/portfo lio/2010/ [Accessed 9 October 2022].

Cortavitarte Carral, E. (2014) 'El movimiento obrero en 2013: Más precariedad, menos cobertura social y más desigualdades', Anuario de Movimientos Sociales. Available from: http://fundacionbetiko.org/wp-content/uploads/2014/03/El-movimiento-obrero-en-2013.pdf [Accessed 9 October 2022].

Crónica Global (2017) 'Así cuenta la Guardia Urbana de Barcelona los asistentes a una manifestación', 24 March. Available from: https://cronicaglobal.elespanol.com/vida/cuenta-guardia-urbana-manifestaciones_70241_102.html [Accessed 9 October 2022].

Crotty, J. and Epstein, G. (1996) 'In defence of capital controls', Socialist Register, 32: 118–49.

Crouch, C. (1977) Class Struggle and the Industrial Relations Crisis: Compromise and Corporatism in the Policies of the British State, London: Humanities.

Crouch, C. (2004) Post-Democracy: A Sociological Introduction, Cambridge: Polity.

Crouch, C. (2009) 'Privatised Keynesianism: an unacknowledged policy regime', British Journal of Politics and International Relations, 11: 382–99.

Crowley, T. (2020) 'This is a revolution, sir', Jacobin, 12 January. Available from: https://www.jacobinmag.com/2020/12/general-strike-india-modi-bjp-cpm-bihar [Accessed 16 June 2021].

Cruz, M. (2010) 'Zapatero rebaja el sueldo a los funcionarios por primera vez en la Historia', El Mundo, 12 May. Available from: https://www.elmundo.es/elmundo/2010/05/12/espana/1273649265.html [Accessed 10 August 2022].

Cué, C.E. and Rebossio, A. (2015) 'Un multitud grita #NiUnaMenos en Argentina contra la violencia machista', El País, 4 June. Available from: https://elpais.com/internacional/2015/06/03/actualidad/1433356172_949785.html [Accessed 9 October 2022].

Cué, C.E., Centenara, M., Barreiro, R. and Rivas Molina, F. (2016) 'Argentina se moviliza contra los más de 200 asesinatos de mujeres anuales', El País, 20 October. Available from: https://elpais.com/internacional/2016/10/19/argentina/1476905030_430567.html [Accessed 9 October 2022].

Cuéllar, A. (2019) 'Qué hacer el 8M si eres hombre', La Sexta, 8 March. Available from: https://www.lasexta.com/noticias/sociedad/que-hacer-hombre_201903065c8217610cf21ff290ea7c57.html [Accessed 9 October 2022].

Daily Observer (2018a) 'State media workers remain off the job', 28 December. Available from: https://antiguaobserver.com/state-media-workers-remain-off-the-job/ [Accessed 10 October 2022].

Daily Observer (2018b) 'Workers at state media stage all out strike', 21 December. Available from: https://antiguaobserver.com/workers-at-state-media-stage-all-out-strike/ [Accessed 10 October 2022].

Daily Observer (2018c) 'Clarevue workers strike', 11 January. Available from: https://antiguaobserver.com/clarevue-workers-strike/ [Accessed 10 October 2022].

Danermark, B., Ekström, M., Jakobsen, L. and Karlsson, J.C. (2002) *Explaining Society: Critical Realism in the Social Sciences*, London: Routledge.

Däubler, W. (2017) 'Das Gesetz ohne Wirkung', *Junge Welt*, 18 July. Available from: https://www.jungewelt.de/artikel/314661.das-gesetz-ohne-wirkung.html [Accessed 9 October 2022].

DBB (2019) 'Tarifeinheitsgesetz: dbb legt erneut Verfassungsbeschwerde ein', 13 March. Available from: https://www.dbb.de/artikel/tarifeinheitsgesetz-dbb-legt-erneut-verfassungsbeschwerde-ein.html [Accessed 9 October 2022].

DBK (2022) 'Katholische Kirche in Deutschland: Zahlen und Fakten 2021/22', July 2020. Available from: https://www.dbk.de/fileadmin/redaktion/Zahlen%20und%20Fakten/Kirchliche%20Statistik/Allgemein_-_Zahlen_und_Fakten/AH332_BRO_ZuF_2021-2022_WEB.pdf [Accessed 20 September 2022].

Del Bado, S. (2012) 'Wir müssen zeigen, dass Bündnisse aus sozialen Bewegungen, Gewerkschaften und linken Parteien eine Alternative zum herrschenden System anbieten', in A. Gallas, J. Nowak. and F. Wilde (eds) *Politische Streiks im Europa der Krise*, Hamburg: VSA, pp 171–8.

DeManuelle-Hall, J. (2019) ' "We believe in ferries": Alaskan ferry workers walk off the job', *Labor Notes*, 1 August. Available from: https://labornotes.org/2019/08/we-believe-ferries-alaska-ferry-workers-walk-job [Accessed 20 May 2021].

DeMartino, G. (1999) 'Global neoliberalism, policy autonomy, and international competitive dynamics', *Journal of Economic Issues*, 33(2): 343–9.

Der Spiegel (2014a) 'Ver.di-Chef Bsirske stellt sich gegen GDL-Boss Weselsky', 22 October. Available from: https://www.spiegel.de/wirtschaft/unternehmen/ver-di-chef-bsirske-kritisiert-blockade-der-lokfuehrer-a-998672.html [Accessed 9 October 2022].

Der Spiegel (2014b) 'Die Zukunft ist gestaltbar', interview with D. Wetzel, 5 November. Available from: https://www.igmetall.de/politik-und-gesellschaft/die-zukunft-ist-gestaltbar [Accessed 9 October 2022].

Der Spiegel (2014c) 'Bahn-Kunden droht längster Streik der Geschichte', 4 November. Available from: https://www.spiegel.de/wirtschaft/service/bahnstreik-kunden-droht-laengster-streik-der-geschichte-a-1000853.html [Accessed 9 October 2022].

Der Spiegel (2014d) 'Bahn will möglichst schnell wieder mit der GDL verhandeln', 7 November. Available from: https://www.spiegel.de/wirtschaft/unternehmen/bahn-unterliegt-vor-gericht-erfolg-fuer-gdl-streik-geht-weiter-a-1001493.html [Accessed 9 October 2022].

Der Spiegel (2015) 'Deutsche Bahn und EVG einigen sich auf Tarifvertrag', 27 May. Available from: https://www.spiegel.de/wirtschaft/unternehmen/bahn-streik-abgewendet-bahn-und-evg-schliessen-tarifvertrag-a-1035764.html [Accessed 9 October 2022].

Der Spiegel (2017) 'Schlichter wenden Bahnstreik ab', 10 March. Available from: https://www.spiegel.de/wirtschaft/soziales/schlichter-wenden-bahn-streik-ab-a-1138167.html [Accessed 9 October 2022].

Der Spiegel (2021a) 'SPD-Chef Walter-Borjans kritisiert Lokführerstreik', 12 August. Available from: https://www.spiegel.de/wirtschaft/spd-chef-walter-borjans-kritisiert-lokfuehrer-streik-a-1572e43c-966d-4277-98fe-662bd49562a0 [Accessed 9 October 2022].

Der Spiegel (2021b) 'Linken-Fraktionschef Bartsch fordert Einschreiten von Merkel', 31 August. Available from: https://www.spiegel.de/wirtschaft/unternehmen/deutsche-bahn-dietmar-bartsch-verlangt-von-angela-merkel-den-gdl-streik-abzuwenden-a-9e1de813-502d-4cda-a4a4-cc3746415339 [Accessed 9 October 2022].

Der Stern (2015) 'Bahn droht ein neuer Lokführerstreik', 17 May. Available from: https://www.stern.de/wirtschaft/news/bahnstreik-der-gdl--verhandlungen-abgebrochen---weiterer-streik-wahrscheinlich-6188980.html [Accessed 9 October 2022].

Dettmer, M. (2021) 'Weselskys Machtspiel ist gefährlich', *Der Spiegel*, 12 August. Available from: https://www.spiegel.de/wirtschaft/unternehmen/deutsche-bahn-und-der-streik-der-lokfuehrer-claus-weselsky-und-sein-gefaehrliches-machtspiel-a-9e1c7015-0ed9-4150-8922-361877f1bc2c [Accessed 9 October 2022].

Deutsche Bahn (2022) 'Integrierter Bericht 2021', 31 March. Available from: https://ibir.deutschebahn.com/2021/fileadmin/pdf/DB_IB21_web_01.pdf [Accessed 9 October 2022].

Dias, H. and Fernandes, L. (2016) 'The November 2012 general strike and anti-austerity protests', *Workers of the World*, 1(8): 16–38.

Dias, T. (2018) 'De la Huelga Feminista de 2018 al 8M 2019: movimientos feministas, visiones políticas en disputa y una nota tecnopolítica', *Technopolítica* blog, 28 June. Available from: https://web.archive.org/web/20220627235933/https://tecnopolitica.net/en/content/de-la-huelga-feminista-de-2018-al-8m-2019-y-mas-alla-movimientos-feministas-visiones [Accessed 22 July 2023].

Die Welt (2014) 'Mit Ersatzfahrplänen und Alternativen in den Lokführerstreik', 5 November. Available from: https://www.welt.de/regionales/rheinland-pfalz-saarland/article133999124/Mit-Ersatzfahrplaenen-und-Alternativen-in-den-Lokfuehrerstreik.html [Accessed 9 October 2022].

Die Welt (2015) 'Deutsche-Bahn-Gewinn dramatisch eingebrochen', 28 July. Available from: https://www.welt.de/wirtschaft/article144525776/Deutsche-Bahn-Gewinn-dramatisch-eingebrochen.html [Accessed 9 October 2022].

Díez, A. (20[08]) 'Zapatero anuncia un plan de austeridad a los 100 días de ganar', *El País*, 23 July. Available from: https://elpais.com/diario/2008/07/23/espana/1216764011_850215.html [Accessed 9 October 2022].

Die Zeit (2013a) 'Warnstreiks behindern Bahnverkehr', 18 March. Available from: https://www.zeit.de/wirtschaft/unternehmen/2013-03/bahn-streik-verspaetungen [Accessed 9 October 2022].

Die Zeit (2013b) 'Deutsche Bahn und Gewerkschaft einigen sich', 25 March. Available from: https://www.zeit.de/wirtschaft/unternehmen/2013-03/tarifstreit-einigung-deutsche-bahn [Accessed 9 October 2022].

Die Zeit (2014a) 'Zwei Drittel der Fernzüge fallen aus', 18 October. Available from: https://www.zeit.de/wirtschaft/2014-10/bahn-streik-lokfuehrer?sort=desc&page=2 [Accessed 9 October 2022].

Die Zeit (2014b) 'Tarifeinheit spaltet DGB', 14 December. Available from: https://www.zeit.de/wirtschaft/2014-12/dgb-streit-tarifeinheit-unterschriftenaktion [Accessed 9 October 2022].

Die Zeit (2015a) 'Wieder Streik bei Amazon: Sechs Logistikzentren betroffen', 22 June. Available from: www.zeit.de/news/2015-06/22/tarife-wieder-streik-bei-amazon---sechs-logistikzentren-betroffen-22140209 [Accessed 22 March 2022].

Die Zeit (2015b) 'Opposition nennt neues Tarifgesetz verfassungswidrig', 22 May. Available from: https://www.zeit.de/politik/ausland/2015-05/tarifeinheitsgesetz-bundestag-die-linke-gruene-kritik [Accessed 9 October 2022].

Die Zeit (2016) 'Ausgang der Bahn-Tarifrunde offen', 8 December. Available from: https://www.zeit.de/news/2016-12/08/tarife-ausgang-der-bahn-tarifrunde-offen-08201407 [Accessed 9 October 2022].

Die Zeit (2017) 'Gilt für Gewerkschaften das Recht des Stärkeren?', 24 January. Available from: https://www.zeit.de/wirtschaft/2017-01/tarifeinheitsgesetz-bundesverfassungsgericht-verhandlungen-klaus-dauderstaedt-dbb [Accessed 9 October 2022].

Die Zeit (2018) 'Deutsche Bahn und EVG einigen sich im Tarifstreit', 15 December. Available from: https://www.zeit.de/mobilitaet/2018-12/bahnstreik-einigung-evg-tarifstreik-gdl [Accessed 9 October 2022].

Die Zeit (2019) 'Bahn verständigt sich mit Lokführern auf Tarifvertrag', 4 January. Available from: https://www.zeit.de/mobilitaet/2019-01/tarifeinigung-deutsche-bahn-lokfuehrer-gewerkschaften-gdl-evg [Accessed 9 October 2022].

DLF (2015) 'Ramelow wirft Bahn "unprofessionelles Vorgehen" vor', 21 May. Available from: http://www.deutschlandfunk.de/schlichtung-zwischen-bahn-und-gdl-ramelow-wirft-bahn.1818.de.html?dram:article_id=320507 [Accessed 9 October 2022].

DLF (2017) 'Proteste gegen Personalmangel. Weinende Patienten – wütende Mitarbeiter', 8 August. Available from: www.deutschlandfunk.de/proteste-gegen-personalmangel-weinende-patienten-wuetende-100.html [Accessed 20 February 2022].

Dogan, M.G. (2010) 'When neoliberalism confronts the moral economy of workers: the final spring of Turkish labor unions', *European Journal of Turkish Studies*, 21 October. Available from: http://journals.openedition.org/ejts/4321 [Accessed 16 February 2020].

Dor, L. and Runciman, C. (2022) 'Precarious workers and the labour process: problematising the core/non-core', *Global Labour Journal*, 13(1): 343–9.

Dörre, K. (2016) 'Die neue Konfliktformation: Klassen-Kämpfe in fragmentierten Arbeitsbeziehungen', *Industrielle Beziehungen*, 23(3): 348–65.

Dörre, K. (2018) 'A right-wing workers' movement? Impressions from Germany', *Global Labour Journal*, 9(3): 339–47.

Dörre, K., Goes, T., Schmalz, S. and Thiel, M. (2016) *Streikrepublik Deutschland? Die Erneuerung der Gewerkschaften in Ost und West*, Frankfurt am Main: Campus.

Dribbusch, H. (2018) 'Das Einfache, das so schwer zu zählen ist: Probleme der Streikstatistik in der Bundesrepublik Deutschland', *Industrielle Beziehungen*, 25(3): 301–19.

Dribbusch, H. and Birke, P. (2012) 'Trade unions in Germany: organisation, environment, challenges', Friedrich Ebert Foundation, May. Available from: https://library.fes.de/pdf-files/id-moe/09113-20120828.pdf [Accessed 29 July 2021].

Dribbusch, H. and Birke, P. (2019) 'Trade unions in Germany: challenges in a transition', Friedrich Ebert Foundation, April. Available from: https://library.fes.de/pdf-files/id/ipa/15399.pdf [Accessed 29 July 2021].

Druciarek, M. (2016) 'After abortion law protest, what stands in the way of gender equality in Poland?', *World Politics Review*, 21 October. Available from: https://www.worldpoliticsreview.com/after-abortion-law-protest-what-stands-in-the-way-of-gender-equality-in-poland/?one-time-read-code=39207166612288952046 [Accessed 9 October 2022].

Dukes, R. and Kountouris, N. (2016) 'Pre-strike ballots, picketing and protest: banning industrial action by the back door?', *Industrial Law Journal*, 45(3): 337–62.

DW (2013) 'Erstmals Streiks bei Amazon', 14 May. Available from: www.dw.com/de/erstmals-streiks-bei-amazon/a-16810614 [Accessed 12 February 2022].

DW (2016) 'Women go on "Black Monday" strike in Poland against abortion ban', 3 October. Available from: https://www.dw.com/en/women-go-on-black-monday-strike-in-poland-against-abortion-ban/a-35947232 [Accessed 9 October 2022].

DW (2018) 'Deutsche Bahn stellt Fernverkehr vorrübergehend ein', 10 December. Available from: https://www.dw.com/de/deutsche-bahn-ste llt-fernverkehr-vor%C3%BCbergehend-ein/a-46661473 [Accessed 18 May 2021].

DW (2020) 'Belarus strike action begins', 26 October. Available from: https://www.dw.com/en/belarus-strike-action-begins/a-55396530 [Accessed 20 May 2021].

Dymski, G.A. (2009) 'Racial exclusion and the political economy of the subprime crisis', *Historical Materialism*, 17: 149–79.

The Economist (1999) 'The sick man of the Euro', 5–11 June, pp 21–3.

EFE (2019) 'General strike in South Africa to protest unemployment, electricity crisis', 13 February. Available from: www.efe.com/efe/english/world/general-strike-in-south-africa-to-protest-unemployment-electric ity-crisis/50000262-3896724 [Accessed 12 February 2022].

Effose, S. (2021) 'Financial empowerment for married women in France: the matrimonial regime reform of 13th July 1965', *Quaderni storici*, 166: 117–41.

Ege, M. and Gallas, A. (2019) 'The exhaustion of Merkelism: a conjunctural analysis', *New Formations*, 96(96): 89–131.

Eichengreen, B. (1996) *Globalizing Capital: A History of the International Monetary System*, Princeton: Princeton University Press.

EKD (2020) 'Statistik über Beschäftigte', August. Available from: https://www.ekd.de/ekd_de/ds_doc/Bericht_Besch%c3%a4ftigte_2020.pdf [Accessed 9 October 2022].

El Confidencial (2020) '¿Por qué este 8 de marzo no hay huelga? El feminismo se manifiesta pero sin paros', 8 March. Available from: https://www.elc onfidencial.com/espana/2020-03-08/huelga-feminista-8marzo_2477683/ [Accessed 9 October 2022].

Elgot, J. (2015) 'Thousands rally in London to protest junior doctor contract – as it happened', *The Guardian*, 17 October. Available from: https://www. theguardian.com/society/live/2015/oct/17/junior-doctors-protest-agai nst-contract-proposals-live?filterKeyEvents=false&page=with:block-56226 f7fe4b094f6bf347e5b#block-56226f7fe4b094f6bf347e5b [Accessed 9 October 2022].

Elk, M. (2018) 'The teachers' strikes prove it: the media is finally seeing America's new labor landscape', *The Guardian*, 28 April. Available from: https://www.theguardian.com/us-news/2018/apr/28/us-teachers-strikes-workers-labor-unions [Accessed 2 July 2021].

Elliott, V. (2018) 'Thinking about the coding process in qualitative data analysis', *The Qualitative Report*, 23(11): 2850–61.

El Mundo (2010) 'Así queda la reforma laboral: despido más barato y mayor control a los parados', 10 September. Available from: https://www.elmu ndo.es/mundodinero/2010/09/09/economia/1284042795.html [Accessed 9 October 2022].

El País (2008) 'Zapatero anuncia la moratoria del pago del 50% de la hipoteca para los desempleados', 11 November. Available from: https://elpais.com/economia/2008/11/03/actualidad/1225701177_850215.html [Accessed 9 October 2022].

El País (2010) 'Las manifestaciones cierran una jornada de huelga desigual', 29 September. Available from: https://elpais.com/elpais/2010/09/28/actualidad/1285661849_850215.html [Accessed 20 October 2021].

El País (2011) 'Escaso seguimiento de la huelga general contra la reforma de las pensiones', 27 January. Available from: https://elpais.com/elpais/2011/01/27/actualidad/1296119819_850215.html [Accessed 20 October 2021].

El País (2012a) 'Las manifestaciones cierran la jornada de huelga en la educación', 22 May. Available from: https://elpais.com/sociedad/2012/05/22/actualidad/1337668996_700737.html [Accessed 9 October 2022].

El País (2012b) 'Cientos de miles de manifestantes cierran la protesta de la huelga general del 14-N', 14 November. Available from: https://elpais.com/politica/2012/11/13/actualidad/1352838703_548795.html [Accessed 9 October 2022].

El País (2013) 'Segunda jornada de huelga general en educación', 9 May. Available from: https://elpais.com/sociedad/2013/05/09/album/1368083591_873673.html [Accessed 9 October 2022].

El País (2017) 'Día Internacional de la Mujer 2017: Manifestación del 8 de marzo', 9 March. Available from: https://elpais.com/elpais/2017/03/08/actualidad/1488970669_451889.html [Accessed 9 October 2022].

El Salto (2019) '8 de marzo de 2019: El feminismo es imparable', 8 March. Available from: https://www.elsaltodiario.com/huelga-feminista/8-de-marzo-de-2019-el-feminismo-es-imparable [Accessed 9 October 2022].

El-Sharif, Y. (2014) 'Deutschlands dümmste Gewerkschaft', *Der Spiegel*, 17 October. Available from: https://www.piegel.de/wirtschaft/soziales/lokfuehrer-gdl-gewerkschaft-provoziert-gesetz-zur-tarifeinheit-a-995541.html [Accessed 9 October 2022].

Engelhardt, A. (2017) 'Know your rights: Portugal zwischen Verfassungsaktivismus und sozialen Bewegungen: Die Staatskrise 2013 aus Sicht der materialistischen Bewegungsforschung', *Kritische Justiz*, 50(4): 417–33.

Enzensberger, H.M. (1991) 'Ways of walking: postscript to utopia', in R. Blackburn (ed) *After the Fall: The Failure of Communism and the Future of Socialism*, London: Verso, pp 18–24.

Erhardt, M. (2019) 'Keine Bahnstreiks bis 2021', *Deutschlandfunk*, 4 January. Available from: https://www.deutschlandfunk.de/tarifeinigung-mit-der-gdl-keine-bahnstreiks-bis-100.html [Accessed 9 October 2022].

Eribon, D. (2009) *Returning to Reims*, Los Angeles: Semiotext(e).

Esping-Anderson, G. (1990) *Three Worlds of Welfare Capitalism*, Cambridge: Polity.

Esser, J. (1982) *Gewerkschaften in der Krise*, Frankfurt am Main: Suhrkamp.

Esser, J., Fach, W. and Väth, W. (1983) *Krisenregulierung: Zur politischen Durchsetzung ökonomischer Zwänge*, Frankfurt am Main: Suhrkamp.

Estanque, E., Costa, H.A. and Soeiro, J. (2013) 'The new global cycle of protest and the Portuguese case', *Journal of Social Science Education*, 12(1): 31-40.

Esteve, A., Schwartz, C.R., Van Bavel, J., Permanyer, I., Klesment, M. and Garcia, J. (2016) 'The end of hypergamy: global trends and implications', *Population and Development Review*, 42(4): 615–65.

Europa Press (2020) 'Las manifestaciones feministas vuelven este domingo a toda España por el #8M', 6 March. Available from: https://www.europapr ess.es/epsocial/igualdad/noticia-manifestaciones-feministas-vuelven-domi ngo-toda-espana-8m-20200306181824.html [Accessed 9 October 2022].

Express (2017) '"Keine Einheit bei Tarifeinheit": Stimmen zum Verfassungsgerichtsurteil', July, p 4.

Fantasia, R. (1988) *Cultures of Solidarity: Consciousness, Action, and Contemporary American Workers*, Berkeley: University of California Press.

Farrow, A. (2017) 'Cleaners strike for equality at university in London', *Socialist Worker*, 21 March. Available from: socialistworker.co.uk/news/ cleaners-strike-for-equality-at-university-in-london/ [Accessed 20 March 2022].

FAZ (2015a) 'Längster Streik der Bahn-Geschichte hat begonnen', 5 May. Available from: https://www.faz.net/aktuell/wirtschaft/streiks-bei-bahn- und-lufthansa/lokfuehrer-beginnen-fuenftaegigen-streik-im-personenverk ehr-13574982.html [Accessed 9 October 2022].

FAZ (2015b) 'Einigung im Tarifstreit zwischen GDL und Bahn', 1 July. Available from: https://www.faz.net/aktuell/wirtschaft/streiks-bei-bahn- und-lufthansa/einigung-im-tarifstreit-zwischen-gdl-und-bahn-13678767. html [Accessed 9 October 2022].

Ferragut, M. (2018) 'El 8M es un hecho histórico, marcará un antes y un después', *Diario de Mallorca*, 7 March. Available from: https://www.diari odemallorca.es/mallorca/2018/03/07/8m-hecho-historico-marcara-desp ues-3252865.html [Accessed 9 October 2022].

Ferrero, Á. (2019) 'Barcelona se convierte en un clamor masivo contra las condenas del Supremo', *Público*, 18 October. Available from: www.publico. es/politica/sentencia-proces-barcelona-convierte-clamor-masivo-conde nas-supremo.html [Accessed 23 March 2022].

Flinders, M. (2005) 'The politics of public-private partnerships', *British Journal of Politics and International Relations*, 7: 215–19.

Foucault, M. (1989) *The Archaeology of Knowledge*, London: Routledge, original work published in 1972.

Fraad, H., Resnick, S. and Wolff, R. (1994) *Bringing It All Back Home: Class, Gender & Power in the Modern Household*, London: Pluto

Franzosi, R. (1995) *The Puzzle of Strikes*, Cambridge: Cambridge University Press.

Fraser, N. (2017) 'From progressive neoliberalism to Trump – and beyond', *American Affairs*. Available from: https://americanaffairsjournal.org/2017/11/progressive-neoliberalism-trump-beyond/ [Accessed 9 October 2022].

Frege, C.M. and Kelly, J. (eds) (2004) *Varieties of Unionism: Strategies for Union Revitalization in a Globalizing Economy*, Oxford: Oxford University Press.

Frey, D.F. (2017) 'Conflict over conflict: the right to strike in international law', *Global Labour Journal*, 8(1): 17–31.

Frese, A. (2014a) 'Tarifeinheit für Mindestlohn: Der DGB in der Zwickmühle', *Der Tagesspiegel*, 14 May. Available from: https://www.tagesspiegel.de/wirtschaft/der-dgb-in-der-zwickmuhle-3562468.html [Accessed 9 October 2022].

Frese, A. (2014b) 'Regierung will Tarifeinheit per Gesetz', *Der Tagesspiegel*, 5 October. Available from: https://www.tagesspiegel.de/wirtschaft/wort-halten-3591994.html [Accessed 9 October 2022].

Frese, A. (2015a) 'GDL gegen Deutsche Bahn', *Der Tagesspiegel*, 21 April. Available from: https://www.tagesspiegel.de/wirtschaft/zehn-monate-str eit-keine-einigung-6890407.html [Accessed 9 October 2022].

Frese, A. (2015b) 'DGB-Chef Hoffmann über den Streik der Lokführer', *Der Tagesspiegel*, 20 May. Available from: https://www.tagesspiegel.de/wir tschaft/weselsky-will-keinen-kompromiss-und-keine-kooperation-8126 290.html [Accessed 9 October 2022].

Frese, A. (2021a) 'Ärger bei der Bahn: Gewerkschafter Weselsky für Personalabbau', *Der Tagesspiegel*, 14 March. Available from: https://www.tagesspiegel.de/wirtschaft/gewerkschafter-weselsky-fur-personalabbau-7760173.html [Accessed 9 October 2022].

Frese, A. (2021b) 'Die GDL spaltet die Belegschaft', interview with R. Hoffmann, *Der Tagesspiegel*, 20 August. Available from: https://www.tagesspiegel.de/wirtschaft/die-gdl-spaltet-die-belegschaft-4271269.html [Accessed 9 October 2022].

Frese, A. (2021c) 'Ein Gewerkschaftsboss kämpft ums Überleben', *Der Tagesspiegel*, 10 August. Available from: https://www.tagesspiegel.de/wirtschaft/ein-gewerkschaftsboss-kampft-ums-uberleben-4269667.html [Accessed 9 October 2022].

Friedman, M. (1962) *Capitalism and Freedom*, Chicago: University of Chicago Press.

Frindert, J., Dribbusch, J. and Schulten, T. (eds) (2022) 'WSI Arbeitskampfbilanz: Normalisierung des Arbeitskampfgeschehens im zweiten Jahr der Pandemie', WSI Report, 74, April. Available from: https://www.wsi.de/fpdf/HBS-008309/p_wsi_report_74_2022.pdf [Accessed 10 October 2022].

Fukuyama, F. (1992) *The End of History and the Last Man*, New York: The Free Press.

Fulton, L. (2021) 'United Kingdom', *Worker Participation*, ETUI. Available from: https://www.worker-participation.eu/National-Industrial-Relati ons/Countries/United-Kingdom/Workplace-Representation [Accessed 9 October 2022].

Furnivall, D., Bottle, A. and Aylin, P. (2018) 'Retrospective analysis of the national impact of industrial action by English junior doctors in 2016', *BMJ Open*, 8(1).

Gago, A. (2012) 'La clase trabajadora hoy y la lucha contra la crisis', *La Hiedra*, 14 February. Available from: https://web.archive.org/web/20160803144 250/http://lahiedra.info/la-clase-trabajadora-hoy-y-la-lucha-contra-la-cri sis/ [Accessed 9 October 2022].

Gago, A. (2013) 'Los sindicatos mayoritarios españoles, CCOO y UGT, ante la crisis económica: ¿Declive o revitalización?', in S. Aguilar (ed) *Anuari del Conflicte Social 2012*, Barcelona: Observatori del Conflicte Social, pp 1075–104.

Gago, V. (2018) '#WeStrike: notes toward a political theory of the feminist strike', *South Atlantic Quarterly*, 117(3): 660–9.

Galdón Corbella, C. (2018) 'Cosmovisiones feministas en clave generacional: Del movimiento 15M a la Huelga Feminista del 8M', *Encrucijadas*, December. Available from: https://dialnet.unirioja.es/desca rga/articulo/6754579.pdf [Accessed 9 October 2022].

Gall, G. (2012) 'Quiescence continued? Recent strike activity in nine Western European economies', *Economic and Industrial Democracy*, 34(4): 667–91.

Gallas, A. (2008) 'Kapitalismus ohne Bourgeoisie: Die "Gentlemanly Association" und der englische Block an der Macht, in U. Lindner, J. Nowak and P. Paust-Lassen (eds) *Philosophieren unter anderen: Beiträge zum Palaver der Menschheit*, Münster: Westfälisches Dampfboot, pp 263–87.

Gallas, A. (2010) 'Brothers in Arms: Zur politischen Strategie der britischen Koalitionsregierung', *links-netz* blog, November. Available from: http://old. links-netz.de/K_texte/K_gallas_brothers.html [Accessed 9 October 2022].

Gallas, A. (2011) 'Singing in the Rain. Nach dem Arabischen Frühling ein britischer Sommer', *links-netz*, November. Available from: http://old. links-netz.de/K_texte/K_gallas_riots.html [Accessed 9 October 2022].

Gallas, A. (2013) 'Did things really get better? Ein Rückblick auf "New Labour"', *Zukunft*, January, pp 24–30.

Gallas, A. (2015) 'The three sources of anti-socialism: a critical inquiry into the normative foundations of F.A. Hayek's politics', *Zeitschrift für kritische Sozialtheorie und Philosophie*, 2(1): 182–99.

Gallas, A. (2016) *The Thatcherite Offensive: A Neo-Poulantzasian Analysis*, Leiden: Brill.

Gallas, A. (2018) 'The politics of striking: on the shifting of dynamics of workers' struggles in Britain', in J. Nowak, M. Dutta and P. Birke (eds) *Workers Movements and Strikes in the Twenty-First Century: A Global Perspective*, London: Rowman & Littlefield, pp 237–54.

Gallas, A. (2019) 'Klassen', in C. von Braunmühl, H. Gerstenberger, R. Ptak and C. Wichterich (eds) *ABC der globalen (Un)Ordnung*, Hamburg: VSA, pp 136–7.

Gallas, A. (2020) 'Mass strikes in a global conjuncture of crisis: a Luxemburgian analysis', in V. Satgar (ed) *Brics and the New American Imperialism: Global Rivalry and Resistance*, Johannesburg: Wits University Press, pp 182–202.

Gallas, A. and Nowak, J. (2012) 'Agieren aus der Defensive: Ein Überblick zu politischen Streiks in Europa mit Fallstudien zu Frankreich und Großbritannien', in A. Gallas, J. Nowak and F. Wilde (eds) *Politische Streiks im Europa der Krise*, Hamburg: VSA, pp 24–106.

Gallas, A., Nowak, J. and Wilde, F. (eds) (2012) *Politische Streiks im Europa der Krise*, Hamburg: VSA.

Gallas, A., Scherrer, C. and Williams, M. (2014) 'Inequality: the Achilles heel of free market democracy', *International Journal of Labour Research*, 6(1): 143–61.

Gambino, F. (2007) 'A critique of Fordism and the regulation school', *The Commoner*, 12: 39–62.

Gamble, A. (1994) *The Free Economy and the Strong State: The Politics of Thatcherism*, 2nd edn, Houndmills: Palgrave.

Gamble, A. (2009) *The Spectre at the Feast: Capitalist Crisis and the Politics of Recession*, Houndmills: Palgrave.

García, B., Alaboa, N. and Pérez, M. (2018) 'Spain's feminist strike', *New Left Review*, II(110): 35–7.

García Grenzner, J. (2017) '2015–2016: Efervescencia feminista social y política para frenar la restauración del 78', *Anuario de Movimientos Sociales*. Available from: http://fundacionbetiko.org/wp-content/uploads/2017/02/03_garcia_feminismo.pdf [Accessed 9 October 2022].

García Grenzner, J. (2018) '2017: resistencia feminista local y global frente a la guerra contra las mujeres y la austeridad', *Anuario de Movimientos Sociales*. Available from: http://fundacionbetiko.org/wp-content/uploads/2018/02/03_grenzner.pdf [Accessed 9 October 2022].

GDL (2014a) 'Frontalangriff gegen alle Berufsgewerkschaften', press release, 11 December. Available from: https://www.gdl.de/Aktuell-2014/Press emitteilung-1418314713 [Accessed 9 October 2022].

GDL (2014b) 'Fünf für fünf', 16 June. Available from: https://www.gdl.de/Aktuell-2014/AushangFakten-1402916543 [Accessed 9 October 2022].

GDL (2014c) '91 Prozent votierten für Streik', press release, 2 October. Available from: https://www.gdl.de/Aktuell-2014/Pressemitteilung-141 2260934 [Accessed 9 October 2022].

GDL (2014d) 'Bundesweiter befristeter Streik bei der Deutschen Bahn', press release, 7 October. Available from: https://www.gdl.de/Aktuell-2014/Pressemitteilung-1412632743 [Accessed 9 October 2022].

GDL (2015a) 'Champagner für den Vorstand, trocken Brot für das Zugpersonal', press release, 17 April. Available from: https://www.gdl.de/Aktuell-2015/Pressemitteilung-1429285418 [Accessed 9 October 2022].

GDL (2015b) 'Arbeitskampf bei der Deutschen Bahn im Personen- und Güterverkehr', press release, 20 April. Available from: https://www.gdl.de/Aktuell-2015/Pressemitteilung-1429545427 [Accessed 9 October 2022].

GDL (2015c) 'DB-Vorstand bestreikt Verhandlungen: Das Zugpersonal streikt für seine Grundrechte', 3 May. Available from: https://www.gdl.de/Aktuell-2015/Telegramm-1430668762 [Accessed 9 October 2022].

GDL (2015d) 'Mehr Zugpersonal hat gestreikt', press release, 10 May. Available from: https://www.gdl.de/Aktuell-2015/Pressemitteilung-143 1261599 [Accessed 9 October 2022].

GDL (2020) 'Keine Unterzeichnung des "Bündnis für unsere Bahn": Mit Bündnispapier und Schriftwechsel', press release, 26 May. Available from: https://www.gdl.de/Aktuell-2020/Pressemitteilung-1590497279 [Accessed 9 October 2022].

GDL (2021) '95 Prozent für Arbeitskampf', press release, 10 August. Available from: https://www.gdl.de/Aktuell-2021/Pressemitteilung-162 8595705 [Accessed 9 October 2022].

Gefken, R. (2021) 'Arbeitsgerichtsurteile zum GDL-Streik', *Streikzeitung*, (2): II.

Gester, J. (2012) 'Tarifbindung und mehr Lohn – Arbeitskampf an der Berliner Charité und bei CFM', *Labournet Archiv*, 18 December. Available from: www.archiv.labournet.de/branchen/dienstleistung/gw/charite_gest er1.html [Accessed 28 February 2022].

GEW Sachsen (nd) 'Das Beamten-Alphabet'. Available from: https://www.gew-sachsen.de/beamte/beamten-alphabet [Accessed 9 October 2022].

Gil Calvo, E. (2014) 'Del desafecto a la contienda: Crisis, austeridad y ciclo de protesta', *Documentación Social*, 173: 37–55.

Goddard, A.F. (2016) 'Lessons to be learned: from the UK junior doctors' strike', *Jama*, 316(14): 1445–6.

Goes, T.E. (2019) *Klassen im Kampf: Vorschläge für eine populäre Linke*, Köln: Papyrossa.

Gómez, M.V. and Marcos, J. (2018) 'Movilización histórica por la igualdad de las mujeres', *El País*, 9 March. Available from: https://elpais.com/economia/2018/03/08/actualidad/1520545956_654616.html [Accessed 9 October 2022].

Gómez, V.N. (2012) 'CC OO y UGT aprueban ir a la huelga general el 29 de marzo', *El País*, 9 March. Available from: https://elpais.com/politica/2012/03/08/actualidad/1331242620_561548.html [Accessed 9 October 2022].

Gómez, V.N. (2016) 'El fin de una era sindical', *El País*, 16 May. Available from: https://elpais.com/economia/2016/04/29/actualidad/1461944863 _948173.html [Accessed 9 October 2022].

Gómez, V.N. and Aunión, J.A. (2019) 'Una movilización masiva exhibe en las calles la fuerza del feminismo', *El País*, 9 March. Available from: https://web. archive.org/web/20220412134820/https://elpais.com/sociedad/2019/03/ 08/actualidad/1552079524_186232.html [Accessed 9 October 2022].

Goméz, V.N. and Quesada, J.D. (2020) 'El feminismo exhibe su músculo movilizador pese al temor al coronavirus', *El País*, 8 March. Available from: https://elpais.com/sociedad/dia-de-la-mujer/2020-03-08/el-femini smo-exhibe-su-musculo-movilizador-pese-al-temor-al-coronavirus.html [Accessed 9 October 2022].

González, C. (2020) '¿El 8-M, el culpable de todos los males? Viajemos al pasado para analizar la demagogia de la derecha con el coronavirus', *Público*, 28 March. Available from: https://www.publico.es/tremending/ 2020/03/27/covid-19-el-8-m-el-culpable-de-todos-los-males-viajemos- al-pasado-para-analizar-la-demagogia-de-la-derecha-con-el-coronavirus/ [Accessed 9 October 2022].

González Begega, S. and Luque Balbona, D. (2014) '¿Adiós al corporatismo competitivo en España? Pactos sociales y conflicto en la crisis económica', *Revista Española de Investigaciones Sociológicas*, 148: 79–102.

González Rodriguez, M.L. (2019) 'Historia sobre la huelga 8-M en el estado español', *El Clarión*, 52: 18–19.

Gordon, T. (2019) 'Capitalism, neoliberalism, and unfree labour', *Critical Sociology*, 45(6): 921–39.

Gordon, A. and Upchurch, M. (2012) 'Railing against neoliberalism: radical political unionism in SUD-Rail and RMT', *European Journal of Industrial Relations*, 18(3): 259–65.

Gorosarri, M. and Sauviat, L. (2016) 'The uneven development of (mass) strikes in France and Spain', *Workers of the World*, 1(8): 39–55.

Gough, I. (1979) *The Political Economy of the Welfare State*, London: Macmillan.

Gowan, P. (2009) 'Crisis in the heartland: consequences of the new Wall Street system', *New Left Review*, II(55): 5–29.

Grabka, M.M. and Göbler, K. (2020) 'Der Niedriglohnsektor in Deutschland: Falle oder Sprungbrett für Beschäftigte?', Bertelsmann Foundation, July. Available from: https://www.bertelsmann-stiftung.de/de/ publikationen/publikation/did/der-niedriglohnsektor-in-deutschland-all [Accessed 9 October 2022].

Grady, J. (2018) Twitter, 23 February. Available from: https://twitter.com/ DrJoGrady/status/967085874931490816?s=20&t=i_rhaswbNAYkE2H uS9SNvQ [Accessed 9 October 2022].

Gramsci, A. (1971) *Selections from the Prison Notebooks*, edited and translated by Q. Hoare and G. Nowell Smith, New York: International Publishers.

Grant, J.P. (1971) 'Marginal men: the global unemployment crisis', *Foreign Affairs*, 50(1): 112–24.

Grice, A. (2016) 'Exclusive: majority of people in the UK supported junior doctors' all-out strike last week', *The Independent*, 1 May. Available from: https://www.independent.co.uk/news/uk/politics/exclusive-poll-majority-of-people-in-the-uk-supported-junior-doctors-allout-strike-last-week-a7007926.html [Accessed 9 October 2022].

Grodira, F. (2019) 'Madrid vuelve a inundarse de feminismo', *Público*, 8 March. Available from: https://www.publico.es/sociedad/huelga-feminista-8-marzo-madrid-vuelve-inundarse-feminismo.html [Accessed 9 October 2022].

Guldi, J. (2019) 'World neoliberalism as rebellion from below? British squatters and the global interpretation of poverty, 1946–1974', *Humanity: An International Journal of Human Rights, Humanitarianism, and Development*, 10(1): 29–57.

Gutschker, T. (2014) 'Mensch, Weselsky', *FAZ*, 22 November. Available from: https://www.faz.net/-gqa-7wnvl [Accessed 9 October 2022].

Haas, T. (2021) 'From green energy to the green car state? The political economy of ecological modernisation in Germany', *New Political Economy*, 26(4): 660–73.

Hain, P. (1986) *Political Strikes: The State and Trade Unionism in Britain*, London: Penguin.

Hall, P.A. (2018) 'Varieties of capitalism in light of the Euro crisis', *Journal of European Public Policy*, 25(1): 7–30.

Hall, P.A. and Soskice, D. (eds) (2001) *Varieties of Capitalism: The Institutional Foundations of Comparative Advantage*, Oxford: Oxford University Press.

Hall, S. (1979) 'The great moving right show', *Marxism Today*, January, pp 14–20.

Hall, S., Critcher, C., Jefferson, T., Clarke, J. and Roberts, B. (2013) *Policing the Crisis: Mugging the State and Law & Order*, Houndmills: Palgrave Macmillan, original work published in 1978.

Hamann, K. (2013) 'The relationship between unions and Zapatero's government: from social pacts to general strike', in B.N. Field and A. Botti (eds) *Politics and Society in Contemporary Spain: From Zapatero to Rajoy*, New York: Palgrave, pp 123–43.

Handelsblatt (2020) 'Bahn und EVG erzielen Tarifeinigung: Keine betriebsbedingten Kündigungen', 17 September. Available from: https://www.handelsblatt.com/unternehmen/handel-konsumgueter/eisenbahn-und-verkehrsgewerkschaft-bahn-undevgerzielen-tarifeinigung-keine-betriebsbedingten-kuendigungen/26197664.html [Accessed 9 October 2022].

Hansard (2016) 'Junior doctors: industrial action', 607, 24 March. Available from: https://hansard.parliament.uk/commons/2016-03-24/debates/16032433000004/JuniorDoctorsIndustrialAction [Accessed 9 October 2022].

Harman, C. (2009) *Zombie Capitalism: Global Crisis and the Relevance of Marx*, London: Bookmarks.

Hart, G. (2018) 'Relational comparison revisited: Marxist postcolonial geographies in practice', *Progress in Human Geography*, 42(3): 371–94.

Hartmann, H. (1979) 'The unhappy marriage of Marxism and feminism: towards a more progressive union', *Capital & Class*, 3(2): 1–33.

Hartocollis, A. and Alcindor, Y. (2017) 'Women's march highlights as huge crowds protest Trump: "we're not going away"', *New York Times*, 21 January. Available from: https://www.nytimes.com/2017/01/21/us/wom ens-march.html [Accessed 9 October 2022].

Harvey, D. (2005) *A Brief History of Neoliberalism*, Oxford: Oxford University Press.

Harvey, D. (2010) *The Enigma of Capital and the Crises of Capitalism*, London: Profile Books.

Harvey, D. (2011) 'Roepke lecture in economic geography: crises, geographic disruptions and the uneven development of political responses', *Economic Geography*, 87(1): 1–22.

Harvey, F. (2020) '"Surprisingly rapid" rebound in carbon emissions post-lockdown', *The Guardian*, 11 June. Available from: https://www.theg uardian.com/environment/2020/jun/11/carbon-emissions-in-surprisin gly-rapid-surge-post-lockdown [Accessed 8 October 2022].

Hayek, F.A. (1960) *The Constitution of Liberty*, Chicago: University of Chicago Press.

Hayek, F.A. (1973–7) *Law, Legislation, and Liberty: A New Statement of the Liberal Principles of Justice and Political Economy*, London: Routledge.

Hayns, J. (2017a) 'Organised rage: the LSE cleaners strike', *Novara Media*, 16 March. Available from: novaramedia.com/2017/03/16/organised-rage-the-lse-cleaners-strike/ [Accessed 20 March 2022].

Hayns, J. (2017b) 'We are not the dirt we clean', *Jacobin*, 17 May. Available from: www.jacobinmag.com/2017/05/strike-cleaners-lse-uvw-univers ity-campus-workers [Accessed 20 March 2022].

Heine, H. (2011) 'Pflegekräfte haben die Arbeit niedergelegt', *Der Tagesspiegel*, 2 May. Available from: www.tagesspiegel.de/berlin/streik-an-der-charite-pflegekraefte-haben-die-arbeit-niedergelegt/4120338.html [Accessed 24 March 2022].

Heine, H. (2015) 'Pflegekräfte kämpfen für mehr Personal', *Der Tagesspiegel*, 27 April. Available from: www.tagesspiegel.de/berlin/streik-an-der-char ite-berlin-pflegekraefte-kaempfen-fuer-mehr-personal/11692014.html [Accessed 24 March 2022].

Heine, H. (2019a) 'Therapeuten streiken erneut an der Charité', *Der Tagesspiegel*, 20 March. Available from: www.tagesspiegel.de/berlin/berli ner-kliniken-therapeuten-streiken-erneut-an-der-charite/24123006.html [Accessed 24 March 2022].

Heine, H. (2019b) 'Senat will Charité-Tochter auflösen', *Der Tagesspiegel*, 27 March. Available from: www.tagesspiegel.de/berlin/nach-therapeu ten-streik-senat-will-charite-tochter-aufloesen/24146836.html [Accessed 24 March 2022].

Heine, H. (2021) 'Charité und Vivantes droht Streik im Sommer: Berliner Pflegekräfte stellen 100-Tage-Ultimatum', *Der Tagesspiegel*, 12 May. Available from: https://www.tagesspiegel.de/berlin/charite-und-vivan tes-droht-streik-im-sommer-berliner-pflegekraefte-stellen-100-tage-ultima tum-im-wahlkampf/27181530.html [Accessed 2 July 2021].

Heinrich, M. (2004) 'Agenda 2010 und Hartz IV: Vom rot-grünen Neoliberalismus zum Protest', *Prokla*, 34(3): 477–83.

Helle, I. (2015) 'A new proletariat in the making? Reflections on the 14 November 2012 strike and the movements of 1968 and 1995', *Transfer*, 21(2): 229–42.

Helleiner, E. (1994) *States and the Reemergence of Global Finance: From Bretton Woods to the 1990s*, Ithaca: Cornell University Press.

Hensche, D. (2012) 'Das Tabu des politischen Streiks in Deutschland. Rechtliche und politische Aspekte', in A. Gallas, J. Nowak and F. Wilde (eds) *Politische Streiks im Europa der Krise*, Hamburg: VSA, pp 219–26.

Herkommer, S., Bischoff, J., Lohauß, P., Maldaner, K. and Steinfeld, F. (1979) *Gesellschaftsbewusstsein und Gewerkschaften: Arbeitsbedingungen, Lebensverhältnisse, Bewusstseinsänderungen und gewerkschaftliche Strategie von 1945 bis 1979*, Hamburg: VSA.

Hernandez, J.C. (2016) 'Across China, Walmart faces labor unrest as authorities stand aside', *New York Times*, 16 November. Available from: www.nytimes.com/2016/11/17/world/asia/across-china-walm art-faces-labor-unrest-as-authorities-stand-aside.html?searchResultPosit ion=14 [Accessed 20 March 2022].

Hinck, G. (2021) 'Irrationale Züge', *taz*, 31 August. Available from: https:// taz.de/Neuer-Lokfuehrer-Streik-bei-der-Bahn/!5792818/ [Accessed 20 January 2024].

Hobsbawm, E.J. (1968) *Industry and Empire*, Harmondsworth: Penguin.

Hobsbawm, E.J. (1984) *Worlds of Labour: Further Studies in the History of Labour*, London: Weidenfeld & Nicholson.

Hoff, J. (1985) 'The concept of class and public employees', *Acta Sociologica*, 28(3): 207–26.

Hoffmann, J. and Schmidt, R. (2008) 'Der Streik der Lokführer-Gewerkschaft GDL', *PROKLA. Zeitschrift für kritische Sozialwissenschaft*, 38(2): 323–42.

Hopkin, J. (2010) 'Comparative methods', in D. Marsh and G. Stoker (eds) *Theory and Methods in Political Science*, Houndmills: Palgrave Macmillan, pp 249–66.

Horn, P. (2003) 'The 1973 strikes: how far have we come?', *Indicator SA*, 20(1): 41–6.

Howell, C. (2005) *Trade Unions and the State: The Construction of Industrial Relations Institutions in Britain, 1890–2000*, Princeton: Princeton University Press.

Hübner, K. (2015) 'Europeanisation and globalisation as drivers of the German growth model', in S. Colvin (ed) *The Routledge Handbook of German Politics & Culture*, Milton Park: Routledge, pp 319–408.

Huke, N. (2016) *Krisenproteste in Spanien: Zwischen Selbstorganisation und Überfall auf die Institutionen*, Münster: edition assemblage.

Huke, N. and Tietje, O. (2014a) 'Gewerkschaftliche Erneuerung in der Eurokrise: Neue Organisationsformen der spanischen Gewerkschaften während des Protestzyklus ab 2011', *Prokla*, 4: 531–48.

Huke, N. and Tietje, O. (2014b) 'Zwischen Kooperation und Konfrontation. Machtressourcen und Strategien der spanischen Gewerkschaften CCOO und UGT in der Eurokrise', *Industrielle Beziehungen*, 21(4): 371–89.

Huke, N. and Tietje, O. (2016) 'Austerity and labour resistance: the shifting shape of strikes in Spain'. Available from: https://web.archive.org/web/20220119101301/http://nhuke.blogsport.eu/files/2016/11/2016_08_13-huke-tietje_spain.pdf [Accessed 19 January 2024].

Huke, N. and Tietje, O. (2018) 'Austerity and labour resistance: the shifting shape of strikes in Spain', in J. Nowak, M. Dutta and P. Birke (eds) *Workers' Movements and Strikes in the Twenty-First Century*, London: Rowman & Littlefield, pp 255–72.

Hunt, J. (2015) *Reports of Review Body on Doctors' and Dentists' Remuneration and NHS Pay*, UK Parliament, 16 July. Available from: https://questions-statements.parliament.uk/written-statements/detail/2015-07-16/HCWS114 [Accessed 9 October 2022].

Hürtgen, S. (2016) 'Authoritarian defense or the German model?', *Workers of the World*, 1(8): 56–70.

Hürtgen, S. (2018) 'Kampf ums Konkrete: Der "Doppelcharakter der Arbeit" und die Gewerkschaften', *Luxemburg*, January. Available from: https://zeitschrift-luxemburg.de/artikel/kampf-ums-konkrete/ [Accessed 26 March 2022].

Hyman, R. (1989) *Strikes*, 4th edn, Houndmills: Macmillan.

Iacobucci, G. (2016) 'TUC urges BMA to join forces on day of action to highlight crisis in NHS', *The BMJ*, 5 May. Available from: https://www.bmj.com/content/353/bmj.i2565 [Accessed 9 October 2022].

Iliffe, S. (2017) 'A tale of three disputes: junior doctors against the government 2015–2016', *Soundings*, 64: 128–42.

ILO (2020) 'As job losses escalate, nearly half of global workforce at risk of losing livelihoods', press release, 29 April. Available from: https://www.ilo.org/global/about-the-ilo/newsroom/news/WCMS_743036/lang--en/index.htm [Accessed 10 October 2022].

Inman, P. (2010) 'George Osborne accused of misleading public over UK bankruptcy claim', *The Guardian*, 4 November. Available from: https://www.theguardian.com/politics/2010/nov/04/george-osborne-misleading-crisis-claims [Accessed 9 October 2022].

IWD (2020) 'Viele Jobs hängen am Export', 4 February. Available from: https://www.iwd.de/artikel/viele-jobs-haengen-am-export-459120/ [Accessed 10 October 2022].

Jaffee, D. (2020) 'Disarticulation and the crisis of neoliberalism in the United States', *Critical Sociology*, 46(1): 65–81.

Jessop, B. (1982) *The Capitalist State: Marxist Theories and Methods*, Oxford: Martin Robertson.

Jessop, B. (1989) 'Conservative regimes and the transition to post-Fordism: the cases of Great Britain and West Germany', in M. Gottdiener and N. Komninos (eds) *Capitalist Development and Crisis Theory: Accumulation, Regulation and Spatial Restructuring*, New York: St Martin's, pp 261–99.

Jessop, B. (1990) *State Theory: Putting the Capitalist State in its Place*, Cambridge: Polity.

Jessop, B. (2000) 'The crisis of the national spatio-temporal fix and the tendential ecological dominance of globalizing capitalism', *International Journal of Urban and Regional Research*, 24(2): 323–60.

Jessop, B. (2002) *The Future of the Capitalist State*, Cambridge: Polity.

Jessop, B. (2013) 'Putting neoliberalism in its time and place: a response to the debate', *Social Anthropology*, 21: 65–74.

Jessop, B. (2014) 'Capitalist diversity and variety: variegation, the world market, compossibility and ecological dominance', *Capital & Class*, 38(1): 45–58.

Jessop, B. (2015) 'Comparative capitalisms and/or variegated capitalism', in I. Bruff, M. Ebenau and C. May (eds) *New Directions in Comparative Capitalisms Research: Critical and Global Perspectives*, Houndmills: Palgrave Macmillan, pp 65–82.

Ji, M. (2020) 'Korean suicide protest as anomic response to labour disempowerment', *Global Labour Journal*, 11(3): 239–53.

Johnston, C. (2014) 'Tens of thousands take to UK streets in pay protest', *The Guardian*, 18 October. Available from: https://www.theguardian.com/world/2014/oct/18/tens-thousands-uk-streets-pay-protest-march-union [Accessed 9 October 2022].

Joyce, R. and Sibieta, L. (2013) 'An assessment of Labour's record on income inequality and poverty', *Oxford Review of Economic Policy*, 29(1): 178–202.

Jiménez Diaz, J.F. (2013) 'Crisis económica, confianza institutioncal y liderazgos politicos en España', *Barataria*, 15: 125–41.

Junge Welt (2018) 'Tarifeinigung zwischen EVG und Bahn', 17 December. Available from: https://www.jungewelt.de/artikel/345575.arbeitskampf-tarifeinigung-zwischen-evg-und-bahn.html [Accessed 9 October 2022].

Kädtler, J. (2012) 'Sozialpartnerschaft in der Krise: Bewährung oder Krise der Sozialpartnerschaft?', *Industrielle Beziehungen*, 19(4): 357–366.

Kalass, V. (2012) *Neue Konkurrenz im Bahnwesen: Konflikt um die Gewerkschaft Deutscher Lokomotivführer*, Wiesbaden: Springer.

Kannankulam, J. (2008) *Autoritärer Etatismus im Neoliberalismus: Zur Staatstheorie von Nicos Poulantzas*, Hamburg: VSA.

Karadag, R. (2010) 'Neoliberal restructuring in Turkey: from state to oligarchic capitalism', MPIfG Discussion Paper, 10/7, July. Available from: ttp://hdl.handle.net/10419/43284 [Accessed 9 October 2022].

Karyoti, O. (2012) 'Es ist leichter, Steine zu schmeißen, als unseren Arbeitsplatz dicht zu machen', in A. Gallas, J. Nowak and F. Wilde (eds) *Politische Streiks im Europa der Krise*, Hamburg: VSA, pp 165–70.

Katsaroumpas, I. and Koukiadi, A. (2019) 'Greece: "contesting" collective bargaining', in T. Müller, K. Vandalae and J. Waddington (eds) *Collective Bargaining in Europe: Towards an Endgame* (vol 2), Brussels: ETUI, pp 267–94.

Kauranen, A. (2019) 'Finnish minister resigns in postal strike furore', Reuters, 29 November. Available from: https://www.reuters.com/article/finland-government-idUSL8N2892UG [Accessed 9 October 2022].

Keller, B. (2016a) 'Berufs- und Spartengewerkschaften: Zur Kritik des Tarifeinheitsgesetzes', *Industrielle Beziehungen*, 23(3): 253–79.

Keller, B. (2016b) 'Berufsgewerkschaften und Streik: Eine Industrial Relations-Perspektive', *Sozialer Fortschritt*, 11: 259–62.

Keller, B. and Seifert, H. (2014) 'Atypische Beschäftigungsverhältnisse im öffentlichen Dienst', *WSI-Mitteilungen*, 8: 628–38.

Kessen, P. (2017) 'Die neue Kampfkultur der Gewerkschaften', *DLF*, 10 January. Available from: https://www.deutschlandfunkkultur.de/streikr epublik-deutschland-die-neue-kampfkultur-der-100.html [Accessed 9 October 2022].

Khomami, N. (2015) 'Junior doctor contracts are threat to NHS, warn Royal Colleges', *The Guardian*, 24 September. Available from: https://www.theg uardian.com/society/2015/sep/24/junior-doctor-contracts-are-threat-to-nhs-warn-royal-colleges [Accessed 9 October 2022].

Kitson, M. and Michie, J. (2014) 'The deindustrial revolution: the rise and fall of UK manufacturing, 1870–2010', *Centre for Business Research Working Paper*, 459. Available from: https://michaelkitson.files.wordpress.com/2014/09/wp-459-2014-kitson-and-michie-the-deindustrial-revolution.pdf [Accessed 20 February 2020].

Knafo, S. (2020) 'Neoliberalism and the origins of public management', *Review of International Political Economy*, 27(4): 780–801.

Koch, M. (2006) *Roads to Post-Fordism: Labour Markets and Social Structures in Europe*, Farnham: Ashgate.

Köhler, H.-D. (2021) *Trade Unions in Spain: Structural Conditions and Current Challenges*, Madrid: Friedrich-Ebert-Stiftung.

Köhler, H.-D. and Calleja Jiménez, P. (2014) 'Conflicto laboral y movimiento sindical en España: ¿Qué queda del "movimiento obrero"?' in J. Pastor and N. Rojas Pedemonte (eds) *Anuari del Conflicto Social 2013*, Barcelona: Observatori del Conflicte Social, pp 750–67.

Koller, C. (2011) 'Weiblich, proletarisch, tschechisch: Perspektiven und Probleme intersektionaler Analyse in der Geschichtswissenschaft am Beispiel des Wiener Textilarbeiterinnenstreiks', in S. Hess, N. Langreiter and E. Timm (eds) *Intersektionalität revisited: Empirische, theoretische und methodische Erkundungen*, Bielefeld: Transcript, pp 173–96.

Kowalla, P. (2021) 'Über den unterschiedlichen Umgang der Eisenbahngewerkschaften mit der Partei AfD', *Labournet*, 31 March. Available from: https://www.labournet.de/politik/gw/gw-in-d/transnet/ueber-den-unterschiedlichen-umgang-der-eisenbahngewerkschaften-mit-der-partei-afd/ [Accessed 9 October 2022].

Krakowiak, F. (2012) 'Una huelga para resistir la flexibilidad', *Página12*, 29 March. Available from: https://www.pagina12.com.ar/diario/elmundo/4-190653-2012-03-29.html [Accessed 9 October 2022].

Krishnan, M. (2012) 'Strike in India hits banking and transport sectors', DW, 28 February. Available from: https://www.dw.com/en/strike-in-india-hits-banking-and-transport-sectors/a-15774001 [Accessed 9 October 2022].

Kuba, K. (2009) 'IG Transport und Nachrichtenwesen (1963–90)', in D. Dowe, M. Willke and K. Kuba, *FDGB-Lexikon: Funktion, Struktur, Kader und Entwicklung einer Massenorganisation der SED (1945–1990)*. Available from: http://library.fes.de/FDGB-Lexikon/rahmen/lexikon_frame.html [Accessed 9 October 2022].

Kuhn, V. (2015) 'Keiner schiebt uns weg! Denn unsere Arbeit, die ist richtig gut...', *SoZ – Sozialistische Zeitung*, 1 June. Available from: https://www.sozonline.de/2015/06/keiner-schiebt-uns-weg-denn-unsere-arbeit-die-ist-richtig-gut/ [Accessed 9 October 2022].

Kvale, S. (1996) *InterViews: An Introduction to Qualitative Research Interviewing*, Thousand Oaks: SAGE.

Labournet (2018) 'Erster Tarifvertrag bei Amazon erkämpft', 8 July. Available from: www.labournet.de/internationales/italien/gewerkschaften-italien/erster-tarifvertrag-bei-amazon-erkaempft-in-piacenza-wird-die-neuordnung-der-schichtarbeit-vereinbart/ [Accessed 22 March 2022].

Labour Party (nd) 'Affiliated trade unions'. Available from: https://labour.org.uk/people/unions/ [Accessed 9 October 2022].

Lacalle, J.D. (2015) *Conflictividad y crisis: España 2008–2013*, Barcelona: El Viejo Topo.

The Lancet (2015) 'Respect, status, and fair pay: what junior doctors deserve', 386(10009): 2117.

Landman, T. (2003) *Issues and Methods in Comparative Politics: An Introduction*, 3rd edn, London: Routledge.

Lapavitsas, C. (2009) 'Financialised capitalism: crisis and financial expropriation', *Historical Materialism*, 17: 114–48.

Lapavitsas, C., Kaltenbrunner, A., Lindo, D., Michell, J., Panceira, J.P., Pires, E., Powell, J., Stanfors, A. and Teles, N. (2010) 'Eurozone crisis: beggar thyself and thy neighbour, RMF occasional report', March. Available from: https://web.archive.org/web/20141222091806id_/http://eprints.uwe.ac.uk:80/23045/1/fullreport.pdf [Accessed 7 October 2022].

Larriu, N. (2019) 'UGT y CCOO convocan también a los hombres a la huelga feminista del 8M', *Cadena Ser*, 22 February. Available from: https://cadenaser.com/emisora/2019/02/22/radio_pamplona/1550831049_201354.html [Accessed 9 October 2022].

La Vanguardia (2013) 'Huelga de educación discreta entre los docentes, manifestaciones masivas', 24 October. Available from: https://www.lavanguardia.com/vida/20131024/54392379926/huelga-educacion-discreta-entre-docentes-manifestaciones-masivas.html [Accessed 9 October 2022].

La Vanguardia (2017) 'Miles de personas se manifiestan en Barcelona y Madrid por la igualdad de la mujer', 8 March. Available from: https://www.lavanguardia.com/vida/20170308/42673864414/manifestaciones-barcelona-madrid-dia-internacional-de-la-mujer.html [Accessed 9 October 2022].

La Vanguardia (2020a) 'Conoce los detalles de la huelga feminista del 8-M 2020', 6 March. Available from: https://www.lavanguardia.com/vida/20200306/473958090224/conoce-detalles-huelga-feminista-8-m-2020.html [Accessed 9 October 2022].

La Vanguardia (2020b) 'El feminismo llena las calles de las principales ciudades de España', 8 March. Available from: https://www.lavanguardia.com/vida/20200308/474036714992/feminismo-llena-calles-ciudades-espana-dia-mujer-8-m.html [Accessed 9 October 2022].

Lembke, U. (2019) 'Recht braucht Courage – und Solidarität! 70 Jahre Grundgesetz und die Gleichberechtigung der Geschlechter', *djbZ – Zeitschrift des Deutschen Juristinnenbundes*, 135–42.

Lenin, V.I. (2004) 'Meeting of the International Socialist Bureau'. Available from: https://www.marxists.org/archive/lenin/works/1908/oct/16b.htm [Accessed 9 October 2022], original work published in 1908.

Lesch, H. (2015) 'Strukturwandel des Arbeitskampfs: Deutschland im OECD-Ländervergleich', *IW Trends*, 3. Available from: https://www.iwkoeln.de/studien/hagen-lesch-strukturwandel-des-arbeitskampfs-230785.html [Accessed 20 October 2022].

Lesch, H. (2016) Spartengewerkschaften: Abspaltungsmotive, Lohnpolitik und Konfliktverhalten, *Zeitschrift für Politikwissenschaft*, 26(supplement 2): 155–74.

Lesch, H. and Winter, L. (2022) 'Langwierige Verhandlungen', *IW Report*, 9, 2 March. Available from: https://www.iwkoeln.de/studien/hagen-lesch-langwierige-verhandlungen.html [Accessed 9 October 2022].

Lichtenstein, A. (2015) '"A measure of democracy": works committees, black workers, and industrial citizenship in South Africa, 1973–1979', *South African Historical Journal*, 67(2): 113–38.

Liedke, J. and Buske, N. (2022) 'So hoch ist das Durchschnittseinkommen in Deutschland', *Handelsblatt*, 22 September. Available from: https://www.handelsblatt.com/unternehmen/durchschnittsgehalt-so-hoch-ist-das-durchschnittseinkommen-in-deutschland/26628226.html [Accessed 9 October 2022].

Lifona, D.G. and Sánchez, M. (2008) 'Zapatero dice que no renunciará al "papel regulador y redistribuidor" del Estado', *El Mundo*, 23 November. Available from: https://www.elmundo.es/elmundo/2008/11/22/espana/1227350652.html [Accessed 9 October 2022].

Lipietz, A. (1996) 'The new core-periphery relations: the contrasting examples of Europe and America', in C.W.M. Naastepad and S. Storms (eds) *The State and the Economic Process*, London: Edward Elgar, pp 112–50.

López, C. (2017) 'Las mujeres paran y se emplazan en la calle', *La Vanguardia*, 8 March. Available from: https://www.lavanguardia.com/vida/20170308/42633563599/dia-internacional-mujer-paro-derechos-feminismo.html [Accessed 9 October 2022].

Lorey, I. (2019) '8-M: the great feminist strike', *Transversal* blog, March. Available from: https://transversal.at/pdf/blog/451/ [Accessed 9 October 2022].

Lucarelli, B. (2012) 'German neomercantilism and the European sovereign debt crisis', *Journal of Post Keynesian Economics*, 34(2): 205–24.

Luckett, T. and Mzobe, D. (2016) '#OutsourcingMustFall: the role of workers in the 2015 protest wave at South African universities', *Global Labour Journal*, 7(1): 94–9.

Luckett, T. and Pontarelli, F. (2016) '#OutsourcingMustFall: unity in action in South African universities', *Brooklyn Rail*. Available from: https://brooklynrail.org/2016/03/field-notes/outsourcing-must-fall [Accessed 26 June 2021].

Luque Balbona, D. (2010) 'Las huelgas en España: Intensidad, formas y determinantes', PhD thesis, Universidad de Oviedo.

Luque Balbona, D. and González Begega, S. (2016) 'Crisis económica y coaliciones anti-austeridad en España (2010–2014): Viejos y nuevos repertorios de protesta', *Sociología del Trabajo*, 87: 45–67.

Luque Balbona, D. and González Begega, S. (2017) 'Declive de las huelgas y cambios en el repertorio de protesta en España', *Arxius de sociologica*, 36–37: 97–110.

Luxemburg, R. (2008) 'The mass strike', in R. Luxemburg, *The Essential Luxemburg*, edited by H. Scott, Chicago: Haymarket, pp 111–82, original work published in 1906.

Lyndon Shanley, M. (1989) *Feminism, Marriage, and the Law in Victorian England*, Princeton: Princeton University Press.

Machuca, P. (2016) 'Voices from the anti-austerity movement that changed Spain', *HuffPost*, 19 May. Available from: https://www.huffpost.com/entry/spain-15m-activists-los-indignados_n_573ca5c8e4b0aee7b8e8a76f [Accessed 9 October 2022].

Malm, A. (2020) *Corona, Climate, Chronic Emergency: War Communism in the Twenty-First Century*, London: Verso.

Manager Magazin (2020) 'Deutsche Bahn steuert auf Milliardenverlust zu', 28 July. Available from: https://www.manager-magazin.de/unternehmen/deutsche-bahn-steuert-auf-milliardenverlust-zu-a-5ab1fd12-7df4-4504-b237-a62dc20c0df1 [Accessed 9 October 2022].

Martens, R. (2014) 'Wir wissen, wo du wohnst', *Die Zeit*, 7 November. Available from: https://www.zeit.de/kultur/2014-11/claus-weselsky-medien-pranger-bild-focus [Accessed 9 October 2022].

Marticorena, C. and D'Urso, L. (2021) 'El poder de los/as trabajadores/as: una revisión crítica de los abordajes conceptuales para su estudio', *Revista de Estudios Marítimos y Sociales*, 18: 171–98.

Martin, R. (2011) 'The local geographies of the financial crisis: from the housing bubble to economic recession and beyond', *Economic Geography*, 11(4): 587–618.

Martín Alcoff, L., Arruzza, C., Bhattacharya, T., Clemente, R., Davis, A., Eisenstein, Z., Featherstone, L., Fraser, N., Smith, B. and Taylor, K.-Y. (2018) 'We need a feminism for the 99%. That's why women will strike this year', *The Guardian*, 27 January. Available from: https://www.theguardian.com/commentisfree/2018/jan/27/we-need-a-feminism-for-the-99-thats-why-women-will-strike-this-year [Accessed 9 October 2022].

Martín Valverde, A. and García Murcia, J. (1998) *Glosario de empleo y relaciones laborales*, Madrid: Mundi Prensa Libros.

Martínez Iglesias, M.M. (2011) 'De la huelga general á las concentraciones', *La palabra y el hombre*, Autumn: 39–44.

Marx, K. (1976) *Capital: A Critique of Political Economy* (vol 1), London: Penguin, original work published in 1867.

Marx, K. (1978) *Capital: A Critique of Political Economy* (vol 2), London: Penguin, original work published in 1885.

Marx, K. and Engels, F. (1959) 'Manifest der kommunistischen Partei', *Marx-Engels-Werke (MEW)* (vol 4), Berlin: Dietz, pp 459–93, original work published in 1848.

Mason, P. (2013) 'Why it's still kicking off everywhere', *Soundings*, 53: 44–55.

May, J., Wills, J., Datta, K., Evans, Y., Herbert, J. and McIlwaine, C. (2007) 'Keeping London working: global cities, the British state and London's new migrant division of labour', *Transactions of the Institute of British Geographers*, 32(2): 151–67.

McCartin, J.A. (2016) 'Bargaining for the common good', *Dissent*. Available from: https://www.dissentmagazine.org/article/bargaining-common-good-community-union-alignment [Accessed 9 October 2022].

McCartin, J.A., Sneiderman, M. and BP-Weeks, M. (2020) 'Combustible convergence: bargaining for the common good and the #RedforEd uprisings of 2018', *Labor Studies Journal*, 45(1): 97–113.

McCartin, J.A., Smiley, E. and Sneiderman, M. (2021) 'Both broadening and deepening: toward sectoral bargaining for the common good, in T. Schulze-Cleven and T. Vachon (eds) *Revaluing Work(ers): Toward a Democratic and Sustainable Future*, Champaign: LERA, pp 163–78.

McMichael, P. (1990) 'Incorporating comparison within a world-historical perspective: an alternative comparative method', *American Sociological Review*, 55(3): 385–97.

McMichael, P. (2000) 'World systems analysis, globalization, and incorporated comparison', *Journal of World-Systems Research*, 6(3): 668–99.

McNally, D. (2009) 'From financial crisis to world-slump: accumulation, financialisation, and the global slowdown', *Historical Materialism*, 17: 35–83.

Mernania, S. (2015) 'Pause nach zehn Tagen', *taz*, 1 July. Available from: www.taz.de/Streik-an-der-Charite/!5208040/ [Accessed 2 February 2022].

Metcalfe, D., Chowdury, R. and Salim, A. (2015) 'What are the consequences when doctors strike?', *The BMJ*, 25 November. Available from: https://www.bmj.com/content/351/bmj.h6231 [Accessed 9 October 2022].

Milankovic, C. (2021) 'Was verdient eigentlich ein Lokführer?', *Stuttgarter Zeitung*, 1 September. Available from: https://www.stuttgarter-zeitung.de/inhalt.gehalt-bei-der-bahn-was-verdient-eigentlich-ein-lokfuehrer.7d3fd736-55af-4b43-938c-03c0448caf5c.html [Accessed 9 October 2022].

Milne, C. (2016) 'Junior doctors' contracts: an introduction to the dispute', *Full Fact*, 29 September. Available from: https://fullfact.org/health/junior-doctors-pay-short-introduction-dispute/ [Accessed 9 October 2022].

Minder, R. (2010) 'Spain hit by strike over austerity measures', *New York Times*, 8 June. Available from: https://www.nytimes.com/2010/06/09/world/europe/09iht-spain.html?searchResultPosition=249 [Accessed 9 October 2022].

Mitchell, P., Short, V. and Eley, T. (2010) 'Spanish unions offer meek protests against pension reforms', *WSWS*, 26 February. Available from: https://www.wsws.org/en/articles/2010/02/spai-f26.pdf [Accessed 9 October 2022].

Molina, O. (2021) 'Working life in Spain: collective bargaining', *Eurofound*, 13 August. Available from: https://www.eurofound.europa.eu/country/spain#collective-bargaining [Accessed 9 October 2022].

Monforte, M. (2020) 'Casado sostiene que el pico actual de contagios procede de las marchas del 8-M y critica al Gobierno por "alentarlas"', *Público*, 20 March. Available from: https://www.publico.es/politica/coro navirus-casado-sostiene-pico-actual-contagios-procede-marchas-8-m-crit ica-gobierno-alentarlas.html [Accessed 9 October 2022].

Montero, J. (2018) 'La huelga feminista del 8M: Haciendo historia', *Dossieres EsF*, 29: 21–4.

Montero, J., Korriche, S.J., Pimentel, R., Tabernero, J., Useros, A., Caravantes, R. and Aroca, I. (2021) 'Del 15M a las huelgas feministas. Claves para los feminismos de hoy', *ctxt*, 12 May. Available from: https:// ctxt.es/es/20210501/Firmas/35993/Justa-Montero-feminismo-15M- manifestacion-8M-indignados.htm [Accessed 9 October 2022].

Montero, S. (2018a) 'Hacia la huelga feminista del 8-M: el día en el que las mujeres intentarán parar el mundo', *Cuarto Poder*, 27 January. Available from: https://www.cuartopoder.es/sociedad/mujer/2018/01/27/8m-hue lga-feminista/ [Accessed 9 October 2022].

Montero, S. (2018b) 'Del 15-M al 8-M: la ciudadanía critica la actitud de los sindicatos mayoritarios', *Cuarto Poder*, 14 March. Available from: https:// www.cuartopoder.es/economia/2018/03/14/8-m-sindicatos-ccoo-ugt/ [Accessed 9 October 2022].

Montoya, N. (2012) 'Es scheint, als ob mit dem Streik eine vereinte Bewegung entstanden ist', in A. Gallas, J. Nowak and F. Wilde (eds) *Politische Streiks im Europa der Krise*, Hamburg: VSA, pp 156–64.

Moody, K. (2017) *On New Terrain: How Capital is Reshaping the Battleground of Class War*, Chicago: Haymarket.

Moreno Badia, M. and Dudine, P. (2019) 'New data on world debt: a dive into country numbers', *IMF* blog, 17 December. Available from: https:// www.imf.org/en/Blogs/Articles/2019/12/17/blog-new-data-on-world- debt-a-dive-into-country-numbers [Accessed 8 October 2022].

Morris, M. (2022) 'What does the UK–EU deal mean for workers' rights?', Institute for Public Policy Rights, January. Available from: http://www. ippr.org/research/publications/uk-eu-deal-workers-rights [Accessed 9 October 2022].

Morton, A.L. and Tate, G. (1956) *The British Labour Movement 1770–1920*, London: Lawrence & Wishart.

Msomi, N. and Team, B. (2018) 'State capture strikes again? Why 95% of medicines are missing at North West clinics', *Mail & Guardian*, 13 April. Available from: mg.co.za/article/2018-04-13-00-exclusive-north-west- could-run-out-of-medicine-within-a-week/ [Accessed 20 February 2022].

Müller, B. (2016) 'Streiklust geweckt', *Süddeutsche Zeitung*, 6 June. Available from: https://www.sueddeutsche.de/wirtschaft/laender-vergleich-streikl ust-geweckt-1.3022209?reduced=true [Accessed 9 October 2022].

Müller, F., Claar, S., Neumann, M. and Elsner, C. (2020) 'Is green a Pan-African colour? Mapping African renewable energy policies and transitions in 34 countries', *Energy Research & Social Science*, 68: 1–9.

Müller, H.-P. and Wilke, M. (2014) 'Gewerkschaftsfusionen: der Weg zu modernen Multibranchengewerkschaften, in W. Schroeder (eds) *Handbuch Gewerkschaften in Deutschland*, 2nd edn, Wiesbaden: Springer VS, pp 147–72.

Müller-Jentsch, W. (1981) 'Vom gewerkschaftlichen Doppelcharakter und seiner theoretischen Auflösung im Neokorporatismus', *Gesellschaftliche Arbeit und Rationalisierung* [*Leviathan* special issue, 4]: 178–200.

Müller-Jentsch, W. (2003) 'Gewerkschaften heute: Zwischen arbeitspolitischer Kompetenz und sozialer Gerechtigkeit', *Gewerkschaftliche Monatshefte*, 10–11: 654–8.

Müller-Jentsch, W. (2014) 'Mittbestimmungspolitik', in W. Schroeder (eds) *Handbuch Gewerkschaften in Deutschland*, 2nd edn, Wiesbaden: Springer VS, pp 505–34.

Muriel, E. (2012) 'La sanidad pública madrileña va a la primera huelga general de su historia', *Público*, 26 November. Available from: https://www.publico.es/espana/sanidad-publica-madrilena-primera-huelga.html [Accessed 9 October 2022].

N24 (2014) 'N24-Emnid-Umfrage zum GDL-Streik: Mehrheit der Deutschen hat kein Verständnis mehr für GDL-Streiks'. Available from: https://www.presseportal.de/pm/13399/2874313 [Accessed 9 October 2022].

Najiels, Y. (2019) 'The demise of the international proletariat of France', *Salvage*, 2 April. Available from: https://salvage.zone/in-print/the-demise-of-the-international-proletariat-of-france-talbot-as-political-turning-point/ [Accessed 10 February 2021].

Navarro, P.A. (2012) 'La Calle gana el 14-N', *El Siglo*, 994: 26–8.

NDR (2018) 'Bahn sieht im Tarifabschluss mit EVG Signal', 15 December. Available from: https://www.ndr.de/nachrichten/info/nachrichten313_con-18x12x15x11y45.html [Accessed 9 October 2022].

Neues Deutschland (2015) 'IG-BCE-Chef grätscht der GDL in den Streik', 5 May. Available from: https://www.nd-aktuell.de/artikel/970082.ig-bce-chef-graetscht-der-gdl-in-den-streik.html [Accessed 9 October 2022].

Nichols, J. (2022) 'Pfizer's revenue doubles: "it's nothing short of pandemic profiteering"', *The Nation*, 10 February. Available from: https://www.thenation.com/article/economy/pfizer-pandemic-profiteering/ [Accessed 20 May 2022].

Nicolson, G. (2013) 'South Africa, a strike nation', *Daily Maverick*, 28 August. Available from: https://www.dailymaverick.co.za/article/2013-08-28-south-africa-a-strike-nation/ [Accessed 26 June 2021].

NIE (2019) 'Foodora cyclists win a labour contract', *News in English*, 30 September. Available from: www.newsinenglish.no/2019/09/30/foodora-cyclists-win-a-labour-contract/ [Accessed 2 February 2022].

Nieselow, T. (2019) 'Cosatu takes to the streets over Eskom, job losses', *Mail & Guardian*, 13 February. Available from: www.mg.co.za/article/2019-02-13-cosatu-takes-to-the-streets-over-eskom-job-losses/ [Accessed 2 February 2022].

Nkosi, B. (2015) 'Huge protest decries Wits's outsourcing practice', *Mail & Guardian*, 6 October. Available from: mg.co.za/article/2015-10-06-huge-protest-decries-witss-outsourcing-practice/ [Accessed 2 February 2022].

Nowak, J. (2015) 'Union campaigns in Germany directed against inequality: the minimum wage campaign and the Emmely campaign', *Global Labour Journal*, 6(3): 366–80.

Nowak, J. (2019) *Mass Strikes and Social Movements in Brazil and India: Popular Mobilisation in the Long Depression*, Cham: Palgrave.

Nowak, J. (2021) 'From industrial relations research to global labour studies: moving labour research beyond Eurocentrism', *Globalizations*, 18(8): 1335–48.

Nowak, J. and Gallas, A. (2013) 'Die aktuelle Streikwelle in Europa ist ein historischer Einschnitt', *Sozialismus*, 9: 33–7.

Nowak, J. and Gallas, A. (2014) 'Mass strikes against austerity in Western Europe: a strategic assessment', *Global Labour Journal*, 5(3): 306–21.

Nowak, P. (2018) 'Prekär populär', *taz*, 17 April. Available from: https://taz.de/!5496049/ [Accessed 20 September 2022].

NSSN (2016) '308: video – TUC rally "call demo to support junior doctors!"', 14 September. Available from: https://shopstewards.net/2016/09/nssn-308-video-nssn-tuc-rally-says-call-demo-to-support-junior-doctors/ [Accessed 9 October 2022].

NTV (2015) 'Gewerkschaftsbosse bei Tarifgesetz uneins', 22 May. Available from: https://www.n-tv.de/politik/Gewerkschaftsbosse-bei-Tarifgesetz-uneins-article15148641.html [Accessed 9 October 2022].

Oberndorfer, L. (2019) 'Between the normal state and an exceptional state form: authoritarian competitive statism and the crisis in Europe', in S. Wöhl, E. Springler, M. Pachel and B. Zeilinger (eds) *The State of the European Union: Fault Lines in European Integration*, Wiesbaden: Springer VS, pp 23–44.

Obertreis, R. (2016) 'Die Zeit der Privilegien ist vorbei', *Tagesspiegel*, 23 November. Available from: https://www.tagesspiegel.de/wirtschaft/pilotenstreik-bei-lufthansa-die-zeit-der-privilegien-ist-vorbei/14884258.html [Accessed 18 May 2021].

O'Brien, L. (2015a) 'Weekend deaths at NHS hospitals', *Full Fact*, 18 May. Available from: https://fullfact.org/health/weekend-deaths-nhs-hospitals/ [Accessed 9 October 2022].

O'Brien, L. (2015b) 'No evidence 11,000 NHS weekend deaths are caused by understaffing', *Full Fact*, 20 October. Available from: https://fullfact.org/health/no-evidence-11000-nhs-weekend-deaths-are-caused-understaffing/ [Accessed 9 October 2022].

OC Media (2018) 'Tbilisi metro resumes service as drivers and mayor Kaladze reach agreement', 6 June. Available from: www.oc-media.org/tbilisi-metro-resumes-service-as-drivers-and-mayor-kaladze-reach-agreement/ [Accessed 2 February 2022].

Offe, C. (2018a) 'Der Niedriglohnsektor und das "Modell Deutschland"', in C. Offe, *Macht und Effizienz: Studien zur kapitalistischen Rationalisierung der Arbeit*, Wiesbaden: Springer VS, pp 161–82, original work published in 2002.

Offe, C. (2018b) 'Two logics of collective action', in C. Offe, *Macht und Effizienz: Studien zur kapitalistischen Rationalisierung der Arbeit*, Wiesbaden: Springer VS, pp 315–62, original work published in 1980.

Osborne, H. and Farell, S. (2016) 'Deliveroo workers strike again over new pay structure', *The Guardian*, 15 August. Available from: www.theguardian.com/business/2016/aug/15/deliveroo-workers-strike-again-over-new-pay-structure [Accessed 2 February 2022].

Oxfam (2018) 'Voces contra la precaridad: Mujeres y probreza en Europa', 15 October. Available from: https://oi-files-d8-prod.s3.eu-west-2.amazonaws.com/s3fs-public/file_attachments/voces-contra-la-precariedad.pdf [Accessed 9 October 2022].

Oxfam (2021) *Not in This Together: How Supermarket Chains became Pandemic Winners while Women Workers are Losing Out*. Report. Available from: https://oxfamilibrary.openrepository.com/bitstream/10546/621194/9/bp-not-in-this-together-220621-en.pdf [Accessed 2 February 2022].

Oxfam (2022) *Inequality Kills*. Report. Available from: https://oxfamilibrary.openrepository.com/bitstream/handle/10546/621341/bp-inequality-kills-170122-en.pdf;jsessionid=C46D19F45A68F21F7796D91674E2BF6E?sequence=9 [Accessed 2 February 2022].

Página12 (2009) 'Huelga y marchas', 29 June. Available from: www.pagina12.com.ar/diario/elmundo/subnotas/127416-40809-2009-06-29.html [Accessed 2 February 2022].

Página12 (2018) 'Paro, ruido y silbatos por la igualdad', 9 March. Available from: https://www.pagina12.com.ar/100377-paro-ruido-y-silbatos-por-la-igualdad [Accessed 9 October 2022].

Página12 (2019) '8M: el tercer paro de mujeres', 8 March. Available from: https://www.pagina12.com.ar/179467-8-m-el-tercer-paro-de-mujeres [Accessed 9 October 2022].

Página12 (2020) 'Otra marea feminista por el 8M', 9 March. Available from: https://www.pagina12.com.ar/251916-otra-marea-feminista-por-el-8-m [Accessed 9 October 2022].

Palley, T. (2016) 'The US economy: explaining stagnation and why it will persist', in A. Gallas, H. Herr, F. Hoffer and C. Scherrer (eds) *Combating Inequality: The Global North and South*, London: Routledge, pp 113–31.

Palley, T. (2019) 'Central bank independence: a rigged debate based on false politics and economics', *Investigación Económica*, 78(310): 67–102.

Palomino, S., Rodríguez, D. and Gortázar, N.G. (2021) 'Las mujeres de América Latina, en la calle o en las redes, claman contra la violencia machista', *El País*, 9 March. Available from: https://elpais.com/sociedad/2021-03-09/las-mujeres-de-america-latina-en-la-calle-o-en-las-redes-claman-contra-la-violencia-machista.html [Accessed 9 October 2022].

Panitch, L. (1976) *Social Democracy and Industrial Militancy: The Labour Party, the Trade Unions and Incomes Policy, 1945–1974*, Cambridge: Cambridge University Press.

Panitch, L. (2001) 'Reflections on strategy for labor', *Socialist Register*, 37: 367–92.

Panitch, L. and Konings, M (2009) 'Myths of neoliberal deregulation', *New Left Review*, II(57): 67–83.

Parfitt, S. (2018) 'Why the UCU strike matters', *Jacobin*, 14 March. Available from: https://jacobin.com/2018/03/ucu-university-staff-strike-deal-pensions-union [Accessed 9 October 2022].

Pateman, C. (1988) *The Sexual Contract*, Stanford: Stanford University Press.

Peck, J. (2003) 'Geography and public policy: mapping the penal state', *Progress in Human Geography*, 27(2): 222–32.

Peck, J. (2010) 'Zombie neoliberalism and the ambidextrous state', *Theoretical Criminology*, 14(1): 104–10.

Peck, J. and Theodore, N. (2007) 'Variegated capitalism', *Progress in Human Geography*, 31(6): 731–72.

Pedrina, V. (2012) 'Ein europäischer Generalstreik?', *Sozialismus*, 29 August. Available from: https://www.sozialismus.de/detail/artikel/ein-europaeischer-generalstreik/ [Accessed 9 October 2022].

Peet, E.R. and Peet, R. (2020) 'Covid-19 – disease of global capitalism: excursion into spatial epidemology', *Human Geography*, 13(3): 318–21.

Pelling, H. (1981) *A History of British Trade Unionism*, 3rd edn, Harmondsworth: Penguin.

Pérez de Guzmán, S., Roca, B. and Diaz-Parra, I. (2016) 'Political exchange, crisis of representation and trade union strategies in a time of austerity: trade unions and 15M in Spain', *Transfer*, 22(4): 461–74.

Pérez Domínguez, C. (1994) 'El sistema de relaciones laborales en España: Una revision de la historia reciente', *Anales de estudios económicos y empresariales*, 9: 273–89.

Peters, J. (2012) 'Neoliberal convergence in North America and Western Europe: fiscal austerity, privatization, and public sector reform', *Review of International Political Economy*, 19(2): 208–35.

Peters, W. (2021) 'Das grenzt an die Methoden der AfD', interview with W. Schroeder, *Süddeutsche Zeitung*, 9 June. Available from: https://www.sueddeutsche.de/wirtschaft/gdl-bahn-streik-schroeder-1.5316439 [Accessed 9 October 2022].

Piciotto, S. (1984) 'The battles at Talbot·Poissy: workers divisions and capital restructuring', *Capital & Class*, 8(2): 5–17.

Pike, J. (2012) 'Strikes', in Chadwick (ed), *Encyclopedia of Applied Ethics*, 2nd edn, Amsterdam: Elsevier, pp 250–6.

Piketty, T. (2014) *Capital in the Twenty-First Century*, Cambridge, MA: Harvard University Press.

Polo, S., Munier, J. and Garcés, C. (2021) 'Día de la Mujer, en directo: Tensión entre Policía y feministas en una manifestación sin autorización en Madrid', *El Mundo*, 8 March. Available from: https://www.elmundo.es/espana/2021/03/08/6045c6d021efa0120f8b458b.html[Accessed 10 October 2022].

Poulantzas, N. (1974) *Classes in Contemporary Capitalism*, London: NLB.

Poulantzas, N. (1978) *State, Power, Socialism*, London: NLB.

Poyo, A. (2020) 'Por qué no habrá huelga feminista este 8M y todo lo que ha ocurrido (y pasará) en tu ciudad', *El País*, 2 March. Available from: https://smoda.elpais.com/feminismo/por-que-no-habra-huelga-feminista-este-8m-y-todo-lo-que-ha-habido-y-habra-en-tu-ciudad/ [Accessed 9 October 2022].

Prasad Philbrick, I. (2022) 'Why union drives are succeeding', *New York Times*, 17 July. Available from: https://www.nytimes.com/2022/07/17/briefing/union-drives-college-graduates.html [Accessed 9 October 2022].

Pringle, T. (2016) 'Strikes and labour relations in China', *Workers of the World*, 8: 122–42.

Projekt Klassenanalyse (1973) *Materialien zur Klassenstruktur der BRD: Erster Teil – Theoretische Grundlagen und Kritiken*, VSA Hamburg.

Público (2009) 'Golpe de Estado en Honduras: los militares deportan a Zelaya', 29 June. Available from: www.publico.es/actualidad/golpe-honduras-militares-deportan-zelaya.html [Accessed 2 February 2022].

Público (2010a) 'La huelga de funcionarios acaba con diferencias en las cifras', 9 June. Available from: https://www.publico.es/actualidad/huelga-funcionarios-acaba-diferencias-cifras.html [Accessed 9 October 2022].

Público (2010b) 'Los sindicatos creen que es un éxito; para la CEOE, no pasó nada', 30 September. Available from: https://www.publico.es/espana/sindicatos-creen-exito-ceoe-no.html [Accessed 9 October 2022].

Público (2012) 'Cientos de miles de personas exigen al Gobierno que rectifique', 30 March. Available from: https://www.publico.es/espana/cientos-miles-personas-exigen-al.html [Accessed 9 October 2022].

Público (2014) 'Intelectuales y activistas llaman a "recuperar la soberanía popular" con una candidatura para las europeas', 14 January. Available from: https://www.publico.es/politica/intelectuales-y-activistas-lla man-recuperar.html#analytics-noticia:contenido-enlace [Accessed 9 October 2022].

Público (2019) '¿Por qué los hombres no están llamados a secundar la huelga feminista y cuál es su rol?', 5 March. Available from: https://www.publ ico.es/sociedad/hombres-no-llamados-secundar-huelga.html [Accessed 9 October 2022].

Público (2020a) 'El 8M de 2020, el año de la revuelta feminista', 8 March. Available from: https://www.publico.es/sociedad/8m-2020-ano-revue lta-feminista.html [Accessed 9 October 2022].

Público (2020b) 'El feminismo exhibe su sororidad y abarrota las calles de España', 9 March. Available from: https://www.publico.es/sociedad/8m-miles-mujeres-espana-toman-calles-reivindicar-igualdad-primeras-mani festaciones-8m.html [Accessed 9 October 2022].

Pym, H. (2016) 'Junior doctors call off five-day strikes over contracts', *BBC*, 24 September. Available from: https://www.bbc.com/news/health-37463 929 [Accessed 9 October 2022].

Quelart, R. (2017) 'Los 8 retos pendientes de la mujer trabajadora', *La Vanguardia*, 8 March. Available from: https://www.lavanguardia.com/vida/ 20170308/42621336927/dia-internacional-de-la-mujer-retos-pendientes. html [Accessed 9 October 2022].

Raehlmann, I. (2017) *Streiks im Wandel*, Wiesbaden: Springer VS.

Rapley, T. (2014) 'Sampling strategies in qualitative research', in U. Flick (ed) *The SAGE Handbook of Qualitative Data Analysis*, London: SAGE, pp 49–63.

RBB24 (2021) 'GDL bricht Verhandlungsrunde ab: Bahnstreik nicht ausgeschlossen', 7 June. Available from: https://web.archive.org/web/ 20210607160426/https://www.rbb24.de/panorama/beitrag/2021/06/ bahn-gdl-tarifverhandlungen-abbruch.html [Accessed 9 October 2022].

Redler, L. (2012) 'Vergessene Geschichte: Politische Streiks in (West-) Deutschland nach 1945', in A. Gallas, J. Nowak and F. Wilde (eds) *Politische Streiks im Europa der Krise*, Hamburg: VSA, pp 194–210.

Rehder, B. (2016) 'Konflikt ohne Partnerschaft? Arbeitsbeziehungen im Dienstleistungssektor', *Industrielle Beziehungen*, 23(3): 366–73.

Rheinische Post (2014) 'Auch Linke nennt den Lokführer-Streik "falsch"', 6 November. Available from: http://www.presseportal.de/pm/30621/2873 266 [Accessed 9 October 2022].

Rhodan, M. (2018) 'Here's why West Virginia teachers are on strike', *Time*, 26 February. Available from: www.time.com/5176094/west-virginia-teac her-strike/ [Accessed 20 March 2022].

Rhodes, M. (2001) 'The political economy of social pacts: "competitive corporatism" and European welfare reform', in P. Pierson (ed) *The New Politics of the Welfare State*, Oxford: Oxford University Press, pp 165–94.

Riedler, U. (2014) 'Kommentar zum Bahnstreik: Rambo der Gleise', *Offenbacher Post*, 6 November. Available from: https://www.op-online. de/politik/kommentar-bahnstreik-claus-weselsky-rambo-gleise-4402118. html [Accessed 9 October 2022].

Rimmer, A. (2014) 'BMA's withdrawal from negotiations was "complete surprise,"says NHS Employers', *The BMJ*, 14 October. Available from: https:// www.bmj.com/content/349/bmj.g6365 [Accessed 9 October 2022].

Rimmer, A. (2015) 'Junior doctors will not re-enter contract negotiations with government', *The BMJ*, 14 August. Available from: https://www.bmj. com/content/351/bmj.h4447 [Accessed 9 October 2022].

Ritchie, J., Lewis, J. and Elam, G. (2003) 'Designing and selecting samples', in J. Ritchie and J. Lewis (eds) *Qualitative Research Practice: A Guide for Social Science Students and Researchers*, London: SAGE, pp 77–108.

Riveiro, A. (2021) 'Sánchez firma con sindicatos y patronal el acuerdo de pensiones: "El sistema es sostenible y lo estamos demostrando"', *El Diario*, 1 July. Available from: https://www.eldiario.es/politica/sanchez-firmar-sindicatos-patronal-acuerdo-pensiones-sistema-sostenible-demostrando_ 1_8094317.html [Accessed 9 October 2022].

Rixen, T. (2013) 'Why reregulation after the crisis is feeble: shadow banking, offshore financial centers, and jurisdictional competition', *Regulation & Governance*, 7(4): 435–59.

Rocha, F. (2012) 'La crisis económica y sus efectos sobre el empleo en España', *Gazeta Sindical*, 19: 67–90.

Rodríguez, B. and González, B. (2012) 'La presión social de una España en huelga busca frenar la austeridad', Reuters, 14 November. Available from: https://www.reuters.com/article/oestp-huelga-espana-idESMA E8AD01S20121114 [Accessed 9 October 2022].

Roediger, D (2017) *Class, Race and Marxism*, London: Verso.

Rogero-García, J., Fernández-Rodríguez, C.J. and Ibañez-Rojo, R. (2014) 'La "marea verde": balance de una movilización inconclusa', *Revista de la Asociación de Sociología de la Educación*, 7(3): 567–86.

Romanos, E. (2016) 'De Tahrir a Wall Street por la Puerta del Sol: la difusión transnacional de los movimientos sociales en perspectiva comparada', *Reis: Revista Española de Investigaciones Sociológicas*, 154 : 103–18.

Rose, S.O. (1992) *Limited Livelihoods: Gender and Class in Nineteenth Century England*, London: Routledge.

Rothenpieler, G. (2020) 'Systemrelevant und mies bezahlt', *taz*, 30 September. Available from: www.taz.de/Warnstreik-der-Pflegekraefte/ !5713313/ [Accessed 20 March 2022].

Ruiz Galacho, E.R. (2011a) 'Crisis económica, reforma laboral y huelga general', *Laberinto*, 32: 7–24.

Ruiz Galacho, E.R. (2011b) 'Crisis económica, reforma laboral y huelga general (YII)', *Laberinto*, 34: 27–38.

Runciman, C. (2019) 'The "double-edged sword" of institutional power: COSATU, neo-liberalisation and the right to strike', *Global Labour Journal*, 10(2): 142–58.

Russell, B. (2010) *Industrial Civilisation*, London: Routledge, original work published in 1923.

Ryder, N. (2016) '"Greed, for lack of a better word, is good. Greed is right. Greed works": a contemporary and comparative review of the relationship between the global financial crisis, financial crime and white collar criminals in the U.S. and the U.K.', *British Journal of White Collar Crime*, 1(1): 3–47.

SA News (2014) 'Sapo welcomes end to strike', 25 November. Available from: www.sanews.gov.za/south-africa/sapo-welcomes-end-strike [Accessed 20 March 2022].

Sales Gelabert, T.S. (2019) 'La democracia en movimiento: Democratización, desdemocratización y ciclos de protesta', *Eikasia*, 89: 65–93.

Salford Star (2016) 'Manchester May Day rally hears the world is upside down', 2 May. Available from: http://salfordstar.com/article.asp?id=3233 [Accessed 9 October 2022].

Salomi, V. (2015) 'Strike hits banking services', *Times of India*, 2 September. Available from: https://timesofindia.indiatimes.com/city/patna/strike-hits-banking-services/articleshow/48779123.cms [Accessed 20 March 2022].

Sainato, M (2022) 'US sees union boom despite big companies' aggressive opposition', *The Guardian*, 27 July. Available from: https://www.theguardian.com/us-news/2022/jul/27/us-union-boom-starbucks-amazon [Accessed 9 October 2022].

Samaddar, R. (2015) 'Forty years after: the great Indian railway strike of 1974', *Economic and Political Weekly*, 50(4): 39–47.

Sanmartín, O.R. (2020) 'Las feministas celebran el 8-M divididas sobre la prostitución, los "vientres de alquiler" y las teorías "queer"', *El Mundo*, 2 March. Available from: https://www.elmundo.es/espana/2020/03/03/5e5bc042fc6c837b5b8b4619.html [Accessed 9 October 2022].

Santoro, S. (2020) 'Paro y marcha por los reclamos feministas', *Página12*, 9 March. Available from: https://www.pagina12.com.ar/251821-paro-y-marcha-por-los-reclamos-feministas [Accessed 20 March 2022].

Sanz Alcántara, M. (2013) 'Análisis del nivel de huelgas en el Estado', *La Hiedra*, January. Available from: https://web.archive.org/web/20140505055928/http://lahiedra.info/analisis-del-nivel-de-huelgas-en-el-estado-espanol-en-el-periodo-2007-2012/ [Accessed 9 October 2022].

Satgar, V. (2018) 'The climate crisis and systemic alternatives', in V. Satgar (ed) *The Climate Crisis: South African and Global Eco-Socialist Alternatives*, Johannesburg: Wits University Press, pp 1–28.

Sauer, S. (2014) 'Die Privilegien der Lufthansa-Piloten', *Frankfurter Rundschau*, 1 December. Available from: https://www.fr.de/wirtschaft/ privilegien-lufthansa-piloten-11048921.html [Accessed 18 May 2021].

Sayer, A. (1992) *Method in Social Science: A Realist Approach*, London: Routledge.

Sayer, A. (2000) *Realism in Social Science*, London: SAGE.

Sayer, A. (2005) *The Moral Significance of Class*, Cambridge: Cambridge University Press.

Schäfer, J. (2017) 'Klassenjustiz in Aktion: Die Entscheidung des Bundesverfassungsgerichts zur Tarifeinheit ist ein Gefälligkeitsurteil für Kabinett und Kapital', *Labournet*, 16 July. Available from: https://www. labournet.de/wp-content/uploads/2017/07/teg_jschaefer.pdf [Accessed 9 October 2022].

Scherrer, C. (2000) 'Global Governance: Vom fordistischen Trilateralismus zum neoliberalen Konstitutionalismus', *PROKLA. Zeitschrift für kritische Sozialwissenschaft*, 30(1): 13–38.

Scherrer, C. (2011) 'Reproducing hegemony: US financial capital and the 2008 crisis', *Critical Policy Studies*, 5(3): 219–46.

Scherrer, C. (2014) 'Neoliberalism's resilience: a matter of class', *Critical Policy Studies*, 8(3): 348–51.

Scherrer, C. (2018) 'Peasant elimination without compensating modern labor market opportunities', in C. Scherrer and S. Verna (eds) *Decent Work Deficits in Southern Agriculture: Measurements, Drivers and Strategies*, Augsburg: Rainer Hampp, pp 209–25.

Scherrer, C. and Kunze, C. (2011) *Globalisierung*, Göttingen: Vandenhoeck & Ruprecht.

Scherrer, C. and Verna, S. (2018) 'Introduction', in C. Scherrer and S. Verna (eds) *Decent Work Deficits in Southern Agriculture: Measurements, Drivers and Strategies*, Augsburg: Rainer Hampp, pp 1–11.

Schmalz, S., Ludwig, C. and Webster, E. (2018) 'The power resources approach: developments and challenges', *Global Labour Journal*, 9(2): 113–34.

Schmid, U. (2014) 'Gewerkschaften im Föderalismus: regionale Strukturen und Kulturen und die Dynamik von politischen Mehrebenensystemen', in W. Schroeder (ed) *Handbuch Gewerkschaften in Deutschland*, 2nd edn, Wiesbaden: Springer VS, pp 367–94.

Schroeder, W. and Greef, S. (2014) 'Struktur und Entwicklung des deutschen Gewerkschaftsmodells: Herausforderung durch Sparten- und Berufsgewerkschaften?', in W. Schroeder (eds) *Handbuch Gewerkschaften in Deutschland*, 2nd edn, Wiesbaden: Springer VS, pp 123–46.

Schumann, M., Gerlach, F., Gschlössl, A. and Milhoffer, P. (1971) *Am Beispiel der Septemberstreiks: Anfang der Rekonstruktionsperiode der Arbeiterklasse: Eine empirische Untersuchung*, Frankfurt am Main: Europäische Verlagsanstalt.

Schwarz, P. (2021) 'Deutsche Bahn: GDL kündigt Arbeitskampf an', *World Socialist Web Site*, 16 June. Available from: https://www.wsws.org/de/artic les/2021/06/16/lokf-j16.html [Accessed 9 October 2022].

Schwarz, R. (2013) 'Call-Center-Agents von Madsack wollen mehr Geld', *Neues Deutschland*, 6 December. Available from: www.nd-aktuell.de/arti kel/917215.streikbesuch-in-hamburg.html [Accessed 23 March 2022].

Scully, R. (2015) 'First results from the new Welsh political barometer poll: the NHS', *Elections in Wales Blog*, 29 June. Available from: https://web. archive.org/web/20150629132533/http://blogs.cardiff.ac.uk/elections inwales/2015/06/29/first-results-from-the-new-welsh-political-barome ter-poll-the-nhs/ [Accessed 9 October 2022].

Segovia, C. (2008) 'Zapatero recorta el empleo público un 70% y congela el salario de los altos cargos del Estado', *El Mundo*, 23 June. Available from: https://www.elmundo.es/mundodinero/2008/06/23/economia/ 1214220343.html [Accessed 9 October 2022].

Sell, S. (2017) 'Ein "weitgehend" grundgesetzkonformes Tarifeinheitsgesetz: Aber geht das überhaupt – ziemlich schwanger, aber nicht ganz? Und wer muss das ausbaden?', *Aktuelle Sozialpolitik Blog*, 11 July. Available from: https://aktuelle-sozialpolitik.blogspot.com/2017/07/ein-weitgehend-grundgesetzkonformes-tarifeinheitsgesetz.html [Accessed 9 October 2022].

Sell, S., Becher, L., Oschmiansky, F. and Bersheim, S. (2020) 'Daten und Fakten: Arbeitslosigkeit', *Bundeszentrale für politische Bildung*, 27 February. Available from: https://www.bpb.de/themen/arbeit/arbeitsmarktpoli tik/305833/daten-und-fakten-arbeitslosigkeit/#node-content-title-0 [Accessed 28 June 2020].

Shah Singh, H. (2012) 'Unions strike across India, results mixed', *CNN*, 28 February. Available from: https://edition.cnn.com/2012/02/28/world/ asia/india-strike/index.html [Accessed 9 October 2022].

Shaller, C. (2021) 'Selbstermächtigung statt Burgfrieden', *woz – die Wochenzeitung*, 21 October. Available from: https://www.woz.ch/2142/ basisgewerkschaft-fau/selbstermaechtigung-statt-burgfrieden [Accessed 2 May 2022].

Shuntov, A. (2021) 'Strike, exile, arrest: what happened to Belarusian workers?', *Open Democracy*, 23 June. Available from: https://www.opende mocracy.net/en/odr/strike-exile-arrest-what-happened-belarusian-work ers/ [Accessed 27 June 2021].

Shyam Sundar, K.R. (2019) 'Dynamics of general strikes in India', *Economics and Political Weekly*, 54(3): 22–4.

Silver, B.J. (2003) *Forces of Labour: Workers' Movements and Globalisation since 1870*, Cambridge: Cambridge University Press.

Silver, B.J. (2014) 'Theorising the working class in twenty-first-century global capitalism', in M. Atzeni (ed) *Workers and Labour in a Globalised Capitalism: Contemporary Themes and Theoretical Issues*, Houndmills: Palgrave Macmillan, pp 46–69.

Singer, R. (2015) 'We need to unite around junior doctors', *Pulse*, 28 September. Available from: https://web.archive.org/web/20200807084 141/https://www.pulsetoday.co.uk/views/we-need-to-unite-around-jun ior-doctors/20030037.article [Accessed 9 October 2022].

Sinn, H.-W. (2003) *Der kranke Mann Europas: Diagnose und Therapie eines Kathedersozialisten*, München: Ifo-Institut.

Sippitt, A. (2015) 'Did 98% of junior doctors vote to strike?', *Full Fact*, 24 November. Available from: https://fullfact.org/health/did-98-junior-doct ors-vote-strike/ [Accessed 9 October 2022].

Smith, M. (2016) 'Support for junior doctors begins to slip away as BMA calls off strike', *YouGov*, 5 September. Available from: https://yougov. co.uk/topics/politics/articles-reports/2016/09/05/public-support-jun ior-doctors-begins-slip-away-bma [Accessed 9 October 2022].

Sperling, H.J. (2014) 'Gewerkschaftliche Betriebspolitik', in W. Schroeder (ed) *Handbuch Gewerkschaften in Deutschland*, 2nd edn, Wiesbaden: Springer VS, pp 485–504.

Steiner, A. (2016) 'Die neue deutsche Streiklust', *FAZ*, 12 May. Available from: https://www.faz.net/aktuell/wirtschaft/wirtschaftspolitik/kitas-pilo ten-post-streiken-neue-deutsche-streikkultur-14215675.html [Accessed 9 October 2022].

Steltzner, H. (2015) GDL im Warnstreik, *FAZ*, 18 May. Available from: https://www.faz.net/aktuell/wirtschaft/kommentar-gdl-im-wah nstreik-13599363.html [Accessed 10 October 2022].

Stephens, P. (1996) *Politics and the Pound: The Tories, the Economy and Europe*, London: Macmillan.

Stevens, R. (2018) 'General strike in Greece against Syriza's latest austerity package', *World Socialist Web Site*, 31 May. Available from: https://www. wsws.org/en/articles/2018/05/31/gree-m31.html [Accessed 8 July 2021].

Strauss, D. (2021) 'UK risks going "backwards" on workplace rights, unions warn', *Financial Times*, 30 December. Available from: https://www. ft.com/content/27cc38ae-6838-4d73-8547-32ea27a979a8 [Accessed 9 October 2022].

Streeck, W. (2009) *Re-Forming Capitalism: Institutional Change in the German Political Economy*, Oxford: Oxford University Press.

Streeck, W. and Hassel, A. (2003) 'The crumbling pillars of social partnership', *West European Politics*, 26(4): 101–24.

Streikzeitung (2014) 1. November. Available from: https://streikzeitung.winfr iedwolf.de/wp-content/uploads/2021/06/StreikZeitung-pro-GDL-01-END.pdf [Accessed 9 October 2022].

Šumonja, M. (2021) 'Neoliberalism is not dead – on political implications of Covid-19', *Capital & Class*, 45(2): 215–27.

SZ (2013) 'Bahn-Mitarbeiter streiken ab Montag', 16 March. Available from: https://www.sueddeutsche.de/wirtschaft/tarifstreit-bahn-mitarbeiter-streiken-ab-montag-1.1626159 [Accessed 9 October 2022].

SZ (2015) '200 Operationen fallen pro Tag aus', 22 June. Available from: www.sueddeutsche.de/wirtschaft/berliner-charite-200-operationen-fallen-pro-tag-aus-1.2532302 [Accessed 23 March 2022].

Tagesschau (2021a) '"Großer Erfolg" oder "Ziel verfehlt"?', 13 August. Available from: https://web.archive.org/web/20210813105206/https://www.tagesschau.de/wirtschaft/unternehmen/bahn-streik-159.html [Accessed 9 October 2022].

Tagesschau (2021b) 'Eine völlig unnötige Belastung der Fahrgäste', 10 October. Available from: https://web.archive.org/web/20210904065100/https://www.tagesschau.de/inland/bahnstreik-gdl-dgb-101.html [Accessed 9 October 2022].

Tailby, S. (2012) 'Public service restructuring in the UK: the case of the English National Health Service', *Industrial Relations Journal*, 43(5): 448–64.

Tapper, J. and Campbell, D. (2016) 'Junior doctors suspend strike plans due to "patient safety" concerns', *The Guardian*, 24 September. Available from: https://www.theguardian.com/society/2016/sep/24/junior-doctors-suspend-plan-to-strike-due-to-patient-safety-concerns [Accessed 9 October 2022].

Tanner, J. (2019) 'Finland's prime minister resigns over postal service dispute', *AP News*, 3 December. Available from: https://apnews.com/article/postal-service-finland-international-news-europe-91572b9267be44419942d69b65c25d03 [Accessed 9 October 2022].

Taylor, F.W. (1919) *The Principles of Scientific Management*, New York: Harper, original work published in 1911.

taz (2014a) 'Der Bahn fehlen die Worte', 11 September. Available from: https://taz.de/GDL-Urabstimmung-ueber-Streik/!5033420/ [Accessed 8 October 2022].

taz (2014b) 'Geste des "guten Willens"', 7 November. Available from: https://taz.de/!5029191/ [Accessed 9 October 2022].

taz (2015) 'Piloten stimmen Schlichtung zu', 13 May. Available from: https://taz.de/Tarifkonflikt-bei-der-Lufthansa/!5008020/ [Accessed 8 October 2022].

Tejada, A. (2019) '8M: el tercer paro de mujeres', *Página12*, 8 March. Available from: www.pagina12.com.ar/179467-8-m-el-tercer-paro-de-mujeres [Accessed 23 March 2022].

Teweleit, A. (2018) 'Gesteigertes Selbstbewusstsein', *Neues Deutschland*, 20 December. Available from: www.nd-aktuell.de/artikel/1108509.therapeutenstreik-gesteigertes-selbstbewusstsein.html [Accessed 23 March 2022].

TOI (2012) 'City's wheels of growth to stand still on Tuesday', 27 February. Available from: http://timesofindia.indiatimes.com/articleshow/12050319. cms?utm_source=contentofinterest&utm_medium=text&utm_campaign= cppst [Accessed 9 October 2022].

TOI (2014) 'Strike cripples transactions in PSU banks', 6 December. Available from: https://timesofindia.indiatimes.com/city/pune/Strike-cripples-transactions-in-PSU-banks/articleshow/45391785.cms [Accessed 23 March 2022].

TOI (2015) 'Brace for two-day bank strike, ATMs to be shut too', 2 September. Available from: https://timesofindia.indiatimes.com/city/kolk ata/Brace-for-two-day-bank-strike-ATMs-to-be-shut-too/articleshow/ 15594994.cms [Accessed 23 March 2022].

TOI (2017) 'Bank strike may hit transactions over Rs 1 lakh cr: Assocham', 28 February. Available from: https://timesofindia.indiatimes.com/business/ india-business/bank-strike-may-hit-transactions-over-rs-1-lakh-cr-assoc ham/articleshow/57391930.cms [Accessed 23 March 2022].

TOI (2019) 'Postal and banking services hit during two days strike', 9 January. Available from: https://timesofindia.indiatimes.com/city/chandigarh/pos tal-and-banking-services-hit-during-two-days-strike/articleshow/67444 128.cms [Accessed 23 March 2022].

Tomlinson, J. (2021) 'Deindustrialisation and "Thatcherism": moral economy and unintended consequences', *Contemporary British History*, 35(4): 620–42.

Tooze, A. (2018) *How a Decade of Financial Crises Changed the World*, New York: Viking.

Toynbee, M., Al-Diwani, A.A., Clacey, J. and Broome, M.R. (2016) 'Should junior doctors strike?', *Journal of Medical Ethics*, 42: 167–70.

TUC (2015) 'TUC supports junior doctors' right to strike', 19 November. Available from: https://www.tuc.org.uk/news/tuc-supports-junior-doct ors-right-strike [Accessed 9 October 2022].

TUC (2016) 'Emergency motion – E5 Support for the BMA and junior doctors', 13 September. Available from: https://www.tuc.org.uk/research-analysis/reports/emergency-motion-e5-support-bma-and-junior-doctors [Accessed 9 October 2022].

Tügel, N. (2017) 'Arbeitskämpfe in frauendominierten Berufsfeldern: Das Beispiel Krankenhausstreik', *Z. Zeitschrift marxistische Erneuerung*, 110: 36–44.

Tzouvala, N. (2016) 'Continuity and rupture in restraining the right to strike', in H. Brabazon (ed) *Neoliberal Legality: Understanding the Role of Law in the Neoliberal Project*, London: Routledge, pp 119–39.

Uhlenbroich, B. (2021) 'Dieser Streik ist unsolidarisch, Herr GDL-Chef!', *Bild-Zeitung*, 7 August. Available from: https://www.bild.de/politik/kolum nen/kolumne/kommentar-zum-bahn-streik-dieser-streik-ist-unsolidari sch-herr-gdl-chef-77318276.bild.html [Accessed 9 October 2022].

Unison (2015) 'UNISON supports industrial action by junior doctors', 19 November. Available from: https://www.unison.org.uk/news/press-release/2015/11/unison-supports-industrial-action-by-junior-doctors/ [Accessed 9 October 2022].

Unite (2019) 'New junior doctors' contract "not good enough", says Unite', [online], 14 June. Available from: https://www.unitetheunion.org/news-events/news/2019/june/new-junior-doctors-contract-not-good-eno ugh-says-unite/ [Accessed 9 October 2022].

Vandaele, K. (2011) 'Sustaining or abandoning "social peace"? Strike development and trends in Europe since the 1990s', ETUI working paper, May. Available from: https://www.etui.org/publications/working-papers/ sustaining-or-abandoning-social-peace [Accessed 26 June 2021].

Van der Linden, M. (2008) *Workers of the World: Essays towards a Global Labour History*, Leiden: Brill.

Van der Linden, M. (2016) 'Global labour: a not-so-grand finale and perhaps a new beginning', *Global Labour Journal*, 7(2): 201–10.

Van der Walt, K. (2015) 'Collective bargaining and labour relations in South Africa', *Mail and Guardian Critical Thinking Forum*, 4 December. Available from: https://www.kas.de/de/web/suedafrika/veranstaltungsberichte/det ail/-/content/collective-bargaining-and-labour-relations-in-south-africa [Accessed 26 June 2021].

Varela, P. (2020) 'Paro Internacional de Mujeres: ¿Nueva tradición de lucha del movimiento feminista?', *Conflicto Social*, 132–61.

Vázquez, C. (2017) 'Miles de personas claman en Valencia por la "igualdad real" de mujeres y hombres', *El País*, 8 March. Available from: https://elp ais.com/ccaa/2017/03/08/valencia/1489002797_829542.html [Accessed 9 October 2022].

Vázquez, C. (2019) 'El movimiento feminista extiende las acciones más allá de la huelga del 8-M', *El País*, 27 January. Available from: https:// elpais.com/sociedad/2019/01/27/actualidad/1548603834_871117.html [Accessed 9 October 2022].

Vázquez, S. (2018) 'Diez claves de la huelga feminista del 8-M: las convocatorias, las movilizaciones…', *El Correo*, 6 March. Available from: https://www. elcorreo.com/bizkaia/legal-huelga-feminista-20180302131631-nt.html [Accessed 9 October 2022].

ver.di (nd) 'Mehr von uns ist besser für alle! Der Kampf um Entlastung und Gesundheitsschutz an der Berliner Charité'. Available from: https://ges undheit-soziales-bb.verdi.de/themen/tarifvertrag-entlastung/++co++ 327c4bce-4f5e-11e7-897c-525400ff2b0e [Accessed 2 July 2021].

Verfassungsschutz (2022) 'Verfassungsschutzsbericht 2021'. Available from: https://www.verfassungsschutz.de/SharedDocs/publikationen/DE/verfassungsschutzberichte/2022-06-07-verfassungsschutzbericht-2021-startseitenmodul.pdf?__blob=publicationFile&v=3 [Accessed 23 September 2022].

Verkehrsrundschau (2013) 'Warnstreik bei Amazon in Bad Hersfeld', 10 April. Available from: www.verkehrsrundschau.de/nachrichten/transport-logistik/warnstreik-bei-amazon-in-bad-hersfeld-3004053 [Accessed 24 March 2022].

Vromen, A. (2010) 'Debating methods: rediscovering qualitative approaches', in D. Marsh and G. Stoker (eds) *Theory and Methods in Political Science*, 3rd edn, Houndmills: Palgrave, pp 249–66.

Wacket, M. (2015) 'Tarifeinigung bei der Bahn – Hoffnung auf Gesamtlösung', Reuters, 27 May. Available from: https://www.reuters.com/article/deutschland-bahn15-idDEKBN0OC1LO20150527 [Accessed 9 October 2022].

Waddell, K. (2017) 'The exhausting work of tallying America's largest protest', *The Atlantic*, 23 January. Available from: https://www.theatlantic.com/technology/archive/2017/01/womens-march-protest-count/514166/ [Accessed 9 October 2022].

Wagner, F.J. (2021) 'Lieber Claus Weselsky, Bahn-Rambo', *Bild-Zeitung*, 2 September. Available from: https://www.bild.de/politik/kolumnen/franz-josef-wagner/post-von-wagner-lieber-claus-weselsky-bahn-rambo-77569280.bild.html [Accessed 9 October 2022].

Wainwright, M. (2009) 'Rubbish and industrial relations moulder amid Leeds bin strike', *The Guardian*, 26 October. Available from: https://www.theguardian.com/politics/2009/oct/26/leeds-council-workers-strike [Available 27 July 2022].

Walker, S. (2020) 'Workers and unions in Belarus launch anti-Lukashenko strike', *The Guardian*, 26 October. Available from: https://www.theguardian.com/world/2020/oct/26/workers-and-student-in-belarus-launch-anti-alexander-lukashenko-strike [Accessed 27 June 2021].

Wallerstein, I. (2005) 'After developmentalism and globalization, what?', *Social Forces*, 83(3): 1263–78.

Wandler, R. (2010) 'Spanien steht am Scheideweg', *Der Standard*, 16 June. Available from: https://www.derstandard.at/story/1276413189947/250-milliarden-euro-spanien-steht-am-scheideweg [Accessed 9 October 2022].

Watkins, S. (2021) 'Paradigm shifts', *New Left Review*, 128: 5–12.

WAZ (2017) 'Verfassungsrichter verhandeln Klage gegen die Tarifeinheit' [online video], 24 January. Available from: https://www.waz.de/video/verfassungsrichter-verhandeln-klagen-gegen-tarifeinheit-id209381349.html [Accessed 9 October 2022].

Weeks, K. (2011) *The Problem with Work: Feminism, Marxism, Antiwork Politics, and Postwork Imaginaries*, Durham, NC: Duke University Press.

Weselsky, C. (2013) 'Brisanz Tarifeinheit', 7 October. Available from: https://www.gdl.de/Aktuell-2013/VorausEditorial-1381152939 [Accessed 9 October 2022].

Weselsky, C. (2020) Letter to K.D. Hommel, 27 May. Available from: https://www.gdl.de/uploads/Aktuell-2020/2020-05-26-Brief%20GDL.pdf [Accessed 9 October 2022].

Wildcat (2021) 'Diamantenmangel', 11 August. Available from: https://www.wildcat-www.de/wildcat/108/w108_diamanten.html [Accessed 27 June 2022].

Williams, N.R. and Davis-Faulkner, S. (2021) 'Worker mobilization and political engagement: a historical perspective', in T. Schulze-Cleven and T. Vachon (eds) *Revaluing Work(ers): Toward a Democratic and Sustainable Future*, Champaign: LERA, pp 121–40.

Wills, J., May, J., Datta, K., Evans, Y., Herbert, J. and McIlwaine, C. (2009) 'London's migrant division of labour', *European Urban and Regional Studies*, 16(3): 257–71.

Wisdorff, F. (2014) 'Nahles' Pläne zur Tarifeinheit spalten den DGB', *WELT*, 6 November. Available from: https://www.welt.de/wirtschaft/article134047462/Nahles-Plaene-zur-Tarifeinheit-spalten-den-DGB.html [Accessed 9 October 2022].

Wissenschaftlicher Beirat (2016) 'Streiks und die Zuverlässigkeit der Verkehrsbedingung', *Wirtschaftsdienst*, 96(2): 114–21.

Woodcock, J. (2019) 'India general strike 2019', *Notes from Below*, 10 January. Available from: https://notesfrombelow.org/article/india-general-strike-2019 [Accessed 8 October 2021].

World Bank (2021) *Women, Business and the Law*, Washington: World Bank.

World Economic Forum (2022) *Global Gender Gap Report*, Coligny: WEF.

WSI-Tarifarchiv (2015) 'WSI-Arbeitskampfbilanz 2014: Deutlich geringeres Streikvolumen, anhaltend viele Konflikte', 4 March. Available from: https://www.boeckler.de/pdf/pm_wsi_2015_03_04.pdf [Accessed 9 October 2022].

WSI-Tarifarchiv (2016) 'WSI-Arbeitskampfbilanz 2015: Ein außergewöhnliches Streikjahr', 3 March. Available from: https://www.boeckler.de/pdf/pm_ta_2016_03_03.pdf [Accessed 9 October 2022].

Wullweber, J. (2019) 'Monism vs. pluralism, the global financial crisis, and the methodological struggle in the field of international political economy', *Competition & Change*, 23(3): 287–311.

Xhafa, E. (2016) 'The right to strike struck down? An analysis of recent trends', Friedrich Ebert Foundation, October. Available from: https://library.fes.de/pdf-files/iez/12827.pdf [Accessed 10 October 2022].

Yilmaz, K. (2013) 'Comparison of quantitative and qualitative research traditions: epistemological, theoretical and methodological differences', *European Journal of Education*, 48(2): 311–25.

ZDF (2021) 'Politbarometer', 27 August. Available at: https://de.statista. com/statistik/daten/studie/1257548/umfrage/verstaendnis-fuer-bahnstr eik/ [Accessed 9 October 2022].

Zelik, R. (2018) *Spanien: Eine politische Geschichte der Gegenwart*, Berlin: Bertz & Fischer.

Zelik, R. (2020a) *Wir Untoten des Kapitals: Über politische Monster und einen grünen Sozialismus*, Frankfurt am Main: Suhrkamp.

Zelik, R. (2020b) 'In Verteidigung des Lebens: Über die Corona-Pandemie, die sozialökologische Großkrise und die Möglichkeit eines neuen Sozialismusbegriffs', *PROKLA. Zeitschrift für kritische Sozialwissenschaft*, 50(2): 345–53.

Zengerling, Z. (2019) 'Ab 15.24 Uhr arbeiten Frauen gratis', *SZ*, 14 June. Available from: www.sueddeutsche.de/politik/schweiz-frauenstreik-prot est-gleichberechtigung-1.4482188 [Accessed 22 March 2022].

Zinn, H. (2003) *A People's History of the United States: 1492–Present*, 3rd edn, New York: HarperCollins.

Index

References to tables appear in **bold** type. References to figures are in *italics*.
References to endnotes show both the page number and the note number (231n3).

deindustrialization
  industrialization, relationship to 32, 50
  unions, impact of on 32, 47, 51, 138
  Western Europe, in 91–6, *92*, 134
demands
  about 16–17
  comparison **201**, 202, 203
  feminist general strikes (Spain) 15, 175,
    177, 182, 187–8, 189–90, 191–2, 193–7
  general strikes (Spain) 162, 163, 165–6,
    167, 169, 171, 173, 174, 191–2, 193, 197
  junior doctors' strike (Britain) 147, 149
  railway strikes (Germany) 113, 114, 115,
    118, 121, 122–3, 125, 126, 130
Denmark **58**
density of unions 55, 58, **58**, 62n5, 91–5,
  92n1, *93*, **94**, **95**, 136–8
Der Spiegel 119
despotism 59, 62, 62n5, 63, 65, 83–4,
  199, 204
Deutsche Bahn (Germany)
  about 108, 124
  interviews 216
  labour relations 109–10, 114–15, 116,
    124–6, 131–2
  strikes at 112, 117–21, 126–9
DGB (German Trade Union Confederation)
  about 7, 102–4, 113
  GDL and 116, 118–20, 122, 124,
    128, 130–1
  membership 107–8
dictatorships 26–7, 32, 46, 92n1
Die Tageszeitung (Berlin) 67, 206, 208
direct class effects 192, 192n14
division of tasks 31–2, 60–1, 62
divisive class effects 193
Doctors' Association UK 147
dominantly economic code *see* mostly
  economic code
domination *see* class domination;
  patriarchal domination
Dörre, Klaus 119, 123
double-dip recession 153–4
Dribbusch, Heiner 125–6
dynamics *see* mobilizing dynamics

E

East German Socialist Unity Party (SED) 106
ecological dominance 60–2, 65, 138,
  175–6
economic and politicized code 70, 71, 72,
  72, 78, 82, 211–12
  see also expansive-politicized strikes
economic crisis *see* global financial crisis
economic extension code 213
economic globalization 28, 30
The Economist 105
Education and Science Workers' Union
  (GEW) 102–3, 119–20

ELA (Solidary of Basque Workers)
  (Spain) 157, **158**
Elliott, Victoria 70
Elsner, Carsten 66
emergent totality 13
employment *see* unemployment
encompassing comparison 5, 12
The End of History and the Last Man
  (Fukuyama) 34n7
Engels, Friedrich 176
Enzensberger, Hans-Magnus 34n7
Eribon, Didier 37
Esser, J. 160, 161
ETUC (European Trade Union
  Confederation) 170
Eurowings 76n4
Eurozone 39, 92, 106–7, 153, 155–60, 202
EVG (Railway and Transport Union)
  (Germany)
  about 111, 112, 114
  collective bargaining, response to 119,
    122, 127
  GDL and 116, 118, 124–6, 129–30, 131
  strike action by 7, 112, 125–6, **201**
exclusively political strikes *see* strikes for
  political aims
exclusive solidarity 107, 114, 115, 193–4, 209
expansive class effects 193
expansive-politicized strikes 72, *72*, 78–82,
  88, 144, 170
  see also economic and politicized code
expansive solidarity 16–17, 74, 193–4, 204
  see also class feeling
exploitation 60, 62, 62n5, 63, 65, 183,
  189, 204
extension strikes 71–2, *72*, 74–8, 88
  see also mostly economic code

F

far-right 27, 45, 47, 112, 180, 189
Federal Republic of Germany 98, 99, 99n3
  see also Germany
#feesmustfall 76
feminism
  intersectional 185
  labour struggle, of 167
  protest movements 180–1
  second-wave 27
feminist general strikes (Spain)
  8M (International Women's Strike) (2018,
    2019) 182–8
  class formations and 190–7
  comparison **201**, 201–2
  constituencies *see* constituencies
  COVID-19 pandemic, during 188–90
  demands *see* demands
  demonstrations 181
  mobilizing dymanics *see* mobilizing dynamics
  as organic 85, 194–5, 197